SEARCHING FOR **AFRICA** IN **BRAZIL**

Stefania Capone

꜀꜀

SEARCHING FOR AFRICA IN BRAZIL

Power and Tradition in Candomblé

꜀꜀

Translated from the French
by Lucy Lyall Grant

Duke University Press   Durham and London   2010

© 2010 Duke University Press

All rights reserved

Designed by Heather Hensley

Typeset in Warnock Pro by Keystone Typesetting, Inc.

Library of Congress Cataloging-in-Publication Data appear
on the last printed page of this book.

Original French edition: *La quête de l'Afrique dans le candomblé: Pouvoir et tradition au Brésil* (Paris: Karthala, 1999).

CONTENTS

List of Illustrations   vii

Preface to the American Edition · ix

Acknowledgments   xi

Some Notes on Orthography and Pronunciation   xiii

Introduction   1

PART I **THE METAMORPHOSES OF EXU** ·

    1. The Messenger of the Gods: Exu in Afro-Brazilian Religions   35

    2. The Spirits of Darkness: Exu and Pombagira in Umbanda   69

PART II **RITUAL PRACTICE**

    3. The Religious Continuum   95

    4. Reorganizing Sacred Space   121

    5. Contesting Power   143

PART III **THE CONSTRUCTION OF TRADITION**

    6. Exu and the Anthropologists   173

    7. In Search of Lost Origins   203

    8. Which Africa? Which Tradition?   233

Conclusion   255

Glossary   263

Notes   269

Bibliography   297

Index   311

LIST OF ILLUSTRATIONS

Tables

1. Spiritual Patrimony of a Medium   127
2. Re-Africanization of Exus   133

Figures

1. Cristovão de Ogunjá, founder of the Rio de Janeiro Efon religious family   22
2. Alvinho de Omolu during the public presentation of a new initiate   23
3. The Efon family-of-saint   24
4. Exu of the gateway   44
5. Exu's *assento* in the Ilê Ifá Mongé Gibanauê   45
6. Plan of Alvinho de Omolu's terreiro   46
7. Exu's functions   47
8. Exu's assento with palm oil, *cachaça*, and honey   48
9. House of Ogun and Oxossi   50
10. *Saida de santo*, final ceremony for an Exu's initiate   55
11. An Exu's initiate dancing   56
12. *Padê* for Exu in an Efon terreiro   59
13. Exu's collective shrines in a Candomblé house   64
14. Exu's assentos in Umbanda and Candomblé   75
15. Afro-Brazilian religious continuum   77
16. A statuette of Pombagira   83
17. Pombagira's *pontos riscados*   88
18. Roots of the tree dedicated to Iroko in the Pantanal terreiro   102
19. The Mercadão de Madureira, a shopping center devoted to Afro-Brazilian religions   115

20. A Madureira store dedicated to an Umbanda Exu   117

21. Religious goods at the Mercadão de Madureira   119

22. Seven Arrows, Alvinho de Omolu's caboclo   125

23. The caboclo's assento   128

24. Offerings to the caboclo   130

25. Representations of Exu in Candomblé and Umbanda   137

26. An Umbanda representation of the Pombagira Maria Mulambo   138

27. A re-Africanized representation of the same Pombagira, baptized Jinda Leba
    Dandasin   140

28. An assento of a re-Africanized Pombagira   146

29. Upward mobility within the same family-of-saint   148

30. The Iroko tree in the Ilê Ifá Mongé Gibanauê   153

31. Initiates working in a terreiro   161

32. Xangô's assento   177

33. *Alabés*, the drummers of the terreiro   185

34. Logunedé's assento   192

35. Alvinho de Omolu during the celebration of the fiftieth anniversary of his
    initiation   199

36. A caboclo's manifestation   211

37. Omolu's assento   219

38. *Olubajé*, the annual festival for Omolu   223

39. Logunedé, Alvinho de Omolu's second *orixá* manifestation   228

40. House of Oxalá   238

41. Ogans in Alvinho de Omolu's terreiro   243

42. Ogun's assento   253

In the Western imaginary, Brazil embodies the myth of a wild and enchanted land, inhabited by hospitable people who are at one with nature. Salvador has long been a city in which contrasts are diminished, colors combine, and beliefs intertwine. But Bahia is also the "Rome of Africa," a place in which religious traditions brought by slaves have been preserved and transmitted most faithfully. Bahia—with its *Nagô* Candomblé, which concentrates an ideal of Africanity—has become the promised land in which racial mixing and harmony reign, although the dream of African purity lives on in the quest for roots which animates conversations in the most traditional houses of worship.

In this work, it is another Brazil that I want to look at, a Brazil with thousands of exceptions to the rules—whether the rule be a law or a model to be respected—making the establishment of orthodoxy or a standard line impossible in the thousands of Candomblé centers spread throughout the country. Multiplicity dominates and is imposed, weakening the elegant—and, at times, too perfect—systematizations that attempt to crystallize the religion.

Writing about Candomblé is certainly a dangerous undertaking, with many pitfalls. Too many illustrious predecessors and too many works presented only one of this religious phenomenon's many forms. For a long time, there was even a feeling that nothing new could be said about this field, perhaps one of the most explored in religious anthropology.

Beatriz G. Dantas's pioneering work, which took Brazilian scholarship by storm, brought crucial criticism of the very idea of "Nagô purity." Many other authors followed her example, analyzing the scholars' role in the making of traditions. A decade has passed since I published the first edition of this book in French, in 1999. The Brazilian edition followed in 2004. Today's American edition gives me the opportunity to clarify my personal approach to this issue.

While Dantas (1988)—like most authors who criticized the valorization of the Nagô model—attributes the imposition of a model of purity to the conscious action of intellectuals, in order to better "control" the cults, my aim in this work is to underline the agency of the Candomblé elites connected to the three houses of worship considered traditional in Bahia. As we shall see, these Candomblé leaders succeeded in imposing their own vision of the tradition upon the intellectuals, reshaping Afro-Brazilian religious practice in their own interest. This work addresses the issue in a way which is fundamentally different from Dantas's argument.

Dantas analyzed the past: the 1930s, a key period in the construction of national identity and in the creation of Afro-Brazilian studies. I decided to write not only of the past, but also of the present, highlighting the ritual negotiation which represents the core of religious life in Candomblé houses. The confrontation between an ideal model of tradition and the reality of ritual practice shows the agency of the initiates and their power of negotiation even at the very heart of ritual hierarchy. The "invention of tradition," then, is the product of a dual movement, a dual project linking religious elites with intellectual elites in the same quest for an ideal Africanity. Today, Afro-Brazilian religions cannot be considered merely as expressions of "Black Brazil," as some authors suggest, because they crossed the color line a long time ago, gathering white, black, and mestizo followers. It is not useful to make racial divisions when discussing the Afro-Brazilian religious universe: in Brazil, race and culture are dissociated, and one can be initiated in a "black" religion without being or considering oneself black.

My analysis of ritual practice shows the impossibility of seeking "uncorrupted" African origins in Candomblé. Nevertheless, young researchers are still too often oriented to reproduce the type of analysis in which Nagô Candomblé is taken as the embodiment of African tradition in Brazil. I hope that this study will help give a better understanding of a very complex universe, showing how tradition, which sees itself as eternal and immutable, is in fact reinvented day after day.

ACKNOWLEDGMENTS

A book is always a collective effort. This project could not have been completed without the support of certain people to whom I would like to express my wholehearted gratitude. Among the many colleagues and friends who have helped me, I would like to thank Marie-Hélène Delamare, Jacques Galinier, André Mary, Stephan Palmié, Susan Rogers, Michka Sachnine, and Antonio Carlos de Souza Lima, as well as the many people who assisted me in this research, especially Leonardo Carneiro and Ana Messias. I would also like to express my gratitude to the Museu Nacional (UFRJ, Rio de Janeiro), where this story began, the Laboratoire d'ethnologie et de sociologie comparative (LESC, University of Paris X), and to the French National Center for Scientific Research (CNRS), which gave me a grant for the English translation.

A special thanks go to my husband Elliott Laffitte and my son Alexandre for their endless patience and support.

Finally, I am forever indebted to the Candomblé initiates and Umbanda mediums who shared their knowledge with me, particularly all the members of the Ilê Ifá Mongé Gibanauê in Rio de Janeiro, and the late Alvinho de Omolu. This work is dedicated to his memory.

The Yoruba language is a tonal language with three relative tone (or pitch) bands represented by acute accents over the high tones, grave accents over the low tones, and no diacritical marks over the middle tones. Yoruba has eighteen consonants, seven oral vowels, and five nasal vowels, plus a syllabic nasal. All the vowels have a tone and can be marked by subdots, as can the consonant "ṣ." For example:

high tone—ọkọ́ (hoe)
middle tone—ọkọ (husband)
low tone—ọkọ̀ (boat)

Subdots indicate the following pronunciations:

e as in gay
ẹ as in net
o as in boat
ọ as in hot
s as in so
ṣ as in show

The letter "n" at the end of a word or before a consonant nasalizes the preceding vowel (as in French), and the sequence "an" becomes almost identical in pronunciation to "ọn," resulting in near homophones such as *efan* and *efọn*. Written "p" is pronounced as the voiceless labial-velar stop "kp" where "k" and "p" are simultaneously pronounced, and the labial-velar stop "gb" is its voiced counterpart.

In Brazil, the language employed in Candomblé rituals is called Nagô. It does not have any subdots and loses the three tones, often transforming the Yoruba high tone into a circumflex accent: the Yoruba *ilé* (house) becoming the Nagô *ilê* (house of worship or *terreiro*). In Brazilian Portuguese, the circumflex accent marks a closed vowel, and the acute accent an open vowel (as in Candomblé). The consonant "x" corresponds phonetically to the Yoruba "ṣ": e.g., *Èṣù* in Yoruba is *Exu* in Portuguese and *Eshou* in English.

I shall use the Yoruba orthography when analyzing the role of this divinity in the Yoruba pantheon, and the Brazilian orthography when referring to its Brazilian counterpart. This choice is a significant one and runs contrary to the current use of Yoruba terms in anthropological writings on traditional Candomblé, which aim to highlight its African origins. My decision to use the Brazilian orthography serves a different purpose: to show how Candomblé is primarily a Brazilian religious product. I shall use capital letters when referring to the name of a god or a spirit, and small letters for generic terms such as *caboclos*, *orixás*, or *pretos-velhos*; therefore I will write of Exu in Candomblé and of exus in Umbanda. Vernacular terms are listed in the glossary.

Unless otherwise noted, translations are my own.

INTRODUCTION

This book is the result of a long personal journey. During my first trip to Brazil in 1983 for bibliographic research about Candomblé, many questions began to take shape. Why had most studies focused on only one of the modalities found in the Afro-Brazilian religious universe?[1] Why did the discourse—of people linked to Candomblé, but also of researchers who wrote on this subject—insist so much on religious "purity"? I was impressed by the apparent uniformity of the cult centers, which contrasted with the constant division of the religious universe into "pure" and "impure" cults along lines of religious genealogy, creating a hierarchy in the Afro-Brazilian religious field. The differences established by native discourse on origins appeared to permeate the discourse of the researchers, with little analysis of the mechanisms of how these differences were constituted. The two discourses, native and anthropological, overlapped curiously.

At first I thought that by presenting another tradition—the Angola tradition, for example—I could contribute to questioning what appeared to me to be an a priori in Afro-Brazilian studies: that the Yoruba (or Nagô) were the guardians of religious "purity," while the Bantu (Angola and Congo) had folklore as their "own special cultural focal point" (Bastide 1971, 194). And so, while defending my master's thesis at the Museu Nacional of Rio de Janeiro in 1991, I was hopeful that I had presented an original worldview, an expression of a lesser known branch of Candomblé, the Angola "nation."[2] Two years earlier, I had found an ambitious and intelligent *pai-de-santo*,[3] who had just founded a *terreiro*[4] in Sepetiba (Rio de Janeiro). My primary interest—studying possession dances—led me into long discussions with him, which gradually revealed a symbolic universe that was truly unprecedented.

Unconcerned with the "purity" of this worldview, I became fascinated by the theoretical construction he presented to me as the heritage of a religious tradition transmitted by his own pai-de-santo, a native of Angola, who had passed away. I thought that the simple possibility of registering this world-view would be an interesting contribution to Afro-Brazilian studies. I was taken by surprise during my dissertation defense when almost all the criti-cisms concentrated on the very singularity of this narrative. Who asserted this universe? How many people shared this worldview? Wasn't my study legitimizing the authority of the pai-de-santo?

These questions appeared unjustified to me. I was accustomed to reading in the classic texts on Candomblé descriptions of a religious universe in which the legitimacy of narratives was never questioned. In most texts (e.g., Bastide 1958), it was impossible even to identify the terreiros where the study was carried out. Almost all the authors referred to one tradition, that of the Nagôs,[5] and emphasized the absence of tradition in the other nations, Bantu[6] in particular.

However, with the tradition I collected, I had suggested that, perhaps, there was also something interesting in the study of Angola Candomblé, although this kind of study could challenge the internal organization of the Afro-Brazilian research field.[7] In fact, how could I give legitimacy to some-thing which, by definition, was the fruit of "degeneration," of the loss of African tradition? Furthermore, I was guilty of a dual audacity, as not only had I dedicated myself to the study of a religious cult considered less tradi-tional, but I had done so in Rio de Janeiro and not in Salvador, the homeland of "true" Candomblé.[8]

I was thus forced to reconsider the mechanisms which made up the opposition between Nagô and Angola Candomblé, structuring both native and scientific discourses (see Capone 2000). Dantas's work—published in 1988—questioned what had appeared to be obvious until then: the pre-dominant model of Nagô tradition. Nagô, synonymous with African purity, revealed itself to be a category arising from converging discourses of researchers and religious elites.

The relativization of the categories—and of the oppositions making up the field of Afro-Brazilian studies—implied, to my mind, the need for a discussion of the power relations that are part of this universe. This is exactly what makes such a work particularly delicate: every researcher working in this field is aware that power issues are at the heart of his object of study, and that it is difficult to analyze this question without entering into conflict with part of his audience, colleagues, or members of the cult. Nevertheless, it seemed to me indispensable to dedicate myself to exploring the making of tradition, as well as the power relations that structure the Afro-Brazilian religious field.

"Pure" and "Degenerate"

One of the most marked characteristics of Candomblé studies is the striking concentration of ethnographic monographs on three terreiros of the Nagô nation, which are then seen as the embodiment of African tradition in Brazil. They are the Engenho Velho or Casa Branca, considered the first Candomblé terreiro founded in Brazil, and the Gantois and the Axé Opô Afonjá, both of which came from the Casa Branca. Other Brazilian cities, such as Recife, São Luís do Maranhão, and Porto Alegre, were considered, respectively, as traditional centers of three other modalities of Afro-Brazilian religions: the Xangô, the Tambor da Mina, and the Batuque. In contrast, the large cities of the Southeast (Rio de Janeiro and São Paulo), were always considered the homes of Macumba, a "degenerate" cult par excellence, stemming from a mixture of African traditions (most of them Bantu), indigenous cults, and European Spiritism.[9]

Raymundo Nina Rodrigues, the pioneer of Afro-Brazilian studies, criticized the idea—supported by linguistic studies and prevalent in his time—of Bantu supremacy among Brazilian blacks. Indeed, the Portuguese language spoken in Brazil is heavily influenced by Kimbundu and, to a lesser degree, other Bantu languages. In order to criticize this predominance, Nina Rodrigues substituted the method based on linguistic analysis for one based on the observation of religious facts, comparing them with available data about the African cultures. At the end of the nineteenth century, the Yoruba social and religious organization was depicted by missionaries and colonial administrators (see Peel 2000). The Bantu, in contrast, were associated with a mythology regarded as inferior, despite the complexity of the social organization of the Kongo kingdom. Several works, such as that of Charles Letourneau on the "religious evolution in different human races," published in 1892 and cited by Nina Rodrigues (1990), postulated the Bantu inferiority.

In his study about Africans in Brazil, Nina Rodrigues clearly asserted the supremacy of the Yoruba (the Nagôs of Bahia), whom he considered the true "aristocracy" among the slaves brought to Brazil. He based this on the studies of Ellis and Bowen, conducted in the late nineteenth century. In the same way, Nina Rodrigues declared that he had sought in vain, among the blacks of Bahia, religious ideas belonging to the Bantu. In reality, his research was concentrated in the Gantois terreiro, created in 1896 (Nina Rodrigues 1988, 239), as a consequence of a split within the Casa Branca. His informant and principal guide in the universe of the Afro-Brazilian religions was Martiniano Eliseu do Bonfim, a historic figure in Nagô Candomblé, who later became one of the founders of the Axé Opô Afonjá (see Braga 1999; Matory 2005). Nina Rodrigues was the first to play down any other cultural contribution of African origin in relation to the culture and religion of the descendants of the Yoruba.

In the wake of Nina Rodrigues, the opposition between the "pure tradition" of the Nagôs and the mythical-ritualistic "weakness" of the Bantu took hold in later studies. Despite the proof of the existence in Bahia of terreiros as old as that of the Casa Branca,[10] the religious superiority of the Nagôs, a product of their supposed "racial superiority" (see Nina Rodrigues, 1988; Ramos 1979, 201), continued to be asserted by most authors studying Bahian Candomblé, thus enhancing the value of one cultural tradition over the others. It was not until Édison Carneiro's work on Bantu Candomblé in the late 1930s that researchers showed interest in another cult modality. Published for the first time in 1937, this study, however, only confirmed Nagô superiority (Carneiro 1991). The difference, initially asserted in the religious realm, was soon transferred into a regional opposition between the Brazilian Northeast (Nordeste), mainly Bahia, which exalted its cultural heritage by means of greater respect for the "superior" black Nagôs, and the Southeast (Sudeste), which—although by the early nineteenth century it had become the administrative and economic center of the country—lacked a cultural tradition of equal value.[11]

Despite the existence of Candomblé at the beginning of the twentieth century in Rio de Janeiro, as shown by João do Rio (1976) and Roberto Moura (1983), most scholars preferred to see in the Bahian terreiros the ethnographic model of "traditional" Candomblé, and in those of Rio de Janeiro, the ethnographic model of the "degenerate" or "degraded" cults.

Roger Bastide is the author who asserted most strongly the opposition between these two forms of religiousness. For him, Nagô Candomblé, a traditional religion, represents the realization of a utopian community. The Bantu cult, in contrast, suffers from a degradation of African beliefs, engendering the "social marginalism" (Bastide 1978, 303) of Macumba. The "subtle philosophy" (Bastide 1958, 10) of African religion remained the monopoly of the Nagôs, with the predominance of Nagô Candomblé confirmed in later studies. A polarization was established between studies on Umbanda[12] —associated, like Macumba, with the degradation of African religions—and the studies dedicated to Nagô Candomblé, the embodiment of African tradition. Nagô Candomblé, concentrated mainly in the city of Salvador, thus represented a pole that reenacted, to use Bastide's term, an African gestalt. In contrast, the cities of the Southeast, swept up by modernity, had irredeemably lost African civilization's most important values. In fact, according to Bastide, immigrants coming from the Northeast in search of work could not recreate in the cities of the Southeast the community spirit that animated the world of Nagô Candomblé. They thus became "infected by a mentality in which material interests and their advancement by political parties and unions are more important than spiritual interests and which regards work as a surer source of reward than magical procedures" (Bastide 1978, 217). In "traditional" Candomblé, magic was transformed from a "potential source of internal conflict" into an element that increases the "integrative force" of the religion, "since all problems can be resolved through the authority of the priests and the discipline they impose upon members" (ibid., 227). In contrast, in the metropolises of the Southeast, this same magic was significantly modified and, in a context where control of the group disappeared, was reduced to a simple means for "the shameless exploitation of the credulity of the lower classes" (ibid., 300).

The opposition between Nagô Candomblé, an expression of the "true" religion, and Macumba, inheritor of European and African magic, once again divided the Afro-Brazilian religious field. But does this opposition between magic and religion really exist in the different modalities of Afro-Brazilian religions? Does it not merely express one of the foundations of the cults' internal logic, reinterpreted by means of oppositions (magic versus religion) that historically have helped construct anthropological discourse?

Magic is intrinsically linked to religion in Afro-Brazilian cults, because to believe in the divinities is to also believe in the magical skills they have to intervene in favor of their "sons." Accusations of black magic therefore represent, as in the classic case of the Zande system (Evans-Pritchard 1937), a tool for political control and legitimation. Thus, what was part of a typically African political discourse (accusations of witchcraft) is seen as the sign of an ontological opposition between "pure" religion and "degenerate" magic, without recognizing that the boundaries between these categories were—and still are—extremely fluid.[13]

The Construction of an Ideal Model of Orthodoxy

The convergence between research carried out by anthropologists and the harmonious systematizations they frequently produced have allowed, over the years, the construction of an ideal model of orthodoxy, identified with the Nagô cult, whose public is both researchers and cult members. A minimal distance between observer and observed is difficult to maintain when working on Afro-Brazilian religions. Most of the anthropologists studying Candomblé became involved in the religion, in one way or another, making a kind of pact with their "object."[14] The hegemonic discourse of heads of terreiros said to be traditional in Bahia has thus been legitimized by the discourse of anthropologists, who for nearly a century have limited their studies, with few exceptions, to the three same Nagô terreiros, although there are thousands of others. According to the September 1997 census, conducted by the Bahian Federation of Afro-Brazilian Religions (FEBACAB), there were 1,144 Candomblé terreiros registered in the city of Salvador alone, as many Caboclo and Angola terreiros as Nagô.

In the 1930s, Raymundo Nina Rodrigues and Arthur Ramos conducted their studies in the Gantois; Édison Carneiro in the Casa Branca; Roger

Bastide, Pierre Verger, Vivaldo da Costa Lima, and Juana Elbein dos Santos, among others, in the Axé Opô Afonjá. These are all terreiros in the line of the Casa Branca, considered the first Candomblé terreiro founded in Brazil. This concentration also led to the establishment of very special ties between the researcher and his object of study. Thus, Nina Rodrigues and Ramos became *ogans*[15] of Gantois (Landes 1994, 72). In the same way, Carneiro was ogan of Axé Opô Afonjá, the terreiro to which Bastide and Verger (who received the title of Oju Oba) also belonged. Many other anthropologists held ritual positions at this same terreiro. The ties between anthropologists and initiates became even stronger when, in the 1950s, trips to and from Africa, which had never completely stopped after the abolition of slavery, gained new impetus thanks to Verger's trips between Brazil and the Yoruba-land (Nigeria and Benin). The role of messenger, performed by Verger on both sides of the ocean, and above all the prestige that stemmed from the titles granted by Yoruba chiefs to the leaders of the Bahian terreiros, repre-sented important elements in the construction of a traditional model, valid for all the other religious groups.

It was, however, Juana Elbein dos Santos, a disciple of Bastide, who in the late 1970s embodied the most complete example of the "alliance" between anthropologists and cult members. This Argentinean anthropologist—an initiate of Axé Opô Afonjá and the wife of Deoscóredes dos Santos, a high dignitary of Nagô Candomblé—was the first to state, inspired by Bastide, the methodological need to analyze Candomblé "from within," or as an active and initiated participant, in order to avoid any "ethnocentric devia-tion" (Juana E. dos Santos 1976, 18). The religious engagement of anthro-pologists in cult groups, which always existed but was rarely acknowledged, thus came to be one of the essential conditions for a true understanding of the culture studied.

The Constitution of the Religious Field

When speaking of Candomblé, it becomes necessary to take into account the other cults that belong to the same religious universe and help to define its borders. In Afro-Brazilian studies, Candomblé is often presented in opposition to Umbanda or Macumba, and Nagô Candomblé as opposed to Bantu Candomblé: the second item in each pair is always marked by inferiority and degradation in relation to an ideal Africanity. This is the result of a continual process of identity construction, by means of a progressive dislocation of the opposition that always defines the "Other" as degenerated, polluted, or inauthentic. But is this opposition truly experienced as such in the ritual practice of Afro-Brazilian religions? Is it possible to distinguish clearly between "pure" religions and "degenerate" cults? What does it mean to be an "authentic" religion? Authentic in relation to what: Africa, Bahia, or Nagô?

Today when we observe the panorama of Afro-Brazilian religions, we find an extreme heterogeneity in the religious field.[16] Each terreiro has its own ritual specificity, which is the fruit of the tradition to which it belongs, but which also stems from the idiosyncrasy of its religious leader. In reality, religious identity is constantly negotiated among social actors. The differences among these religions are, therefore, much less clear than anthropologists and Afro-Brazilian religious elites maintain. For this reason, an opposition between Umbanda and Quimbanda—in other words, between the realms of religion and black magic—asserted, for example, in Bastide's writings (1978), is recognized by several authors as merely a pattern of accusation seeking to demarcate different modalities of cult in the "religious market." David Hess (1992) asserts that there is a continuum between Umbanda and Quimbanda, which is not the expression of two opposing forms of magic (white and black). According to Hess, Macumba, Quimbanda, and Umbanda represent a unified and coherent system articulated around what he calls a "syncretic dynamic" (ibid., 151). In the same way, in her work about the Mina cult from Belém, Véronique Boyer-Araujo (1993, 19) has chosen a methodological approach emphasizing the profound unity of the Afro-Brazilian religions (Umbanda, Mina, and Candomblé) in that city.

In his analysis of the formation of Umbanda, Ferreira Camargo also puts forward the hypothesis of the existence of a religious continuum among the "African" forms of Umbanda and the most orthodox Kardecism. Camargo maintains that there is a "popular awareness of the continuity, if not of the religious identity, between Umbanda and Kardecism" (1961, 14). This continuum is not limited to the Spiritist cults in southern Brazil but is also found in regions with "the strongest influence of the cultures coming from

Africa": "in cities such as Salvador and Recife, a considerable part of the population adopts the religions of African origin, which are now beginning to suffer strong influence from Kardecism, thus tracing the formation of the 'continuum' studied, which appears to be more functional, in urban areas, than traditional Sudanese and Bantu practices" (ibid., 92). The presence of ideas of Spiritist origin among those who practice "orthodox" Afro-Brazilian religions is also claimed by Alejandro Frigerio (1989, 77), who highlights the growing influence of Umbanda in even the most traditional terreiros of Salvador. It would seem that the modalities of Afro-Brazilian religions observed in Brazil constitute different combinations of the elements of this continuum. The differences are thus established more by initiates' discourse than by a real opposition in ritual practices. In reality, even the terreiros considered most pure are not immune to the influence of Spiritism.[17]

Yvonne Maggie (1989) emphasized the coinciding of the discourse of anthropology and that of Afro-Brazilian religions: as in the social sciences, Candomblé, Umbanda, or Kardecist practitioners create their own classifications. They order the field of the Afro-Brazilian religions according to a hierarchical logic, based on categories of high and low, pure and degenerated, authentic and corrupted. In establishing an opposition between "pure" religions and "degenerated" cults, anthropologists use the same classifications as their informants. It is not necessary to say that mediums always claim that they belong to the cult considered most pure. Thus, no one would define himself or herself as a Quimbanda adept, just as no terreiro said to be *umbandomblé*[18] would identify itself as such—i.e., mixed, degenerated, corrupted. Self-identification always occurs with the most respected pole, "traditional" Candomblé in this case.

The same idea of a continuum linking the various cult modalities is defended by Inger Sjørslev (1989), who reinterprets Bastide's theories about purity and degradation as an example of "anthropological myth." According to Sjørslev, the observable changes in the new modalities of Afro-Brazilian religions—"the playing with elements or forms"—are not due to the degradation of something which should remain unchanged: "on the contrary, it is a precondition for the continuation of ritual" (ibid., 106). Candomblé and Umbanda thus represent two intermediary forms on the same continuum.

Exu's Mediation

This continuity is well expressed by the figure of Exu, the divine messenger, master of magic, and the great manipulator of destiny. The central god in Candomblé, for it is through his intercession that communication takes place between the *orixás* (gods) and man, he is equally present in all the other modalities of Afro-Brazilian religions. Exu appears to serve as a pivot between the religious systems. He embodies the contact point between religion and magic: indispensable to the realization of any religious ritual in Candomblé, he is also the manipulator of magical forces in favor of those he protects. Exu's existence was denied for a long time, because his very presence was proof of the prohibited practice of magic and witchcraft. He was thus strategically erased in order to help the process of religious legitimation.

Candomblé, like most Afro-Brazilian religions, was repressed to various degrees by the police until the 1970s. Along with the illegal practice of medicine, Brazilian law expressly prohibited the practice of magic. Therefore it was necessary to "hide" any indication that gave credence to accusations of witchcraft, while at the same time asserting at any price the legitimacy of the terreiros, associating them with the practice of the "true" African religion. Furthermore, it was necessary to deny the presence of Exu, whom missionaries identified with the devil, in order to assert the cult's purity and legitimacy. But what could be done when the majority of rituals inevitably pass through the mediation of Exu?

Anthropologists who defended the traditionalism of the Nagô cult modality confined themselves to the study of its public rituals and cosmogony, avoiding analysis of the most problematic aspects: "magical works" in private rituals. As Reginaldo Prandi (1991) rightly maintains, it is through magic that Candomblé weaves its relations with the clients to whom it offers its services. A terreiro's importance is therefore proportional to its success in the religious market, marked by a large number of clients and sons-of-saint (initiates) attracted by the "mystical strength" of the pai-de-santo and his ability to manipulate magical powers. Paradoxically, its religious legitimation depends on the very denial of the origin of its success: a traditional terreiro should not practice magic!

In the writings of most anthropologists, magic thus remains limited to the "degenerate" or "syncretic" cults: Bantu Candomblé, Macumba, Quimbanda, and Umbanda. The latter has become, in Bastide's work (1978, 324), the privileged space for the expression of white magic, with its function limited to the treatment of misfortune, linked to the problems of daily life in a particularly difficult urban and industrial context. The contradictions raised by modernity find a powerful symbol in Exu. He personifies the ambiguous hero, the trickster, whose weapons are shrewdness, mobility, and luck. However, Brazilian society is ambiguous and structured around a small elite. It is a society that offers individuals social objectives which are almost impossible to achieve and which create needs that cannot be satisfied. In the context of Afro-Brazilian religions, Exu thus represents a possible solution to the conflict between an unrealizable ideal and a reality in which the possibilities for upward mobility are greatly reduced. Exu is the owner of magic and the master of destiny: through his mediation, it becomes possible to influence daily life. The African Exu must, then, transform himself to adapt to a new reality. He becomes Brazilian.

Circulation between the Cults

The relation between the African Exu and the Brazilian Exu—including the multiple exus and *pombagiras* of Umbanda—is even more complex if we consider the great extent to which Candomblé spread in the cities of the Southeast. Until the 1970s, "white" Umbanda was held in higher esteem than Candomblé, which continued to be fundamentally "a black thing"; but since then Candomblé's image has changed considerably. Its social prestige increased with the growing participation of whites and, above all, intellectuals who gave it renewed social visibility and cultural weight. Today to be initiated in Candomblé raises the status of a medium[19] from Umbanda in the religious market.

In Rio de Janeiro and São Paulo, the large cities of the Southeast, mediums' passage from Umbanda to Candomblé constitutes a very important phenomenon that has entailed the reorganization of the Afro-Brazilian religious field. Umbanda is considered by many mediums to be an access route to Candomblé, a kind of preparation to achieve a higher level. To become initiated in Candomblé signifies a return to roots—a way to become "African."

Nevertheless, in this quest for Africa as a focus of legitimation, the mediums bring with them the "entities" (spirits) that they embodied in Umbanda: the *caboclos* and the exus. The caboclo—an indigenous spirit reinterpreted as being the "master of the land"—is venerated even in the most traditional terreiros, despite all efforts to maintain "African purity."[20] In contrast, the persistence of exus and pombagiras in the passage from Umbanda to Candomblé causes several problems. Umbanda exus are considered disincarnated spirits, and possession by them conflicts with the prohibition in Candomblé of any possession by *eguns*, the souls of the dead. The proximity of the eguns is regarded as spiritually polluting. Umbanda exus are thus considered negative and harmful to the son-of-saint's life.[21]

Therefore if, on the one hand, heads of terreiros need a great number of initiates in order to establish themselves in the religious market, on the other hand, the initiation of mediums from Umbanda can be a source of conflict with those who maintain cult orthodoxy. There is a dual response to this paradox: either the leader of the terreiro imposes a spatial separation —that is, he does not accept possession by exus in his terreiro but tolerates it outside the terreiro (in the medium's home or terreiro, if he has one)—or he reinterprets these spirits by "Africanizing" them. Umbanda exus then become the "slaves" of the orixás, reproducing one of the ritual functions of Exu, who can be the servant of the other African divinities. They are thus inscribed in Candomblé ritual logic. Even if most mediums assert that Pombagira is a typically Brazilian creation, she can also be reinterpreted and legitimized as the "slave" of a divinity—in other words, as one of the aspects of an African Exu in Candomblé.

In Umbandist writings we find constant ideological reformulations that seek to resolve the conflict between doctrinaire and conservative demands and the immediate interests of a cult's adepts. This has led to the reintegration of the once denied and weakened figure of Exu into the Umbandist system. In the same way, the reinterpretation of these spirits in Candomblé reveals a parallel strategy of adaptation of an ideal orthodoxy to the real interests of the mediums. We find the same opposition existing in Umbanda between the official discourse that seeks the "whitening" of the religion and the ritual practice of its followers, who see in Exu's power a form of adaptation to the social reality of large cities. Mediums overcome the difficulties of daily life using the same instruments as their protective spirits: cunning, guile, and the manipulation of destiny, all characteristics of Exu.

The complex rearrangements of Candomblé orthodoxy in ritual practice indicate that Afro-Brazilian religions are neither completed, fixed religious constructions nor mutually exclusive entities. Furthermore, ideal models bear little resemblance to ritual reality: neither the ideal Umbanda described by its theologians nor the "pure African" Candomblé preferred by the tradition's spokespeople ever really existed.

In Umbanda, as in Candomblé, official discourse seeks to reproduce an ideal of purity defined differently according to the situation: the whitening of black culture in Umbanda in the 1930s, or the re-Africanization of Candomblé through the struggle against syncretism since the end of the 1970s. The two "orthodoxies" constitute ideal, historically determined models that are linked to terreiros' legitimation in the religious market. Both (more aspirations than realities) must learn to coexist with the multiple arrangements that allow the ideal model to adapt to the complexity of ritual practice.

Africa in Brazil

The re-Africanization process that we see at work in the ritual reinterpretation of Umbanda exus originates in the tireless search for "Africanisms" in Afro-Brazilian religions. Since Afro-Brazilian studies began—and the very name of the discipline highlights this—researchers' attention has often focused on cultural traits that show African origins. Religions were analyzed with regard to elements that cannot be explained as social facts belonging to Brazilian society, "given that their origins are in Africa" (Birman 1980, 3).

Thus, the quest for these Africanisms constitutes the principal approach of the majority of anthropologists who have studied Afro-Brazilian religions. If for Nina Rodrigues (1900) the surviving African elements confirm the primitive and inferior character of Brazilian blacks (despite an internal distinction between more or less inferior blacks), for Bastide (1978) remaining true to an African past becomes a positive sign of social and cultural cohesion. "Black memory" becomes a sign of faithfulness to one's origins, and therefore of ritual purity. On the other hand, "betrayal" of these origins, caused by the loss of collective memory, characterizes "degenerated" or "degraded" cults.

Remaining true to the past defines "pure" religions as traditional, but the very idea of tradition raises epistemological problems that must be considered. Tradition commonly involves the survival of the past in the present. However, for something to become traditional implies not only repetition but also transformation. Traditions, in reality, tend to constitute a system of references that establish distinctions between what is traditional and what is not. Being part of a tradition, therefore, means establishing a difference. It is then necessary to question the political functions of traditions: they are not merely systems of ideas or concepts, but models of social interaction.

Asserting tradition, however, was often interpreted as intentional in Afro-Brazilian studies. People from "traditional" terreiros assert their loyalty to tradition because they are conservative, because they have maintained ties that keep them close to their origins. This assertion is often presented as a fact, or as a universal trait of human psychology, without further explanation. This trait, however, is not a common heritage. In the case of Candomblé, it is distinctive only to the Nagô cult, becoming a sign of superiority in relation to other African cults which have lost their roots forever.

The traditionalism of Nagô Candomblé, a notion already found in the writings of early researchers, was reiterated by Bastide (1978 and 1970b), based on the concept of collective memory. This notion—which Maurice Halbwachs (1925) associates with the construction of a symbolic space set in a material space—enables, according to Bastide, an African space and metaphysics to be reconstituted in Candomblé. However, the very idea of collective memory implies a superorganic view of culture. This vision is still found in the writings of several intellectuals linked to Nagô Candomblé who use, as we shall see, this recollection of an original *arkhé* as a political instrument.

The notion of tradition associated with Africanisms in Afro-Brazilian religions began to be questioned, starting in Maggie's (1977) work. Patricia Birman's (1980) analysis of Afro-Brazilian studies, for example, sees Africanisms—and indigenous elements found in the terreiros—as direct reproductions of what, in Brazilian society, was conventionally considered representative of the African and the indigenous in religious practices. Birman suggests that the origin of these surviving cultural elements is not to be found in a collective black memory, as Bastide claims, but in Brazilian (and non-Brazilian) intellectuals' scientific literature, and in their reconstruction of this tradition. Their responsibility has been brilliantly analyzed by Dantas (1988). However, while she sees this tradition as the invention of intellectuals used to better control the cults, this relationship of domination is by no means in one direction only. In reality it is also a political instrument which legitimizes the hegemony of the pure over the degenerate, being the product of scholars' "evangelization" (Maggie 1989) by Nagô religious elites. Africa—or at least the image of it constructed in Brazil—thus becomes the source of religious legitimation, in which the initiates' and anthropologists' discourses overlap in the same quest for roots.

Ritual Reorganization

This quest is also found in some studies of Umbanda. Liana Trindade, who analyzed the figure of Exu in Umbanda, sees in this divinity's characteristics proof of Africa's survival in a "white" religion. However, what seems important in this context is not to rediscover the Umbanda Exu's original African characteristics, but to see how a symbol from another context becomes part of a mythical and ritual structure, according to a specific operating logic. Religious systems, therefore, should be analyzed as codes for structuring the world—that is, as systems of signification. The mythical and ritual structure tells of the relations binding followers to the social system, by means of a complex network of symbolic mediations and solutions to social contradictions. In this way, each element does not have autonomous and absolute value, because its significance changes according to the position it occupies in a given context. The elements of heterogeneous origin are part of a vast process of symbolic bricolage, in which origin counts less than the significations currently attributed to them by believers.

The figures of Exu and Pombagira are, then, simultaneously symbols of faithfulness to African roots in Umbanda (Trindade 1985) and heterogeneous elements, signs of degeneration from their original purity, during the medium's passage from Umbanda to Candomblé. These spirits should therefore be reinterpreted and re-Africanized, in order to be assimilated back into Candomblé's religious structure. The separation between the ideological level—the "pure African" orthodoxy, as the source of legitimacy—and the ritual practice level is perpetuated, and the various ritual arrangements constitute the difficult mediation between the ideal and the reality.

Thus, while the principal concern of some authors has been to demonstrate the continuity of African thought in Umbanda, mine, in contrast, will be to analyze the ritual arrangements enabling the formation of a religious continuum which runs through the entire Afro-Brazilian religious field. At the same time in which Africa survived the "whitened" Umbanda, thanks to the daily practice of mediums and clients of Umbanda centers, the adaptation of Candomblé initiates coming from Umbanda has kept its links with the original religious context. The factors that were preserved—fiercely defended and reaffirmed—are those that more directly evoke a critique of the hierarchical system on which Candomblé ritual organization is based. What is at stake, then, is no longer the survival of an African heritage, but the operating strength of these symbols—the exus and pombagiras—and their importance in the interpretation of mediums' experience.

While Exu certainly acts as an element of adaptation to the chaotic reality of urban Brazilian society, offering symbolic assistance to resolve conflicts, he also is the protector, the "compadre" or friend of the individual, and the mediator of social conflicts between different hierarchical positions, between pais-de-santo and initiates, and between men and women. Through the discourse of Exu and that of his female counterpart, Pombagira, religious, social, and sexual power is constantly called into question.

The words of the spirits allow the power relationships within the cult or the family group to be criticized directly. Initiates, who owe obedience to their initiator, can thus create for themselves a space of autonomy and rebellion. The medium is not responsible for what is said, because officially possession leads to total loss of consciousness. Any critical judgment thus becomes legitimate because it comes from the spirit. The only way to react to these criticisms is to contest the spirit's presence and accuse the medium of simulating possession.[22] Such criticism, however, is not limited to the religious structure. Pombagira frequently becomes a pivotal figure in marital dramas, when gender relations are directly questioned. Thanks to the words of the spirit, female mediums can contest their partners' primacy and manage to impose their own conditions, renegotiating their inferior position.

These spirits' persistence in the passage from Umbanda to Candomblé also provokes rivalry between the medium and his pai-de-santo, who asserts his "power" in the religious market through his clientele and spiritual kinship. The practice of divination using cowries (*búzios*) is the pai-de-santo's principal means of resolving his clients and initiates' problems. On the other hand, possession by Exu or Pombagira puts the client in direct contact with the spiritual realm, since it is the spirit itself who offers a solution to his problem. The widespread practice of consulting mediums possessed by these spirits is thus a gauge of success—having many clients guarantees the mediums' economic independence and social status, resulting in their being in direct competition with the head of the terreiro.

Scholars and Tradition

We saw how the writings of intellectuals—physicians, sociologists, and anthropologists—on Afro-Brazilian religions have a direct influence upon the object of their study. The reformulation of the religious field through anthropologists' discourse is evident when studying Exu. How can we explain the fact that from the early twentieth century until the 1950s, Exu was identified with the devil, and then—in the works of Carneiro (1950), Bastide (1958), and above all Juana Elbein dos Santos (1976)—became the great mediator, the great communicator, the conveyor of the divine force (*axé*)? What is the explanation for this semantic shift based on a "pure African" tradition which is suddenly echoed in Bahian terreiros?

Is information gathered from the last slaves and reported in Nina Rodrigues's work at the end of the nineteenth century more "traditional" than that of African *babalawo* (diviners) which formed the basis of Juana Elbein dos Santos's analysis almost a hundred years later? Why did the last freed slaves hide Exu's fundamental importance in the Candomblé universe? Is it because the figure of Exu was associated with magic and, because of this, denied in the discourse of religious elites and anthropologists linked to traditional terreiros?

The alliance between scholars and Candomblé elites was able to disguise the quest for legitimacy of one sector of this religious universe with a scientific discourse, thanks to the pretended neutral and objective systematizations made by anthropologists. After the research of Juana Elbein dos Santos in Africa, Exu could occupy once again the central place in the internal logic of the cults, which led me to ask the fundamental question: what does tradition really mean?

In fact, we must not forget that what is told to anthropologists is always in accord with the ideological background of the informant, according to his own strategy of social adaptation and legitimation. There is no scientific objectivity because there is no objective discourse on the part of the subject. The Exu who was "forgotten" in the first part of the twentieth century could be "remembered" when his presence became coherent with the informants' goals and the reconstruction of an African tradition. The importance of the alliance between the terreiros and the scholars is confirmed by the emphasis given to the anthropologist's presence in a terreiro. To be studied by a researcher is equivalent to a certification of traditionalism and of one's close ties with African tradition.

Furthermore, when analyzing the re-Africanization process at work in the reinterpretation of the exus and pombagiras of Umbanda, it is important to understand that to "be re-Africanized" does not mean being or wanting to be black, or African. The re-Africanization process, as shown by Prandi (1991), implies, on the contrary, familiarity with all the literature on African and Afro-Brazilian religions. To "become African" signifies, therefore, the quest for a scientific explanation for religious practice.

The enormous success of the Yoruba language and civilization courses in Brazil demonstrates Candomblé initiates' constant quest for all the elements of the religion, now lost, which are thought to reconstitute an African purity. In this way, books—especially the vast amount of anthropological literature about Africa—become keepers of the lost tradition. Re-Africanization appears as an exercise of bricolage, in which each element is carefully sought in scientific literature. Initiates are thus transformed into researchers attempting to reconstruct their own culture, piece by piece.

The continual search for information about African religions, and the resumption of journeys to Africa (which played an important role in the legitimation of Afro-Brazilian religions in the beginning of the twentieth century), are the expression of this quest for African purity.

Mediums' Discourse

I chose to use the life stories of mediums possessed by Exu and Pombagira to better understand the central role performed by these spirits in their mediums' lives. The constant reinterpretation of everyday troubles as the sign of spirits' intrusion in the medium's life is indispensable for understanding these spirits' persistence in Candomblé, despite the problems it creates for maintaining an orthodox model.

During each interview, the medium organizes his experience: he presents himself as a social actor and, at the same time, offers an image of the society in which he lives. The majority of writing on Candomblé, however, does not accord much room to the individual; religion seems always to stem from an immutable past imposed upon its followers. Initiates appear as dispossessed of their material and spiritual lives: they are controlled by the gods and rarely described as social actors or political subjects. In interviews, on the other hand, they clearly reveal what Jeanne Favret-Saada calls a "specific experience of time" (1991, 671): the reinterpretation of misfortune through mediumship implies a reorganization of time, personal (and biographical) as well as social. The spirit is presented as the medium's only ally when faced with the difficulties of daily life.

My main concern was to avoid what Pierre Bourdieu, as well as Jack Goody, calls the "privilege of totalization" (Bourdieu 1977, 106). Therefore I kept a dialogical relation between my informants' speech and my perspective and interpretation. In this way, I sought to explain the constant process of creation and reformulation that forms the basis of every cultural construction. It was necessary to escape from the illusion of a perfect formal coherence that had tempted me in the past, and that appears to be the dominant line in Afro-Brazilian studies. I did not want to erase the contradictions among my informants' different theories and political projects, or to erase the authors of the statements by replacing them with an undefined collective subject: the *povo-de-santo* (Candomblé initiates). It is important to remember, however, that these narratives are not all equally significant, because the position that each informant occupies in the group modifies the information that he presents. It is very different if the person speaking is a pai-de-santo or a son-of-saint, and if he is regarded as belonging to the African tradition or to the syncretic cults.

I am aware that the continuous dialogue between the medium and his spiritual companions, as well as the constant shifts between the I and the Other, may shock more than one rational mind. In Brazil, however, the material world and the spiritual world are often very close—in no other country is mediumship (and the proximity of men and spirits) treated so naturally in television soap operas, such as *Mandala*, *Carmem*, or *A Viagem*. In Brazil, spirits live with and within people.

My aim is not, then, to cast doubt upon or to prove the reality of the spirits. The issue of the rationality of mediums' discourse arises only when interlocutors who do not have the same beliefs enter the scene. Spirits' intervention in daily life is as rational to the mediums as any relationship of cause and effect is to us. What seems important to me, then, is understanding how the mediums reinterpret their experience as an encounter—not always painless—between human beings and spiritual powers.

The two sides—the earthly and spiritual worlds—are part of a single reality: one cannot exist without the other, both in Candomblé and Umbanda. The close interaction of the adept with his orixá is reciprocal. The orixá (as the spirit, in Umbanda) possesses the initiate, but the initiate also metaphorically possesses his god: the incarnated god is referred to as being the Oxalá of Maria or the Oxossi of João, while the initiate is identified as Maria of Oxalá or João of Oxossi. Possession functions more as a multiplier of identity than as a simple loss of consciousness in favor of an external possessing agent. In the interviewees' narratives, we find a plurality of voices, in which identity is defined by multiplicity.[23]

My objective, therefore, was to reveal the close relationship linking mediums to their spiritual protectors, as well as their capacity to reinterpret the elements available to them in different religious contexts. The subtle articulation of symbolic thought—which offers a new place to elements from other religious contexts, using them in projects whose nature is essentially political—can be analyzed only through the discourse of the mediums themselves.

The complex relationships binding mediums to their spiritual allies— what Birman (1980) defines as the mediums' "symbolic capital"—are also linked to daily life in an extremely difficult socioeconomic context. To defend these spirits also means defending one's very means of subsistence. Becoming a medium is often one of the few options that can guarantee economic survival in the suburbs of large Brazilian cities. Asserting one's ties with the spirits is, therefore, a means of upward mobility for individuals who have little opportunity to improve their lot.

The Efon "Nation"

Various reasons led me to choose the Efon nation. First was the fact that it has developed greatly in southeastern Brazil, mainly in Rio de Janeiro and São Paulo. Other researchers (Prandi 1990, 1991; Gonçalves Silva 1992) have emphasized this nation's importance in spreading Candomblé in São Paulo. Furthermore, the Efon nation, along with the Ketu and Ijexá nations, is part of the group of Nagô nations, the cult modality considered to be the most "traditional." We have seen how this notion of tradition has been historically and politically elaborated. Paradoxically, the Efon nation's traditionalism has been constructed in the city of Rio de Janeiro, while the motherhouse in Salvador is now closed and practically abandoned.

The second reason for my choice is that there exists within this nation an opposition between orthodoxy, defended by religious leaders (Cristóvão de Ogunjá and Alvinho de Omolu, his son-of-saint), and the necessary adaptation to new contingencies, determined by the arrival in the religion of mediums from Umbanda. The ritual drama, which leads to a structural reorganization of the cult, focuses on the figures of Exu and Pombagira. This internal reorganization of the cult is common to other traditions, but almost all those I interviewed are part of the same religious family, even if they were affiliated successively to other Candomblé nations (see figure 3).

The Efon and Ijexá nations are very often confused with each other. According to the current mãe-de-santo of the Pantanal terreiro in Rio de Janeiro, founded by Cristóvão de Ogunjá, these two nations are very similar. The difference resides in the cult dedicated to the patron divinity of the Efon nation: Oloque or Oloroquê. The existence of a cult to this divinity, almost unknown, was noted by João do Rio and mentioned later by Arthur Ramos (1951b, 53). The presence in Salvador of black Africans from the Efã group (Efã, Efon, and Efan are generally used synonymously in specialized literature) was indicated by Gilberto Freyre (1946), Ramos (1979, 186), and Manuel Querino (1988, 31). According to Ramos (1979, 202), the Efan came from central Dahomey and were known as "burnt faces" due to a tribal mark on their faces. In his dictionary of Afro-Brazilian religions, Olga Guidolle Cacciatore (1977) uses Ramos's definition and includes the Efan in the Fon group. She also notes the presence in Rio de Janeiro of Cristóvão's Efan

1. Cristovão de Ogunjá, founder of the Rio de Janeiro Efon religious family.
PHOTO BY AUTHOR.

terreiro, while Gisèle Binon-Cossard (1970), in her list of terreiros in the Baixada Fluminense area of Rio de Janeiro, identifies the house of Cristóvão as belonging to the Ijexá nation.

In his Yoruba-English dictionary, Roy Abraham (1958, 301) speaks of the Efon of Ekiti, from the Ondo Province (Ilorin Division). The Efon have tribal marks, in which "the lines are so many and so close to each other that they form a dark patch on each cheek." The word "Efọn" can be pronounced in Yoruba *Efon* or *Efan*, depending on regional variations. In Brazil, these two terms refer to the same cult.

The Ekiti (Yoruba) origins of the Efon nation are even more likely if we consider the cult to Oloroke, the principal god of one of the districts of the Nigerian city of Ilemesho, in the kingdom of Ishan (Apter 1995, 389). The same cult exists in one of the "foreign" districts (of Iyagba origin) in the

2. Alvinho de Omolu during the public presentation of a new initiate. PHOTO BY AUTHOR.

neighboring kingdom of Ayede, still in Ekiti territory. The Iyagba (or Yàgbà) were allies of the Ekiti, along with the Ijeṣa and the Akoko, in the war between the Ekiti-Parapo and the Oyó and Ibadan until 1886 (Abraham 1958). This alliance can also explain the confusion in Brazil between the Efon and the Ijexá nations.[24]

Fieldwork, or Anthropologists and Belief

Since the seminal work of James Clifford and George Marcus (1986), an-thropologists have been aware of the essential role played by fieldwork narratives in claims for ethnographic authority, as well as of the complexity and ethical implications of the ethnographic encounter. However, con-ducting research on possession religions, structured by initiation rituals,

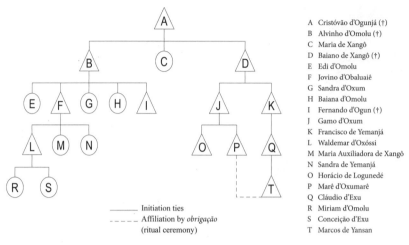

A   Cristóvão d'Ogunjá (†)
B   Alvinho d'Omolu (†)
C   Maria de Xangô
D   Baiano de Xangô (†)
E   Edi d'Omolu
F   Jovino d'Obaluaiê
G   Sandra d'Oxum
H   Baiana d'Omolu
I   Fernando d'Ogun (†)
J   Gamo d'Oxum
K   Francisco de Yemanjá
L   Waldemar d'Oxóssi
M   Maria Auxiliadora de Xangô
N   Sandra de Yemanjá
O   Horácio de Logunedé
P   Marê d'Oxumarê
Q   Cláudio d'Exu
R   Miriam d'Omolu
S   Conceição d'Exu
T   Marcos de Yansan

_____ Initiation ties
_ _ _ _ _ Affiliation by *obrigação*
(ritual ceremony)

3. The Efon family-of-saint.

also involves serious problems of methodology. To what point is it necessary to make a commitment? How is it possible to maintain a minimal distance when the object of the study requires total transformation, enrollment into a new order, and a change in one's body and spirit? Should one remain an "outsider" and observe without surrendering, or must one enter into the initiatory religion in order to penetrate its secrets and better understand it? Where does research end and belief begin?

These questions are the basis of all fieldwork in Afro-Brazilian religions, but, despite their importance, they are rarely made explicit and remain limited to the existential experience of the researcher. Nevertheless, since anthropological writings are a source of prestige and legitimation among practitioners, a scholar's involvement in a terreiro is not without consequences.

Most anthropologists who have studied Candomblé have become involved, in one way or another, in the religion[25]—a logical consequence of the anthropological method of participant observation. The anthropologist's first step in this universe is the divination session, through which he discovers his protective divinity. This is normally the first contact with the terreiro. From this moment on, the individual finds his place in the symbolic universe of Candomblé. He is the "son" of Xangô or Yansan, reproducing the fundamental personality traits of the other children of that god. The researcher is no longer a stranger: he participates in a structured world whose meaning is given by the gods.

The following step, the washing of the sacred necklaces, represents the first ceremony—the minimum level of religious engagement—and marks entrance into the cult. This is the first degree attained in Candomblé hierarchy. The anthropologist thus becomes a novice (*abian*), a potential candidate for initiation (*feitura de santo*).[26] At this stage, the researcher is already subject, to some degree, to the authority of the pai or mãe-de-santo. He (or she) has "read" his destiny; he (or she) has prepared the necklaces, activating them with his (her) *axé*.[27] Gradually, the researcher becomes engaged in the ritual life of the terreiro. He makes offerings to the divinities, participates in rituals, and helps initiates in their ritual tasks.

This first commitment frequently leads to initiation or to other rituals that mark religious affiliation to a certain terreiro. This is what happens with most anthropologists who study Candomblé. For men, there is an ad hoc ritual responsibility, allowing them to mark their affiliation to the cult without having to submit completely to the hierarchical order: receiving the honorary title of ogan, bestowed upon men who do not experience trances. An ogan is a protector of the terreiro, a person generally of higher social standing who helps the terreiro materially and financially. A male anthropologist would easily fit in this category.[28] To be chosen as an ogan is a sign of distinction because the choice comes directly from the gods, through the intermediary of one of their "sons" in trance. At the same time, there is nobody better than a doctor, professor, or man of letters to represent the cult group.

The same situation does not hold for women. Although there is a similar honorary title for women (*ekedi*),[29] it does not constitute a female anthropologist's principal mode of affiliation to Candomblé. Is this a question of, as Nina Rodrigues and Manuel Querino claim, women's greater inclination toward "altered states of consciousness," a type of inherent feminine weakness which leads them more easily into trance? Whatever the case, women appear to have closer direct experience with the sacred.

A researcher's belonging to the universe studied lends a particular authority to his voice, because it implies, *ipso facto*, a deep knowledge of the culture. The anthropologist thus becomes a kind of organic intellectual of the cult. This direct religious commitment appears to be a prerogative of Candomblé studies in Salvador. René Ribeiro, a specialist of the Xangô from Recife, defended his nonaffiliation to a terreiro in order to "separate himself from ritual commitments and the taboos that would certainly interfere with the discussion of the most esoteric subjects or with the assistance to the most private rituals; the observer seeks thus to escape from the *babalorixá's* domination, and remain, at the same time, on his level" (Ribeiro 1978, 6).[30] Nevertheless, nonaffiliation makes it impossible to participate in many rituals which are restricted to initiates.

What, then, is the best route to follow to conduct fruitful research? Is it necessary for the researcher to limit his role to that of a "sympathetic confidant," as René Ribeiro would wish, or should he become initiated to be able to know the religious reality from within?

Anthropologists are certainly not trained to conduct research in initiatory societies. The impact of research on the group studied, as well as on the researcher himself, is analyzed even less. To increase their knowledge, anthropologists must penetrate the initiatory secrets, but this knowledge, once acquired, cannot be revealed. To speak about or describe the initiation would be equivalent to betrayal.

This problem is even more serious in a society such as Brazil's, in which increasing numbers of initiates read anthropological texts with interest. Anthropological writings now make up part of the day-to-day reality of Afro-Brazilian religions. The implications for the researcher are difficult to manage: some things can be written, while others cannot. It is not only ritual logic, however, which imposes a silence that is difficult to violate; the discipline of anthropology also leads researchers to leave unmentioned experiences that are too close to the sacred.

In his Aquinas Lecture, given at the Hawkesyard convent in March 1959, Edward Evans-Pritchard (1962) analyzed sociologists' (and social anthropologists') attitudes toward belief and religious practice. For the most part, these attitudes were openly hostile. The social sciences developed along what is known as the process of disenchantment of the world from the end of the eighteenth century. Religious beliefs and faith had to be analyzed as social phenomena, and the social function they performed had to be demonstrated. Religion was merely an illusion, the product of an immature state of social evolution, which had to be reduced to another order of reality in order to be understood. Religious faith was considered definitively irreconcilable with science.

This attitude has been perpetuated until today. Studying a belief system or a religion means constantly reducing it to something different. Religious phenomena were thus reduced to social organization, economic order, or political balance between groups, sexes, age groups, and social classes. Incontestably, all this can be measured in the organization of religious cults. Religion has to do with a given society and the relations uniting the individuals within it. It is a "total social fact." But where does that leave religious experience? Can one reality be reduced to another without dismissing what is most clearly its specificity? Does our axiomatic need to relativize not engender a paradox?

It is indeed paradoxical to claim that the aim of relativization is to comprehend a native belief that is foreign to us, when those who believe do so absolutely. Their horizon of explanation is given by the belief itself and not by another order of reality (see Segato 1992). This paradox between the essence of the object and its interpretation is reinforced by the relationship linking the product of this relativization to the academic milieu, its primary interlocutor. How can we give the necessary space to another order of reality which can speak more directly of the specificity of religious experience?

The question becomes even more complex when the anthropologist really experiences the foundation of these cults: spirit possession. Is it possible to be "scientific" and "mystical" at the same time? Does participation in the studied object eliminate the possibility of understanding it? Why is the work of an anthropologist who analyzes the kinship system of a given society, and is incorporated into this system through adoption into a clan or lineage, not invalidated by this proximity, while an anthropologist who studies possession religions and experiences trances is seen with a mixture of suspicion and disdain by other scientists? Is this mistrust due to the excessive proximity to one's object, or the condemnation of any "out-of-body" experience?

José Jorge de Carvalho (1993, 105) examines the difficulty of analyzing the trance as a lived experience: if trance constitutes a departure from oneself, then the location of the subject becomes problematic, given that "basic rationality is short-circuited, both for observation as well as for interpretation." If it is difficult to interpret the processes of subjectivity which make up the multiplicity of I's, the analysis of situations in which the same ethnographer experiences an ecstatic trance becomes even more problematic: "These cases, apparently much more numerous than imagined, are, as a rule, relegated to the margins of 'professional' anthropological texts, and are unfortunately restricted to the sphere of scholars' private lives" (ibid.).

Arthur Ramos (1951b, 70), one of the most important anthropologists to have studied Candomblé, accepted initiation as an ogan, but only "for purposes of scientific research." Another attitude is that of Roger Bastide, who came to identify himself completely with the religion he studied. In the introduction to *The African Religions of Brazil* (1978, 28), Bastide writes "*Africanus sum*," thus claiming he belonged to the universe he studied. But no anthropologist, openly initiated or not, has spoken of his experience of trances.

Like all researchers, I too had to become involved in the cult "for purposes of scientific research." There are no other options for Candomblé researchers. It goes without saying that the pais and mães-de-santo show great ability to attract researchers into their sphere of influence. In my master's study of Candomblé Angola Kassanje, in 1991, I clearly indicated my involvement with the terreiro in question and my desire to give a more precise picture of the initiates' worldview, one different from what is usually presented. However, like other anthropologists before me, this commitment prevented me from relativizing the religious practice, one of the obvious limitations of my master's study. The criticisms I received led me to keep a certain distance from the studied object, which I now consider to be indispensable. Above all, however, they led me to ask unavoidable questions about anthropologists' roles in religion. Terreiro leaders' constant desire to establish an alliance with the researcher—offering him an honorary title or caring for his divinities—is part of a strategy to assert their religious power, which is also political, in the complex universe of Afro-Brazilian religions. My engagement with the terreiro I studied at the end of the 1980s was, in reality, a way for the pai-de-santo to assert himself among his peers.

What George Marcus (1997) calls the "complicity" in fieldwork—to define collaborative relationships that link anthropologists to their informants —is also based on a mutual awareness of the motivated interest in the ethnographic encounter. This "complicity" is not solely defined by the anthropologist's research agenda but rather includes the informant's own political agenda in a highly structured religious field. As Marcus (2006, 116) states, collaborations with our "epistemic partners" require "a very different sense of the politics of fieldwork, one that blurs the boundaries between the professional community of observers and those observed." But what happens when this collaboration entails the reasserting and validating of a symbolic relation of domination within the Afro-Brazilian religious field? The "complicity" between anthropologists and Nagô Candomblé elites leads to the exclusion of other possible epistemic partners: Angola Candomblé or Umbanda practitioners, for example.

If we are to recognize the subject as an epistemic partner who produces, in his own terms, what George Marcus and Douglas Holmes (2005, 1101) call a "para-ethnography," we also need to recognize the political function of these narratives. The anthropological studies resulting from this encounter, based on "complicity," often serve to restate and validate the difference between epistemic partners of different levels, such as the traditional Nagô and the syncretic Bantu or Angola.

For personal reasons, I left the terreiro I studied for my master's thesis and severed my ties with the cult group. Some years later, on resuming my research, I made every effort to separate my anthropological work from any involvement with the groups I was studying. But despite my "nonengagement," to my informants, I was one of them, because my divinities were "seated" (assentadas) and I had experienced the trance of the gods. As they say in Brazil, "when you enter Candomblé, you never leave." My presence in the heart of the religious family, made easier by my friendship with the pai-de-santo who initiated most of my informants, was legitimized by the contact I had with the sacred. In their view, I belonged in all respects to their religious universe.[31]

All the information I received was given to me as an anthropologist who, above all, had experienced in the flesh what it is to become the "Other." I always maintained a very clear distance from the logic at work within the terreiros or religious kin, avoiding taking sides in conflicts, which are far more frequent than I had imagined. I always clearly explained my intentions to all those I interviewed, sons-of-saint or pais and mães-de-santo. Because of the controversial nature of my research, which highlighted the opposition between a pai-de-santo who defended "orthodoxy" and a large proportion of his sons-of-saint who were possessed by exus and pombagiras, I attempted to remain neutral—as far as possible—with regard to the differing positions. I never saw my collaborative relationships with informants as a mere way to facilitate the gathering of data for authoritative frameworks. For me, fieldwork was not—and is still not—a simple professional rite of passage, as it is often perceived by anthropologists, but an enduring and transformative experience.

Exu, or Ariadne's Thread

The analysis presented here, then, is the fruit of a long journey into Afro-Brazilian religions, a difficult journey but also an extremely rich human experience. The questions that arose—about the internal logic of the cults and the role of anthropology—constitute the principal object of my analysis. I chose the figure of Exu as the leitmotif of this work and as an escort through and interpreter of this universe. He will be a kind of "Ariadne's thread," serving as a constant point of reference and giving ethnographic density to my arguments.

The "orthodox" discourse on Exu and his various avatars helps reveal the links between the different cults, too often regarded as separate and independent entities. First, we are confronted with a paradox (Exu's specific domain): most of Exu's characteristics in Africa—his unpredictability, his unbridled sexuality, his provocative role—were attenuated in Brazil, ironically in the cult groups that have always insisted on their traditionalism. This was so they could better adapt to the dominant social values, which considered Exu the incarnation of the devil, magical arts, and African savagery. In this way, the cult of Exu in Brazil became a characteristic mark of the "syncretic" cults, the Bantu cults that were accused of being unfaithful to Africa because they were too "permeable" with regard to outside influences.

In reality, it is precisely at the heart of the cults considered more "degenerated" or more "degraded" in relation to the "true" African tradition that the god of West Africa, the god of the Yoruba and of the Fon (under its Legba aspect), finds a space to exist and transform himself—one of his characteristic traits. The symbol of Exu, a figure in constant movement, continues his metamorphosis: the exus of Umbanda, the exus-eguns, and the pombagiras. The temptation of an impossible orthodoxy in a world where each terreiro is completely independent from the others cannot prevent the reappropriation of this African divinity, who has become a Brazilian spirit thanks to Umbanda. In ritual practice, orthodoxy must, therefore, adapt itself to the interests of ritual actors, men and women who live with their spirits, who share their concerns with them, and whose daily lives are pervaded by these spiritual powers. This orthodox model, difficult to reproduce in a highly complex reality, reveals itself to be the product of a process of tradition construction. Construction, not necessarily invention, for it is due to anthropologists' writings and, of course, to the strategies set up by the elite of Nagô Candomblé that this "traditional" image was developed over the years.

Through the re-Africanization movement and the circulation of mediums from one cult modality to another, Exu helps us to clarify the internal dynamic of these religions, founded on strategies of power and legitimation. Tradition acquired a "political" character: Africa, or its many incarnations, becomes the principal issue in this religious universe.

The Use of the Term "Afro-Brazilian"

In the first pages of this introduction, I alerted the reader to the problems involved in the use of the term "Afro-Brazilian." Within the Afro-Brazilian religious field, cults such as Kardecism or "white" Umbanda, which do not see themselves as practices of African origin, are in reality closely linked to religious modalities ("African" Umbanda, Omolocô, Candomblé) claiming African heritage. Furthermore, even religions that consider themselves the keepers of an African tradition, such as Nagô Candomblé, are no longer—and have not been for a long time—the monopoly of descendants of Africans. Even in the most traditional terreiros of Bahia, we find initiates who are white or mestizo. "African" identity is, therefore, completely dissociated from one's real ethnic origins. It is possible to be white, blond, and blue-eyed and say one is "African," as Bastide did, because of initiation into a terreiro considered traditional.

The term "Afro-Brazilian" is obviously loaded with significance and associated with the idea of a legitimating Africa, the sole and ideal birthplace of a religion which has now become a symbol of resistance. But what would be a more suitable term?

The simple use of specific terms identifying each religious practice (Omo-locô, Candomblé, etc.) prevents emphasizing the relationship of continuity (symbolic and ritual) that links the different cult modalities. In Brazil, "Afro-Brazilian" has become a common notion in popular and academic discourses. The concept came into being when blacks became part of the Brazilian nation, at the abolition of slavery, when Brazilian intellectuals began to question the nature of society and its human components. "Afro-Brazilian" thus refers to this blending of cultures which gave birth to the very idea of the Brazilian nation. Today the politics of affirmative action in Brazil means that Afro-Brazilian has become synonymous with "Afro-descendant," a hazardous shift when the matter is religious practices open to followers of all origins. The question is complex and needs to be discussed with other researchers who work in similar contexts (such as Cuba) so that, together, we can find new ways and a new terminology to recognize these religious realities. So I ask the reader to bear these observations in mind when reading the term "Afro-Brazilian." For my part, I will attempt to question the constant reference to Africa as the sole and exclusive origin of these cults. I will emphasize, in contrast, the process of cultural construction that gave birth to these cults, a process linked to the political issues running through the entire religious universe known as Afro-Brazilian.

THE METAMORPHOSES OF EXU

THE MESSENGER OF THE GODS
Exu in Afro-Brazilian Religions

The figure of Exu[1] attains a complexity in Afro-Brazilian religions that is rarely seen in other divinities. Exu, the emblematic representation of the trickster,[2] is the most human of the gods, neither completely good nor completely evil. Although the ritual role of this divinity has been shaped in an original manner in Brazil by the creation and internal organization of Candomblé, the constant reference to Africa, present since the religion's origins and particularly accentuated by the current re-Africanization and desyncretization movement in Brazil, makes it necessary to define the role of Èṣù in the Yoruba pantheon. In fact, information about Africa available in anthropological writing, limited to Benin and Nigeria in "traditional" Candomblé, serves as a model to religious members in their quest for an original purity. Thus, myths lost in Brazil are frequently rediscovered in the texts of Africanists.

To define this divinity and his ritual role in an African context is, then, an indispensable comparison for those who defend a "return to roots." Likewise, the discussion about the existence of a female Èṣù in Africa plays a central role in the legitimation process of the figure of Pombagira, the "wife of Exu," in Brazil. Thus, the constant dialogue between Afro-Brazilian and African religions makes it necessary to introduce the Yoruba figure of Èṣù–Ẹlẹ́gbẹ́ra and his Fon counterpart Legba, in order to better understand how the figure of Exu is currently constituted and articulated in Brazil.

The African Trickster: Èṣù and Legba in Africa

The Yoruba god Èṣù Ẹ̀lẹ́gbẹ́ra, called Legba by the Fon of Benin, plays a multiple role, rich in contradictions and often openly paradoxical.[3] He is the great communicator, the intermediary between gods and men, restorer of order to the world. However, at the same time, as master of chance in human destiny, he casts doubt upon conformist approaches to the universe by introducing disorder and the possibility for change. As the personification of challenge, will, and irreverence, Èṣù allows men to change their destiny thanks to the magic practices he controls. His irascible, violent and cunning character, however, has also caused the figures of Èṣù and Legba to be identified with the Christian devil. This identification, perhaps due to the most startling aspects of the effigies of these divinities, such as the large phallus that characterizes them, has existed since the first writings on West African religions.

According to the abbot Pierre Bouche (1885, 120–21), Èṣù Ẹ̀lẹ́gbẹ́ra incarnated the spirit of evil: "the Béelphégor of the Moabites, the Príapo of the Latins, *Deus turpitudinis*, as Orígenes said . . . Moreover, is he not given the name of *échou*, in other words, excrement or waste matter?" In the same way, the Reverend Samuel Johnson, a native of Nigeria and a convert to Christianity, attributed the demonic characteristics of Judeo-Christian mythology to Èṣù, calling him "Satan, the malign, the author of all evil" (1957, 28).

Legba is frequently associated with the notion of *aovi* (misfortune). In the Christianization process, Legba became the source of all evil: "Legba or Aovi is the worst of the evil fetishes. He is responsible for all the disputes, all the accidents, the wars and the catastrophes. He seeks only to hurt men and must be placated constantly with sacrifices and presents" (Kiti 1926, 2).

Èṣù's identification with Satan became the norm in dictionaries edited by missionaries. Thus, in Bishop Samuel Crowther's 1852 Yoruba dictionary, Èṣù is the "god of evil," misfortune, error, and damage. In Dahomey, where the missionaries' influence was very strong, "every black who knows some words of French thinks he must translate Legba by 'the devil,' just as he translates Bokonō [the priest dedicated to the god of divination] by 'charlatan'" (Maupoil 1988, 76). Currently, the most important Yoruba-English dictionary translates Èṣù (or Sátánì) as devil, "the supreme power of evil" (Abraham 1958, 166).[4]

The identification of Èṣù with absolute evil clearly implies his opposition to a positive principle identifiable in the Judeo-Christian God. However, the supreme divinity of the Yoruba pantheon, Olódùmarè, a kind of *deus otiosus*, does not act directly in the world, but through intermediaries. The opposition between good and evil, order and disorder, is therefore sought by missionaries in the relationship linking Ifá (Fa in Benin) to Èṣù-Legba. The Ifá divinatory system, of Arabic origin, was probably introduced to Yorubaland by the Hausa, an Islamicized people of northern Nigeria. From the beginning of the eighteenth century, the Ifá system (which became Fa among the Fon) spread through Dahomey, having been introduced by Yoruba merchants (Maupoil 1988, 49–50). In this system, Ọrùnmìlà, the god of divination, often designated by the name of Ifá, is defined as the mouthpiece of the supreme god (Olódùmarè or Ọlọ́run for the Yoruba and Mawu-Lisa for the Fon) and is associated with the divine trickster. This relationship was interpreted by the missionaries as a struggle between two opposing principles. Thus, the missionary Richard Dennett (1910, 95) identified Èṣù with the negative principle of the universe, "the Being of Darkness," opposed to the principle of goodness, embodied by Ifá, "Being of Light and Revelation."

In reality, the relationship between Ifá-Fa and Èṣù-Legba is far more complex. It cannot be reduced merely to an opposition between two principles: good and evil, order and disorder. Various myths reveal the interdependence that exists between the two gods, in which Ifá (Ọrùnmìlà) is the representative on earth of Ọlọ́run, the supreme god, and Èṣù is responsible for transmitting the supplications and offerings of men to the gods. This trinity, as William Bascom (1969a, 118) defines it, guarantees and protects men in accordance with the destiny attributed to each individual before birth. Èṣù assists Ọlọ́run and Ọrùnmìlà, translating the language of gods into the language of men and punishing all those who do not perform the sacrifices demanded by the Ifá divination, men as well as gods. In addition, he rewards those who scrupulously perform the sacrifices, therefore assuming the role of an "impartial police officer" who punishes those who disturb the order of the universe (Abimbola 1976a, 186).

The diabolical role of Èṣù is also closely connected with the order sanctioned by Ifá. If Èṣù-Legba tricks men, forcing them to offend the gods, it is to guarantee the survival of the latter, who feed off the sacrifices made by those who are obliged to atone for their errors and invoke divine protection. The Yoruba and the Fon say that Èṣù-Legba is the anger of gods. He is Ifá-Fa's executor, his chief commander. It is he who sets in motion the Ifá system, establishing the necessary bond between men and gods. According to the words of a diviner recorded by Maupoil: "Fa is like a judge: one cannot be both judge and executioner, this does not exist anywhere. *Agbanukwe*, one of Legba's aspects, is the anger of Fa. Each of Legba's aspects is an anger, and the great Legba is the wrath of God" (1988, 83). In the human body, Legba resides in the navel (*hon*), from where he breathes in anger. For this reason in Benin he is called *houdan* (the agitator of the navel) or *home-singan* (chief of anger), "because anger comes from the womb like happiness, pain and compassion" (Le Hérissé 1911, 138).

Èṣù-Legba is, therefore, simultaneously "police officer," "executioner," and "*agent provocateur*." Without him, communication between men and gods would be lost forever. The order established by Ifá cannot survive without the "diabolical" intervention of Èṣù-Legba.

As well as being a translator, messenger, and mediator, Èṣù-Legba is the master of magic. A Fon myth tells how Legba was the first to prepare the *gbo*.[5] At that time, the gods were starving because no offerings were made to them, so Legba decided to place snakes, which he created by magic, in the path that led to the market. When a snake bit someone, Legba was there, ready to save him in exchange for payment. One day a man called Awé asked Legba to explain how he had prepared the snake magic, and Legba, after having been suitably rewarded, revealed the secret of his *gbo* to the man. This is how Awé became the first man to know how to prepare a *gbo*, and he became the great chief of the fetishists (Herskovits 1938, 257). Legba is the master of magic because he has the power of transformation, but he and Èṣù are also masters of paradox: they reorder the world by causing chaos; they delude in order to reveal and lie in order to tell the truth. While Èṣù is considered the firstborn of the universe, he is also the youngest son.

In his form of Èṣù Yangi, the red laterite stone, he personifies the first form created, made from the same mud with which Ikú (death) created human beings. Yangi, then, becomes humankind's firstborn; he is simultaneously the ancestral father (the Èṣù-Àgbà) and the first descendant.

Various myths related to the birth of Èṣù are mutually contradictory, describing him both as an old man and a mischievous boy. This apparent contradiction, however, expresses paradox as a cognitive possibility of the universe. Thus, one of the ritual names of Èṣù is Táíwò (tọ́-aiyé-wò, or the "taster of the world"), and it is given by the Yoruba to the firstborn of twins. But Èṣù is never considered the elder—on the contrary, he is considered the younger twin,[6] for among the Yoruba the younger one must always go before the older to "test the path before him," to the degree that the firstborn is called the explorer (Wescott 1962, 341). The identification with the younger reveals Èṣù's paradoxical nature.

Master of paradox, Èṣù is equally the master of multiplicity, assuming various forms, each one of them named according to its characteristics. The exact number of these forms is not known, but the quantity recorded clearly indicates the elusive nature of this divinity.[7] Thus, Èṣù is called Ẹlẹ́bọ, the master or regulator of ẹbọ (the ritual offering), or Ẹlẹ́rù, the master of ẹrù (or carrego, religious obligation).[8] The myth of Òṣẹtùá, linked to the Ifá system, tells how Èṣù was able to bring all the offerings to the feet of Olódùmarè and how he became Òjíṣẹ́-ẹbọ, the bearer of offerings.[9] In this myth, Èṣù is the only one able to cross the gates to the spiritual world and be heard by Olódùmarè. Through the restitution of the vital energies symbolized by the ẹbọ, the offering, Èṣù reestablishes harmony on earth.

In the same way, the power of Èṣù and Legba to reorganize the universe is linked to their highly sexual nature. Travelers in ancient times and early missionaries always emphasized the obscene side of these two divinities. Pruneau de Pommegorge, who lived in Ouidah from 1743 to 1765, described Legba as "a Priapic god, crudely made from earth, with his principal attribute, which is enormous and exaggerated in proportion to the rest of his body" (quoted by Verger 1957, 120). This picturesque description of Èṣù Ẹlégbẹ́ra is from Bouche:

> The phallic cult is exhibited without shame. One sees everywhere the horrible instrument that Liber invented to serve the abominable maneu-

vers of his passion: in the houses, in the streets, in the public squares. The phallus is found in isolation; at times the priests carry them with great pomp. In certain processions, they are shaken with great ostentation and pointed at young girls, amid the dancing and laughter of a population without shame. The blacks are very inspired when they make this instrument the attribute of Elegbara, the personification of the demon. (Bouche 1885, 121)

Nevertheless, Èṣù-Legba's relation to sexuality is not limited to the obvious symbol of the disproportionate phallus, as shown in statuettes of him. Èṣù is always represented with a cap, the long point of which falls over his shoulder, or with his hair combed in a long braid, sometimes sculpted in the form of a phallus (Wescott 1962, 348). Most often, Èṣù is whistling or sucking his thumb. According to Wescott (ibid., 347), whistling is taboo around the royal palace because of its sexual symbolism, and the same is true of thumb sucking. Èṣù carries on his back various calabashes with long necks, called calabashes of power (àdó irán), and holds in his hand a club called ọgọ̀, a euphemism for penis (ibid.).

Èṣù's sexual connotations, however, are not directly linked to reproduction. His phallus represents potentiality, boundless energy, sex as a creative force and the possibility of realization. Èṣù is also responsible for erotic dreams, adultery, and all illicit sexual relations. At the end of the nineteenth century, Ellis established an interesting parallel between the cult of Legba and the sorcery of the Middle Ages: "As in the case in the western half of the Slave Coast, erotic dreams are attributed to Elegba, who, either as a female or male, consorts sexually with men and women during their sleep, and so fulfils in his own person the functions of the incubi and succubae of mediaeval Europe" (Ellis 1894, 67).[10]

Legba, like Èṣù, is closely linked to the beginning and end of an individual's life. Every rite of passage is marked by the revelation of the fa (individual destiny) and of the "personal Legba." When a man dies, his personal Legba should be destroyed, as well as the representation of his fa (destiny). That is because, the Fon say, during death a door closes, and if Legba cannot accompany the deceased, the door to the world will remain open forever (Pelton 1980, 126). The same occurs with Bara, the existential representation of Èṣù shaped during the Candomblé initiation ritual. Èṣù, in his individualized form of *Bara*,[11] also accompanies men until their death.

The existential Èṣù is represented by a mound of clay or red laterite (in the form of Yangi) in a vaguely human shape, his eyes and mouth sometimes accentuated by cowries, with nails driven into the top of his head to symbolize that he "bears no weight"—meaning that he is not subject to any of the obligations to which men are subject. Legba's representations are more markedly characterized by sexual attributes—an enormous phallus, or a pipe in his mouth. The association of Èṣù and Legba with all the places linked to exchange and transaction (market squares, crossroads, front doors) clearly shows that they occupy a position of mediation. Piles of earth moistened with palm oil or covered with yams or cola nuts constitute their sanctuaries at crossroads, called *Èṣùríta* (Èṣù of the crossroads). The representations of Èṣù found on the roadside are called *Èṣù-ọ̀nà* (Èṣù of the road), and those in the market, *Èṣùọjà* (Pemberton 1975, 20). There is also a shrine dedicated to Legba or Èṣù in each Fon or Yoruba market square.

Authors do not agree about the existence of an organized cult and priesthood for Èṣù and Legba. Melville Herskovits (1938, 229) and Geoffrey Parrinder (1950, 82) deny its existence, while Honorat Aguessy (1992, 95), having claimed the absence of priests devoted to the cult of Legba, contradicts himself when quoting the discourse of Akpowena, "high priest of Legba" (ibid., 307). Le Hérissé (1911, 100) writes of the "Vodun Legbanon," the priest that embodies Legba. In the same way, Pemberton (1975, 22) quotes songs dedicated to Èṣù chanted by the *elemoso* (Èṣù priestess of the first rank), just as Bascom (1969b, 79) quotes Èṣù priests "who are identified by a string of small opaque maroon or black beads worn around the neck."[12]

Verger (1957, 114–15), meanwhile, writes as much about initiates and priests dedicated to Èṣù as he does about Legba's adepts, the *legbasi*. The latter dress in purple straw skirts, wearing hats decorated with various objects, also purple, and numerous cowrie necklaces slung over their shoulders. The legbasi dance with enormous wooden phalluses concealed under their skirts, showing the audience the phalluses, raising them, and simulating the sexual act. Others carry in their hands a purple fly swatter which hides a club in the form of a phallus.

Annual festivals in honor of Èṣù are organized at Oyó (Wescott 1962,

344) and Ilé-Oluji (Idowu 1962, 84), during which women dedicated to Èṣù parade in procession. They carry different insignias, the most common of which are a pair of statues representing a man and a woman with their hair styled in a crest. Èṣù is often symbolized by a couple. According to Robert Farris Thompson (1984, 24), among the Egbado Yoruba, these two statues represent Èṣù-Ẹlẹ́gbá and his wife. Wande Abimbola (1976a, 36) also writes of Èṣù's mythical wife, called Agbèrù (she who receives sacrifices), and Abraham (1958, 167) confirms the existence of male and female images of Èṣù.

Legba also has feminine representations, according to Herskovits (1938, 222), who cites Richard Burton's description of 1864: "Legba is of either sex, but rarely female. Of the latter I have seen a few, which are even more horrid than the male; the breasts project like halves of a German sausage, and the rest is to match." Herskovits (ibid., 225), like Maupoil (1988, 82), notes the presence of statues representing Legba's wives next to the central figure of Legba in shrines dedicated to him.

Èṣù-Legba, whether male or female, inhabits all the places in which separated worlds come into contact. He or she passes from one to another, making them communicate with each other. The places over which Èṣù-Legba reigns are places for encounters, mediation, and exchanges, and like any place of transition and intersection, they are charged with a dangerous tension. The market is the representation par excellence of the place where men's transactions can engender conflict and disharmony. Only Èṣù-Legba, with his power of transformation, can change conflict into harmony.

Èṣù-Legba, god of multiple faces and multiple origins, is also a critic of power and those who wield it. He is the only divinity who can do this, introducing liberty into a closed and fixed system. Through his irreverence, questioning of social rules, and lack of respect, Èṣù-Legba incarnates what Georges Balandier (in Motta 1985, 66) calls the "logic of politics" in African tradition. In reality, most of the myths related to Èṣù-Legba are myths of inversion of the social order.[13] Thus, Èṣù has a dual role: on the one hand, he is the transgressor of rules, questioner of the established order; on the other hand, he is the symbol of change within this same order, exploring the possibilities inherent in the status quo. As Joan Wescott states (1962, 345), Èṣù-Legba has a dual and paradoxical role, both social and antisocial, making him the most human of all the divinities.

The Multiplicity of the Ritual Figures of Exu in Brazil

In Brazilian Candomblé, the figure of Exu appears to have retained the majority of his African characteristics. Today, any initiate questioned about Exu would confidently respond that he is the messenger of the orixás. Another characteristic of this divinity, also known to all initiates, is that Exu is the firstborn of the universe, the first created being, which distinguishes him from the other divinities by making him closer to mankind. Marcos de Yansan, a Ketu pai-de-santo, reveals these close ties between men and Exu: "As the Catholics have Adam and Eve, the followers of Candomblé have Exu."[14]

Exu is also the master of destiny because he opens or closes paths, meaning the paths of life. Thus, for an individual to be completely realized, he needs to attract Exu's benevolence by means of ritual offerings. Exu also represents the principle of change in an individual's life, or—as Palmira de Yansan, a Ketu mãe-de-santo, puts it, the "principle of revolution":

> Exu is the principle of revolution. He is responsible for the path you take on earth. When things are going badly, Exu gives you the desire to change everything. What is the point of living in a luxurious penthouse and being terribly unhappy, while a washerwoman from the *favela* is singing happily next to her children? This washerwoman has no prob lem with Exu, but the rich lady is extremely dissatisfied. If she has the strength to drop everything and start a new life, she will seek change. She will seek Exu.

Identified for a long time as the devil in Afro-Catholic syncretism, Exu is today considered an indispensable element of the religion's smooth functioning. Without him, nothing can be done. His role as a go-between for men and gods has become even more important in Candomblé. This is because divination by *opelé*,[15] linked to the Ifá system, has been abandoned and replaced by divination by *dilogun*[16] (*jogo de búzios*), through which Exu speaks directly to the person via the way the cowries fall. The predominance of *dilogun* in Candomblé is linked to the disappearance of the figure of *babalaô* (diviner, priest of Ifá) in Brazil. Cowries can be cast by the pais or mães-de-santo, facilitating the functioning of ritual activities, which always depend upon the consultation of the divine oracle.

4. Exu of the gateway. PHOTO BY AUTHOR.

There are always at least two Exus in every Brazilian terreiro.

Near the entrance door of the house of worship there is always a small construction where the *assento*[17] of the Exu of the gateway is placed. He is the guardian of the house, the one who wards off negative influences. The second Exu, known as friend or compadre, is buried in the main room (*barracão*) where public ceremonies take place.

Exu's assento is usually made of a mound of clay, to which an anthropomorphic form may be given, with cowries in the place of the mouth and eyes. Another method of preparing it consists of placing a *ferramenta* (a piece of forged iron) in the clay, which is always ritually prepared with herbs and ingredients specific to each "quality."[18] Next to the assento may be found iron statuettes endowed with large phalluses and horns, long-necked calabashes, cowries, and knives. The assento is always encircled by lighted candles and sprinkled with palm oil. This oil, called *azeite de dendê*[19] in Brazil, is closely connected to the figure of Exu, who is also known as Exu Elepó or Exu, master of palm oil (*epó*).

As the incarnation of multiplicity, Exu splits into Exu-orixá and the orixá's Exu. Each orixá has his Exu, who is considered his servant or "slave."[20]

5. Exu's assento in the Ilê Ifá Mongé Gibanauê. PHOTO BY AUTHOR.

He works for the orixá with whom he is connected, bringing the offerings (ebó) from the material world to the spiritual world. Without Exu, the orixás would never be aware of the needs of their followers and, consequently, would not be able to come to their aid. Distinguishing between the qualities of Exu-orixá and those of Exu-slaves is complicated and leads to complex discussions about the nature of these spirits. The orixá's Exu is sometimes identified as the Exu-Bara, the personal Exu who is linked to an individual's destiny and who accompanies the initiate until his or her death. Indeed, one of the most important moments of the initiation process is the revelation of the initiate's personal odù (his destiny) and the fabrication of his existential Exu. However, these two types of Exu seem to represent two distinct forms of individualization of the Exu-orixá's energy: the orixá's Exu or Exu-slave being the individualization of the Exu-orixá with regard to the

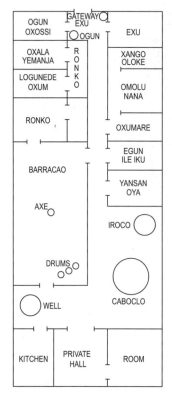

6. Plan of Alvinho de Omolu's terreiro.

spiritual world, while the Exu-Bara or existential Exu is his individualization with regard to the world of men.

Most Candomblé houses have many statuettes representing the existential Exu of the sons-of-saint. Modeled from clay in the shape of a head, with cowries or nails, they are placed in the house of Exu, at the entrance of the terreiro. They symbolize the initiate's existence and receive offerings of palm oil and *cachaça*, a distillation of cane sugar. But, as we have seen, Exu is also the master of magic, manipulation, and transformation; so, in every house of worship, it is necessary to "seat" various Exus destined for magic works according to their specialties. Thus, if you wish to harm someone, you would choose a dangerous Exu such as Buruku (which means evil in Yoruba). On the contrary, if you are looking for protection and well-being, you would choose Exu Odara (meaning good in Yoruba) or Onan, who opens the way. In practice, however, Exu can always act for good or for evil, whatever his specialization.

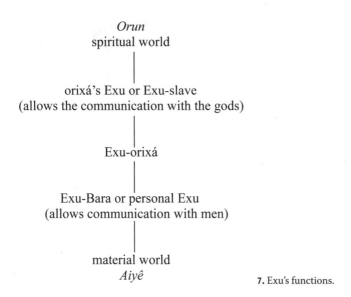

Orun
spiritual world

orixá's Exu or Exu-slave
(allows the communication with the gods)

Exu-orixá

Exu-Bara or personal Exu
(allows communication with men)

material world
Aiyê

7. Exu's functions.

The difficulty in pinning down the real nature of this divinity is shown clearly in Claude Lépine's definition of Exu-slave, who may even be confused with one of the manifestations of Exu-orixá: "each orixá has his own Exu, who is his servant and has a specific name; this Exu may occasionally appear in the place of the orixá, and the mãe-de-santo must be capable of distinguishing them—similarly, she should not confuse this Exu with the manifestation of a quality of the general Exu: Lalu, Ijelu or another" (1978, 264).

In this case, possession by the orixá's Exu (the Exu-slave) would be considered impure and must be avoided at all costs. The plurality of Exu's roles has given rise to a peculiar perception of this mythical figure. According to some authors, he is not a true orixá, but a servant of the orixás and an intermediary between men and gods.[21] The number of Exu's "qualities," then, becomes the expression of his elusiveness. Exu ought to have twenty-one qualities, but, as he is connected with multiplicity, this number is often much greater and varies according to the terreiro under consideration. The only common denominator is the number seven, which is particularly closely linked to magic: "there are twenty-one Èṣù, say some in Bahia; others speak of seven, or twenty-one times twenty-one, but he is multiple and one at the same time" (Verger 1957, 119).

8. Exu's assento with palm oil, *cachaça*, and honey. PHOTO BY AUTHOR.

Exu plays a central role in the initiation process. Some of Exu's "qualities" are, in fact, linked to the crucial moments of the initiation. Thus, Exu Jelu, the symbol of the growth and multiplication of living beings, is connected to the creation process of the new being—the initiate who is reborn into a new life. Exu Jelu is the master of *waji*, the dark blue pigment extracted from the indigo plant that is used in the ritual painting of the initiate's head, after it has been completely shaved. This procedure is also performed under Exu's protection, in this instance Exu Idosu. Similarly, the incision made on the top of the head to allow the fixation of the connection with the orixá who is master of the head, and the preparation of the *oxu*, the cone placed upon this ritual cut, are two operations linked to Exu's actions. In this way, the oxu symbolizes the red laterite stone, the very first creature, Exu Yangi, the elder of the universe, and the new initiate will be called an *adoxu*, the bearer of oxu.

In his quality of *enugbárijo* (the collective mouth), Exu is invoked at another moment of the initiation ritual, the "opening of speech." This ritual allows the manifestation of the new orixá on the day of naming, the public ceremony during which the orixá reveals the ritual name of his "son," and the new initiate is admitted as a member of the religious group. The final step of initiation is the preparation of Exu-Bara, which can come with a calabash containing twenty-one cowries: sixteen constitute the dilogun; four others make up what is known as Exu's oracle, consulted for the problems of daily life or to confirm a divine response; and the last symbolizes Exu Oxetuá, the firstborn of the universe.

Possession Denied

In works dedicated to Candomblé, as in those on Èṣù and Legba worship in Africa, information about initiation to Exu is extremely contradictory. Thus, while Nina Rodrigues confirmed in 1900 that Exu was an orixá like the others, with his own initiates,[22] in 1948 Carneiro recounted the difficulty of accepting the cult of a divinity identified as the devil in Afro-Catholic syncretism. In the event of a person whose master of the head was Exu, initiation was carried out to Ogun, another orixá considered as his brother:

> Although not exactly an orixá, Exu may manifest himself as orixá. In this case, one would not call the person "daughter" of Exu, but she would have a *carrego* of Exu, an obligation towards him throughout her whole life. This carrego is delivered to Ogunjá, who lives with Oxossi and Exu, and who feeds off raw food, so that Exu does not take possession of the person. If, in spite of this, he manifests himself, Exu may dance in the Candomblé, but not among the other orixás. This did occur once, in the Tumba Junçara (Ciriaco) Candomblé, in the Beiru district (Salvador): the girl was dancing, crawling on the ground, her hair unkempt and her clothes filthy. The manifestation has, it would seem, a provocative nature. It is the only instance, to my knowledge, of possession by Exu in the Candomblés of Bahia. (Carneiro 1986, 70)[23]

In his study on the Candomblé of Bahia, Bastide uses Carneiro's definition: "Exu does not take on incarnations, even though he sometimes has children" (1958, 21). For Bastide, possession by Exu would be completely distinct from other possessions; it would not be a question of "a simple difference of degree in, for example, the violence of the manifestation, but a veritable difference in nature" (ibid., 153). Possession by Exu would, in reality, be perceived as both a "heavy burden to be dragged laboriously"

9. House of Ogun and Oxossi. PHOTO BY AUTHOR.

and, under "Christian influence," a "divine punishment" (ibid.). To illustrate what he says, he presents the case of Sofia, an initiate who received the ritual name of Gikete in the Angola Candomblé terreiro of Ciriaco, already mentioned by Carneiro. The initiation to Exu seems to be the pai-de-santo's "mistake":

> The *babalaô* may occasionally be wrong in the consultation of destiny; it is certainly very rare—I know of only one controversial case, that of a daughter of Exu, but it was the girl who was displeased with her "saint" [orixá] and made herself out to be a daughter of Ogun; the *babalorixá* who had initiated her, however, insisted that S. was really a daughter of Exu. In any case, one can never be completely sure that the babalaô did not make a mistake. But it would have been a very grave error—the true orixá of the horse [the person possessed] could not fail to show his discontent on seeing sacrifices and food go to someone other than himself; for revenge he would cast disease and misfortune upon the horse in question, and it was precisely because S. was ill that she considered herself "wrongly initiated." (Bastide 1958, 32)

Sofia's refusal to accept her divinity seems, then, to be motivated more by public disapproval—because of Exu's being identified with the devil—than by the initiate's real ambivalence. What's more, this ambivalence is called into question when Verger (1957, 119) tells us that Sofia kept a great number of Exus in her home, which she must certainly have considered as her protectors:

> She had many Èṣù in her home: at the bottom of the garden in a little house there was a trident-shaped iron which supported Esu Baba Buya, and an iron chain for Esu Sete Facadas. He was accompanied by Esu Elegbara and Esu Mulambinho. Behind the door of her house was lodged Esu Pavena. Under the front door there was Esu Vira (a female Esu), and in the floor was Esu Intoto. She could also have at her disposal Esu Tibiriri Come Fogo who wandered here and there without being seated, as well as Esu Tamanquinho and Esu Ligerinho, the latter bearing a bow. She herself was dedicated to Esu Mavambo from Angola [Candomblé].

It would seem improbable that someone who did not publicly accept her orixá would have such a large number of Exus for private worship. In reality this ambivalence, says Verger (1981, 79), derives more from social constraints—Exu's identification with the devil—than the initiate's real refusal, due to the pai-de-santo's error. The true cause of this avoidance of Exu thus reveals itself to be connected to the weight of syncretism, and not to the degradation of the African tradition in Bantu religions.

Bastide contradicts himself when, seeking to demonstrate that the initiation to Exu was an error exclusive to the Bantu religions, he quotes, among the "extremely limited" number of sons and daughters of Exu, Maria of the Mar Grande terreiro; Julia from the Lingua de Vaca terreiro, who was known as Exu Biyi; and the brother of Pulcheria from the Gantois (1958, 152). These three terreiros are considered traditional, all connected to the Nagô orthodoxy.

Bastide also quotes another of Exu's initiates belonging to the temple of Bernardino, the pai-de-santo of Bate-Folha (of the Angola nation). His possession, like Sofia's, seemed to be characterized by much violence and extreme suffering: "I saw another at Bernardino's house during my last journey to Bahia—his face hardened in a grimace of conventional evil, whose dance was nothing but spasmodic movements or sacred fury" (1958, 152).

And to highlight the disapproval connected with this possession, he says: "possession by Exu differentiates itself from that of orixás' by its frenzy, its pathological, abnormal nature and its destructive violence; if one needs a comparison, it is similar, in Catholics, to the difference between divine ecstasy and demonic possession" (ibid., 21).[24]

The interdiction of the possession by Exu is affirmed later by other authors, for whom it is no longer the result of Afro-Catholic syncretism but a mark of traditionalism: "In traditional terreiros, Èsù must not manifest himself" (Juana E. dos Santos 1976, 134). "Seating" Exu in the head of a son-of-saint cannot then come under the true African tradition! However, Juana E. dos Santos's categorical statement is tempered by Marco Aurélio Luz (1983, 94–95): "The Catholic priests and Protestant vicars sought to para-lyze the Nagô system, by fighting against Exu whom they associated with the devil. So, in order to get around this repressive campaign, the African tradition initiated his priests in the cult of Ogun, considered to be Exu's brother in the terreiro's jargon."

The first person initiated to Exu recorded in anthropological writings was Sofia de Exu Mavambu, from the Angola terreiro Tumba Junçara of Sal-vador. Her pai-de-santo, Manoel Ciriaco dos Santos, was criticized harshly for having "made" (seated) the devil in Sofia's head. Toward the end of the 1940s, Ciriaco transferred his terreiro from Salvador to Rio de Janeiro and established his house of worship to the Baixada Fluminense at Vilar dos Teles. The first to be initiated to Exu in Rio de Janeiro was Djalma de Lalú, in the Jeje terreiro of Tata Fomotinho (Antonio Pinto). This pai-de-santo had been initiated in the Terra Vermelha terreiro at Cachoeira de São Felix, in the heartland of Bahia's Jeje tradition. It is a very interesting case, because officially the initiate was the son of Oxossi, but on the day of naming—at the end of the initiation period—it was an Exu who manifested himself: Exu Lalú. Djalma de Lalú went on to become one of the best known figures of Candomblé in Rio de Janeiro. All my key informants spoke of him with respect and admiration, and all admitted that after him, it became much easier to initiate an Exu's son in Candomblé.

The existence of a veritable prejudice against initiation to Exu is re-counted by a son of this divinity, Cláudio de Exu, who was initiated in 1967 at the age of fifteen:

At the time it was difficult to be initiated to Exu. The worst was finding someone who knew how to do it . . . and who was brave enough, of course! If a mistake were made, the initiate could go mad or have serious problems. Even João da Goméia, the most important Angola pai-de-santo, did not have the courage to seat Exu in my head. I'd known him since I was twelve . . . and he was well aware of the problems I had because of this orixá.

In reality, João (or Joãozinho) da Goméia initiated at least one daughter-of-saint to Exu before his death in 1971 (Binon-Cossard 1970, 338). But if, in Angola terreiros, initiation to Exu is considered completely normal, this is not so for other Candomblé nations, such as the Efon nation. Thus Maria de Xangô, mãe-de-santo of Pantanal and granddaughter of its founder Cristóvão Lopes dos Santos, states categorically that "in Efon, we do not initiate to Exu but to Ogun Mejé" (a quality of Ogun, linked to Exu)."

However, Alvinho de Omolu, pai-de-santo of the Ilê Ifá Mongé Gibanauê and son-of-saint of Cristóvão,[25] initiated one of his sons-of-saint to Exu at the beginning of his religious career. His pai-de-santo, Cristóvão de Ogunjá, participated in this initiation, while declaring that to "make" an Exu was to "dirty the razor" (*sujar a navalha*), meaning "to contaminate the axé."[26] This contradiction illustrates the tension that exists between an orthodoxy that is desired, but difficult to carry out, and ritual practice. Indeed, the testimonies gathered reveal a very marked ambivalence between the desire to obey the ideal model proposed by Nagô tradition, and the temptation to "make" an Exu. In order to initiate someone to Exu, the necessary knowledge must first be acquired, for he is a dangerous god; at the same time, "making" an Exu brings prosperity and well-being to the terreiro. Alvinho de Omolu, of the Efon nation, explains how to initiate a son of Exu:

A son of Exu cannot be initiated in Exu's house. The ritual of shaving the head is done outside, in a specially built hut of oil-palm leaves. But first, Exu-Bara must be seated [*assentado*]. It is difficult to initiate an Exu for one has to know the "paths" he will take [the odùs to which he is connected] and the offerings to make in determined places. They are not the same things as we would offer to the Umbanda exus, grilled meat, and so on—the orixá eats nothing of that kind!

The pai-de-santo's explanation reveals the constant preoccupation with demarcating the distance between an Exu "of the street" (*da rua*), considered an inferior category and too close to the domain of the Umbanda exus, and an Exu-orixá.

One of the most remarkable characteristics of the people involved with Candomblé is their capacity to analyze, dissect, criticize, or justify the slightest detail of a ritual. In this way, in a constant effort to reorganize the religious universe, each detail is discussed and is the subject of long and elaborate argumentation. All my informants presented their own vision of the ritual characteristics of the Exu-orixá. For example, ritual colors can vary from the classic red and black (connected to the Christian devil in syncretism) to white, red, and black (or dark blue, which is considered a variation of black), to completely white (a symbol of peace), or even multicolored, because "Exu is Ifá's envoy" and thus represents all the other orixás.

However, when discussing the plants used in the initiation process, all agree that Exu's leaves are hot leaves, such as those of nettles or *atá* and *ataré* peppers. During a public ceremony, Exu may also carry in his hands *peregun* leaves (*Dracaena Fragans* Gawl), which are connected to the initiation process. According to José Flavio Pessoa de Barros (1993, 109), the peregun leaf invokes trances.

We have seen how Bastide (1958, 152) defined Exu's possession as a pathological manifestation of ritual trance, with a dance characterized by spasmodic movements. This is not the case in the description of possession by Exu given by Ana Maria Correa (1976, 53): "During a ceremony in the Ilê Oiá Otum, the *terreiro* of a daughter-of-saint of Olga de Alaketu, I was able to observe one of these possessions which, in spite of an attitude of characteristic defiance, was hardly any different from possessions by other orixás."[27]

On the evening of April 23, 1994, I was at a celebration dedicated to Ogun, Oxossi, and Exu in the Ilê de Omolu e Oxum at São João de Meriti (Rio de Janeiro). In Rio, this Ketu terreiro is considered one of the most traditional, linked to the axé Alaketu and the Ilê Ogunjá in Salvador.

The ceremony for Ogun, Oxossi, and Exu opened with an invocation to Exu, composed of five ritual chants dedicated to him. During the *xirê* (the invocations and dances for the orixás), the son of Oxossi for whom the ceremony was organized went into a trance, followed by other sons of the

10. *Saida de santo,* final ceremony for an Exu's initiate.
COURTESY OF LEONARDO CARNEIRO.

same divinity. Then Marcos de Exu suddenly entered into a trance. His movements were far more violent, although not spasmodic, and far more energetic than those who incarnated Oxossi, Ogun, Xangô, and Oxalá. His face was hard, as also happens when being possessed by Ogun, and he was dancing with large movements of his back. He was sweating profusely, and the ekedi constantly wiped away his sweat. His movements were expansive and energetic, seeming to spread out over the whole room. He lifted his head with an air of defiance, often turning around and around. When there was a pause in the music of the sacred drums, the initiate made a faint whistling sound, a sign of Exu's presence. His chest was covered with a long band of fabric (*ojá*), tied at his back so tightly that it looked as if he could hardly breathe. He passed in front of the mãe-de-santo and threw himself on the ground in ritual salutation, as forcefully as if he were diving through the air.

11. An Exu's initiate dancing. COURTESY OF LEONARDO CARNEIRO.

After a pause, the initiates in trance reappeared adorned in the clothes of their respective orixás. The first was Exu. He was wearing a bonnet entirely covered with cowries, with the brown tip of a calabash fixed to the top. He had covered a corset with straw and decorated it with cowries, and he wore a multicolored skirt (red, black, yellow, green, blue, white, and orange) cut in rounded panels over another skirt of purple gauze on starched lace. Over the panels of multicolored material fell other layers of braided straw with decorative motifs in cowries. Small calabashes were attached to his belt, symbolizing the power of Exu. Over his left shoulder he wore a *laguidibá*, a necklace made of black horn, and from his right shoulder hung a long-necked calabash. On his arms he wore bracelets of shining iron, and in his hand he held a small lance of polished steel with a ring at one end, which he used as a handle. Behind Exu came the other divinities: Ogun, Oxossi, Yemanjá, Oxum, Logunedé, and Oxaguian.

Marcos began to dance frenetically. When the music stopped, unlike the other orixás who kept still, he swayed from side to side with an air of dominance and superiority that was almost provocative. Although his dance was very similar to Ogun's, his movements were far more expansive than those of his brother. The ogans played the Odara chant, an invocation to Exu. Marcos then began to dance in a circle, taking small steps. He stopped in front of the sacred drums and started to turn around and around, with a mischievous smile on his lips. He lifted his arms to shoulder height, held them wide open, and promptly threw himself backward with great force.

Exu then started to dance with Ogun and Yemanjá. Sweat was running down his body, for he did not hold back his efforts or his energy. A new chant began. The ekedi came to wipe his brow, but Exu pushed her away—he wanted to dance. He began to spin again, beating his fists and hopping on one foot. His face was overcome with an expression of pleasure such is rarely seen on the faces of initiates in a trance. Another chant began. Exu continued to spin, rubbing his hands or pointing with his index finger alternately to his forehead and the nape of his neck. Yet another chant began, and Exu danced lasciviously, swaying from side to side and spinning with a sly smile of pleasure. Then Oxum came to dance with him. Once this dance was over, Exu withdrew from the public area, the barracão.

As we see, there is nothing pathological or demonic about this description. What differentiates Exu from the other orixás—especially Ogun, who resembles him the most—is his particularly expansive movements, supposed to express the nature of this divinity, his role, and his energy. Exu is movement, energy, communication. He is also the mischievous child, the cunning, clever one. There is nothing abnormal about his performance—it is neither savagery nor sacred fury. Furthermore, the presence of Exu in the midst of the other orixás removes any suspicion of the trance's having a pathological nature.

Despacho, or Padê

Before any public celebration, the ritual of Exu's despacho, or padê, is performed. The first researchers saw in this ritual a way of distancing Exu from the sacred space because of his identification with the devil. However, as Carneiro (1986, 69) pointed out, *despachar* in Portuguese is not only used in the sense of chasing away, but also to mean sending. Exu is the messenger, the necessary go-between of men and gods. It is he, then, who is sent to inform the orixás of the celebration that is to take place in the terreiro. Abraham's (1958, 540) English-Yoruba dictionary defines *pàdé* or *ìpàdé* as: "(a) (I) the act of meeting. (II) *ibi ìpàdé*, the place of meeting. (b) the holding of a meeting. (c) celebration." The padê thus signifies the orixás' reunion with their sons.

There are two types of padê: a very complex ceremony also known as *rodar a cuia*,[28] in which the spirits of the terreiro's founders are invoked, and the despacho, which consists of offering water and manioc flour to Exu. Not all terreiros practice the first ritual. In the simplified form of padê, one of the oldest daughters-of-saint in the house, known as *dagan* in Nagô terreiros, celebrates the ritual, assisted by the *sidagan*. Many chants are performed by the sons-of-saint in the barracão, the public ceremonies hall. A small clay amphora (*quartinha*) is placed in the center of the room, with water and a plate of Exu's food—manioc flour moistened with palm oil (*farofa*). The dagan then dances around the two vessels until the moment when she takes the amphora and goes outside to throw the water in the street. She will then leave the food at a nearby crossroad.

In the Efon nation, the despacho, prepared before any public ceremony, is slightly different. Instead of a single plate of manioc flour, also called padê, four plates of manioc flour are prepared, each mixed with a different ingredient: palm oil, honey, cachaça and water. Next to the quartinha is placed the water that has been used to cook white corn (*canjica*), which is used in all purification rituals. The offering to Exu is then left at seven nearby crossroads: it consists of a *mamona* (*Ricinus communis*) leaf wrapped around a little of the ingredients used—popcorn (*pipoca*), the four padês, eggs, acaçá,[29] salt, honey, and palm oil (*dendê*)—to which is added some blood and the *exés*[30] of the animals sacrificed to Exu before the beginning of the ritual. A cigar, matches, and a lighted candle are left next to the mamona leaf. All is then ready for the public ceremony to commence. The invoked Exu is the guardian and protector of the terreiro, and the aim of the seven offerings to Exu is to attract the god so that he will watch over the celebration, ensuring its smooth functioning.

12. *Padê* for Exu in an Efon terreiro. PHOTO BY AUTHOR.

The most complex padê ritual has been described in great detail by Juana Elbein dos Santos (1976, 187–95).[31] According to her, it is an extremely dangerous ritual as it evokes formidable powers: *essas*, the founding forefathers of the terreiro, and *iyamís*, the female ancestors. The padê takes place before each public ceremony dedicated to the orixás where a four-legged animal is sacrificed, and before the funeral ritual of the *axexê*, always at sundown. In the Axé Opô Afonjá, the invocations are made by the *asogbá*, the high priest of Obaluaiê's cult, and the offerings are prepared by the *iyamorô* and the dagan. The ritual opens with an invocation to Exu Inan, so that he protects the terreiro and comes to carry out his functions. Three times the iyamorô mixes the water, flour, and palm oil in the calabash, and goes out to carry the offering to the foot of a sacred tree. Exu Odara is then called, so that he may deliver the offering to Baba Orișa, "the collective symbol of all the male ancestors" (Juana E. dos Santos, 1976, 191). All the Eguns (male ancestors) and essas are then asked to accept the offering brought by Exu.

The ritual culminates with the invocation of Iyamí Oxorongá, the principle of feminine power. This is the most dangerous moment, as she represents a formidable force. The rhythm accelerates, and the offerings are carried outside the terreiro, almost at a run. Exu Agbo, the guardian Exu of the Axé Opô Afonjá terreiro, is then invoked, and with him the other orixás. An Ogun priestess sprinkles the ground with water to make Iyamí Oxorongá favorable and so prepare the path for the iyamorô, who comes quickly out of the terreiro with the acaçá, the offering for Iyamí. When she returns, everyone stands and chants for the ritual to end well. Exu, under his aspects of Inan (fire), Ojise (the messenger), and Agbo (the guardian), establishes communication between the male ancestors (Eguns), the founders of the religion (essas), and the iyamís. This term designates collectively the female ancestors, the mythical mothers; in reality, however, it signifies our mothers and, in its *agba* or *iya agba* variant meaning elderly mothers, it symbolizes all the female orixás.

Considered for a long time as the representation of negative forces and linked to witchcraft, the iyamís were associated with destructive and antisocial powers. In fact, iyamís and the *ajés* (witches) associated with them are feared because they are so powerful and aggressive, and so extremely dangerous. It is believed that a large quantity of axé is concentrated within the iyamís. Like Exu, who can do good as well as evil, iyamís, especially in their individualized form of Iyamí Oxorongá, can work for both sides. One story from the Ifá corpus (*Odù ogbé òsa*) tells how, on coming to this world, the *iyamís-eleiye* (our bird-owning mothers) go to perch on seven different trees—on three of them, they work for good; on three others, they work for evil; and on the seventh, they work for good and evil (Verger 1965, 147).[32]

The symbol of the iyamís is a calabash containing a bird, representing woman's power of procreation—the calabash is the belly, the bird, the son. However, the ajés may transform themselves into "birds of evil" known as Agbigbó, Elùlú, Atioro, and Osoronga (Rego 1980). The bird is then the witch's familiar and works for her. During the bird's expeditions at night, the witch's body remains inert. In order to kill the ajé, always identified as an old woman, it is enough to rub her body with ataré pepper, her ritual bane (Verger 1965, 143).

Iyamí Oxorongá, chief of all the iyamís, is said to be in a permanent state of anger which she is always ready to unleash upon human beings, and she must be appeased with specific rituals. But there is also another side to the iyamís, according to Marianno Carneiro da Cunha (1984), referring to a divinity, now fallen, called Odu, who received from Olodumare (the supreme god) power over the orixás. Odu was always angry, always ready to attack, while her companion Obarixá (or Orixalá) was patient, contemplative, and wise. As Odu abused her power, Olodumare took it back and gave it to Obarixá, thus giving him control of the world. Similarly, another myth tells how, at the beginning of time, Odu was the leader of the eguns, the male ancestors, but she did not know how to wear the Eguns' ritual garments or how to talk as they did, in a deep, gravelly voice. So Obarixá stole the Eguns' robes and began to speak with their voice, terrifying everyone who was present, including Odu (ibid., 2–3).[33]

The Eguns represent the whole of society. Their cult, the prerogative of men, tries to maintain social order,[34] an order that cannot be established without controlling the antisocial power of the witches. All women are considered as potential ajés because the iyamís control them by altering their menstruation. Thus the myth of the transfer of the control of the Egun society from Odu (Iyamí) to Obarixá (Orixalá) clearly symbolizes the transfer of social power from women to men.

Judith Hoch-Smith (1978, 250) recounts a Yoruba tale in which Exu bestowed malevolent power upon women who, transformed into ajés, made the men with whom they had sexual intercourse impotent, or stole their penises. This bond between Exu and Iyamí is reiterated by Marianno Carneiro da Cunha (1984, 14) who defines the iyamís as the "Exu's great-grandmothers." He also writes that outside the house of a high priest of Ifá at Lagos were placed Obaluaiê's shrines ("a hot divinity, closely linked with Iyamí Oxorongá"), Exu's shrine, and next to that, Iyamí's.

We have also seen that the iyamís' principal bane is red pepper, and that contact with it deprives them of their evil powers. One of Exu's *orikís* (laudatory epithets), recorded at Ketu by Verger (1957, 132–33), associates Exu, pepper, and the "step-mother"—i.e., an old woman:

Nilori irun (a)be o gbo idi ana lo ka dodo.
The hairs of his stepmother's vagina hung around her buttocks because they're old.

Agbo l o wò soso dà (o)mi ala s(i) abe anan.

Agbo [Exu] who watches calmly to pour pepper into his stepmother's vagina.

One of the invocations to Iyamí Oxorongá during the annual festival of Geledé in Yorubaland is: "Mother, whose vagina terrifies us all. Mother of the pubic hair that wraps around us. Mother who has set her trap, set her trap" (Cunha 1984, 3). We saw that Agbo is the name of one of Exu's qualities, and it is as such that he is called upon during the part of the padê when Iyamí Oxorongá is also invoked. Exu Agbo's intervention, then, is a means of neutralizing the dangerous power of Iyamí.[35]

In Nigeria, the festival of the *geledé* masks[36] is intended to appease Iyamí's anger as is expressed by the very Yoruba word *gèlèdé*: "*Gè* means 'to soothe, to placate, to pet or coddle'; *èlè* refers to woman's private parts, those that symbolize women's secrets and their life-giving powers; and *dé* connotes 'to soften with care or gentleness'" (Drewal and Drewal 1983, 3). The geledé cult was practiced in Bahia, probably until the end of the nineteenth century. Carneiro (1986) states that Maria Julia Figuereido (Omonike) organized a festival of geledé masks every December 8 in the district of Boa Viagem, in Salvador. Omonike was a daughter-of-saint of Marcelina da Silva (Obá Tossi), iyalorixá of the Casa Branca, the first Ketu terreiro founded in Brazil. Upon da Silva's death, Omonike succeeded her as high priestess. Some of the ritual geledé masks are conserved in the Axé Opô Afonjá terreiro in Salvador, and others are to be found in the city's Geographical and Historical Museum.

Today, thanks to the influence of Juana Elbein dos Santos's writings, and courses on Yoruba language and culture, all the Candomblé initiates that I met were aware of the role and mythical nature of Iyamí Oxorongá. Her association with female sexual power also places Iyamí in complementary relation with Exu, the symbol of male sexual power.

From Porto Alegre to Maranhão

In Brazil, Exu is not only present in the Candomblé of Salvador and Rio de Janeiro, but also in other religions of African origin. In Batuque at Porto Alegre, in Rio Grande do Sul, Exu is known by the name of Bará. Bastide, who led research into Batuque in the beginning of the 1950s, gives a list of terreiros at Porto Alegre where, out of twenty-seven houses of worship, at least five were dedicated to Bará (1978, 448). He also uses a report from 1936, quoted by Ramos (1951b), where a despacho is described, carried out by a woman possessed by this divinity. In Batuque, then, initiation to Bará is accepted, since this god is not identified with the devil: "Bará has children, and during a ceremony I was able to see one of his daughters dancing" (Bastide 1952, 199).

In Xangô in Recife, Exu displays the same characteristics as in Candomblé: he is the master of crossroads and messenger of the orixás. He is always the first to be venerated. According to one of Ribeiro's (1978, 56) informants, his assento is prepared from the earth of an anthill, from which a mound is formed by adding palm oil, nettle leaves, and cowries, sprinkled with the blood of a sacrificed rooster.

In contemporary Xangô centers, Exus are divided between those who are baptized and those who are pagan. Baptized Exus may appear next to orixás, while the uncontrollable pagans are venerated in the houses of the Jurema cult. This ritual, close to Catimbó, a cult from the Northeast, is strongly influenced by indigenous rituals. Today it is often confused with Umbanda, and the names of these pagan Exus—such as Zé Pelintra, Tranca-Ruas, Tiriri, and Tata-Caveira—are found in both religions (Carvalho 1990, 141).

However, in the Xangô terreiros of Laranjeiras in Sergipe, Exu is associated with evil and the devil—he is even called the enemy—being opposed to Lebará (Elegbá, Elegbará) who "does both Good and Evil" (Dantas 1988, 102), and his presence must be scrupulously avoided in houses of worship considered traditional.[37] The two divinities are seen to be antagonistic: in Nagô terreiros it is said that "Lebará chases out Exu," for Exu is the devil and "Lebará is an African saint who takes care of the house and the world, and liberates it from evil and misery" (ibid., 103).

In Nagô terreiros in Sergipe there are two Lebarás: one outside the house of worship in the courtyard, the other in the orixás' room. Lebará also receives an offering of the first sacrificed animal, and each time the orixás eat—i.e., receive their offerings—Lebará also has some. However, Exu also receives an offering, but secretly. Two initiates whose duty is to serve him carry a small amount of sacred food to the entrance of the terreiro and throw it into the street, saying *"Exu bá, Exu bá, guia, guia,"* but the words

13. Exu's collective shrines in a Candomblé house. PHOTO BY AUTHOR.

are recited furtively (*xubá*), for Exu "does not have the right to enter the *terreiro*" (ibid., 104). This dissimulation does not escape the author's analysis: "Exu's identification with the devil has turned him into a proscribed entity, at least to the extent of manifest expression, which has led to dissimulation on a ritual level" (ibid., 102).

In the Tambor da Mina[38] of São Luís do Maranhão, the cult of Exu or Legba uses the same evasive strategies that we see at work in the Xangô of Sergipe. In Nagô terreiros (the ones linked to the oldest among them, the Casa de Nagô), the *embarabô* is sung before any ceremony to invoke the divinities (Santos and Santos Neto 1989, 41). Embarabô is one of the names given to Exu in the Nagô cult and for whom an invocation chant is performed. During the preparations for public ceremonies in the Casa de Nagô, always before midnight, a secret ritual is carried out only for high priests and the people closest to the house of worship. The ritual includes invocations "to Exu and the guardians" of the terreiro, "so that they close the way to negative energies and disruptive spirits, and so that they give strength and protection to the terreiro and to all those who participate in the religion" (ibid., 42). Even if the authors do not say so explicitly, this description is very close to that of the Nagô padê.

On the other hand, at the other extreme of African tradition in São Luís, the Casa das Minas, of Jeje (Fon) origin, the Legba cult is categorically denied by the initiates. In 1947, Manoel Nunes Pereira (1979) had already noticed the absence of a cult of Legba. Forty years later, Sergio Ferretti (1986, 123) explained this absence by Legba's association with Satan. According to him, the initiates of the house considered Legba an evil god, for it was because of him that the founding mothers of the religion were sold as slaves. Ferretti is referring to a letter mentioned by Luis da Câmara Cascudo (1972, 509), which the king of Dahomey, Adandozan (or Adonzan), sent to Prince Dom João of Portugal. In this letter, dated November 20, 1804, the Dahomian king claims to be protected by the god Legba. So if it is true that members of the royal family of Abomey were sold as slaves by King Adonzan, and that the founding mother of the Casa das Minas was part of the group, as stated by Verger (1953), the prohibition of the cult of Legba would be justified.

However, Sergio Ferretti (1986, 123) also reveals certain ritual attitudes that are linked to the cult of Legba, accentuating the reticence that is always expressed when it comes to this divinity:

> We managed to discover that it is habitual to leave water next to the entrance of the house of worship before the ceremony opens. This is the despacho, made from water from the shrine (comé or peji). Thus he [Legba] drinks the water, but outside the house and he receives no food. We also saw that on festival days, before the ceremonies opened, they chanted on the veranda, to ward off Legba, so that he would not appear. We believe that other chants exist with the same purpose, but the initiates do not like to reveal them, and avoid the subject.

The same reluctance to talk about Legba was noted by Bastide (1978, 444), when, during his journey to São Luís, Mãe Andresa, a former mãe-de-santo of the Casa das Minas, revealed to him, "smiling," that she knew Legba well, but she would not say more. However, the prohibition of the cult of Legba seems not always to have existed. In fact, Sergio Ferretti (1986, 122) quotes "an old lady," the daughter of a former player of sacred drums, who confirms the existence until the 1920s of cases of possession by Legba in the Casa das Minas. At the time it appears that someone worked magic with Legba against a well-known person in the town, which caused many problems, and it is since then that possession by Legba has been banned in the terreiro.

The same story was told to me by one of the initiates of the Casa de Nagô, a house of worship with close links to the Casa das Minas and also considered traditional. D. Sinhá denied Legba's identification with the devil. For her, he was a god like the others, and, even if he did not have initiates, he was always part of the religion: "That is why we sing at the beginning for him. Legba does not have initiates—we only know of one woman from the Casa das Minas who had a problem because of magic work with Legba." It would seem, then, that the denial of the cult of Legba in the Casa das Minas has more to do with the accusations of witchcraft and the resulting repression, than with a revolt against the god who protected the enemy of the terreiro's founding mother (King Adonzan).

Eduardo Octávio da Costa (1948), who carried out his research in the rural areas of the state of Maranhão under the direction of Melville Herskovits, states that Legba is identified with the *encantado* Legua Boji, who is considered to be a spirit who does both good and evil, and who is much solicited for the treatment of diseases and for finding lost objects. When he is incarnated in an initiate, the encantado displays a joyful disposition and is treated with affection by all present, who consider him a "resourceful and humorous trickster" (ibid., 59).

This identification between Legua Boji and Legba is not accepted in the Casa das Minas (Sergio Ferretti 1986). However, in other houses of worship, the encantado's bad behavior and his predilection for alcohol and arguments lead to his association with Legba. Mundicarmo Ferretti (1993, 207) quotes Jorge Itací, pai-de-santo of a well-known terreiro at São Luís, who sees in Legua Boji the result of a fusion of two *voduns*, the Dahomian divinities: Legba and Poliboji, from whence the name Legua Boji. The author seems to doubt this explanation, especially because of the repulsion that Legba inspires in the Casa das Minas, where Poliboji is one of the most respected voduns.[39] She seems to prefer the idea of the existence of a relationship between Legba (Exu) and Averekete, for in the ritual of the Tambor da Mina at Codó (in the state of Maranhão), known as Tambor da Mata (drum of the bush), the ceremony opens with chants dedicated to Averekete (or Verequete), rather than to Exu, as is the case in other Afro-Brazilian religions.

In the Casa das Minas, Averekete is a *toquem* (*token* or *tokhueni*), a young vodun whose role is to act as messenger and guide for older voduns in his family: "The *toquens* have a role equivalent to that of Exu in the Nagô religions, instead of Legba who is not accepted as the voduns' messenger" (Sergio Ferretti 1986, 126).[40] But even if he is identified as Legua Boji or Averekete, it seems to me that Legba's invisibility in the Casa das Minas ritual is nothing more than the result of an attempt to conjure away a disturbing divinity.

THE SPIRITS OF DARKNESS
Exu and Pombagira in Umbanda

Umbanda was officially created in Rio de Janeiro in the 1920s, by a dissident group of Kardecists disappointed with the orthodoxy of Spiritism, which had spread throughout Brazil thanks to the works of Léon Hippolyte Dénizart Rivail, better known as Allan Kardec. His doctrine consisted of a combination of religion, science, and philosophy, based on the codification of messages received from the spirits during séances involving psychography, or writing while in a trance. Kardec's method was presented as scientific: starting with an effect (the phenomenon of turning tables), he discovered its cause (the existence of spirits) by methodically asking the evoked spirits questions during Spiritist séances. His aim was to compile the most comprehensive work possible on knowledge of the spirit world. It was the spirits themselves who dictated *The Spirits' Book* (1875/1857) to Kardec, called "the codifier," and their knowledge was to be transmitted through this book.

Other books, such as *The Book on Mediums* (Kardec 1970/ 1861) and *The Gospel Explained by the Spiritist Doctrine* (Kardec 2000/1864), were written with the aim of reinforcing the Kardecist doctrine, confronting it with Christianity. Thanks to their dissemination, the Spiritist doctrine was an unexpected success in Brazil. Its scientific pretensions immediately seduced the Brazilian bourgeoisie, eager to distance themselves from the practices of the working class which they esteemed too primitive. The Kardecist doctrine, then, fell on fertile ground and initially took root in the "African" city of Salvador, in Bahia. The first Kardecist meeting took place there on September 17, 1865, organized by Luis Olímpio Teles de Menezes, the founder of the Spiritist Family Group. At the time, Kardecist theory was already dividing opinion among the intellectuals of Bahia, to the point of influencing emblematic figures in the struggle for the abolition of slavery, such as the poet Antonio de Castro Alves (Aubrée and Laplantine 1990, 110).

In 1873, Teles de Menezes managed to obtain a legal status for what he called his religion. This official recognition encouraged the creation, that same year, of the first Spiritist movement in Rio de Janeiro, the Society of Spiritist Studies. Spiritism in Rio was bound up with republican and abolitionist ideas, and it spread mostly in political and scientific circles. The emphasis was on the recognition of its scientific and philosophical status, differing from the tendency in Bahia, where its religious aspect was predominant. In 1875, the Garnier Bookstore in Rio de Janeiro published the complete works of Allan Kardec, and many Spiritist groups were created, culminating in the foundation of the first Brazilian Spiritist Federation in 1884, which fulfilled the need to unify the movement and define the contents of the Kardecist doctrine.

Spiritism spread like wildfire. In 1900, Spiritist federations were present in almost every state in Brazil, but it was not until the 1930s that Brazilian Spiritism acquired its main characteristics, thanks to Francisco Candido Xavier, better known as Chico Xavier. He neglected the idea of scientific experimentation, in order to emphasize the importance of the principle of karmic evolution and the practicing of charity as the sole condition for salvation. His works were very widely read. Of the three hundred books that he wrote, most sold more than a hundred thousand copies (Camargo 1961, 5). Basically, he formulated a national theory of Spiritism, underlining Brazil's role in the evolution of the planet.

By the mid-1920s, a group of Spiritist dissidents began to incorporate elements linked to the fetishistic practices so carefully avoided by the Kardecist orthodoxy, and Zélio de Moraes founded the first center of a new religion known as Umbanda.[1] The Centro Espírita Nossa Senhora da Piedade began to operate in Niterói, in the state of Rio de Janeiro, before moving to the center of Rio in 1938. Most of the members of this group were dissatisfied Kardecists who considered the African and indigenous spirits and divinities of Macumba to be more powerful than the evolved spirits of Kardecism. However, they refused all the aspects that, in Macumba, were associated with the "savagery" of African cults, such as animal sacrifices or possession by "diabolical" spirits (the exus). Umbanda thus incorporated the symbolic universe of the ancient African religions while purifying it of its more disturbing aspects. To understand how this reinterpretation was carried out, it is necessary to analyze briefly the formative process of African religions in the Southeast of Brazil.

From Calundu to Macumba

Information about African religions in Brazil during the colonial period confirms a predominance of cultures of Bantu origin. In 1728, Nuno Marques Pereira, known as the pilgrim of America, claimed that as he traveled in the Minas Gerais region, he could not sleep a wink at night because of the *calundus*, the "festivals of witchcraft held by the Negroes which were the custom in their land, and which they continue to hold here, with the aim of having answers upon most varied topics" (Marques Pereira 1939, 124).

"Calundu" is a word of Bantu origin,[2] designating all the religious practices of slaves in Brazil in the eighteenth century. The slaves of the mining region of Minas Gerais performed a dance called Acontundá, or the Tundá Dance, which, according to Luiz Mott (1986, 138), greatly resembled those from Candomblé and Xangô that we know today. Someone who practiced an African religion was called a *calundureiro*.[3] The ritual was characterized by playing sacred drums and by direct communication with the spirits, who spoke through the mouths of those possessed. In Bantu mythology, Calunga-ngombe, the king of the underworld and the personification of death,[4] reigned over these spirits.

The cult of Cabula, described in 1901 in a pastoral letter from D. João Nery, the bishop of the state of Espírito Santo, would seem to come directly from the same Bantu heritage. At the beginning of the twentieth century, this religion was already widespread in the region, with eight thousand followers. Cabula adepts were known as *camanás* (initiates); they met under the direction of the *embanda* (the head of the religion) for ceremonies called *mesas* (tables). Meetings, or *engiras*, took place in the middle of the night in the *camoucite* (temple). The embanda was helped by an assistant, the *cambono*, and the followers were barefoot and dressed in white. During the ritual, they invoked Calunga, Tatá (spirits), and Baculo (ancestors). The chants were punctuated by hand clapping while the embanda was possessed by spirits. The ritual's aim was to acquire one or more protective spirits through the mystic trance:

> Once a man has been possessed by the *santé*, he may try to get to know his familiar guardian spirit in the following way. He goes into the forest with an unlighted candle and returns with it burning, having taken along nothing to light it with. In this way he brings back the name of his protector. There are many of these—for example, Tatá Warrior, Tatá Flower of Calunga, Tatá Break-Mountains, Tatá Break-Bridge, etc. (Bastide 1978, 204)

Information we have about Macumba in Rio de Janeiro clearly shows the parallel that exists between this religion and the Cabula of Espírito Santo: the head of the religion was also called embanda, and his assistant also called cambono. The religious gathering was called the *gira*. Possession was determined not by a saint or divinity, but by a familiar spirit. In 1939, Arthur Ramos wrote: "In the Honorato temple this spirit is Pai Joaquim, who was active there twenty-five years before, according to the claim of the believers" (1951a, 101). The word pai (father, in Portuguese) corresponds to the Bantu *tata*. Once incorporated in the initiates, this spirit gave advice to everyone present and resolved any disputes, exactly as the ancestors' spirits used to do in Angola.

Macumba adepts were called mediums "because of the influence of Spiritism" (Ramos 1979, 229). They participated in ceremonies associated with a line or nation, according to the spirits evoked. In reality, the word "macumba" was used in Rio de Janeiro to signify all the religions of African origin, as was the case with the word "calundu" in colonial times. Ramos, one of the first scholars to take an interest in Bantu traditions, defined Macumba as follows:

> The Macumba of the Brazilian Negro is a religious and magical ritual. It was transformed in its Brazilian atmosphere, taking new shapes and

becoming mixed with religious and magical beliefs and customs existent in the new land . . . In Brazil, the Macumba as a religion or sort of magic, assumes various forms and expressions according to the locale. It is called Candomblé in Bahia. (Ramos 1951a, 92)

In Macumba, the relation between religion and magic was doubly marked —by African heritage and by strong roots in the magic tradition of Iberian origin. During colonial times, African religious practices had survived alongside the magical and demonic beliefs of European origin. They were often mistaken for each other in the repression led by the Inquisition overseas. Laura de Mello e Souza, in her study of sorcery in colonial Brazil (1986, 273), underlines their important interpenetration:

The Devil, magical practices, and sorcery were usually regarded as being completely natural and part of everyday life. They arrived in the colony with the Portuguese, their roots lost in the darkness of time in popular European tradition. Here, by integrating with other cultures, they took on new colors. *Patuás*, the *mandinga* purses worn around the neck synthesizing African, Amerindian and European beliefs, were, along with calundus, the two great creations of colonial magic and sorcery.

During this colonial period came the start of the process of cultural translation, which gave birth to Afro-Brazilian religions. Popular religion, which the Portuguese colonials had brought with them to Brazil, was characterized by an extremely utilitarian approach. The continuous demand for all kinds of aids and material advantages was the basis of the relationship between the faithful and the saints, as though it were a contract made between mankind and God's representatives. Gilberto Freyre (1946) witnessed the persistence of a popular religiosity marked by an extreme familiarity with the Virgin Mary and the saints, the subjects of an intimate and personal worship. The believer's relationship with his patron saint was no different from that which bound the African slave to his divinities or spirits. As Bastide states (1978, 68–69), the philosophy of the African religion is "essentially utilitarian and pragmatic; the only thing that counts is success." In the same way, popular European religiosity was preoccupied not with eternal salvation, but the resolution of numerous daily problems.

However, there was another side to this intimate relationship with the spiritual world: men lived not only with saints, but also with devils. In the sixteenth and seventeenth centuries, devils, she devils, and imps populated the daily life of the colonials as if they were inoffensive domestic divinities. Even though the colonials knew that commerce with these almost-human devils was illicit, the colony's inhabitants would invoke them whenever difficulties arose in daily life. Such devils, who acted for good as well as evil and who were protectors and patrons, closely resemble Exu in the African slaves' beliefs.

The Macumba of Rio de Janeiro, therefore, was born of this union of the beliefs of African slaves, indigenous practices, and magic of Iberian origin. From the beginning of the twentieth century, the African Exu, reinterpreted as a mischievous but obliging spirit, much like the familiar imp of Iberian tradition, started to multiply in the Rio Macumbas, under the influence of Spiritist beliefs about the dead:

> In all the religions, the messenger multiplies into many exus, with very various names and functions. In most cases, he is associated with Ogun and Oxossi, his inseparable companions; in Rio de Janeiro, as well as presenting his multiple personality, adepts have fused him with another divinity, Omolu, to create the Exu Caveira [Skull], responsible for protecting graveyards. (Carneiro 1964, 134)

The Rio Macumbas also incorporated the aspects of the African Exu that Bahia Candomblé had scrupulously hidden or repressed, notably his symbolism of unbridled sexuality. With their exus associated with the devil, the Macumbas held a fascination for even the most "evolved" segments of the bourgeoisie. In Rio de Janeiro in the late nineteenth century, Satanism was fairly widespread, as João do Rio's report (1976, 113) shows. The way was clear for Exu's transformation into a spirit of darkness.

Umbanda and Quimbanda

Macumba incorporates and reinterprets European beliefs according to an African worldview. The assimilation of the Christian devil by black culture has transformed him into an ambiguous figure, a magic entity like the African Exu. Umbanda was born, then, from an attempt to recover the strength and efficiency of the spirits venerated in Macumba, while erasing—

14. Exu's assentos in Umbanda and Candomblé. PHOTO BY AUTHOR.

at least in the official discourse of the Umbandist intelligentsia—its ties with a backward and uneducated Africa.

The first congress of Umbandist Spiritism took place in Rio in 1941. The debate was animated by two major concerns: to create a de-Africanized Umbanda, whose roots could be found in the ancient traditions of the Far and Near East, and to whiten Umbanda and purify it of its barbaric and demonic origins (Brown 1985). In this way, there was an attempt to legitimize a new religion, by reinterpreting the Afro-Brazilian symbolic world according to the dominant values of white society. By slightly blackening Kardecist Spiritism, Umbanda was made into a national religion, a symbol of the myth of the racial and cultural melting pot, which was at the center of the debate on national identity in the 1930s.

Umbanda took from Spiritism the belief in reincarnation and in karmic evolution, as well as practicing charity and direct communication with guides (*guias*), spirits incarnated in mediums. In Kardecism this communication did not entail suppressing the conscience of the medium, who should, on the contrary, control the messages of the spirits on an emotional, logical, and ethical level. But in Umbanda, trance was supposed to be unconscious, with the spirit taking full control of his horse. Another charac-

teristic which marks the influence of Kardecism on Umbanda is the importance given to the medium's training through the study of sacred literature.
Umbanda places great value in books as a source of knowledge and, above
all, as a "model for action" (Camargo 1961, 147).

These points in common between Umbanda and Kardecism enable a
kind of continuum to be formed between the two religions, according to the
position defended by each religious center. This continuum extends from
the least "white" extreme of Umbanda (its most Africanized forms, such
as Omolocô) through to Candomblé. In fact, Umbanda includes a wide
array of variants, ranging from the centers most closely connected to the
Kardecists' *mesa branca* (white table) through to "African" Umbanda, still
known as popular Umbanda. In spite of enormous internal differences, the
elements common to all Umbanda centers may be defined generally as a
division of venerated spirits into seven lines, each ruled by an orixá or
Catholic saint, and a division of each line into phalanxes or legions of
disincarnated spirits.

As in Kardecist Spiritism, Umbanda uses séances to help the spirits'
evolutionary process. But while in Kardecism this process is linked to the
indoctrination of the spirits through the conscious action of the mediums,
their evolution in Umbanda can only be realized through the work of a
medium, meaning the charity practiced by the spirits themselves once they
are incorporated in their mediums. The direct intervention of spirits in
men's lives, helping them to solve their problems, thus becomes the only
way to evolve, since they must work in order to progress. Umbandist spirits
are divided into four groups: caboclos (indigenous spirits), pretos-velhos
(literally, old-blacks; the spirits of slaves), exus, and *crianças* (children).[5]
The orixás, as the heads of the lines, do not manifest themselves, leaving
their charitable work to spirits invested with their strength or vibration.
These spirits must give consultations, through mediums, to human beings
in need of their help.

Exu is the only orixá to have survived the adaptation process from African religious tradition. As in Candomblé, he occupies an important place in
the spatial organization of an Umbandist center: his shrine is always situated at the entrance, and in the most Africanized centers, before the start of
a séance, Exu's despacho is performed, with its invocations (*pontos cantados*) and offerings of sacred food. One of the characteristics of the gradual

| KARDECISM | "WHITE" UMBANDA | "AFRICAN" UMBANDA | OMOLOCÔ | ANGOLA CANDOMBLÉ | NAGÔ CANDOMBLÉ | RE-AFRICANIZED CANDOMBLÉ |

15. Afro-Brazilian religious continuum.

passage of Umbanda to Kardecism is the disappearance of Exu's shrine and the despacho ceremony. Thus Exu has become the guardian of African heritage in Umbanda. But Exu is also the object of a complex reinterpretation, in which "African" is synonymous with "inferior." In reality, Exu is incorporated into the Umbandist religious construction as an inferior, unevolved spirit, unlike caboclos or pretos-velhos, who are "beings of light." Umbandist exus are very close to human beings, incarnations of souls who have yet to complete the process of karmic evolution: "God has granted unevolved spirits the possibility to remain upon Earth, either as incarnated beings, or as 'beings without light' who are in transit in the lower planes of the astral world until they succeed in reaching perfect equilibrium, which will take them in the future to perfection, through suffering which will redeem their sins" (Fontanelle n.d., 26). Exus are, therefore, unevolved spirits, who must be indoctrinated and comply with the rules of the Umbandist cosmos. If they work for good, they will, little by little, be transformed into beings of light, but until the process of karmic evolution has been completed, they remain spirits of darkness.

While it is true that Umbanda offers an adaptation to urban life through the assimilation of the dominant discourse, implying a "domestication of the lower classes" (Birman 1980, 42), at the same time, it entails an opposition to this discourse through Quimbanda, its dark side—if one works toward good, practicing charity, the other dedicates itself to evil and black magic. In reality, Quimbanda occupies an extremely ambiguous position with regards to Umbanda. The two cults are presented as irreconcilable enemies, but actually they live in symbiosis. Quimbanda may be defined by the following characteristics: it uses black magic; it uses a specific technique to obtain particularly powerful magical effects; and it therefore possesses magical powers superior to those of Umbanda and Kardecism. However, no center calls itself a Quimbanda center because of the cult's association with black magic, even though almost all Umbanda centers practice Quimbanda rituals during special séances. Quimbanda is thus more a pattern of accusation than a cult completely opposed to Umbanda. To practice Quimbanda signifies being more African, backward, and uncivilized, an equation made evident by one of Umbandist authors:

> Quimbanda, low spiritism, black magic, Afro-Brazilian religion practised by the blacks in Brazil . . . Quimbanda attempts to perpetrate the ancient traditions of the African descendants, while Umbanda, on the contrary, seeks to suppress completely the uncivilized side of these practices, thanks to the influence of the white man, who, by reason of his level of education, cannot accept them. (Fontanelle 1952, 77)

To fight Quimbanda is to fight the stain of a past that is barbaric, ignorant, diabolical, and, to put it succinctly, African. In order to eliminate evil, it is necessary to domesticate Exu, the symbol of Afro-Brazilian heritage, the spirit who incarnates the forces of darkness. The path to Umbandist salvation goes through the acceptance of the position of black people in the class system, through the reproduction, in Umbanda, of the relationship of domination in global society. However, to be part of the Umbandist cosmos, exus must be baptized, and they are divided into pagan exus and baptized exus. The first group is on the margins of spirituality, deprived of light and knowledge, far from the path to evolution, and consecrated to black magic, while baptized exus are educated in goodness, accepting the logic of spiritual evolution and practicing charity. On the contrary, Quimbanda exus do not accept the relationship of domination that makes them subordinate to the beings of light.

Quimbanda exus revolt against the Umbandist order, which reflects the order of Brazilian society, and—like their female counterparts, the pombagiras—give their mediums the chance to criticize the social structure: power belongs to the outcasts, spirits who are ignorant but immeasurably more powerful. For Marco Aurélio Luz and Georges Lapassade (1972), Quimbanda became the symbol of the resistance of the oppressed classes and their revolt, while Umbanda incarnated repression. In reality, Quimbanda and Umbanda have never been opposed, except in the Umbandist theologians' attempts at systemization. Quimbanda, then, is the heir of the old Macumba, the most African pole of Umbanda, in the religious continuum that links Kardecism to Afro-Brazilian religions. In spite of the Umbandist theorists' efforts, Quimbanda guarantees Macumba's continuation by continuing its magical practices: "Quimbanda is nothing other than Macumba seen through the moralizing eyes of the Umbandists and integrated in a more general theory of evolution. It represents one school of thought's attempt to order the world according to moral, social and religious criteria" (Ortiz 1988, 146). In the stereotypes of the Umbandist universe, the fundamentally good black is incarnated by the preto-velho, the slave who accepts his fate with resignation. On the other hand, the fundamentally evil black is represented by the exus of Quimbanda, the blacks on the margins of society who threaten the social status quo and the order of the universe. Fontanelle (1952, 74) emphasizes the relation between the birth of Quimbanda and the rebellion of African slaves against their masters:

> Quimbanda was born in Brazil with the arrival of slavery, when the first Portuguese colonialists brought black slaves from among their possessions in Africa. These slaves carried in their hearts the wounds, hatred and resentment against the white men who had enslaved them, and so tried by every means possible to work against their masters, with the help of demonic beings.

Therefore exus are slaves who do not accept their destiny, who rebel against their masters and kill them with poison or witchcraft. In the Umbandist cosmos, they are degraded and set apart from the world of evolved spirits, in the shadows of ignorance; yet at the same time, they are valorized because of the power that this position of being outcast accords them. They are powerful because they are impure.

The Exu People

In Umbandist literature, the exus are interpreted differently according to the author's proximity to the African branch of the religion. Thus, Matta e Silva, linked to "white" Umbanda, sees in exus "spirits who resist spiritual progress, representing the wretched of the sacred Umbandist cosmos" (quoted in Ortiz 1988, 91). On the other hand, Molina (n.d.a., 7), linked to the "African" Umbanda, defines Exu as the "universal agent of magic," the intermediary between men and gods.

In general, Umbandist authors identify Exu with the Christian devil, the fallen angel. However, some authors, more connected to "African" Umbanda, do not accept this identification, disproving it in a subtle way by using Kardecist logic. So, according to Antônio de Alva, the genesis of evil, due to the rebellion of "the most beautiful and most important of the cherubim" (n.d., 18), is nothing but an absurd story invented by the Roman Catholic Church to dominate believers through terror. This idea is contradictory to Kardecist theory, which, as we have seen, was revealed to men by the spirits themselves. To claim that the first cherub brought evil into the world would be equivalent to claiming that cherubim are not pure spirits, for they would still be dependent upon the material world, a source of degradation. On the contrary, according to Kardec's *The Spirits' Book*, cherubim belong to the first of the three orders that populate the universe and are part of the world of pure spirits, to whom the order of good spirits and evil spirits are subordinate. Only spirits of the first order are not subject to the law of karmic evolution. To consider Exu as like the devil of the Bible would thus be to invalidate Kardec's classification, which rules out the idea that a pure spirit may still be connected to matter. And how can Kardec's work be contested if it was transmitted directly by the spirits? God himself created good and evil, and therefore the devil, Satan, or Exu are divine creations, "necessary, indispensable and appropriate, logical and acceptable, good and perfect" (Alva n.d., 20).

Alva cleverly uses Kardecist arguments to differentiate internally between the Umbandist category of exus, dividing them into higher and lower exus. Exu-King, the chief of all the exus, is himself divided into three people: Lucifer, Beelzebub, and Aschtaroth. Lucifer is in direct command of Exu Marabô and Exu Mangueira; Beelzebub is the chief of Exu Tranca-Rua (Block-the-Street) and Exu Tiriri; and Aschtaroth, also called Exu-King of the Seven Crossroads, commands Exu Velvet and Exu of the Rivers (ibid., 27). These higher exus always work for good, helping the orixás in their mission with their magic powers, seconded by the lower exus who are at their service. The lower exus then become "spirits who, having wandered from the path of righteousness during their incarnations, are transformed into diabolical spirits" (ibid., 50).

In this opposition between higher and lower exus, the exus' fundamental ambiguity is retained in the internal organization of the Umbandist pantheon. The inferior exus, or diabolical spirits, are called exus-eguns, meaning disincarnated spirits. This incorporates the notion of egun (spirit of the dead) in Candomblé, where two sorts of egun exist, the Egun who is a deified ancestor and who does not possess human beings, but manifests himself in his specific cult; and the eguns who are disembodied souls, and with whom contact may be harmful for mankind, provoking physical and spiritual problems. These disruptive souls must therefore be chased away and exorcised. At the most African extreme of Umbanda, another distinction is made later between exus-eguns and Exus-orixás. The first have been incarnated: they were human beings who, after a violent death (murder or suicide), became exus. In these spirits' passage from Umbanda to Candomblé, the term "exu-egun" is used to distinguish the disincarnated spirits from the Exu-orixá, the divinity who keeps his African characteristics.

But to come back to the opposition between higher and lower exus, this is an opposition which is also reflected in the division of spiritual labor. Thus, the exus considered as coming from the privileged social class are excused from the vilest labors, which are carried out by their subordinates. It is the latter who lead magic attacks (*demandas*) against people. The lower Exu is identified with the soul of a person who led a morally dissolute life: thieves, murderers, outcasts (*malandros*), or prostitutes. He may also be a pagan or obsessive Exu, who, in addition to having lived in an immoral way, does not accept the reality of his own death. These spirits, often called *quiumbas*, do not comply with the logic of evolution.

Higher exus, heads of phalanxes and legions, are credited with behavior identical to that of the upper classes. Here is an Umbandist author's description of one of them (quoted in Ortiz 1988, 159): "He speaks slowly, pausing often with extreme delicacy. He has an elegant allure, and always chooses the most refined cigars, and the finest wines or liquors to drink. But his real drink is absinthe. He speaks and writes fluent French." On the other hand, the same author describes exus of the lower level as "horrible blacks, whose faces are covered with smallpox scars."

This valorization of French culture as a sign of evolution for men as well as spirits is still very present in the imagination of mediums today. I attended a ceremony dedicated to Exu Barabô in Duque de Caxias (Rio de Janeiro). There, Exu was the perfect incarnation of the ideal of superior exus' politeness. According to the medium, his Barabô had lived in France during the reign of Louis XV and had been addicted to absinthe, and, even though it was difficult to procure, absinthe was still his favorite drink.[6]

The ceremony took place on Tuesday, April 26, 1994, about ten o'clock in the evening. The courtyard of the house, transformed into a terreiro for the exclusive cult of Exu, was already filled with people. In front of Exu's house a shrine had been erected, upon which were placed lighted candles, a bottle of Martini Bianco vermouth, pink champagne, glasses, and cigars. A little further were the sacred drums. Soon the invocations to Exu began, accompanied by the sound of drumming and chanting. Suddenly the medium went into a trance, animated by movements typical of possession by Exu—his back arched, his body waved, his arms went rigid, and his face contracted. After a rapid change of clothes, Barabô came back into the yard with great elegance and calm. In one hand he held a cane of dark wood, in the other, a crystal champagne glass; he wore a black cape covered in silver sequins over his shoulders. Barabô began to dance while distributing champagne to those around him. He then ordered the drums to stop, and, going from one side of the yard to the other, launched into a long speech, in very elegant Portuguese, explaining the principal aim of the ceremony—to resolve the economic or relationship problems of those present. At the end, he concluded, still with the same extreme elegance, that had he been able to choose, he would never have agreed to live in Brazil, for "the best perfume is not French perfume, but the perfume of the French land" where he lived during previous incarnations. Barabô kept up this haughty, refined attitude throughout the night. Regally seated on a large chair, he watched the successive trances of various mediums possessed by Pombagira. With the same nonchalance, he listened to the problems of each of the people present, who patiently waited their turn until dawn.

While higher exus are characterized by stereotypes of a superior culture, lower exus are always the expression of a marginal condition; thus bohemian exus, such as Zé Pelintra, are incarnations of the stereotype of the malandro, who prefers to live by his wits rather than work. This Exu seems to be the representation of someone who really existed in Recife, José Pelintra, a notorious crook in the police chronicles of the 1930s (René Ribeiro 1957). Statuettes in his image placed on Umbandist altars show a mulatto in a white linen suit, white shoes, and Panama hat. Lower exus can also be part of the cemetery, called Petite Calunga, where they take charge of the heaviest labors under the responsibility of Exu Caveira (Skull), also known as João Caveira. He is considered to be the secretary of Omolu (or Obaluaiê), who is

16. A statuette of Pombagira. PHOTO BY AUTHOR.

transformed from the god of smallpox in Candomblé into master of the graveyards. Omolu is connected to the decomposition of corpses and hence to death itself.

Although in comparison to the spirits of light, Exu is a negative being, linked to the world of shadows, he nevertheless contains a duality, a negative side and a positive side. The negative side of Exu is his female representation, Pombagira. Fontanelle (n.d., 104) defines her as "the Biblical devil, Klepoth" who took the form of a buck with a woman's breasts, presenting all the characteristics of the buck of the Sabbath. However, Alva (n.d., 121), defending the most African branch of Umbanda, contests the name of Pombagira (or Pomba Gira), preferring that of Bomo-Gira, thus establishing a direct link between the female Exu and the Bombogira of Bantu Candomblé, equivalent to the Yoruba Exu.

Pombagira, a negative spirit par excellence, is the Exu of women, very closely linked to witchcraft. For Fontanelle, she is "a black magic being, incarnating evilness in the guise of a woman" (n.d., 140). She is also responsible for witches' revenge against their enemies. In general, Pombagira incarnates the stereotype of the prostitute, but also that of the woman who rebels against any male domination; it is she who is invoked in magic to do with love. Furthermore, Pombagira is the "wife of seven exus," meaning that she is no one's wife. Here is a description of the spirit, recorded by Liana Trindade (1985, 98): "Pombagira lived in the Freguesia do O [a popular district of São Paulo]. She rebelled against her mother's life. She killed four men and castrated one of them. She killed the men who exploited her mother. She ended up a prostitute."

Pombagira is also associated with marginal, dangerous places, and there are Pombagiras of the Crossroads, of the Calunga (graveyard), of the Seven-Calungas, of the Gateway, of the Sepulcher, of the Seven Shallow Sepulchers, etc. There are also the family of the Tzigane Pombagiras; the family of the Maria Mulambos (Mary in rags), who often receive their offerings next · to garbage dumps and who, for that reason, may also be called Pombagiras of the Garbage; and the family of Young Pombagiras (Pombagiras *Meninas*), who, unlike the former, are virgins. Pombagiras crossed with the line of souls are known as Pombagira of the Graveyard Cross, Rose-Skull (Rosa Caveira), or Pombagira of Souls. Their offerings are left in cemeteries, and their sacred necklaces have white beads and a skull made from horn or the bone of a dead person among the black and red beads typical of Exu (Molina n.d.b., 17).

All pombagiras have in common the colors red and black (as well as white in the example we have just seen). They are offered red roses (always in full bloom, never in bud); drinks such as cachaça or champagne (according to how refined the spirit is), cigars or cigarettes; and candles that are (according to the spirit's level of light) white; white and red; red, black, and white; or black.

These offerings, called despacho as in Candomblé, are usually made at midnight on a Friday, the day of the exus in Umbanda. For a Pombagira "traced" with the line of souls, the day of the despacho will be Monday, the day of the souls of the dead. The place of the despacho varies, as we have seen, according to the type of Pombagira and the kind of work she does. According to Umbandist authors, each Pombagira has her own specialization. In reality, they all receive as many requests to cure disease or help solve a problem (financial or sentimental) as they do requests for magic attacks to harm someone. Human beings are solely responsible for the evil deeds of exus and pombagiras, for the latter are "venal beings, who, as soon as they receive a present, are willing to satisfy any request, whether it be for Good or for Evil" (Molina n.d.a., 6–7).

Like exus, pombagiras are divided into higher and lower spirits. If Maria Mulambo appears to occupy the lowest position among the pombagiras, Maria Padilha is considered the most refined. She, too, is often identified with stereotypes associated with the upper classes—she speaks French, drinks champagne, uses a cigarette holder, and has refined behavior.[7] Maria Padilha does not accept "the heaviest labors"; she leaves them to her subordinates.

Generally, mediums possessed by pombagiras (who only incarnate women or homosexuals) adopt a provocative sexual behavior. Their going into a trance is always marked by guffaws; their movements become lascivious, their regard shameless, and their language obscene. This is the dramatization of female sexual power, the witch hidden in every woman.

European Witchcraft and African Witchcraft

Pombagira seems to have been created in Rio de Janeiro. The first reference to this entity was discovered by Arthur Ramos (1951b, 221) in a Rio de Janeiro newspaper, *O Jornal*, of October 12, 1938. During an operation targeting centers of what was called low spiritism, the police raided a Macumba center of the Ramos district in the outskirts of Rio, which was accused of illegally practicing medicine (*curandeirismo*). Among the objects seized that day was a list of prices: seven thousand *reis* (the Brazilian currency at the time) for Exu or Pombagira's magical works, and five thousand for a consultation with Pombagira.

Pombagira was therefore already present in the 1930s in Rio de Janeiro Macumba. For most authors, she is the reinterpretation of Bombogira from Bantu Candomblé, a divinity corresponding to the Yoruba Exu. But why would a male god be transformed into a symbol of female sexual power? What are the origins of the mythical figure of Pombagira?

We have seen how, in Africa, Èṣù-Legba also has female representations, and we have seen how, in Bantu Candomblé, there is at least a cult of a female Exu, Exu Vira.[8] Today, however, the stereotype of the dangerous woman, the witch, linked to the figure of Pombagira seems to be the result of a bricolage of symbols referring simultaneously to various traditions. Here is a ponto cantado,[9] a chanted invocation dedicated to Pombagira Maria Padilha, recorded by José Ribeiro (n.d., 76):

> She is the wife of seven exus,
> The wife of Lucifer.
> She is the wife of seven husbands,
> She is the wife of seven husbands,
> Do not provoke her,
> Pombagira is dangerous.
> When the rooster crows,
> The Dead arise,
> The birds fly in circles.
> Greetings, Pombagira
> Woman of the street.
> Vivat! Alleluia! Vivat! Alleluia!
> Pombagira tames
> The wild donkeys.
> I have tamed my husband
> With six hundred thousand devils.
> Pombagira has received
> A bottle of cachaça,
> Took it to the chapel
> For the priest to bless it.
> She asked the sacristan
> If under the priest's cassock
> There was palm oil,
> Palm oil,
> Palm oil.
> Into the family of Pombagira,

May enter only those who can do this.
She is Maria Padilha,
I am the wife of Lucifer.

Pombagira is dangerous. She belongs to no one and is a woman of the streets, a prostitute. She dominates her husband with witchcraft ("with six hundred thousand devils"); she lives in graveyards and reigns over the shadows. She receives cachaça, the typical offering for exus, which she takes to church "for the priest to bless it." Thus the symbolic inversion between good and evil becomes clear: the priest blesses the devil's liquor and, under his cassock, keeps the palm oil which, as we have seen, is the principal offering to Exu. This relation between Pombagira and sorcery has been developed by two authors, each of whom in her own way has carried out research into the cultural origins of the figure of Maria Padilha: Marlyse Meyer (1993) in the Iberian Peninsula, and Monique Augras (1989) in Africa.[10]

Meyer uses as her starting point data presented by Laura de Mello e Souza (1986) in her valuable analysis of witchcraft during Brazil's colonial period. She records a seventeenth-century prayer dedicated to a certain Maria Padilha, invoked along with Lucifer, Satan, and Barrabás (ibid., 235). Prayers to Maria Padilha, in those times as well as our own, always have a purpose related to love: they aim to bend another's will in one's favor, or to facilitate an "illicit friendship" between a man and a woman. Maria Padilha's origins, then, may be found in a character in the hispanic ballads called *romances viejos* and collected in the *Romancero General*, published in Castile in 1600. Among these narratives about the history of Spain may be found the cycle of Pedro I of Castile (1334–69), known as "the Cruel" for having killed a large number of his relatives, friends, and allies. He was under the influence of a *mala mujer*, an evil woman—the beautiful and vindictive María de Padilla,[11] and for love of her he abandoned his legitimate wife, Blanca of Bourbon, whom he had killed. The king had been bewitched by María de Padilla, who dominated him completely.

The first collection of romances viejos was prepared by the editor Martin Nucio, probably in 1547, for Spanish soldiers in Flanders. This collection was republished three times; the 1581 edition from Lisbon contained many romances in which Maria Padilha (the Portuguese translation of María de Padilla) was presented in an unfavorable light. Less than a century later,

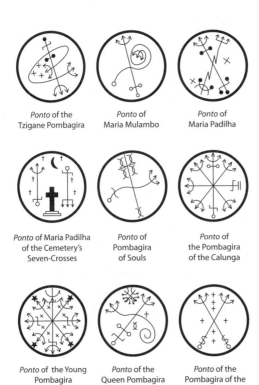

Ponto of the Tzigane Pombagira	*Ponto* of Maria Mulambo	*Ponto* of Maria Padilha
Ponto of Maria Padilha of the Cemetery's Seven-Crosses	*Ponto* of Pombagira of Souls	*Ponto* of the Pombagira of the Calunga
Ponto of the Young Pombagira	*Ponto* of the Queen Pombagira	*Ponto* of the Pombagira of the Calunga

17. Pombagira's *pontos riscados*.

Maria Padilha was being invoked in Brazil in black-magic practices, along with the demonic triad of Barrabas, Satan, and Lucifer. In many of the prayers preserved in the Inquisition's archives in Lisbon, Maria Padilha, presented as Lucifer's wife, is already the incarnation of the witch dedicated to love magic, a spirit who appears each time she is invoked (Meyer 1993, 15).

In 1843, Prosper Mérimée wrote a history of Pedro I, which was published by the *Revue des Deux Mondes* in 1847. The character of María de Padilla, transformed into a witch, appears again in his famous novel *Carmen.* The story's heroine practices love magic by singing the magic formulas which "invoke Marie de Padilla, Don Pedro's mistress, who was said to be the *Bari Crillisa,* the great queen of the Bohemians" (Mérimée 1994, 60). The Carmen who sings for Maria Padilha is described as "a wild and strange beauty," whose regard "both voluptuous and untamable" was proof of the power with which she led men to their downfall. She was a "Bohemian," a "witch," and a "servant of the Devil" (ibid.). The diabolization of María de Padilla and her adepts was thus recognized. On December 26, 1841, Gaetano Donizetti produced an opera titled *Maria Padilla* at La Scala in Milan, which was performed at least once in Rio de Janeiro—on December 7, 1856 (Meyer 1993, 155). The myth of Maria Padilha appears to stretch over six hundred years of history.

Maria Padilha's association with the Tziganes, as established by Mérimée, is also present in the Brazilian imaginary that links Maria Padilha to her "sisters," the pombagiras. Among the latter is a group of Tziganes (*Ciganas*), endowed with strong magical powers. Indeed, during the colonial period, the Tziganes received the same punishment as those accused of witchcraft: exile from Portugal to Brazil, the land where they had to purge their sins. They were principally concentrated in Salvador and Rio de Janeiro, where they lived in the poor districts with the black people. It is therefore highly probable that there was contact and exchanges of magical practices between the two cultures.

Maria Padilha is also a powerful symbol of dissolute femininity. The contemporary association between Pombagira and the figure of the prostitute already existed in the seventeenth century between the witch and the "woman who led a bad life." Unmarried women or those who worked for a living were almost always regarded as prostitutes. In the same way, in colonial Brazil, "sexual magic and prostitution seemed always to go together" (Souza 1986, 241). We have seen how Pombagira is constantly associated with sexual magic, and her power derives from her ability to manipulate men's and women's sexual potency. Maria Padilha's noble origins have been conserved in the Umbandist imaginary, which makes her a queen, a higher Exu, Lucifer's wife—she is refined, drinking champagne, smoking expensive cigarettes, and speaking French.

Monique Augras (1989) takes the opposite path as she searches for Pombagira's origins in Africa. She sees in the female orixás, collectively known as *iyagbás*, the revival of the mythical figure of Iyamí Oxorongá. Augras suggests that Pombagira incarnates the power which, in Africa, is the monopoly of the iyamís, for, like her, Iyamí is not submissive to any man—she talks loudly, like men; she is self-sufficient; and she kills her husband once she has been fertilized. Her terrible power is individualized in every Candomblé goddess: Nanã, linked to death, the beginning and end of things; Obá, head of the women's secret society; Oxum, who possesses the power of fertility;

Yemanjá, the castrating mother; and Yansan, the queen of the Eguns and graveyards. All the goddesses who "bear a sword," and who are therefore warriors, incarnate some of the strength and power of Iyamí. In Umbanda, it is through the toning down of Yemanjá (who has come to represent the asexual mother) that Pombagira seems to have concentrated all the subversive potential of the Yoruba witch, to the point of her becoming the most sensual and aggressive spiritual being in the Brazilian terreiros.

For Augras (1989, 25–26), even the name of this spirit, which she considers to be derived from the Bantu god Bombogira (or Bombojira), reveals her ambiguity:

> For us, there are no doubts about the origin of the name Pombagira. Through a process of dissimulation Bombojira was transformed first into Bombagira, then to Pomba Gira, thus recovering words that had meanings in Portuguese; *gira*, a word of Bantu origin (*njila*, *njira*, "direction, way") from the verb *girar* ("to turn"), refers to the Umbanda ritual circle (*roda*), and *pomba*, as well as meaning "dove," also signifies the genitals, male in the Northeast and female in the Southeast. Her name conceals ambiguity and a sexual reference.

However, while Pombagira is associated with sexuality, it is not for reproductive purposes, for she uses sexuality as an end in itself. She is the negation of the mother figure. The fact that she is the wife of seven exus shows excessive sexual power rather than submission. Her position on the margins of society (she is a prostitute) also constitutes her strength: her independence threatens the balance between the sexes involving women's subjugation. Furthermore, Pombagira is often associated with blood, which must flow profusely from the wounds of her enemies. Apart from its evident warrior connotations, this relationship seems to confirm that the true power of women lies in blood.[12] Pombagira is also associated with death and the cemetery, a marginal place par excellence.

Pombagira, then, seems to be born of the popular religious imaginary peopled by spirits, devils, and witches. Her identification with the "African devil" is part of the reinterpretation process of this imaginary in an "African" context. The hypothesis advanced by Augras is particularly interesting because it shows, as we will see, the same path of reinterpretation that initiates follow in their attempt to re-Africanize the spirits when they pass from

Umbanda to Candomblé. This logical path has already been presented in Umbandist literature: "each female medium has a Pombagira by her side who acts in accordance with the initiate's father or mother orixá, around whom she fulfills the functions of an intermediary in the same way as the other exus" (Molina n.d.c., 17). Here we are in the presence of a spirit from Umbanda transformed into an Exu slave of the orixá, following the best "African" tradition. In this way, Pombagira moves from spirit, a disembodied soul, to an intermediary divinity of the Candomblé pantheon, and so the contradiction with Candomblé orthodoxy, which does not allow possession by the souls of the dead, is blurred. The way is clear for the Africanization of these spirits.

PART II

RITUAL PRACTICE

THE RELIGIOUS CONTINUUM

The figures of Exu and Pombagira are good illustrations of the intense circulation of symbols and ritual practices among the different modalities of Afro-Brazilian religions. In Candomblé, the African Exu is the subject of a very complex reinterpretation that transforms him into an Umbandist spirit. We have seen how the different Afro-Brazilian religions are part of a religious continuum. It is always difficult to classify a religious center, be it Candomblé or Umbandist, because the classification systems used by anthropologists do not always correspond to those used by the religions' members. In practice, religious identity is always renegotiated between the different interlocutors. Therefore, it is extremely important to take into account the position in the terreiro's structure of the person who classifies and the person classified: the opposition between pure and degenerate will be subject to constant shifting according to the aspects of the religion under consideration.

Despite the existence of a series of definitions to categorize the Afro-Brazilian religious field, what constitutes the day-to-day activity of these religions is not the "pure" form—which is more an ideal model than a reality—but a "mixed" form.[1] In fact, the fluidity seen in the Afro-Brazilian religious field among the different categories (Candomblé, Macumba, Umbanda, and Quimbanda), where the potential combinations are constantly renegotiated, is matched by the reinterpretation of the gods spirits in the terreiros described as *traçados* (mixed). In Umbanda, there is a distinct category of spirits, known as *cruzados* (crossed), who come from two different lines simultaneously: a caboclo or preto-velho may be "crossed" with an exu, taking on the characteristics of the first for six months and those of the second for the rest of the year (Maggie 1977, 23).

Members of the terreiros, whether they are Candomblé or Umbandist, have a very clear perception of the interweaving of ritual practices. However, even if most terreiros are meeting places of different religious experiences, the "mixed" one will always be the "Other," the neighbor or rival. No one admits to being a member of a crossed terreiro; members always identify themselves with the branch considered the most traditional. The opposition between the ideal model of purity, which lays the foundation for orthodoxy and refuses any mixture, and the ritual practice, which illustrates the interpenetration and the reinterpretation of elements coming from different religious modalities, constitutes, in my eyes, the major issue for Afro-Brazilian religions.

Rio de Janeiro: A History of Afro-Brazilian Religions

CANDOMBLÉ

The city of Rio de Janeiro has been a center for Candomblé since at least the beginning of twentieth century, despite its identification with the degenerate pole of Afro-Brazilian religions. In specialist literature, Rio is the homeland of Macumba, the "less traditional" syncretic cult that gave birth to Umbanda. For this reason, information about the existence of religious houses which reproduce the Jeje-Nagô model in Rio at the beginning of the twentieth century (Rio 1976; Moura 1983) have not been taken into account by most researchers. Since the work of Ramos, they have preferred to see in Bahia terreiros the anthropological model of traditional Candomblé, and in Rio terreiros the anthropological model of Macumba, the "degraded" Bantu cult.[2]

The earliest information on religions of African origin in Rio de Janeiro is found in a series of chronicles written in 1900 by the journalist João Paulo Alberto Coelho Barreto, better known by his pseudonym, João do Rio. These chronicles, collected in 1904 in a book titled *Religions in Rio* (Rio 1976), were, until very recently, the sole source of information available to us, apart from the oral tradition passed down in the terreiros. The author was attracted by the contrast between "the rumblings of modern life" (ibid., 8) and the survival in the heart of huge urban areas of countless cults and religions opposed to the ideal of material progress that was linked to positivist beliefs, predominant at the beginning of the twentieth century.

Rio de Janeiro underwent great changes under President Campos Salles's government (1898–1902). The first stretch of the railway line that was to link the city center with the suburbs was inaugurated in 1886. From 1889 to 1891, an epidemic of yellow fever, a very common infectious disease at the time in the Rio area, motivated a whole series of reforms to sanitize the city. The year 1902 saw the start of important urbanization, leading to the extensive demolition of entire districts and two hills in the center of Rio, inhabited mostly by freed slaves. The population of African origin was concentrated in the city center, especially in the Saúde district and around Praça Onze, in what was known as "Little Africa."

There former slaves had created a network of social relations based around houses of worship built on the hills surrounding the port. The decline of the sugar industry in the Northeast, due to competition from the West Indian colonies and the growing economic importance of coffee, had resulted in the large-scale selling of slaves and their displacement farther south in the country. For this reason, the province of Rio de Janeiro, whose population in 1844 included 119,141 slaves, had more than 300,000 in 1870, brought from Africa or Salvador. Between 1872 and 1876, 25,711 slaves arrived in Rio from the north and northeast of Brazil (Moura 1983). However, the deterioration in living conditions in Bahia had also resulted in a large migration from Salvador to Rio de Janeiro of freed slaves who wanted to try their luck in the country's new capital. By the end of the nineteenth century, there was already a large community from Bahia living in Rio de Janeiro.

With the abolition of slavery in 1888, the migrants from Bahia asserted themselves in Rio de Janeiro as the leaders of the black community, organizing around the Candomblé terreiros. But with the sanitization of the city, the "Africans" had to move farther toward the outskirts, following the railway line, driven out by the rise in rents in the city center. In fact, the demolition of the unhealthy districts where they had been concentrated was a response to a predominant preoccupation of the time—as Nina Rodrigues

(1988, 7) puts it, a nefarious trilogy was ruining Brazil: an "intertropical climate harmful to the white man," "the black who hardly could be civilized," and the "humdrum and retrograde Portuguese." With the sanitization policy, the city thus rid itself of diseases due to the climate and, at the same time, of "savage" blacks, who were pushed to the margins of a city which was civilized at last.

Among the pais and mães-de-santo who used to live in the city center were important religious figures, still evoked today in the oral tradition. The best known at the beginning of the twentieth century was João Alagbá, a son of Omolu. His house was one of the most important meeting places of the Bahian community. Tia Ciata (Hilária Batista de Almeida), a daughter of Oxum and probably the best-known priestess of Rio de Janeiro, was his *mãe pequena*.[3] Tia Ciata, whose name is also very closely linked to the birth of samba "in the yards of Candomblé *terreiros*" (Sodré 1979), had been initiated by Bamboxé (Rodolfo Martins de Andrade), a very well known figure in Bahian Candomblé. At the same time Cipriano Abedé (or Agbedé) was living in Rio de Janeiro, an African who had been initiated by Maria Júlia Figuereido from the Casa Branca. He was a son of Ogun and bore the titles of babalawo (diviner), and *babalosaniyin* (leaves specialist). Baba Sanim, another African living in Rio at the beginning of the twentieth century, was renowned as a great "fetishist" (João de Rio 1976, 51), for which he was persecuted by the police, as the Brazilian constitution condemned the practice of magic and the illegal practice of medicine (curandeirismo). Born in Nigeria, Baba Sanim, also known as Tio Sani Adio (Ornato da Silva 1988, 29), is often identified in the oral tradition as Joaquim Vieira da Silva (Obá Saniá), who founded with Aninha (Eugenia Ana dos Santos) the terreiro of the Axé Opô Afonjá at Salvador (Verger 1981, 30). According to Monique Augras and Jõao Batista dos Santos (1985, 47), Joaquim Vieira da Silva came to Rio with his friend, Rodolfo Martins de Andrade, and both opened terreiros at Pedra do Sal, in the Saúde district. Today, Obá Saniá is venerated in the terreiro during the padê ritual, under the name of Essa Oburo.

Many "fetishists" lived in Little Africa, such as Tia Dada, Tia Inês, Tia Oni, and Torquato Tenerê, who were in great demand by a huge clientele to resolve problems of various natures. Their terreiros alternated between Nagô Candomblé and religions of Bantu origin, which had existed for a long time in Rio de Janeiro. As Moura (1983, 90) points out, "Macumba in Rio springs from the Bahia Houses in the districts of Saúde and Praça Onze, even if the idea of Nagô superiority resulted in an undeclared war between Macumba and Candomblé."

Another important figure in the founding of Candomblé in Rio de Janeiro was Felisberto Américo Souza, who anglicized his name to Sowser and who was one of the last diviners from Bahia, like the famous Martiniano Eliseu do Bonfim. Maria Oganlá was another high priestess from the beginning of the twentieth century; she ran her house of worship in the district of São Cristóvão. She initiated only one woman, Filinha de Oxum, who went on to become the mãe pequena of the Axé Opô Afonjá terreiro in Rio, founded by Aninha. The latter, one of the most famous mães-de-santo in Brazil, lodged at the home of Maria Oganlá in 1925, as well as at the terreiro of Obá Saniá (Augras and Santos 1985, 47), during her long visits to Rio, where she opened a terreiro of the same name as the one she founded in Salvador.

From the end of the 1940s onward, a wave of migration from the Northeast reached the city of Rio de Janeiro. A large number of pais and mães-de-santo, looking for new places to establish their cults, set up terreiros in the outskirts of the city around Guanabara Bay. This region, known as Baixada Fluminense, was linked to the center of Rio by the railway line. The initial movement from the city's center toward its periphery at the beginning of the century changed to a migration from the Northeast directly to the poorest quarters of Rio de Janeiro. A new generation of pais and mães-de-santo arrived from the state of Bahia. Among the most important terreiros was the Axé of Mesquita, one of the first houses of worship to open in the Baixada Fluminense. Today, this Ketu house, called Ilê de Omolu e Oxum, is led by Mãe Meninazinha (Maria Arlete do Nascimento), in the São João de Meriti district.

At the same time, many pais and mães-de-santo from "traditional" Candomblé terreiros in Bahia established themselves in Rio. According to oral tradition, the first house of worship of the Jeje nation in Rio de Janeiro was that of Gaiaku Rozenda, an African who had come to Brazil around 1850; it was located on rua America, a street next to the port. However, the Jeje "family" that now exists in Rio has its roots in the terreiro of Tata Fomotinho (Antonio Pinto) who initiated, among others, Zezinho da Boa Viagem and Djalma de Lalú, the first person to be initiated to Exu in the city. Tata

Fomotinho, now deceased, had been initiated in the Terra Vermelha ter-reiro, in Cachoeira de São Felix, at the heart of the Bahia Jeje tradition.

The Angola nation was represented in Rio by Ciriaco (Manoel Ciriaco dos Santos), who had transferred his terreiro from Salvador in the 1940s, and had founded a new house of worship, called Tumba Junçara, in Vilar dos Teles in the Baixada Fluminense. Coming from the Bate-Folha terreiro of Salvador, which was led by the pai-de-santo Bernardino of the Angola na-tion, João Lessengue moved to the Catumbi district in Rio in 1938. Around 1940, he bought the site of the current Bate-Folha of Rio. When he died in 1970, his niece Mameto Mabeji, a "daughter" of Omolu, replaced him as the head of the terreiro.

Without a doubt the most famous pai-de-santo of the Angola nation was Joãozinho da Goméia (João Alves Torres Filho). Having moved from Bahia to Rio de Janeiro in 1946, he was the first to systematically use the media to increase his prestige and authority. Joãozinho da Goméia had been initiated by Jubiabá, the pai-de-santo immortalized in the homonymous novel by Jorge Amado, who was from a Caboclo Candomblé, mixed "with a lit-tle Angola" (Binon-Cossard 1970, 278). Young and charismatic, João worked with Carneiro in his anthropological study of the religions of Bantu origin, which enabled him to gradually establish himself in Salvador Can-domblé. However, his unorthodox religious origins (Caboclo Candomblé) prevented him from being part of the exclusive circle of "pure" Candomblé.

In 1946, Joãozinho da Goméia decided to set up a terreiro in Rio de Janeiro, where he soon became very well known. He founded his house of worship in the Baixada Fluminense, at Duque de Caxias. He took part in radio programs, and interviews with him were published in various news-papers. An excellent dancer, he was invited to interpret the orixás' dances on the stage of the João Caetano Theater in Rio. For many years, he also participated in the parades of the samba schools during carnival. His name soon became synonymous with Candomblé. When he died, Joãozinho da Goméia left behind an impressive number of sons-of-saint, whom he had initiated or who were affiliated with him. According to his own count, which appeared in a 1970 issue of the journal *Pasquim* and was quoted by Ziegler (1975, 213),[4] he initiated 4,777 people throughout Brazil.

At the end of the 1940s, Cristóvão de Ogunjá (Cristóvão Lopes dos Santos) arrived in Rio de Janeiro, becoming the patriarch of the Efon family in the city. He had been initiated by the founders of the first Efon terreiro, the Ilê Axé Oloroquê, in the Engeno Velho de Brotas district of Salvador: Tio Firmino (José Firmino dos Santos) and Maria do Violão (Maria Bernarda da Paixão). According to Maria de Xangô (Maria José Lopes dos Santos), Cristóvão's granddaughter, the Oloroquê terreiro had been founded more than a century earlier.[5]

The first document from the terreiro (its title deeds) dates from August 15, 1908. Five years later Tio Firmino died, and Maria do Violão became the house's iyalorixá; upon her death she was succeeded by Matilde de Jagun (Matilde Muniz Nascimento). Cristóvão opened another house of worship in Salvador, called Ilê Ogun Anauegi Belé Ioman, where he initiated many sons and daughters-of-saint, among them Waldomiro de Xangô (Waldomiro da Costa Pinto, or Baiano) who followed him to Rio de Janeiro.

In 1947 Cristóvão decided to close his terreiro and leave for Rio de Janeiro. A small group of followers and friends went with him to the big city in the south, with the aim of founding a new house of worship in the Baixada Fluminense. In 1951, Cristóvão bought the plot of land at 69 rua Eça de Queiroz, known as Pantanal, in Duque de Caixas. In May of the same year, he planted a tree dedicated to the god Iroco, and at the foot of the tree he dug a well for Oloque,[6] the patron divinity of the Efon nation. The house of worship as it is today was not inaugurated until 1955, and it was given the same name as the Bahian terreiro: Ilê Ogun Anauegi Belé Ioman.

In 1952 Cristóvão's daughter, Mãe Lindinha (Arlinda Lopes dos Santos), accompanied by her daughter Maria José, came to join her father. She had been initiated in Salvador by Mãe Runhô, mãe-de-santo of the Jeje terreiro of Bogun.[7] Mãe Lindinha became the mãe pequena of the Pantanal terreiro. Maria José was initiated to Xangô by her grandfather in 1954, when she was eight years old. Seven years later, she received the title of future iyalorixá from Cristóvão, who chose her as his heir. Three months after Maria's Xangô initiation was held came the initiation ceremony of Alvinho de Omolu (Alvaro Pinto de Almeida), one of the pais-de-santo who contributed most to the spread of Candomblé in the Southeast, especially in São Paulo.

In 1970, upon the death of Matilde de Jagun, the iyalorixá of the Ilê Axé Oloroquê, Cristóvão took over the direction of the house at Salvador, dividing his time between the terreiros in Rio and Salvador. In his absence,

18. Roots of the Iroko tree in the Pantanal terreiro. PHOTO BY AUTHOR.

Arlinda de Oxossi, a daughter-of-saint of Matilde de Jagun, looked after the Salvador terreiro's activities. During his trips to Bahia, Cristóvão continued initiating new sons-of-saint in the Oloroquê's terreiro. When he died on September 23, 1985, in Rio de Janeiro, Crispina de Ogun (Crispiniana de Assis) took over the direction of the Salvador terreiro until her death in 1993. Today the terreiro is closed; its direction has been the subject of dispute between Cristóvão's sons-of-saint.[8]

Maria de Xangô, who had left for São Paulo at the beginning of the 1970s after a disagreement with her grandfather, came back to Rio de Janeiro after a long absence, to be reconciled with him just before he died. After a long period of mourning, during which the terreiro remained closed, she became the new iyalorixá of the Pantanal. Baiano, also known as Waldomiro de Xangô, was one of the first sons-of-saint of Cristóvão, initiated when he was still at his terreiro in Salvador. Like Alvinho de Omolu and Maria de Xangô, Baiano opened a terreiro in São Paulo at the end of the 1960s, but he soon returned to Rio de Janeiro, where his house of worship is found today, in the Caxias district. Around 1970, Baiano "changed waters," joining the religious family of the Gantois.[9] Because of this change in religious affiliation, today his former brothers-of-saint no longer consider Baiano a member of the huge Efon family-of-saint.

Alvinho de Omolu was the first white person to be initiated in the Pantanal and one of Cristóvão's first sons-of-saint at Rio de Janeiro. He relates having suffered much discrimination because of the color of his skin, for at the time it was said that a white man had no orixá. This was in 1954, when it was far less common to initiate a white person than it is today. Alvinho should have been initiated to the god Logunedé, but he was a divinity "full of enchantment" who therefore could not be "seated" in a white man's head,[10] so Alvinho was initiated to Omolu (Azauane), who decided to take possession of the young novice. Alvinho spent many years with his pai-de-santo, taking part in all the ritual activities. In 1960, Alvinho de Omolu opened an improvised terreiro in Rio and initiated his first *iyawós* (sons-of-saint), with the help of Cristóvão. A year later, he decided to move to São Paulo, where he lived until 1972, becoming as famous as Joãozinho da Goméia, who was also very active in the city at that time.

During the years that he spent in São Paulo, Alvinho initiated a whole generation of pais and mães-de-santo.[11] In 1962, he was invited to host a television program about Afro-Brazilian religions on TV TUPI called *When the Cowries Fall*.[12] The program continued until 1968. In 1972, he returned to Rio de Janeiro, where he opened a house of worship in the Santa Luzia district, in the Baixada Fluminense. He then founded the Ilê Ifá Mongé Gibanauê terreiro in the Engenheiro Pedreira district, at the very edge of the city. Alvinho de Omolu initiated hundreds of sons-of-saint in the states of Rio de Janeiro, São Paulo, and Minas Gerais, as well as in the city of Brasilia. He died on July 21, 2008, in Rio de Janeiro.

UMBANDA

In chapter 2 we saw how Umbanda was born in Rio de Janeiro in the 1920s, and the efforts made to purify the religion of the elements most closely linked to the Candomblé tradition of initiation and sacrifice. The Portuguese language took over from African, initiation was simplified and almost eliminated, and animal sacrifice was banned. The Candomblé pantheon was reduced, and the "entities" who were incarnated in mediums were no longer orixás, but spirits who "came down" to "work"—i.e. to advise people.

In 1939, Zélio de Moraes founded the first Umbanda federation, the Umbandist Spiritist Union of Brazil (UEUB).[13] It followed the example of the federations of Afro-Brazilian religions created in Salvador in the 1930s to respond to social discrimination and obtain social recognition by distinguishing between legitimate religions and syncretic cults. In the same way, the "white" Umbanda, created by Zélio de Moraes's group, in ridding itself of the negative elements linked to its African origins was seeking a legitimation to differentiate itself clearly from "inferior" cults.

It was after the Second World War that Umbanda acquired its national aspect, with the decrease in government repression of cults that had characterized the Estado Novo (the New State, 1937–45) under Getúlio Vargas's dictatorship. During those years, Freemasons, Kardecists, Umbandists, and initiates of Afro-Brazilian religions in general were under the jurisdiction of the Department of Narcotics and Fraud of the Brazilian police. The department dealt with any problems relating to drugs, alcohol abuse, gambling, and prostitution. Terreiros had to apply to the police for a special registration in order to function freely, because their practices were associated with antisocial, deviant activities.

From the 1950s onward, half a dozen other Umbanda federations were created in Rio. Three of them included the centers which considered themselves part of "white" Umbanda, like that of Zélio de Moraes. These centers did not accept the use of drums or animal sacrifices, or any mixing with Candomblé. The three other federations defended a form of Umbanda of African orientation. The most important among them was the Umbandist Spiritist Federation, founded in 1952 by Tancredo da Silva Pinto, who soon became the spokesman for the adepts of "African" Umbanda and rapidly gained popularity. He defended a popular Umbanda which claimed origins in African traditions, and he published a large number of books in which he presented Umbanda as part of the African heritage. Thus, Umbanda began to organize itself around two opposing poles—"white" Umbanda, influenced by Kardecism and the desire to create a socially respectable image, and "African" Umbanda, which defended its links with the Afro-Brazilian religions. The Umbandist terreiros aligned themselves along this continuum from the white form to the African form.

By the 1960s, some federations were renaming themselves to include explicit references to African heritage, such as the Spiritist Federation of

Umbanda and Afro-Brazilian Sects. With the arrival of the military dictatorship in 1964, Umbanda shed its marginal image. In fact, because it included many members of the army among its followers, Umbanda benefited from the protection of the military government, which effectively used Umbanda to combat the influence of the Roman Catholic Church, a religion too close to the political left since the 1950s. During the dictatorship, Umbanda centers were no longer under police jurisdiction, and Umbanda was recognized as a religion among the others in the official census. Various Umbandist festivals, such as the ritual for Yemanjá on December 31, were even declared national holidays.

The opposition between a white model and an African model has remained very strong in Afro-Brazilian religious circles. Thus, starting with the Candomblé terreiros in Rio since the end of the nineteenth century, a religious continuum takes shape, which goes from the "whitest" forms of Kardecism through to the most "African" variants of Afro-Brazilian religions (see figure 15). This continuum is also demonstrated by the creation of an intermediary religion between Umbanda and Candomblé, called Omolocô, which claims origins in Bantu religions such as Cabula. Tancredo da Silva Pinto was the charismatic leader of this religion, which originated in Rio de Janeiro and presented itself as a kind of "African" Umbanda. Numerous Umbandist mediums were already moving along this religious continuum, passing from Umbanda to Omolocô, then affiliating themselves with Angola Candomblé. Today, Omolocô has all but disappeared due to the considerable number of its initiates who joined other cult modalities thought to be more prestigious, such as Nagô Candomblé.

From Umbanda to Candomblé

The circulation of mediums among different cults seems to be one of the characteristic traits of this religious field. Prandi (1991) analyzed the valorization of Candomblé compared with Umbanda, and its wide diffusion in the city of São Paulo. Until the 1970s, Umbanda seemed destined to be the most important religion in the urban areas of the Southeast. Candomblé was seen as merely a distant relative of Umbanda, and before 1960 only one house of worship calling itself Candomblé existed in the state of São Paulo: the house of Seu Bobó, founded in 1958 in Santos. Candomblé began to spread in São

Paulo in the 1960s, with the arrival of various pais-de-santo from Salvador and Rio de Janeiro; it went on to expand massively in the 1970s, growing more than ten times faster than in the previous decade (Concone and Negrão 1985, 48). Hence, Candomblé flourished at the expense of Umbanda, just as the latter had done to the detriment of Kardecist Spiritism in the 1950s.[14]

According to Reginaldo Prandi and Vagner Gonçalves da Silva (1989, 226), there were two reasons for the spread of Candomblé in São Paulo: one was linked to the initiation process of Umbanda adepts, who in moments of religious crises sought the help of Candomblé pais and mães-de-santo from Bahia and Rio de Janeiro, because they were reputedly more powerful; the other was due to the influx of Candomblé initiates who came from the Northeast in search of a better life. Writing in the 1950s, Bastide (1978, 216-17) presents three cases of what he calls "the migration of rites and gods":

> I know of at least three such attempts in São Paulo. The first was made by a *babalorixá* from the Bahia *sertão* who moved to the city on two separate occasions but could not find a job to support himself. The second case was a *babalorixá* from Alagoas who arrived with great trunks full of cult objects, having moved his *xangô* lock, stock, and barrel. Although he found compatriots, he did not succeed in establishing his sect and had to return home after a year. The *babalorixá* from Bahia who had done so well in Rio later decided to set up a kind of branch *candomblé* in São Paulo, where a dozen or so of his former *filhas* were living. Indeed he had several times been invited by Paulistas [São Paulo inhabitants] who were resisting Vargas to celebrate sessions of black magic there. Nevertheless the *terreiro* he founded is evolving in the direction of Umbanda Spiritism instead of remaining faithful to purely African norms.[15]

The success of the progressive initiation of Umbanda adepts to Candomblé led to a considerable movement of pais and mães-de-santo from Rio and Salvador to the city of São Paulo. Alvinho de Omolu, from the Efon nation, was one of the most representative figures of the spreading of Candomblé to São Paulo. The Efon nation quickly established itself there to the detriment of other forms of religion, such as the Angola rite propagated by

Joãozinho da Goméia, principally because of its resemblance to the Ketu (Nagô) model, considered purer and consequently more prestigious.

The importance of the Efon nation in Candomblé in São Paulo, and the role played by Alvin hode Omolu and his brother-of-saint Waldomiro de Xangô (Baiano) have been pointed out by Vagner Gonçalves da Silva (1992, 80), who also attributes the widespread diffusion of the Efon rite to the quest for a "pure religious model" (ibid., 82). But what caused Candomblé's spread to São Paulo? Why did such a great number of Umbanda adepts decide to convert?

According to Prandi (1991, 20), when Candomblé came to São Paulo, it was no longer an ethnic religion whose aim was to "conserve the black cultural patrimony," but a universal religion open to everyone, regardless of skin color, origin, and social class. In reality, Candomblé had much earlier been transformed into a religion for all. As Vivaldo da Costa Lima (1977, 61) reminds us, this religion which at the time of Nina Rodrigues was "that of the Africans," and in Carneiro's and Ramos's time was "that of the blacks," had by the 1970s become a popular religion, "without well-defined ethnic and social limits":

> it can be claimed without a doubt that the current Candomblé of Bahia— even in the most orthodox and most "African" houses of worship—is, day after day, initiating people from other social classes, white people from Bahia and even foreigners with no ethnic or cultural relation to the dominant models of Candomblé. (Ibid.)[16]

Candomblé's transformation into a universal religion is also at the root of the construction of the opposition between pure religions and degenerate cults. Bastide (1978) sees in the ethnic dissolution in the Southeast religions a sign of loss of fidelity to the purely African traditions. The true religion, then, is the one that is based on maintaining an ethnic patrimony. However, Bastide was well aware of the presence of whites in the most traditional houses of worship, since he himself, a white foreigner, was accepted into the Axé Opô Afonjá. He was led to assume the existence of two different types of white people, just as there were assumed to be two different types of black people. He associated the "cultural disorganization" or "degeneration" of the Afro-Brazilian religions in the big cities of the Southeast with inter-breeding due to European immigration (1978, 300). Bahia Candomblé is thus designated as a black people's religion, and white people who come into contact with its "metaphysics" come to accept "naturally" "African law" and becoming "African." On the contrary, Macumba (of Bantu origin) is the product of the "cultural 'mulattoism'" (ibid., 303) of black people subjected to the rules of a class-based society. When they come into contact with white people (especially poor immigrants), the blacks soon lose their roots and their Africanity.

In this case, then, there would seem to exist not only two, qualitatively different, types of white—the "aristocracy" (white intellectuals) linked to the Nagôs, and the "plebeians" linked to the Bantus—as Fry (1984) notes, but also two different types of blacks: the Nagôs who impose their traditions on the whites, and the Bantus who are, on the contrary, receptive to change. Thus, "pure African" Candomblé can continue to establish itself as a "cultural niche," where African tradition (the "ethnic patrimony") is perpetuated, and whites who participate in it can assert, along with Bastide (1978, 28), "Africanus sum."

So, two types of white and two types of black—why, then, go from a national religion (Umbanda) to a religion which, despite its being open to everyone, regardless of their skin color or social background, manifests profound identification with African origins and traditions?

We have seen how religious affiliation with a Candomblé family always occurs with regard to an ideal of African purity, and how the Efon nation asserted itself in São Paulo to the detriment of Joãozinho da Goméia's Angola nation, by claiming a closer proximity to its African roots. Each new initiate then comes to identify himself with an African origin which has nothing to do with his own family or racial origins: a white man of Portuguese origin, initiated into a Nagô terreiro, will then claim "Yoruba" cultural origins without hesitation. What is at play here is not the melting down of racial differences in a universal religion, but the affirmation of a cultural identity with positive connotations and independent of each person's real origins.

In fact, from the 1960s onward, belonging to "pure African" Candomblé became a source of prestige in Brazilian society. It was during this period that African countries began the process of decolonization, becoming effective and independent actors in the political and economic international scene. Brazil was extremely interested in these new markets, especially in West African countries, with which it already had very close commercial ties, but with imports vastly exceeding exports. In 1964, the Senegalese president, Léopold Sédar Senghor, visited Brazil and signed the first Senegalese-Brazilian trade agreement. In 1965, the Brazilian government sent a trade mission to six West African countries, inaugurating its commercial policies with non-Portuguese-speaking African countries.[17]

This change of attitude with regard to Africa also brought about a sweeping reformation of national policies toward Afro-Brazilian religions, which became one of the main assets for establishing diplomatic relations with West African countries, by expressing shared cultural origins. This is how the supposedly pure and traditional origins of Nagô Candomblé from Bahia came to be held in high esteem. At the time, it was common to see Brazilian civil and military authorities side by side with representatives of African governments at public ceremonies in traditional Candomblé terreiros.[18] Candomblé became one of the symbols of Brazil, along with carnival and samba, and it began to be offered in tourist offices (notably the Bahiatursa) as one of the national folklore attractions.

This new image of blacks, no longer synonymous with ignorance and cultural backwardness, corresponded to the spread of the counterculture movement in the 1970s, in response to the authoritarianism of the military dictatorship. It was the period of the establishment of the blacks', homosexuals', and women's movements. At the same time, black Brazilians began to have access to universities, and their higher levels of education and the resulting social mobility laid the foundation for the emergence of a black middle class. The cultural symbols linked to Candomblé then became part of an identity with positive connotations. Gradually, Candomblé acquired a social visibility on a national level that it had never had before. It was the era of Mãe Menininha do Gantois (Maria Escolástica Nazaré), without doubt the most famous priestess of Bahia, and the first to be known nationally, even outside the religious sphere.[19] It was common to see her on television or in magazines; singers and poets paid homage to her. In 1972, for her initiation jubilee, Dorival Caymmi composed a song titled "Prayer to Mãe Menininha," which was performed by Caetano Veloso, Gal Costa, and Maria Bethania, all three Gantois's sons-of-saint. The novels of Jorge Amado and the films of Nelson Pereira dos Santos had already started to introduce the world of orixás into the national culture. At the end of the 1970s, the movement culminated in the abandoning of the Candomblé terreiros' obligation to register with the police, a decision which put a definitive end to the long period of repression of Afro-Brazilian religions which had begun in the 1930s. Being a Candomblé initiate had lost its negative connotations of social and cultural backwardness, a thing for blacks and poor people, and had become a source of prestige.

The "Scientific" Nature of Religious Discourse

In mediums' discourse, the passage from Umbanda to Candomblé is always justified by force: the direct calling of the orixás, manifested by an illness or misfortune, requiring the initiation. At some point in the medium's life, his inscription in the symbolic framework of Umbanda is no longer sufficient to master existential difficulties, and a crisis erupts. The solution is then sought in a universe considered to be more powerful—Candomblé. Thus, the conversion is always regarded as inevitable, independent of individual choice, caused by the divinities imposing their will directly on men. But this type of explanation constitutes a kind of code in Afro-Brazilian religions— discovering one's mediumship often occurs during existential crisis, and the more reticent the medium, the greater the veracity of the divine calling is esteemed to be. So why go from Umbanda to Candomblé? Why relive the same crisis, this time because of the orixás, when an alliance with Umbandist spirits has already been accepted?

In mediums' discourse, the inescapable aspect of the conversion is related to a belief in the superior religious and magical powers of Candomblé, which is stronger and can resolve problems more easily than Umbanda. This preeminence is confirmed above all when magical attacks are involved. This is how an Umbandist medium analyzes the magical war which set an Umbanda mãe-de-santo against a Candomblé initiate: "What a crazy old woman! She has gone and provoked the devil, even though she knows she's not strong [enough]. He's [an initiate] of Candomblé, and stronger than her" (quoted in Brumana and Martinez 1991, 432).[20]

However, mediums' conversion from Umbanda to Candomblé is above all a means of acquiring prestige, as shown by the discourse of a Ketu mãe-de-santo, Dina de Yansan, who was from Umbanda and initiated to Candomblé in 1971:

A person from Umbanda who is present at a Candomblé public cere-mony cannot take part in the ritual dance because he or she has not been through all the initiation rituals. Thus Candomblé confers upon us a different status from that of Umbanda people—even if you're an iyawó, newly initiated, when you come to a Candomblé terreiro, you're held in esteem. I'm an iyalorixá, so if I go into a terreiro during a celebration, the drummers stop to greet me, but if an Umbandist mãe-de-santo arrives, nothing of the sort happens!

It is this public recognition that leads most Umbandist mediums to be initiated into Candomblé, which also leads to an improvement in their position in the religious market, and opens the door for a religious career that would have been impossible in Umbanda. During his time in Bahia, Melville J. Herskovits (1967, 100) had already noted that one of the principal functions of Candomblé is to enable the initiate to simultaneously satisfy his aspiration to a prestigious position and to improve his social stand-ing. Indeed, the Candomblé economy, based on exchanges, is never simply about seeking profit but above all about asserting the prestige—both per-sonal and collective—of the pai or mãe-de-santo and his or her religious group. The affirmation of religious leadership through the accumulation of prestige is common to "pure" religions in Salvador, as much as it is for the "degenerate" cults of the Southeast. It forms the basis of the initiates' con-stant movements within the different Afro-Brazilian religious modalities.

Candomblé's increase in social standing from the end of the 1960s broke down the barriers between religions; until the 1950s, Umbanda represented a respectable option compared with the primitive nature of the blacks' religions, but this relationship was turned around with the rediscovery of symbols linked to Africa. This change is very clearly noticeable in initiates' discourse. Palmira de Yansan, a Ketu mãe-de-santo connected with the Axé Opô Afonjá of Rio de Janeiro, experienced the difficulties and constraints of initiation to Candomblé in 1957, when prejudice against the religion was still very strong, especially for a white woman from a Portuguese family: "Candomblé was taboo. If you practised Spiritism, you were marginalized from society. And it was even worse if it was Candomblé! You couldn't even talk about Candomblé, because it was a black thing, wasn't it? A thing for atheists, a diabolical thing!" Gradually, however, the country's cultural climate began to change, starting at the end of the 1960s. Candomblé began to occupy a central place in the religious market and benefited from widespread diffusion throughout the country, especially thanks to radio programs. Palmira de Yansan explains the change as follows:

> Candomblé really began to change towards 1970, when it opened up to everybody. Despite the dictatorship, I think that suddenly everyone wanted to talk, to say openly "I practice Candomblé." Until then, people had not said so. We began to discuss our experiences and produce radio programs. We began to talk of odùs [configurations connected to the divination system]. This is when people learnt that something called odù existed. But where did it come from? Many educated people became interested in Candomblé . . . they began to visit the terreiros and study what Candomblé was about.

The trend for radio programs about Candomblé ran parallel to a desire to understand the founding principles (*fundamentos*) of the religion, and initiates began to seek out books about Candomblé in Brazil and the very few that dealt with African religions that had been translated into Portuguese. These books became a source of sacred knowledge, alongside the direct religious experience.

We have seen how Umbanda was formed at the same time as the systemization in writings about the religion advanced. Umbanda is, then, the result of a cobbling together of various elements, organized into a scientific discourse. In this way, mystical experiences must be explained in the context of rationality, enabling it to be understood and legitimating it. Like Candomblé, Umbanda is no longer just for ignorant, superstitious people. The scientific explanations of magic and the magical universe of the spirits prove that the values of the modern world are compatible with Umbandist values, allowing the religion to be accepted by a modern, rational society. Books become the irreplaceable instruments of religious instruction.

Today, this Umbandist scientificity, considered to be positive, has become the subject of reinterpretation in the search for the African roots of Candomblé. If, through books, Umbandists participate in the values of the dominant society, where school and learning are the normal channels of social mobility and legitimation, these same values also reorganize the rediscovery of Candomblé: the cultural roots are not only linked to tradition, but also to a supposed scientificity original to this tradition. We go, then, from a religion of African origin, where traditions are placed beneath faith and superstition, to Umbanda, which combines faith and scientificity, to arrive at a re-Africanization, a rediscovery of Candomblé and its Africanity, where tradition connects with this search for the scientific components of the religion. The quest for scientificity implicit in African theological thinking thus drives the passage from Umbanda to Candomblé.

The radio programs, the search for anthropological texts, and courses in Yoruba language and civilization are all signs of the same quest for a rationalization of the religion:

> I'd like to know how the Africans invented all that, because I haven't studied theology—I didn't go to university. But how did it all start? What did the Africans understand about biology to dedicate an *igbin* [large snail] to Oxalá? Had they observed that when these animals copulate, both of them reproduce? [Oxalá is an orixá considered to be hermaphrodite.] How could they have known all that? So, to understand the system, we want to know why—why we must pour water on the ground three times, why we use palm oil, why we use honey, and in books we can find answers to all these questions.[21]

Candomblé has become a field of incessant research into the wherefores of life. Mediums no longer content themselves with simple mystical experiences and communication with the gods—they want to understand, and they look for the expression of a rationality which escapes them in each ritual action. This change of attitude regarding what is sacred has led to great upheaval in the way in which people join the religion. Thus, we have gone from a culture where the spoken word is the bearer of the sacred force, and where knowledge is gained over many years spent in a religious group, to a culture which is based upon a body of systemizations of its religious universe, produced by anthropologists but also by high priests. Candomblé initiates dedicate themselves to the study of their own culture, in search of the "true" Candomblé, for study is now an integral part of a religious career.[22]

Furthermore, in the absence of any centralizing institution to which to refer in questions of orthodoxy, some initiates wish to create training centers for future heads of terreiros. This is the case with Ornato da Silva (1988,

10), a babalorixá and the author of works on Candomblé who has proposed the creation of a "center for the training of priests in Afro-Brazilian religion" at an "academic level." This burning desire for legitimation through a scientific religious discourse is shared by most Candomblé initiates today.

Prestige and Hierarchy

Moving from Umbanda to Candomblé is synonymous, then, with greater efficiency ("Candomblé is more powerful"), increased knowledge (the scientific study of the religion), and prestige, thanks to the public recognition of the status of son-of-saint. If previously initiation into Candomblé was justified as a necessity, a divine obligation, today it is openly sought: "The orixá sends the illness to make his very skeptical son take notice, because people often turn to orixás only when they really need to, for example, when they are ill. But recently they have begun to see the beauty of the religion, and they want to become initiated into it."[23]

It is precisely this beauty that attracts a majority of the initiation candidates. Candomblé differs from Umbanda aesthetically: the luxuriousness and creativity of the clothes used in Candomblé contrast starkly with the simplicity and austerity of the white uniforms worn by Umbandist mediums. Although the profoundly festive nature of Candomblé ceremonies is contrasted with the "utility" of Umbandist work, this luxury acts as a magnet for mediums. On the other hand, it is difficult for mediums coming from Umbanda to accept the greater cost of all the Candomblé rituals. Initiation represents a considerable expense for candidates who, on the whole, have little disposable income. This commercialization of Candomblé gives rise to frequent criticism from initiates from Umbanda:

> Candomblé has become too commercial and those of us coming from Umbanda, there's still this side to us that says: "Well, this guy, he needs some work done, but he can't afford it." So we help those in need, by lowering the price. But those who were born into Candomblé don't have that attitude—carrying out a certain task costs this much, lighting a candle costs that much. But we would never behave in that way![24]

Anybody familiar with Candomblé knows that the more one spends, the more prestige one acquires. Furthermore, the much-criticized commercial-

19. The Mercadão de Madureira, a shopping center devoted to Afro-Brazilian religions.
PHOTO BY AUTHOR.

ization of Candomblé is the basis of a huge parallel economy—one need only visit the large market of Madureira,[25] a veritable Macumba supermarket, to be aware of that. However, despite—or perhaps precisely because of—the costs, most Umbanda mediums and their customers do not hide their fascination for the world of Candomblé. Everything pulls them in this direction: if, in Umbanda, mediums embody spirits whose mission is to practice charity, in Candomblé, initiates are transformed into powerful gods who control thunder and wind, and whose simple presence on earth is the object of veneration. For a Candomblé ceremony to be crowned with success, the combination of music, dance, the luxuriousness of the gods' clothes, and the decoration of the terreiro, plus the indispensable abundance of the feast offered, must irresistibly fascinate the spectator.

Becoming a Candomblé initiate, therefore, signifies accumulating prestige—a prestige proportionate to one's capacity to excel in ceremonies and to master mystical forces. Admittance into Candomblé also opens doors to a religious career inaccessible for an Umbandist medium, and so Umbanda becomes a sort of preparation for Candomblé: "Umbanda is the route toward Candomblé, for if one wants to be able to get on well in Candomblé, one has to have already lived in Umbanda. Initiation into Umbanda helps entry into Candomblé, as much for the capacity to understand people as for the way to behave in the terreiro and in hierarchical relations."[26]

In the eyes of Umbandist mediums, Candomblé is a fundamentally authoritarian cult where respect for the hierarchy must be learned. Many authors, such as Prandi (1991, 59), have defined Umbanda as a democratic religion. In reality, it also has a hierarchical organization, but it is difficult to compare that with Candomblé. Umbanda differs from Candomblé because it lacks a hierarchy of mediums according their initiatory age. The Umbanda centers closest to the African pole are the only ones to have an initiation ritual, called feitura as in Candomblé. The others make do with a "baptism" which legitimizes their spiritual work. The lack of importance attached to initiation causes a whole series of potential conflicts at the heart of the hierarchy, since the medium has no need of the pai-de-santo to embody spirits for he is born with them: "He who has mediumship, who has a crown [a group of spirits by whom the medium may be possessed] in order to work [spiritually] from birth, does not need someone to shave his head for his "guide" [an Umbanda spirit] to possess him . . . You are born with your mission; it is a gift from God" (quoted in Brumana and Martinez 1991, 189). Belonging to an Umbanda center is connected to the necessity of spiritual development, but the subordinate relation to the pai-de-santo may be called into question at any moment, because it was not he who "seated" the entity.[27] This increases the potential of conflict within the group. In reality, a medium needs the mediation of the pai-de-santo to protect him from the magical attacks of his peers. His position of hierarchical superiority is then guaranteed by the potency of his spirits. So, as Brumana and Martinez (1991, 154) state: "The relational typology of the terreiro reproduces the general typology of the cult: protection, submission, punishments and rewards move along a vertical axis, where one needs to protect oneself from the dangers coming from the horizontal axis of relations between peers."

The compromise between religious independence and the necessary submission to someone more powerful in order to protect oneself, is the basis of the equilibrium—perpetually called into question—of Umbanda. Power relationships are the subject of constant negotiation through the

20. A Madureira store dedicated to an Umbanda Exu. PHOTO BY AUTHOR.

word of the spirits.[28] In fact, any modification in Umbandist ritual is legitimized by the spirits' intervention. It is they who dictate their doctrines (their characteristics and ritual specifications) to the mediums they possess. During rituals, they can introduce themselves by name, explain their role in the Umbandist pantheon, and tell their story, and it is through their discourse that the details making up part of the religious rules are continually renegotiated.

The medium's relative independence in Umbanda is greatly reduced when it comes to Candomblé. The internal organization of any Candomblé terreiro is founded on a rigid religious hierarchy, determined by the initiatory age (the principle of seniority). Any new member of a terreiro occupies an inferior position to those initiated before him. The position that each person occupies in the religious hierarchy is marked by complex rituals of greeting and courtesy. After seven years of being an iyawó (newly initiated), one becomes an ebomi, and once the *deká* has been received (the ceremony symbolizing the gaining of one's independence from one's pai-de-santo), one can open a new house of worship. But rising through the ranks can also happen by obtaining ritual responsibilities. Thus, even if they have been initiated for the same amount of time, a son-of-saint owes respect and submission to his initiation brother (a person initiated with him during the same ceremony) if the latter has received a ritual responsibility from the pai-de-santo. The distribution of ritual responsibilities and the resulting transmission of knowledge constitute the most efficient way for the head of the religion to establish and keep his authority over his initiates.

This internal differentiation between sons-of-saint is a major source of conflict in the religious group. Conflicts are very often resolved thanks to what can be defined as one of Candomblé's veritable institutions—gossip (*fuxico-de-santo*). Indeed, in Candomblé terreiros, attacks upon an enemy are never direct, and accusations can be made about the legitimacy of the religious origin of the person targeted, about his practice of black magic, and even about the authenticity of his trance. In Candomblé, gossip plays a role of internal reorganization, like the intervention of spirits in Umbanda. It acts as a mechanism for reducing tension and reorganizing power relations at the heart of the group. In this way, accusations against people who are part of another terreiro serve to define the external boundaries of the religious group, since contesting the legitimacy of someone else enables one to affirm one's own legitimacy. On the other hand, internal accusations against someone who occupies a distinct hierarchical position calls into question the terreiro's organization.

Therefore, Candomblé offers the Umbandist medium a place where he may "have a taste of power" (Prandi 1991, 88), power linked to rising in the religious hierarchy, and thus to the ensuing accumulation of prestige. The initiate's capacity to master mystical forces gives him access to the magical manipulation of the world through magical work (*feitiço*). This manipulation is a function of the position the medium holds in the religious hierarchy—and thus of the knowledge that he has acquired—but also of his relations with the gods or spirits. Contesting the legitimacy of a medium, by contesting the veracity of his alliance with spiritual entities, calls into question his mystical powers.

21. Religious goods at the Mercadão de Madureira. PHOTO BY AUTHOR.

In Candomblé, with fuxico-de-santo—similar in this to the Umbandist demanda—the religious group reproduces the internal logic of Brazilian society, a society that is extremely hierarchical and stratified. However, if Afro-Brazilian religions reproduce the inequalities, they also offer initiates the possibility of expressing the conflicts between them and their hierarchical superiors. The complete absence of references to power struggles and conflicts within and between terreiros in writings about Candomblé is an expression of a romantic vision of a place—the "pure" Candomblé—where harmony should reign supreme. This attitude, present in most studies of Afro-Brazilian religions, reveals the difficulty in thinking of Brazilian society as a hierarchical society, and Candomblé as a product of this society. As Roberto Da Matta (1983, 46–47) remarks:

> In fact, it is easier to say that Brazil was formed by a triangle of races, leading us to the myth of a racial democracy, than to accept that it involves a hierarchical society which is set up along gradations, and precisely because of this, accepts a whole series of classification criteria between the superior white and the poor, inferior black.

For Gilberto Freyre (1946), who inspired the founding myth of Brazilian society, if the society's origins resulted in the meeting of the three races (white, black, and indigenous), the different contributions of each blend harmoniously, eliminating (a priori) any antagonism or social conflict. The image of Brazil as a melting pot views the meeting of the races as a harmonious cultural integration of their symbolic universes, where any power struggles must be hidden, and where the absence of conflict becomes a sign of democracy. Denying the existence of conflict in Afro-Brazilian religions enables them to be held in a state of immobility, clearly different from global society, presenting them as cultural entities deprived of history and therefore also of political strategy and agency. The importance of the notion of prestige, and the recourse to gossip or magical attacks in power struggles reveals a different, far more complex reality.

REORGANIZING SACRED SPACE

When mediums move from Umbanda to Candomblé, the presence of the Umbandist spirits of darkness—exus and pombagiras—poses serious problems on a ritual level. In fact, these spirits are regarded as eguns—i.e., spirits of the dead.[1] However, in Candomblé, any contact with the dead must be accompanied by a series of rituals to neutralize the negative power and inescapable pollution. Being possessed by the spirit of a dead person inevitably has nefarious consequences—disease, madness, or even death.

The island of Itaparica, in the Bay of Salvador in Bahia, has conserved the cult to Egunguns (or Eguns), in which ancestors' spirits manifest themselves during ritual ceremonies. In this cult of Yoruba origin, the great care taken to separate the space of the living from that of the ancestors is proof of the risks involved in having contact with the dead. During a ceremony, priests (*ojés*) use long canes to keep the dancing Eguns away from the spectators, for accidental contact with an Egun's clothes may lead to illness or even the death of the person touched. This necessary distance between the world of the dead and the world of the living becomes even more obvious in the relations that men have with Eguns. In Brazil, unlike the orixá, who takes possession of his initiate's body, the Egun does not possess a person, he "manifests himself." He who dances and speaks with a guttural voice, completely covered by clothes which hide him from the others present, is not a possessed man but the materialization of the ancestor's spirit, his manifestation. Close contact with the dead would entail risks that no man would undertake.[2]

How, then, can it be acceptable for a Candomblé initiate to be possessed by the spirit of a dead person, an egun? How can an initiate who has been ritually prepared to receive a divinity allow himself to be contaminated by the presence of death?

In fact, Umbandist spirits are regarded as disembodied souls who, after their passing, return to earth in the bodies of mediums to accomplish their mission and thus progress through the different stages of spiritual evolution. Spirits—pretos-velhos, caboclos, exus, and pombagiras—tell of their lives on earth, their deaths, and the reasons for the behavior that characterizes them, and are thus linked to life as they are linked to death. They put the two worlds in contact with one another. The potential contamination of living people by the dead is even more serious when it involves exus and pombagiras, who are associated, as we have seen, with a world of debauchery, immorality, and perdition. They are spirits of darkness, bound to all that is on the fringes, and with whom contact may be extremely dangerous.

From Exu-Orixá to Exu-Egun

The conflict between the persistence of Umbandist spirits and the ideal orthodox model, which denies any contact with the dead, is expressed in the series of rituals accompanying the initiation process in Candomblé. The pai-de-santo first carries out a divination, which dictates the steps to follow in the novice's initiation. If the novice comes from Umbanda, purification rituals are performed to ward off the spirits accompanying him. So-called cleansing offerings (*ebós de limpeza*) are used to remove any of the influence of the eguns (the dead) by purifying the novice's head (the seat of spirituality). So, to ward off an Exu from Umbanda, an ebó is prepared, and a rooster is sacrificed (or a hen in the case of a Pombagira). The Umbandist spirit must then consider himself satisfied and distance himself from the medium, who is then under the protection of his orixá. At birth, every individual has a protecting orixá, a kind of guardian angel who becomes, during initiation into Candomblé, the master of his head. However, in Umbanda, it is usually the spirit who possesses the medium, and not the orixá to whom he is attached.

But what happens when spirits do not want to leave their mediums? In certain houses of worship, possession by exus and pombagiras is accepted only a year after initiation. During this first year, the initiate is supposed to be completely dependent upon his pai-de-santo, owing him absolute obedience, often working for him at his home or in his terreiro, and going into uncontrollable trances, which emphasize even further his dependence on his initiator. The new initiate is considered extremely vulnerable because he is open to any negative influence, which is why special care rituals such as that of the *contra-eguns*—the strings of braided straw that are attached to the new initiate's arms and waist for three months to protect him from contact with the spirits of the dead—are lavished upon him to protect him. Contact with a spirit from Umbanda, an egun, would be detrimental to maintaining the initiate's spiritual equilibrium, especially when it involves spirits who are not very evolved, such as exus or pombagiras.

The confusion arising from the use of the same term to mean the Exu from Candomblé—with all his ritual functions (Exu-slave, Exu-Bara, etc.)—and the exus from Umbanda—is at the heart of very complex discussions as to the precise nature of these spirits. Therefore, in order to distinguish them from the Exu-orixá (or Exu-vodun, as some key informants call him) Umbandist exus are assimilated with eguns, the spirits of the dead, under their most dangerous aspect. This assimilation is shared by most of my informants, even if the possible confusion between eguns, the spirits of the dead used in Candomblé mostly for offensive magic, and the Eguns, deified ancestors, is disturbing for some of them. Thus, for Albino de Oxumarê, an Angola pai-de-santo, it is not a question of Exus-eguns, but of Exus-quiumbas, quiumba being the least evolved spirit of the Umbandist pantheon. Quiumbas are perturbing spirits, known as *encosto*, who attach themselves to human beings, transmitting illness or madness, or even driving them to suicide. They are inferior to exus who enjoy a certain spiritual evolution. In the Umbandist world, quiumbas are the closest to the category of dangerous and impure eguns, and contact with them is forbidden in Candomblé.

The same subtle distinction is made by Celinho de Barabô, a Candomblé

pai-de-santo who owes his fame to his Exu. According to him, the Umbandist exus are really eguns, for they have lived and are dead, but they occupy a
higher plane than the latter "because they belong to the category of exus"—
which does not mean, however, that they are identified with the Exu-orixá:

> It's completely different. The Exu-orixá is a force of nature like the
> other orixás. The orixá Exu is an African god, and must be worshipped as
> such—we can't go mixing everything up! Exu entities do not come under
> this category. The exu entity has no connection with the orixá; or, rather,
> there is really a connection—for an entity to come and practice charity in
> a house of Candomblé, she has to have been "determined" by an orixá.
> She must act as that orixá's messenger. She cannot remain free and do
> whatever she wishes!

In the discourse of mediums, Umbandist exus and pombagiras are identified with eguns, with whom, as we have seen, contact must be avoided at
all cost in Candomblé. To be able to continue to manifest themselves in the
bodies of their mediums once the latter have been initiated into Candomblé, they therefore have to submit to the higher authority of the orixá, the
master of the head of the initiate.[3]

The Separation of Ritual Spaces

The arrival of mediums from Umbanda, with their exus and pombagiras,
necessitates an internal reorganization to allow the integration of these new
elements into the ideal orthodox model of Candomblé. In the previous
chapter, I analyzed the reasons that lead a medium from Umbanda to be
initiated into Candomblé. But those who "receive" (are possessed by) Exu or
Pombagira have a further reason to do so, because it can become very
dangerous to be spiritually bound to either of those spirits alone. Marcos de
Yansan gives the following explanation for the need to be initiated: "When
you are not initiated, Exu has very easy access to your body, to your blood-
stream and head, because of his very close links with life and death. When
you do not have a master in your head, when you're not initiated (feito), you
are like something open, like an abandoned house—Exu can do anything he
wants with you!" And while it is therefore necessary for an Umbandist
medium to submit his Exu to the orixá's authority so that nothing bad may

22. Seven Arrows, Alvinho de Omolu's caboclo. PHOTO BY AUTHOR.

befall him, he must also accept the authority of the pai-de-santo who, through initiation, makes the new personal orixá be "born."[4]

However, while mediums from Umbanda need the Candomblé pais-de-santo, the latter also need mediums. In reality, Umbanda represents a veritable reservoir of future sons-of-saint and potential clients for Candomblé. Initiating a mãe-de-santo from Umbanda implies spreading one's sphere of influence over the new initiate's whole religious group—and, of course, her clientele.

In the huge Efon family-of-saint linked to Alvinho de Omolu, many initiates come from Umbanda. This pai-de-santo personifies the religious career typical in the Southeast. Alvinho became aware of his mediumship at the age of six, when, after a crisis, he was taken to a Kardecist center, where he was told that his problem was not a matter for that cult. He was then taken to an Umbandist center, where he began to be possessed by the caboclo Sete Flechas (Seven Arrows). At the time, Alvinho knew nothing of Candomblé. One day, while he was at a ceremony in a Candomblé terreiro with friends, he suddenly went into a trance. They were in the house of worship of Djalma de Lalú, the most famous Exu initiate in Rio de Janeiro.

According to tradition, it was then, when the divinity manifested himself for the first time, that Alvinho should have been initiated, but his family, who saw Candomblé as "a thing of the devil," came with the police to force him to leave the terreiro. Later, when he was fifteen, Alvinho met Cristóvão de Ogunjá, the founder of the Pantanal terreiro, and his initiation could finally take place.

This is how Alvinho tells of his passage from Umbanda to Candomblé and of the construction of what could be called his "spiritual patrimony" (see table 1):

> Before my initiation I used to receive Exu, but after having been initiated, never again—Exu in my head was finished! The only spirit from Umbanda who stayed, after all these years of initiation, was the caboclo —as for the others . . . but if Exu never came back into my head, I always tell my sons-of-saint, how do you think that an exu *de rua* [from Umbanda] could come into an initiate's head? I do not accept him!

The conflict between the pai-de-santo's experience and that of his initiates reveals the gap that exists between the ideal orthodox model and its necessary adaptation in ritual practice. But the resulting tension is not simply a consequence of Candomblé's current dominance over Umbanda. On the contrary, the history of the Efon nation may be read as the constant quest for structural balance—always threatened from within—between the orthodox model that is impossible to achieve and the obligation to seek symbolic mediation in order to adapt to this model.[5]

We have seen how, in the early 1950s, the Pantanal terreiro structured itself around part of Cristóvão de Ogunjá's family. His daughter, Mãe Lindinha, became the terreiro's iyá kekeré, the pai-de-santo's personal assistant. She had been initiated by the prestigious mãe-de-santo from Bahia, Mãe Runhô, from the old Jeje terreiro of Bogum. She "received" the caboclo Capangueiro, who had been manifesting himself since the time she was living in Bahia. Her daughter, Maria de Xangô, the current iyalorixá at Pantanal, justifies this possession as being a family inheritance, for her grandmother (Mãe Lindinha's mother) used to participate in mesa branca séances (a Kardecist ritual) in Bahia, and her great-grandmother had been the president of a Kardecist center, the mesa branca Ogun de Lei. Even though, by this time, the caboclo was present almost everywhere in Bahia and in most

Table 1 Spiritual Patrimony of a Medium

Candomblé		Umbanda		Passage from Umbanda to Candomblé	
agent supernatural	*possession*	*agent supernatural*	*possession*	*agent supernatural*	*possession*
orixá (master of the head)	"orthodox"	orixá (master of the head)	rare	orixá (master of the head)	"orthodox"
adjuntó second orixá	criticized	second orixá	rare	second orixá	rare
Erê	"orthodox"	Erê crianças	"orthodox"	Erê	"orthodox"
exu	criticized	exu and Pombagira	"orthodox"	exu and Pombagira re-Africanized	accepted
caboclo	tolerated	caboclo	"orthodox"	caboclo	accepted
egun	forbidden	preto-velho	"orthodox"	preto-velho	rare

Candomblé houses, Cristóvão would not accept his daughter's being possessed by such a spirit. When it happened, she was made to leave the ceremony hall (barracão) and stay outside the sacred space, in the open air.

Alvinho de Omolu confirms his pai-de-santo's aversion for the caboclo. When the young Alvinho "received" Seven Arrows, the only Umbandist spirit who continued to manifest himself after his initiation, he was obliged to leave the barracão straight away and stay outside in the terreiro yard until the end of the possession. The caboclo's presence in the terreiro's sacred space, especially in the barracão where most of the religious ceremonies take place, represented, to Cristóvão's mind, a veritable spiritual contamination.

Over time, however, Cristóvão had to accept possession by caboclos and had to bow to their strength. His granddaughter, Maria de Xangô, justifies this by a cause common in mediums' conversions: illness. Cristóvão was cured of a serious illness by the work of his wife's caboclos (she had not followed him to Rio de Janeiro), and those of his daughter Lindinha. But according to Maria de Xangô, this mystical healing was not the only reason

23. The caboclo's assento.
PHOTO BY AUTHOR.

for his change of attitude: "Cristóvão understood that he had to evolve, that the caboclo was part of [spiritual life], as most of the sons-of-saint came from Umbanda and embody caboclos. And so he agreed." Mystical healing, proof of the power of the spirits, provided a way to accept the adaptation of ritual practice to the new conditions of the religious market, since most of the sons-of-saint came from Umbanda and brought their caboclos with them.

After this healing, a shack called the "caboclo village" (*aldéia do caboclo*) was built on the perimeter of the Pantanal terreiro, outdoors "because caboclos like the bush." The separation of the symbolic spaces—inside, the orixás' space; outside, the dangerous divinities' and spirits' space—was thus preserved. Every year, at the end of June or beginning of July, a festival for the caboclo is organized in the Pantanal. But this ritual adaptation did not concern the figure of Exu, or the Umbandist exus. In fact, Cristóvão would not agree to initiate an Exu: a novice son of Exu was invariably initiated to Ogun Mejé, a dual god half-Ogun, half-Exu. Cristóvão said that initiating an Exu was equivalent to "dirtying the razor" (*sujar a navalha*)—i.e., contaminating the axé.[6] The initiation of the first son of Exu by Alvinho de Omolu was, then, a sign of his distancing himself, albeit temporarily, from his pai-de-santo. He became closer to another very famous pai-de-santo at Rio de Janeiro, Tata Fomotinho, of the Jeje nation, who had initiated Djalma de Lalú, the best-known son of Exu in the city. But in his narrative, Alvinho underlined the fact that Cristóvão stood by his side during the initiation.

The insistence on the fact of Cristóvão's presence, despite his apparent disagreement, is very important, for it is precisely this presence which legitimizes an initiation, which otherwise could be criticized as being unorthodox. In reality, Alvinho's going to another terreiro (Fomotinho's) and his departure for São Paulo were signs of the existence of a disagreement which explains this new alliance.

While Cristóvão did not like initiating an Exu, he liked even less the exus who came from Umbanda. Maria de Xangô, who succeeded him, tells how she was possessed by Pombagira for the first time in 1969, fifteen years after her initiation. This Pombagira was neither an inheritance,[7] nor the consequence of previous experience in Umbanda—she was Oxum's slave, meaning the servant Exu of Oxum, and thus "African."

This impromptu possession by Pombagira exacerbated the conflict between the pai-de-santo and his initiate, which had begun a year earlier with another affront to orthodoxy—possession by the second orixá. Oxum, Maria de Xangô's *adjuntó* (second orixá), took possession of her during the ceremony organized for the fourteenth anniversary of her initiation. Cristóvão did not accept this innovation, as Maria de Xangô explains: "Cristóvão did not accept the fact that I had received the responsibilities of mãe-de-santo, that I was possessed by an exu, and, what's more, I was embodying my second orixá. He accepted and venerated only the orixá that he had "made" and who was the master of the initiate's head."

Maria de Xangô's possession by Pombagira coincided with her leaving for São Paulo, where she opened her own house of worship. She did not return to Rio until just before her grandfather's death, to be finally reconciled with him and to take on the responsibility of Pantanal's mãe-de-santo.

24. Offerings to the caboclo. PHOTO BY AUTHOR.

Their separation was the result of a power struggle in the heart of the terreiro, between the pai-de-santo and his future successor. Maria's possession by Pombagira, just after the ceremony of the fourteenth anniversary of her initiation, where she was humiliated by having her Oxum rejected, was a direct challenge to her pai-de-santo's authority.

Why did Cristóvão accept caboclos, but not exus? Why could caboclos be integrated into the orthodox model, but not exus? Are caboclos not eguns just as exus are, with their history and their life on earth?

The response of Maria de Xangô, today the repository of Efon orthodoxy, is categorical: "In our nation, we do not consider the caboclo in this way. He is a living Indian (*indio vivo*), just like the Amazonian Indians. He lives in villages populated with living beings." If caboclos are "living beings," this means that they cannot come under the category of eguns, for they are never dead. Possession by them is then perfectly acceptable, on condition that the separation between symbolic spaces is respected.

In reality, the caboclo is subject to the same treatment as that reserved for the Exu in anthropological writings linked to a Nagô-centric vision of Candomblé—strategic erasing in order not to question the purity of the so-called traditional houses. Bastide (1974, 21) maintained that traditional Candomblé refused any intrusion of indigenous religions, despite the caboclo's presence in most Nagô houses of worship. To him, the caboclo was only one of the aspects of Oxossi, god of hunting and the bush.[8]

Although Donald Pierson (1942, 305) declared that "the most orthodox sects do not escape indigenous influence," information that could invalidate official discourse about African legitimacy has too often been neglected by anthropologists (Teles dos Santos 1992). One of the rare exceptions is Alejandro Frigerio (1989, 22), who noticed the presence of caboclos even in the Axé Opô Afonjá, the religious house regarded as the birthplace of Nagô tradition, where they are venerated in private, not in public ceremonies. This information is confirmed by Claude Lépine who recalls the presence of caboclos in Ketu (Nagô) terreiros. The very words of the mãe-de-santo of the Axé Opô Afonjá in Salvador, as the author recalls them (1978, 79), reveal the strategy adopted, a strategy we have already seen at work in Pantanal, and which we see again when exus and pombagiras are involved:

> If one of my daughters-of-saint is possessed by a caboclo, what am I to do? I'm not going to kill her, am I? The daughter-of-saint would then make her orixá [be initiated] in the São Gonçalo terreiro [the Axé Opô Afonjá], but would "seat" her caboclo with someone else. The axé's iyá kekeré does not want a caboclo in her house, but believes piously in their existence.

In fact, usually the unorthodox spirit is "seated" not in another terreiro, which would mean that the daughter-of-saint would be under the authority of someone other than her mãe-de-santo, but in the initiate's house itself. The initiate then worships her orixá in the terreiro where she was initiated, while the worship of her spirit (caboclo or exu) is limited to her domestic space. This same division of space constitutes the ritual solution to the problem of possession by Exus-eguns. In Alvinho de Omolu's discourse, the banning of possession by these spirits in his terreiro is once again justified by the mystical intervention which marks the limits of orthodoxy:

> In my house of worship, I do not accept possession by the Umbandist Exu. In their house of worship, initiates may do as they like, but not in mine! I have many sons-of-saint who practice Umbanda in their house of worship; I go there, I respect them because they deserve it, but I won't have it in my house! In my house, as soon as they step over the threshold, Umbandist Exu cannot enter. I tried to give a party for the Umbandist Exu, but I had a lot of problems—the shack [built for Exu] caught fire, we don't know how, for there were no candles—there was nothing, it was just natural light. Since that happened, I will never do it again!

Each time, then, the conflict between the orthodox ideal and the reality experienced by the mediums is resolved on a mystical level. The caboclos are accepted and reinterpreted within the limits of orthodoxy, for they prove their power by miraculous healing; the exus, on the contrary, confirm their ungovernability and their dangerous nature, in this instance by a mysterious fire. They must, therefore, be left outside the sacred space, in the indistinct and frightening territory populated by spirits without masters.

The Re-Africanization of the Spirits

If Exus-eguns, the spirits who follow mediums when they move from Umbanda to Candomblé, have no place in the orthodox model of Candomblé, how can they continue to be worshiped? By making them conform to the model and "Africanizing" them.

The first argument advanced by those who consider possession by Umbandist exus and pombagiras as illegitimate is the nonexistence of female Exus in Africa. When one talks of Pombagira, it is really a Bantu Exu, Bombogira, a male spirit who metamorphosed into a female Exu or *Exua*. There are also two other names that signify Pombagira: Leba, from the Fon Legba; and Lebará, deriving from the Yoruba Elegbara, one of Exu's names in Nigeria.

The question of spirits' African origins constantly animates mediums' discourse. Dina de Yansan, a Ketu mãe-de-santo with almost thirty years of

Table 2 Re-Africanization of Exus

Candomblé	Umbanda	Passage from Umbanda to Candomblé
Exu-orixá (divinity)	Exu-egun (disincarnated spirit)	Exu-slave of the orixá (from disincarnated spirit to avatar of the orixá Exu)
Exu-slave Exu-Bara	exus pombagiras	

experience in Umbanda, identifies her Pombagira, Maria Padilha do Fogo, as being the slave of her orixá:

> Exu is the orixá's messenger. I, myself, am [daughter] of Yansan, and therefore Yansan's slave is Maria Padilha, who goes under the name of Lebará Jiraloná. It's really a [male] Pombo Gira, not a [female] Pomba. She is called Maria Padilha do Fogo and is Yansan's messenger in the terreiro. She tells us what Yansan accepts and what Yansan does not accept—everything is transmitted through her!

Dina's discourse shows, once again, the distance which exists between the ideal orthodox model and its necessary adaptation. If female Exus do not exist in Africa, Pombagira may then be only "a [male] Pombo Gira," referring to the Bantu god Bombogira. If the name Maria Padilha do Fogo is too closely linked to the Umbandist world, it is transformed into Lebará Jiraloná, thus signifying its Africanity. If the Umbanda Exu must be relegated beyond the limits of the sacred space, he is metamorphosed into a slave of the orixá, the master of the initiate's head, thus becoming Yansan's messenger, and expresses the wishes and will of the orixá (see table 2).

One of the principal characteristics of the divinity Exu, both in Africa and in Brazilian Candomblé, is his role as messenger. It is he who brings about communication between the world of gods and that of men. To assert that the Umbandist spirit is really the orixá's slave legitimizes him against the attempts to banish him beyond the boundaries of orthodoxy. Furthermore, the fact that Pombagira, once she has become African, preserves the role of divine interpreter (she "is Yansan's messenger") renders her even more important in the sacred space which is, in principle, exclusively reserved for the orixás. It is the Pombagira (or Pombo Gira) who establishes the ritual behavior of the house's most important orixá (the mãe-de-santo's divinity). In fact, in Candomblé, orixás speak very rarely during possessions, and they mostly express themselves through divination, needing the ritual mediation of the pai or mãe-de-santo, specialists capable of interpreting the gods' words, in order to communicate with the group. The re-Africanized Pombagira, on the other hand, can directly transmit the orixá's wishes, by deciding what is correct and what is not. It is this capacity of expression which renders the Umbandist spirit essential for the powerful Candomblé orixá— without Lebará Jiraloná's mediation, the Yansan of Dina would not be able to impose her will during ritual ceremonies.[9] Her word is legitimate, for the Umbandist spirit has been re-Africanized. But how can spirits who ought to have disappeared with initiation into Candomblé be re-Africanized? Why do they continue to manifest themselves?

The answer to these questions may be sought in the pai or mãe-de-santo's relationship with spiritual beings. What is called into question here is the efficiency of the so-called cleansing rituals (ebós de limpeza) they perform. In reality, it is not the initiator who "gives" the spirits and orixás to the medium; he or she is but a mediator between a gift (mediumship) and its bearer (the medium). His or her role is to connect the individual and his divinities, and to make them work together.

How, then, can a pai-de-santo chase away spirits which have accompanied Candomblé initiation candidates for a long time? By defining space, where the pai-de-santo's role is to take care of the orixá while respecting the spirits' existence, even if they are pushed to the outer limits of the sacred space. Torodê de Ogun, a son-of-saint of Joãozinho da Goméia, who is one of today's representatives of re-Africanized Candomblé and one of the first to have organized divination courses in Rio de Janeiro, agrees with this theory:

> Personally, I don't know what can be done to prevent possession by Umbandist spirits. The medium is a receiver and may receive an orixá just as he may receive an Umbandist entity. I do not see why these beings should be qualified as inferior. I don't understand the distinction between egun and orixá, when a society of Eguns exists in Bahia, which is nothing other than a form of trance!

This last statement is all the more interesting because it brings up the conflict which generally arises between possession by the orixás and the manifestation of the Eguns, a conflict which is the basis of all orthodox discourse. If the cult of the Eguns at Itaparica is organized around ritual trance (which is vehemently denied by those involved), no obstacle remains to the complete insertion of Umbandist spirits in the African world of Candomblé. Even more explicitly, Fernandes Portugal, another representative of re-Africanized Candomblé who organizes courses in Yoruba language and civilization in Rio de Janeiro, compares the category of Umbandist exus with that of Egun ancestors, who are, then, the ancestors of the mediums who embody them. He even makes a distinction between Exuseguns, whom he calls *ayé kuru*—eguns who work for good—and eguns *buruku*, who are malevolent.

However, this connection between Eguns and orixás, which, for Torodê occurs through the sharing of the same experience (the trance), is not accepted by all informants. The identification of the Umbanda Exu with the Exu-slave, the orixá's servant, seems to prevail in mediums' discourse. Therefore, the same Exu has one name in Umbanda and another name in Candomblé. The treatment to which he is subject is related to the chosen ritual modality.

The assimilation of the entities (spirits) with the "saints" (orixás) therefore enables the re-Africanization of Umbanda spirits who do not necessarily come from a world which claims to be African. In this way, the Umbanda Exu and Pombagira are metamorphosed into the slaves of African divinities, and the relationship which binds the orixá's slave to his master (the African god) determines his essence:

> There is not one single Maria Padilha or one single Maria Mulambo. For example, the Maria Mulambos who are Oxum's guardians [slaves] have very different characteristics from Yemanjá's guardians. Oxum's guardians are richer, and they speak differently. Those of Yemanjá are slightly inferior [the speaker is a daughter of Oxum]. For example, the Cigana [Tzigane] is a free entity, for she can manifest herself with Oxalá, Oxum, or Yansan, etc. Mine has very close ties with Oxalá and Oxum. That is why her colors are white and gold.[10]

Umbandist spirits' relative submission to the orixá, who is the master of the medium's head, is not always accepted by the spirits in question. Indeed, a latent conflict between the spirits (slaves) and their masters always transpires in the discourse of mediums who embody Umbandist exus and pombagiras and who are initiated into Candomblé. Talking of her Pombagira (Maria Mulambo), Maria Auxiliadora de Xangô, of the Jeje nation, emphasizes the spirits' rebellion against the orixás and their power:

> The Pombagira says that Xangô is Xangô and that she is herself. She minds her own business and so Xangô should mind his own too, because Pombagira won't allow it. If Xangô wants to dress in white and red, she's not going to interfere, and so Pombagira cannot accept that Xangô does not let her wear black, because that is the color she likes and he must respect that. She respects Xangô's rights, and he ought to respect hers!

These words, officially those of the spirit and not the medium, reveal the ambivalence of this dependence. The disagreement about the use of ritual colors involves questioning the relationship of power, defined by the reinterpretation of the position occupied by spirits in their passage to another symbolic universe where the masters are the orixás. While in Sandra de Oxum's discourse the choice of colors (white and gold) is determined by the Pombagira Cigana's relationship with Oxalá and Oxum, the medium's two orixás, in Maria Auxiliadora's speech it is the spirit who demands her own choice, independent of the orixá's characteristics. The spirit defends the color black—forbidden in Candomblé for it is extremely dangerous—as one of her Exu's characteristics.[11]

Pombagira, Leba, or Iyamí?

For an Exu (or Pombagira) from Umbanda to become "African," he or she must submit to a series of rituals which mark his or her inscription into an African universe. The first of these rituals is the ceremony of assentamento, which aims to "seat" the spirit's energy into a material representation connected to the initiate. It is important to remember that in Umbanda, exus and pombagiras are not "seated"; they are considered to be free energies, relatively independent of their mediums. Usually the spirit is represented

25. Representations of Exu in Candomblé and Umbanda. PHOTO BY AUTHOR.

by the statue of an extremely seductive or scantily clad woman if it is Pombagira (with her variants Cigana or Maria Padilha, the richest of them), or of an uncanny man with goat's hooves and diabolical features in the case of Exu. In Umbanda, these statues, suitably prepared, take the place of Candomblé assentos.

A second operation to "seat" the exus' or pombagiras' energy, within the framework of the African ritual, enables the reinterpretation of these spirits, who then receive an African name and are considered fully pledged slaves of the orixás. They must then be "seated in the nation"—i.e., according to the ritual rules of Candomblé. To do this, a *tabatinga* (a piece of clay) is used to fashion a head, representing the Exu connected with each initiate. The clay is mixed with various ingredients, such as the blood of sacrificed animals and special herbs. For a female Exu (Pombagira, Exua, or Leba), a hen is sacrificed during the preparation of the tabatinga, and then its blood and exés (the parts of the animal considered sacred) are mixed with the clay. For a male Exu, a rooster is killed. Each statuette prepared in this way has its own characteristics, which distinguish it from others. They have in

26. An Umbanda
representation of the
Pombagira Maria Mulambo.
PHOTO BY AUTHOR.

common cowries, which are used as the eyes and mouth, and nails em-
bedded in the top of the head, for, according to tradition, Exu does not carry
any load. Once Exu is "seated," he is considered African.

For Candomblé initiates who have come from Umbanda and already
have their own house of worship, the statue of the Umbandist Exu is placed
next to the Exu slave's assento. In the same space (Exu's house), but separated by a partition, it is common to find two representations of the same
spirit, one "African" and one Umbandist. Thus, in the house of worship of
Fernando de Ogun, initiated by Alvinho de Omolu, one small construction
housed the statue of his Maria Mulambo and the clay assento representing
his African side, baptized with the name of Jinda Leba Dandasin.[12]

In the Efon nation, the Umbandist Exu is "seated" in an independent house of worship—in other words, when a new terreiro is opened. In the case of a son-of-saint of Alvinho de Omolu, such as Fernando de Ogun, the same spirit can then manifest himself in two different lines: that of Umbanda and that of the "nation"—i.e., in the Candomblé—where he will be re-Africanized. So, during a festival dedicated to his Maria Mulambo, Fernando de Ogun appeared in the main room of his terreiro clothed in a sumptuous red robe, over which he wore the ojá (a large piece of fabric wrapped around the chest) and two *atakan* (strips of material attached to the shoulders and crossed over the chest below the ojá), the sacred elements characteristic of the orixás' costume, in this way assimilating the spirit from Umbanda with the African divinities.

This blending is strongly criticized by Celinho de Barabô, who supports the separation of places of worship:

> Personally, I always say that my work with Exu never touches the orixá, because even if I'm a Candomblé pai-de-santo, my work with Exu is completely separate. What's more, many exus present themselves as Exus-orixás or orixás, even in the way they dress, and these pombagiras become Maria Padilha and Maria Mulambo, and use ojá or atakan. Nothing like that happens with my Exu!

Celinho de Barabô makes a clear distinction between, on the one hand, his terreiro entirely dedicated to the cult of the Umbandist Exu (Barabô), who made his medium's fortune, and, on the other hand, his Candomblé terreiro where the orixás are cared for. However—and this seems very significant to me—if his Candomblé terreiro is very far away (Piabetá, a district of Magé, on the very periphery of Rio), the terreiro consecrated to Barabô coincides with the domestic area of his medium. Usually, however, these two spaces overlap, which makes the re-Africanization of the spirit from Umbanda necessary.

It even occurs, occasionally, that this re-Africanization leads to the initiation (feitura) of a Pombagira, as though she were an orixá.[13] Identifying with such a spirit, the representation of the prostitute, the archetypal fallen woman, reveals a fundamental change in the image we have of this spirit. From being a stigma, possession by Pombagira has today become synonymous with being "chic" and "nice," as Marê de Oxumarê recounts:

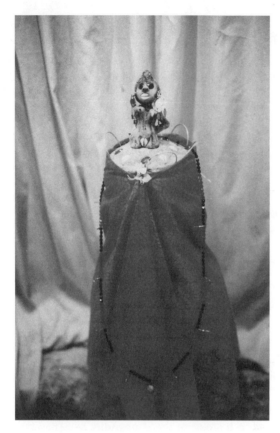

27. A re-Africanized representation of the same Pombagira, baptized Jinda Leba Dandasin. PHOTO BY AUTHOR.

In Umbanda, Pombagira used to come to show girls' mistakes and women's bad behavior. These days, we don't hear anything like what used to be said about possession by Pombagira: that the girl was a prostitute, and so on. There used to be a lot of prejudice. Now it's different—now it's chic, it's nice!

If today being possessed by Pombagira no longer has negative connotations, this does not mean that a medium can be initiated openly to this spirit without entering into conflict with the orthodox ideal. How, then, can a medium be initiated to Pombagira, a female Exu, if there are none in Africa? By finding a female equivalent of the Exu-orixá in the African universe of Candomblé: Iyamí Oxorongá, the great witch evoked along with Exu in the padê ritual. This identification, which makes most Candomblé purists wince, is based upon a very detailed comparison of the symbolic universes of Umbanda and Candomblé. They have in common the mastery of black magic and a relationship with all that is on the fringes of society. Antonivaldo, a Ketu pai-de-santo, very concerned with African purity, recognizes the closeness of the two entities, without going so far as to identify them with each other: "Each woman is ajé [witch]. Women are all witches because of Iyamí. Perhaps that is why people confuse them, but they are nothing to do with one another, as Pombagira is Umbandist and Brazilian, and Iyamí Oxorongá is African."

The same concern to distinguish the two symbolic universes—Brazil and Africa—while looking for possible similarities between the elements with their different origins, animates Alvinho de Omolu's discourse:

> I think there is something very similar between them, as iyamís are connected to everything that is spoiled, everything rotten. But Iyamí does not submit to the same things as Pombagira, who claims she takes possession of people in order to corrupt their lives. Their relation with black magic is perhaps equal. Iyamís eat everything placed before the orixá; for three days they eat all this rotten food—eggs, mostly rotten eggs, that's what they like best. They won't accept fresh things!

Here, once again, the comparison is made between Pombagira and Iyamí Oxorongá, as previously formulated by Augras (1989). But if Pombagira seems to keep some characteristics of the African witch, this does not indicate the survival of African traits in the Umbandist universe, but rather the spirit's legitimation within the framework of the African universe. Asserting that Pombagira has things in common with Iyamí Oxorongá, even while keeping the two original universes separate, is equivalent to taking the spirit from Umbanda out of the "degenerate" context of mixed cults, in order to reinterpret the spirit in an African—and therefore legitimate—perspective.

Consequently it is at least theoretically possible to "make" a female Exu as though she were an Iyamí. This is true for Waldemar de Oxossi, who initiated a young man to Exu Akessan and a woman to Iyamí, regarded as a female quality of the orixá Exu. This initiation, which outraged guardians of tradition, is, however, perfectly logical, as we have seen, in light of the existing correspondence between the divinities and the spirits. Obviously, for a pai-de-santo to be able to initiate an Iyamí, she must be considered one of Exu's qualities, meaning an Exu-orixá, and not an Exu-egun from Umbanda. Therefore, Waldemar is not a partisan of the identification of Iyamí with Pombagira; they are different, for Iyamí is, according to him, a quality of the African orixá Exu. In this way, her legitimacy is confirmed.

In order to remove Umbandist spirits from the domain of death and its inevitable pollution, they must be transformed into something else. The existence in Candomblé of one of Exu's many functions—the Exu slave of the orixá—renders possible the reinterpretation of Umbandist exus and pombagiras in African terms. The disincarnated spirit finds itself subjugated to the African orixá, master of the initiate's head. What is involved here is not respect for a preestablished orthodoxy, but the adaptation of an ideal model according to "African" logic. The example of the re-Africanization of exus and pombagiras shows us the very great plasticity of these religious phenomena, whose ritual practice is made up of constant rearrangements and readjustments.

*

⚜ 5 ⚜

CONTESTING POWER

When explaining the alliance between men and exus and pombagiras, mediums constantly emphasize two factors in their narratives: on the one hand, the help that their protecting spirits give them on a material level and in improving their social status; and on the other hand, the power and assurance given by the spirits in the event of conflict with the religious hierarchy. Exus and pombagiras prove themselves to be mediators facilitating mediums' accomplishments, by perpetually questioning —at least in their discourse—the power of those who occupy higher positions in the hierarchy. However, despite the declared rebellion against authority which accompanies most of these narratives, mediums do not really contest the structural order of Brazilian society; rather, they use the logic at work within this society. Brazilian society revolves around multiple mediations between the different levels of the social hierarchy—a veritable relational society (Da Matta 1983) where the intervention of someone powerful can resolve any problem, and where connections are more important than individual capabilities. Following the same relational logic, the protection of these spirits transforms into reality that which mediums could never obtain by their efforts alone.

Indeed, in Brazil, social upward mobility is rarely considered as simply the result of work. One does not get rich through working, but rather thanks to good luck and the intervention of a sponsor or patron (or patroness), or someone else who helps one's advancement. When telling the story of his life, a medium constantly relives the miraculous intervention of a mediator who has changed his life. Exu personifies perfectly this ideal mediator—he is the compadre, the comrade to whom the medium owes his success. His presence by the medium's side is indispensable to the latter's success. The spirit cohabits with his medium, as a completely separate subject, and directly influences his life. Exus and pombagiras, then, are at the center of a series of dramas, as much personal as ritual, questioning the relationships of power in the heart of the hierarchy.

Conflict with the Hierarchy

The passage from Umbanda to Candomblé is, more often than not, characterized by difficulty in accommodating to a new ritual reality, in which exus and pombagiras can no longer find their place. The struggle to assert oneself as a recognized medium, with one's own patrimony of protecting spirits, is often transformed into a mystic battle between the spirits of the new son-of-saint and a pai or mãe-de-santo who does not accept them. The candidate for initiation into Candomblé often goes from one house of worship to another until he finds one which accepts his Exu or Pombagira and does not question his alliance with the spirits.

Celinho de Barabô, who, at the time of his initiation into Candomblé, was already a confirmed Umbandist medium with his own terreiro and clientele, describes the negotiation preceding his conversion:

> Even if my pai-de-santo accepted [exus], my Exu wanted to discuss the situation with him. He made no demands and said that he accepted and was in complete agreement with the initiation, but he wanted to know what conditions would be made by Candomblé, how long he would have to wait before incorporating himself [in his medium] and if he really would be able to come back without any difficulty. The pai-de-santo replied that, obviously, he would be free to come whenever he wished, without any problem. This is how, a year later, he came back [incorporated in the medium].

The very great respect shown in this discussion between the Candomblé pai-de-santo and the spirit of his future initiate is an indication of the power that a representative of a religion considered superior and more powerful than Umbanda saw in this Exu. Celinho did not have to submit to the humiliations to which most mediums coming from Umbanda are subject, including being forbidden to receive their spirits for the first year after initiation, for he was already a confirmed medium at the time. His renown enabled him, "with his pai-de-santo's authorization," to keep his terreiro, which was transformed into a Candomblé house. This passage without interruption from Umbanda to Candomblé—although against the Candomblé hierarchical rules, which set a minimum time of seven years before an initiate is able to open an independent house of worship—was legitimized by a gift granted by the gods at birth—the mission of pai-de-santo. Claiming this responsibility as a birthright was, for the new initiate, an efficient strategy to bypass the period of subordination, which would have placed him at the bottom of the hierarchical ladder and led to his losing power and liturgical authority. In Celinho's case, at his initiation, the years he had spent in Umbanda were taken into consideration—an implicit recognition of the reality of the alliance between the medium and his spirits.

It is worth noting, however, that in most cases, the recognition of the legitimacy of the spirits and their alliance with the initiates is the result of a long process involving conflicts with the hierarchy. Exus or pombagiras constitute, by their very presence, a direct challenge to the pai-de-santo of a terreiro, who has a monopoly on all that is sacred. It is he who must guarantee the mediation between divinities and individuals, either clients or initiates. The unfair competition exercised by the spirits of exus and pombagiras is thus a direct attack upon the superiority of the pai-de-santo, whose principal method of communication with orixás is divination. Clients, the terreiro's main source of income, often prefer direct contact with a spirit, talking to him and receiving his advice, to consulting the oracle where it is a man (the pai-de-santo) who speaks. Exus are the most sought-after spirits by clients, for they are "venal," and resolve problems more quickly. For Candomblé pais and mães-de-santo, accepting exus and pombagiras means acknowledging two constraints: showing tolerance for these strategically re-Africanized spirits in order to increase the terreiro's number of initiates, and demarcating different ritual spaces—the terreiro for orixás, and domestic spaces (or an independent terreiro) for exus—in order to guarantee the monopoly of the pai or mãe-de-santo on mediation with all that is sacred.

28. An assento of a re-Africanized Pombagira.
PHOTO BY AUTHOR.

Any conflict between initiator and initiate therefore has economic implications, because criticism of the hierarchical structure of Candomblé is closely linked to the economic success of the medium, who must have spiritual allies to ensure his survival. For example, this is the reason which led Palmira of Yansan, a mãe-de-santo of the Ketu nation, linked with the Axé Opô Afonjá of Rio, to accept the possession by Pombagira of Edí de Yemanjá, one of her daughters-of-saint:

> Edí had been an Umbandist mãe-pequena for eight years. She had been initiated to Yemanjá in an Angola terreiro, but seven months after her initiation, her Pombagira Mulambo manifested herself, because she had not been "seated." This Pombagira gave consultations; she always gave the money [to her medium] and offered her the necessary means of survival for her and her children. So I could not forbid it [being possessed

by her]. Each time that the Pombagira wanted to leave, I forbade her, for Edí was a widow and had four young children to feed with just a minimum wage, and I wasn't going to deprive her of her sole means of survival!

Edí's Pombagira, Maria Mulambo da Figueira, was re-Africanized and received the (Candomblé) nation's name of Leba Mulambo Baraji, thus becoming Yemanjá's slave. Every Tuesday, Edí gives consultations, remaining possessed from four o'clock in the afternoon until three o'clock the next morning. In an average séance, she receives fifteen to twenty clients, who come to consult the spirit as much about questions of a material nature as about marital disputes, illness, or professional difficulties. In reality, consultations constitute the income of most mediums from Umbanda who are initiated into Candomblé, even if that is contrary to the ideal Candomblé orthodoxy. The mediums justify this use of the spirits by the need to practice charity, as ordained by Umbanda, for, they say, when you enter into Umbanda, you swear never to close the door on those in need.

In houses of worship where the leader already "receives" an Exu or Pombagira, the newly initiated are encouraged to enter into a trance with this spirit, to which some of them object. In the case of Sandra de Yemanjá, initiated by Abrão de Oxum, this obligation resulted in a drama which led to a restructuring of the relationship between the initiator and the initiated. In Abrão's terreiro, ceremonies during which the sons-of-saint were possessed by Exu or Pombagira were very frequent. Seven months after her initiation, Sandra was subjected to a ritual to let through (manifest themselves) the exus, with her orixá's permission. Like the other initiates in the house, she incorporated two exus, one male and one female. Every Tuesday she had to be in the terreiro, "ready to receive the exus so that the clients could consult them." This obligation to go into a trance led to the crisis which pitted Sandra against her initiator. She decided to speak to Jovino de Obaluaiê, her great-grandfather-of-saint in her religious family, as he had initiated the pai-de-santo (Waldemar de Oxossi) of her pai-de-santo (Abrão de Oxum). However, by this time, Jovino had become her grandfather-of-saint, as Abrão had held his ceremony of seven years of initiation in Jovino's terreiro, thus becoming his son-of-saint by *obrigação*.[1] Jovino proposed that Sandra put herself under his spiritual protection by joining his terreiro. In this way,

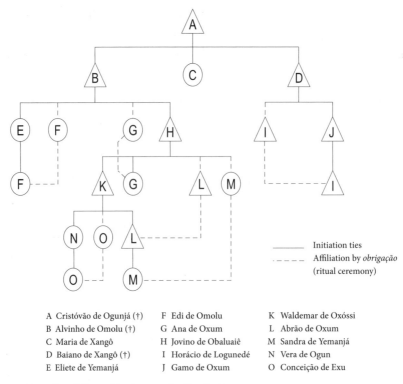

A Cristóvão de Ogunjá (†)   F Edi de Omolu   K Waldemar de Oxóssi
B Alvinho de Omolu (†)   G Ana de Oxum   L Abrão de Oxum
C Maria de Xangô   H Jovino de Obaluaiê   M Sandra de Yemanjá
D Baiano de Xangô (†)   I Horácio de Logunedé N Vera de Ogun
E Eliete de Yemanjá   J Gamo de Oxum   O Conceição de Exu

29. Upward mobility within the same family-of-saint.

Sandra resolved the conflict with her initiator by becoming his sister-of-saint, and the initiate's obligation to be subservient to her initiator was neutralized by Sandra's moving to the same hierarchical level in the family-of-saint. It is thanks to this upward mobility within the family-of-saint that hierarchical order is circumvented and the balance of power is renegotiated in Candomblé.[2]

Affiliation to a new pai-de-santo in the same family-of-saint or between different nations is, then, a very efficient method of negotiation. In this way, mistakes are always rectifiable, without any particular authority putting an end to negotiations: the adept simply changes mediator. Mediums' movements are not limited to passing from one religious modality to another, since the movement may also be within a given family-of-saint. The balance of power between initiator and initiated, like the religious categories analyzed in the previous chapter, proves to be in a state of constant reorganization.

The Words of the Spirits

Despite considerable change in the image of Afro-Brazilian religions, being initiated to Exu or incorporating Exus-eguns continues today to be synonymous with danger and power. Alliance with Exu is always surrounded by an aura of marginality. This peril, inherent in all contact with Exu, is reflected in the perception that others have of sons of Exu. Being linked to Exu means occupying a dangerous place, between good and evil, which others carefully avoid. It also means that a person is hotheaded, someone with whom it is wise to be prudent.

In reality, what seems to best characterize Exu's sons is their extreme frankness, which often leads them to disrupt the terreiro's hierarchy—Exu's sons do not mince their words and do not accept Candomblé's established code, in which conflicts are often resolved by gossip and rumor. They are not afraid of provoking conflict within the religious group, for their hotheaded nature, defined by the master of their heads, leaves open a path toward transgression.

This is a spiritual sign, then, but also one which appears physically. In all the narratives of those initiated to Exu in Candomblé, or of his mediums from Umbanda, a constant element may be found: Exu-orixá or the Exus-eguns (exus and pombagiras) like to mark their horses. The frequency with which Exu's mediums fall, have accidents, or hurt their legs seems to be one of their characteristics; in Candomblé, it is said that Exu likes to leave his mark upon his sons. The first manifestation of the spirit (Exu or Pombagira) is often brutal. This is why Maria Auxiliadora of Xangô bears the scars of her alliance with Maria Mulambo:

> During her lifetime, my Maria Mulambo was the wife of a rascal [malandro], a petty criminal, and she suffered a lot. In the beginning, when she started possessing me, she cut me. My arms are completely cut up [she shows her scars]—can you see the gashes? She never explained why she cut me like this. One day when we were in Exu's house, there was a piece of glass on the ground—she picked it up and pushed my arms back.

When she left [when the medium returned to her normal state], I let my arms fall and I was covered in blood. Another girl from the terreiro told me that she had talked with Maria Mulambo. I don't know what they talked about, what she asked for and what she promised—all I know is that from that moment on, she stopped! But in the beginning she cut me a lot, and they weren't superficial wounds, they were deep gashes, you could see the white flesh.

If pombagiras are the wives of those outside mainstream society, their mediums must also have inscribed in their flesh the signs of being outcast. In Brazil, being the wife of a malandro means being a battered wife, a woman who will accept anything from her partner. The spirits of exus and pombagiras sign their alliance with human beings by corporal punishment. Accepting this means establishing a relationship of dependence with the spirit, no matter which sex the medium is, for the spirit, even if it is female, reproduces the male model of domination over the medium who is dominated. It is because he has bowed to the will of his spirit that the medium is no longer subjected to violence and obtains riches, strength, and power.

Another constant in the narratives of mediums possessed by exus and pombagiras in Candomblé is the relationship of protection linking the pai-de-santo to the spirits of his sons-of-saint. The head of the house of worship always appears obliged to accept these spirits, as recognizing the spirits' power implies recognizing the legitimacy of his initiates' power. Thus, in all these narratives, exus and pombagiras help their mediums' initiators and prove their reality at the same time. Although confined to domestic space, they reaffirm their authority thanks to the element which forms the basis of all conversions: mystical healing.[3] The subordinate relationship linking the initiate to his initiator is thus reversed—if the initiate needs his pai-de-santo for all ritual mediation with the divinities, the pai-de-santo relies upon his son-of-saint's spirits for protection, and therefore a debt binds the father to the son through the spirits' assertion of their power.

Failure to recognize the spirits' power results in conflict. However, if in Candomblé a son of Exu can attack the terreiro's hierarchy in a direct manner, this is not true for a medium who has come from Umbanda. An initiate to Exu, because of the role played by this orixá on the mythical level and the fear of witchcraft which he instills, has no need of what could be called

Candomblé's parallel discourse—gossip and rumor. He does not participate in this dynamic common to all the initiates in Candomblé terreiros, consisting of apparent submission to the hierarchical structure and of criticizing it through accusations conveyed by this parallel discourse. However, when not possessed by their spirits, initiates who embody Umbandist exus and pombagiras would never dare to directly attack the terreiro's hierarchy. Making use of mediums' supposed unconsciousness during possession, they can resort to the words of the spirits who are solely and uniquely responsible for what is said. Criticism becomes legitimate, for it was offered by the spirit and not the initiate. In order to counter these attacks, the criticized pai-de-santo must dismiss the spirit by accusing the medium of simulation.

Sandra de Oxum's story is a very good illustration of this tactic. At the time of her initiation twenty-one years earlier, she already incorporated a Cigana Pombagira, a Hungarian Tzigane by the name of Vadinha Ratzá. After a long time in Umbanda, she decided to be initiated by Gamo de Oxum, the Efon son-of-saint of Baiano de Xangô. However, "given the Efons' difficulty in accepting possession by Exu," no one would take care of her Pombagira. During the first year, Sandra obeyed the rule that forbade her to incorporate an Exu, but soon the Cigana began to manifest herself again, for "she wanted to work." So Sandra distanced herself from her initiator's terreiro and joined that of Alvinho de Omolu. In her narrative, the resulting conflict with the pai-de-santo, due to her Pombagira, was resolved by the intervention during divination of Sandra's orixás, who asked the pai-de-santo to accept the medium's spirits along with her orixás.

The day after our first interview, Sandra was giving consultations with her Cigana in her apartment. She invited me to meet her spirit and even allowed me to record the interview. When I arrived at her home, it was already ten o'clock in the evening, and Sandra had been in a trance since that morning, receiving one after another the clients that one of her daughters-of-saint greeted in the living room. After I had waited for almost three hours, she received me, dressed all in white, with a golden scarf around her waist and small white clogs on her feet. A large plastic red rose in her hair lent her a bohemian air. She wore large earrings, several gold necklaces, bracelets, and rings. The Pombagira introduced herself as the "queen of the Tziganes" and as "the wife of Lucifer, and more than twenty husbands." It was no longer Sandra doing the talking, but her spirit, Dona Cigana.

After a lengthy digression about the nature of her mission in the world and her relationship with her horse, the spirit came to her medium's pai-de-santo. About Exu, "without whom the orixá would not exist," the Pombagira Dona Cigana said that her words would probably be contrary to the pai-de-santo's convictions, but that "it is she [Sandra] who must obey him, not I!"—thus reconfirming the distance existing between the orixás' space, which is the monopoly of the pai-de-santo, and that of the spirits, where the relationship between the medium and her entities is direct. The Pombagira has no need of the pai-de-santo's mediation and so does not owe him obedience. The Cigana claimed her independence, even with regard to the orixá, the master of the head of her medium, whom she ought nevertheless to obey, being her slave: "It is she [Sandra] who submits to the pai-de-santo's authority. She is mad about him, she's grateful to him, her orixá is grateful to him, she loves his caboclo, but he [Alvinho] has never liked me . . . he can barely tolerate me."

This is where the conflict arises—the pai-de-santo does not accept the spirit, he only tolerates it. Despite the spirit's constant attempts to avoid conflict with the pai-de-santo, because "he is important for my horse," the Pombagira told me of the ritual drama of which she was the pivot in Alvinho's terreiro. During the ceremony to mark her seven years of initiation, Sandra, who was in the initiation room (ronkó), began to feel unwell, a sign of the Cigana's imminent manifestation. According to the spirit's words, Alvinho was busy making sacrifices to the Eguns (ancestors) in the outer part of the terreiro. Sandra was brought into the ceremony hall where the ekedi tried in vain to call her orixá, Oxum. But the orixá did not manifest himself "because it was not he who was there." She was possessed by Dona Cigana, and so an argument broke out. Alvinho would not allow the presence of an Exu-egun in his terreiro and brutally chased it away. At that moment the Pombagira declared that she would never come back to the terreiro "because she would not go where she wasn't accepted."

Years later, the conflict between the pai-de-santo and the spirit (Dona Cigana) remains unresolved. Although hurt by the lack of recognition of her mystical powers, Sandra cannot allow herself to defy her pai-de-santo's authority, because he cares for her orixás very successfully. So it is the spirit who will attack. The medium is not responsible for what her spirit does or says. Embodying an Exu would seem, then, to fulfill two needs—

30. The Iroko tree in the Ilê Ifá Mongé Gibanauê. PHOTO BY AUTHOR.

to improve one's social standing through building up a clientele linked to the spirit, and, at the same time, freeing oneself from the weight of the religious hierarchy.

However, in passing from Umbanda to Candomblé, the role played by Exu and Pombagira is subject to a reversal. In Umbanda, the principal object remains practicing charity, together with working—consultation séances with the spirits, whose aim is the spirits' evolution and indoctrination. In Candomblé, however, exus and pombagiras give consultations and earn money for their mediums in their homes or their own terreiros. From a spirit driven by the need to evolve, who, in order to do so, pays through his work on earth, we move to a spirit free of any indoctrination who ensures his medium's material well-being.[4] One pays for his evolution, and the other is paid for his services.

On a political level, the use of exus and pombagiras, which we have seen at work in conflicts with hierarchical superiors ("orthodox" pais and mães-de-santo), is even more obvious when the conflict sets an initiate against her husband or partner. Spirits, especially pombagiras, thus play a pivotal role in the profound reorganization of the balance of power within the couple: the invisible ally grants her horse her power and protection against a husband who rarely possesses the same spiritual mediation. For the man to be accepted, he must submit to the authority of his wife's protecting spirit, usually establishing a pact with the invisible being.

This pact is always the result of a long process whose objective is the recognition and acceptance of the woman's mystical power. The man, who must bow to the spirits' strength, is then obliged to negotiate his relationship with the woman, whose principal master is the spirit. Accepting the supremacy of the protecting spirit is the sine qua non of any relationship with a female medium. Recognizing her spiritual patrimony means recognizing her power. Alliance with the spirit thus becomes the place where the woman's role is redefined. In fact, although the patriarchal family constitutes the ideal model within Brazilian society, in everyday practice this model is very far removed from reality—at least among the working classes, where the woman is generally the family's real pillar. Men come and go, without really taking responsibility for the children born of their unions with women. Very often the woman is the head of a family made up of children with different fathers; it is she who works hard to ensure the children's survival.

In mediums' narratives we constantly find the theme of the difficult alliance between spirit and medium, experienced as a veritable power struggle. Conversion is the result of spirits' victory over men. However, if mediums submit to the spirits' will, they also impose this will upon those around them—a man must accept his wife's spiritual mission so as not to provoke the spirits' wrath. Accepting his wife's allies is also to accept her mystical superiority; through the spirits and their words, a woman may reverse the submissive role to which she is generally confined.

Therefore, while it is true that possession acts as a place where "sexual roles are transformed," where whatever the sex attributed to the spirit, he or she always plays the dominant male role with regard to the medium who takes on the dominated female role (Boyer-Araujo 1993, 108), women's alliance with exus—and especially pombagiras—reverses women's role of submission in everyday life and imposes their will upon men through the spirits' words. In most narratives, the relation between the woman and her protecting spirit, Exu or Pombagira, is always experienced as an alliance enabling the woman to deal with men's violence or betrayal. It is, then, the spirits who intervene directly in the most dangerous moments of their horses' existence, protecting them and punishing those responsible.

While spirits punish men when they are violent, they also intervene when they leave their wives for other women. In fact, marital problems are one of the main reasons clients consult pombagiras. This spirit, identified with a prostitute, then becomes the guarantor of a harmonious marriage. If a woman, especially one possessing mystical powers, is not obliged to submit to a man's authority, she is, however, forced to accept spirits' mediation or risk very serious consequences.

An illustration of this is the story of Rosinha de Mulambo and her alliance with the Pombagira Maria Mulambo da Figueira, as she told it to me:

At the age of seven, Rosinha was living in the Manguinhos favela (a suburb of Rio de Janeiro), with her widowed mother and six young brothers and sisters. In the favela lived many Pentecostalists as well as *macumbeiros* (Umbanda and Candomblé adepts). Every day she went to find food in the vegetable garden. One day, hidden in a cave nearby, she found some money—first a coin, then another, and finally a tied bag. It was a work of black magic. Rosinha lost control of herself: she started to cry and could not stop. People thought she had been raped because it was said that a man was abusing children in the favela (shantytown), enticing them with sweets or money. She was taken to the police station and then to a medical center, where the doctor could find no sign of violence. But Rosinha could not stop crying. Her mother, in spite of her fear of black magic, took her to an Umbandist center, "crossed with Quimbanda," where Rosinha's orixá, Oxum, finally manifested himself. But Rosinha fell ill because her mediumship had not been treated (developed).

At the age of eleven, Rosinha was possessed by Maria Mulambo for the first time. She was paralyzed in her bed with rheumatic fever. Having taken possession of Rosinha, Mulambo told her mother that if she did not decide to give her her daughter, Rosinha would be ill for the rest of her life. Her mother acquiesced, for Rosinha had been paralyzed for a whole year. When she was cured, Rosinha began to give consultations with her Pombagira in her mother's house. Gradually, the spirit took control of the young girl and those around her—when Rosinha's mother wanted to do something, she had first of all to discuss it with the spirit, with whom she had made a pact.

When Rosinha was sixteen, Mulambo told her mother that the girl wanted to get married, but that she was against this marriage—she wanted Rosinha simply to live with her boyfriend. But Rosinha's mother did not agree. She fell to her knees before the spirit, crying and begging her not to impose such a shameful thing. She managed to convince Mulambo to let her daughter marry. By this time, Rosinha was working in a factory and was the household's sole breadwinner. Her future husband was the son of a rich Spaniard, the owner of a large house "like a castle" in the district of Bonsucesso and of six other apartments in Rio de Janeiro. Rosinha had met the boy at the favela church door where he had come to a wedding. Rosinha's mother wanted them to marry as soon as possible, before her daughter "lost herself." Nineteen days before the day set for the wedding, the boy's father died suddenly. The day before the wedding, Mulambo took possession of Rosinha and told her fiancé: "Listen, I shall make you an offer. I will let her get married, but you shall let her come here [to her mother's house] each week to hold consultations." Mulambo then asked him to take a vow with her at the foot of a waterfall dedicated to Oxum, Rosinha's orixá. He did so but let Rosinha hold her consultations only twice after their wedding.

The crisis came just after the very difficult birth of their first child, when Rosinha's husband forbade her to visit terreiros. Rosinha fell ill and remained paralyzed for four months. Mulambo was punishing the couple for having broken their pact. It was a period of misery, of "black hunger," to use Rosinha's words. Her husband lost everything he owned —his car, all his property was frittered away by his mother, who had met a younger man. Rosinha, her legs paralyzed, could no longer walk. It was her mother who brought food for her and her child.

One day, when Rosinha was alone in her apartment, the doorbell rang. It was a very dark man with sleek hair, offering to sell her paintings. She was not interested but allowed herself to be persuaded to look at them more closely. The man, who was "tall and black with perfect teeth," then told her that his real aim was to "possess" her. Rosinha began to cry and call for help, but no one heard her. Her child suddenly fell into a very deep sleep. She lost all notion of time, hours passed . . . And the man could not cross the threshold because Rosinha had called all her spirits to help her. Suddenly she heard the neighbor's radio announce the time—it was six o'clock exactly. The man looked at her and said, "Goodbye until next time." He had just left when Rosinha's mother arrived. There were only eleven steps to the main entrance, but she had seen no one come down. Rosinha fainted, and her mother went to speak to a neighbor who knew people connected with "spiritism."[5] So they went to consult a medium by the name of Ilka who lived on the other side of Avenida Brasil, in the Nova Brasília favela. Rosinha dragged herself there, as her legs would not obey her. Ilka examined her hands and asked how many men she had in her life. Exhausted, Rosinha replied that she had only one, her husband, Manuel. It was then that she lost consciousness, and Mulambo manifested herself, declaring that Rosinha was paying "the price of her life" and that she would end up "like all the other women," as a prostitute "taking pleasure" from her fate. Pombagira demanded proof by fire,[6] to show that she was not handicapped—it was Rosinha who would continue to be so after the spirit's departure. She danced in a circle of fire. Before leaving, Mulambo told Rosinha's mother that it was all because of the wedding, and that she was Rosinha's only master. After this, the mother said to Rosinha's husband: "Listen, Manuel, you have taken my daughter, who gave me everything, from my house. You knew she practised spiritism. You have to let my daughter go back there!" He refused, and Rosinha remained paralyzed.

Relations between husband and wife deteriorated with each passing day. They had stopped having sexual intercourse two months after the wedding. Rosinha thought it was because of her humble background or her "dark skin," and felt inferior. She says that there was only one exception, and it was then that she became pregnant for the second time. Her husband did not want the baby and asked her to have an abortion, which she refused. Her first child was eighteen months old, and Manuel worked nights as a taxi driver. One night Rosinha fell asleep with her hands pressed together—the next morning she was unable to separate them. The pain was so great that Rosinha cried, hoping to die. Suddenly she got up and left the apartment, having recovered the use of her legs, and she ran, crying, into the street in despair. People from an Umbanda terreiro called her to give her something for the pain, but she was afraid to go into the cult house. Eventually she accepted, and when the mãe-de-santo, possessed by the caboclo Sete Estrelas (Seven Stars), placed her hands upon Rosinha's head, Mulambo manifested herself. Straight away she demanded cachaça to drink and spread fire on her medium's arms to · show her strength. She declared that if Rosinha did not look after her, her life was going to get worse and worse. But after the trance, Rosinha left and did not return to the terreiro.

A few days later, Rosinha dreamed that Sete Estrelas was calling her, so she went to the terreiro, where the caboclo was waiting for her. She went into a trance and held consultations with her Pombagira throughout the night. When she got home, Rosinha felt better than she ever had done, but one problem remained—her husband. One day his family came to the house to humiliate her, claiming that it was thanks to them that she had left the favela. A crisis erupted. Mulambo took possession of her and called her husband to talk to him. She told him that if he did not allow his wife to dedicate herself to her spiritual mission, she, Mulambo, would separate them. The husband agreed to let her work, but only in Dona Alice's terreiro, where she had been called by the caboclo Sete Estrelas.

Rosinha then began visiting the terreiro, apart from the days her husband came home early. But his behavior was still somewhat odd; he continued to neglect her sexually. Rosinha had met Luiz, a Candomblé pai-de-santo, at whose house she had carried out the first ceremony for her orixás. He revealed to her that her husband was leading a "double life." Rosinha, who despite her recriminations had become pregnant for a second time, asked the Mulambo to help her prepare a magic spell which she placed under the marital bed.

One evening Rosinha was at her sister's house, in the same block, when her husband came home. She found him already in bed, asleep. She was brushing her teeth in the bathroom when the brush slipped from her hands and fell on the floor, next to the laundry basket. She moved the basket and behind it found a pornographic magazine. When she picked it up, something slipped from the pages—her husband had just been masturbating on the magazine. It was like a slap in the face for Rosinha:

> It was such a disappointment! I was shouting and screaming. My hair was long and I started to tear it out. I stayed for a long time with no rest, looking after him, so that he would stop doing such things, because I loved him. I told myself, if I have a saint [a divinity], if Oxum and Mulambo exist, I will never abandon spiritism again! But, please, get me away from this man. I'll have a man, but I'll never leave spiritism, whatever happens!

Rosinha's mother went to the house of her daughter's mother-in-law, to explain what had happened and the danger of Rosinha's losing the baby. Together they went to see a diviner, who told them that Rosinha was also in danger of dying. During the night, Rosinha started to lose a lot of blood. She dragged herself to the apartment of her sister, who took Rosinha to hospital. Her husband, however, who was at home, did not lift a finger. When Rosinha's mother went to talk to her son-in-law, he finally explained the reason behind all these dramas—when he "looked for" his wife, she was always in a terreiro.

Once she was out of hospital, Rosinha begged her husband to let her return to the favela with her child. She asked for nothing but the few belongings she had brought with her when they married. But Rosinha's mother would not agree. Little by little, Rosinha realized that she loved her "saint" (her spiritual mission) more than her husband. The couple moved to another district in the suburbs of Rio de Janeiro, Vila da Penha. There Rosinha met a woman, Ondina, who was going to teach Mulambo "the value of money." In fact, Mulambo worked hard in Dona Alice's terreiro but did not accept any payment, and the money went to the terreiro. Mulambo began holding consultations in a small room in Rosinha's new apartment, and from then on, Rosinha earned her financial independence. With the spirit's help, Rosinha's material life changed completely. Mulambo obtained enough money for her to build a nice house on some land given to her by a client, and to buy a car and everything she could want. She was independent: "Never again will I have a husband to tell me what to do!" In reality, he continued to live with her, but now he was economically dependent on his wife and her spirit. Because he was beginning to mistreat his wife's clients and sons-of-saint, Rosinha decided to leave him, which delighted Mulambo, who had never accepted sharing her with her husband. Mulambo "paid the lawyer" with the money her clients gave her.[7] Rosinha did not have to make any effort—everything was taken care of for her, for it was her spirit, at last, who had taken control of her life.

After her husband left, Rosinha never fell in love again. She had affairs with younger men but did not commit herself to a relationship. Rosinha received everything from her spirit: a house, sexual satisfaction, financial well-being; she even managed to receive a seamstress's pension (she had worked as one for a certain time) as well as social security. When I interviewed her, with Mulambo's earnings, the spirit had enabled her to build a house for her son. The whole family lived thanks to Mulambo's help.

We find in Rosinha's story characteristics common to all mediums' narratives, primarily a strong sexual component in the spirits' relationships with human beings. Thus Rosinha's first contact with black magic was originally interpreted as a rape. When Mulambo wanted to force Rosinha to respect the pact they had made, instead of being spiritual, the harassment became sexual—the tall, black man who tried to come into her apartment to "possess" her was an Exu, one of Mulambo's spiritual partners. Finally, the fact that Rosinha's husband no longer wanted sexual intercourse with her is indicative of the exclusive nature that joins the medium to her spirit. Once the pact with the spirit is accepted, sex stops being a problem. However, while a woman may make love with a man, she cannot marry him—the spirits' jealousy ruins the relationship because a wife is supposed to be subservient to her husband:

> Mulambo told me that she is deadly jealous, and that I can have intercourse with men, there is no problem with that, but Mulambo will not allow me to let a man into my life and meddle in my business with the spirits! There's no shortage of men. I have a boyfriend, but I cannot marry him—we can live together, but never get married!

31. Initiates working in a terreiro. PHOTO BY AUTHOR.

The spirit cannot accept the intrusion of a husband in his relationship with his medium—it must be an exclusive one. The sole authority to which the woman must submit is that of the spirit, male or female, who is her only master and mate. The spirit's authority does not bend to that of the husband; if the latter agrees to submit to the will of his wife's protector, he may continue his relationship with her, but if he insists upon defying the spirit, he will be forced to leave home. In Rosinha's case, she took a long time to accept the preeminence of the spirit over her husband, and her suffering stemmed from this difficulty in accepting the alliance with her protector.

The second constant element in mediums' narratives is the opposition between the financial well-being procured by the spirits and the relative and precarious economic situation connected with marriage. Indeed, the rise in social status (Rosinha's marriage with the rich "stranger") implied accepting the authority of the husband who did not accept his wife's alliance with her spirit. Therefore the rich husband lost all his worldly goods and became dependent on his wife and her mystical protector, and thus the roles were reversed. In reality, great ambivalence is found in most married women's accounts of their role. Most crises occur at the time of their change of status from young woman to that of a married woman, and the spirits manifest themselves in order to express their rejection of the marriage. The resulting mystical war is only resolved by the husband's submission to his wife's spirit, or by his definitive departure.

However, the central point is the constant negotiation of the extent of women's freedom. A religious career represents financial independence for women from the more deprived social classes, even if, as we have seen, this social and economic ascension requires a necessary division of space. Rosinha left Dona Alice's terreiro to open her own. Economic success is never bound to an area belonging to someone else, but to the domestic area or an independent sacred space.

Because she is able to use her mediumship freely, Rosinha has become completely independent from her husband and all other men. Her spirit alone—Maria Mulambo da Figueira—offers her everything she has ever desired.

The Mystic Triangle

Making a pact with one's wife's protecting spirit can lead to a *ménage à trois*, in which the man must negotiate his role and his marital prerogatives. This is the price that must be paid for the couple to lead a peaceful life. Obviously, they are never alone, since the spirit is always with them, the central figure of a mystic triangle.

In complete contrast to the stereotype of the prostitute or the Tzigane embodied by Pombagira, the Pombagira Menina (Young Pombagira) portrays a prepubescent girl[8] who died defending herself from an attempted rape, or who was killed by her father who would not accept her love for a boy. She is usually a virgin and behaves in an upstanding manner. During a ceremony dedicated to her, the Pombagira Menina dos Campos Verdes of Edí de Omolu told me her story. During her lifetime she had been the daughter of Pombagira Maria Padilha, "who had many men and many children." But the men did not want children, and Maria Padilha abandoned them in order to keep her lovers. So Pombagira Menina lived as a street child, on a soccer field, where today she receives offerings. In order to survive she had to work in a cabaret, where the men seemed much taken with her. One day, when she was only eleven years old and still a virgin, a man tried to force her to have sexual intercourse with him. Desperate, she struggled with the man, who killed her.

During our conversation, Pombagira Menina expressed very clearly her hatred and mistrust of men. She claimed that she did not like them because "they were all liars" and that her mission on earth was to protect women, "for they are more sincere, and always deceived by men." She also explained to me that two types of pombagiras exist—those who enjoy leading women to their downfall, and those who, like herself, do not, and who do not laugh in a vulgar manner but speak calmly. She even went as far as to apologize for using the word *safada*, which is not the crudest word in Portuguese for a woman of low morals. She was completely different from other pombagiras.

She was as restrained in her deeds as she was in her words. While she controls men, she also controls women according to a very moral conception of the world:

> Wherever I see a fault, I correct it. I punish those who behave badly. If a man has left with another woman, I bring him back home. But some women are—excuse the expression—sluts [safadas]. So while I put things in order, they go looking for men. They find fools, who stay to heel, and they are not satisfied—they want more. So I punish them by cooling them completely, and they can no longer make love with any man!

Once again the sexual aspect of Exu and Pombagira's intervention appears in the spirit's words. Men—and women—have to accept the spirits' mediation in order to benefit from a harmonious emotional and sexual life; if they refuse this mediation, their sex lives will be affected.

The tale of Edí de Omolu and her singular household is typical in this regard. Furthermore, Edí is a perfect example of a medium who moves from one religion to another. Edí was possessed for the first time when she was twenty-seven years old. Her family practiced neither Umbanda nor Candomblé, but her grandmother was connected to Spiritism, and Edí inherited her "saints."[9] She began her religious career making offerings to her grandmother's orixás, then started visiting an Umbandist house, where she carried out her first ceremony. From Umbanda she went on to Omolocô (a more African Umbanda), and from there to Angola Candomblé. But as her orixá did not accept the Angola ritual, she adopted the Efon ritual, the only one that proved to work for her.

The first spirit that she embodied when she was twenty-seven was Exu Tranca-Rua:

> He left me unconscious, in a faint. No one understood what was happening to me. A mãe-de-santo told me that I was a medium, and one day, when I was unconscious, I found myself in her terreiro, where Tranca-Rua introduced himself and explained his mission on earth. He also told me that, one day, I would have to be initiated [into Candomblé].

One of the first things Tranca-Rua told his medium was that she should not marry, and he promised her that if she remained single, he would give her everything she desired. She could see men but should never marry them. Edí had already been engaged for eleven years to Moacyr, her current husband, and at the time everything was going well for her: she studied and did some work embroidering and cooking, which earned her a little money. The day she decided to get married, her tranquility was over: spirits began intervening in her life, and shortly before her wedding, Edí began to be possessed by Pombagira Menina, who would soon be at the center of a conjugal drama:

> The day of the wedding, Pombagira was so close to me that I don't remember much. I didn't want to get married any more. On the day of the ceremony, my husband argued with my father and wanted to kill him, and my father didn't want me to marry any more. I felt very odd, as if I were big, huge . . . as if I were something extraordinary!

That very evening, Pombagira took possession of Edí and left a message with Moacyr, now her husband, destined for the spirit's horse: Edí could not marry because she, Pombagira Menina, did not like men, and neither did Tranca-Rua agree with this marriage. Moacyr replied that it was too late, that she should have told him before. The spirit answered: "I do not want this marriage. I am a maiden and you cannot touch my horse!" The first possessions were very violent:

> She was hitting me and making me waltz around the room; she wanted to set fire to my hair. At the time I had long hair, and she wanted to burn it,

she wanted to burn my clothes . . . I saw flames on me . . . I was shouting and screaming!

The wedding night was the first in a long series of crises, as the spirit prevented the young couple from leading a normal life. The repeated attacks drove the newlyweds to seek the mediation of a mãe-de-santo. This is how Moacyr recalls the experience:

During our first night as a married couple, Edí went to take a bath and, at quarter past midnight, she fainted. She stayed like that all night and only regained consciousness at four or five o'clock. We were talking when she fainted again. This went on for three years. I would go to work in the morning, and when I came home I would find her unconscious. I took her to hospital, and then to the terreiro, where I performed some [magical] work for her, and she got a little better. But it continued. Edí started to lose her memory. The day it came back, she did not even know that she was married. She had a two-year-old child and didn't know. "What is it? Where am I? What has happened to me?" I told her that we were married, and she replied, "I don't know if I am, you didn't tell me!" It was Pombagira doing this to her. She [Pombagira] wanted to split us up as she was a virgin, and because of that, could not accept our marriage. This went on for three years. When she [Edí] wasn't working at home, she was unconscious or in the hospital. And if she wasn't in the hospital, she was with the mãe-de-santo. It was terrible!

Pombagira's behavior attempted to prevent, or at least make difficult, the couple's sexual relationship, and so, even though Edí was married and a mother, she did not know it. Her spirit did not let her lead a normal life, as she explained:

She [Pombagira] left me unconscious all night until the morning. Exu makes you lose consciousness so that no one could touch you. You stay like that, inert and motionless, while he, your guardian angel, stays there, watching over you.

Desperate, Edí and her husband went to consult another mãe-de-santo, who performed a ritual at the crossroad to soothe Pombagira Menina. The latter had requested seven offerings, one a year; after seven years, she would leave the couple in peace. During this period Moacyr gradually learnt to accept Pombagira's will, not without some difficulty, as Edí recalls:

> He could not accept it, because when she manifested herself, she lifted my skirt over my head, and he didn't like that! So they argued a lot. She said that she didn't like him, because he was going to take me away . . . she threatened to tear my clothes and leave me naked in the middle of the terreiro!

An undeclared war set the man and the spirit against each other for the control of Edí's life. However, knowledge of spiritism enabled Moacyr to understand the crisis:

> I did not accept all this easily. Pombagira and I often argued, because it is a very difficult situation for a man, a recently married man, not to have his wife there! Even Edí's brothers told me that they would have given up and left. However, I knew a bit about all that [spiritism], because my aunt has a terreiro and I lived with her for a long time, and so, coming from a spiritist background, I more or less knew what was going on, and that's how I managed to tolerate it [the situation].

Moacyr was obliged to make a pact with the Pombagira: he had to respect everything related to his wife's religious work. He began to take part in the preparation of rituals for Pombagira and offer her each time a red rose, the symbol of her mystical power. These days, Moacyr is like an Umbandist *cambono* (assistant), responsible for organizing the ceremonies for his wife's Pombagira and supervising their smooth functioning. Moacyr is head of the drummers and directs the ritual chanting to invoke the spirits. The entire family is involved in the religious ceremonies in honor of Pombagira Menina.

Nevertheless, tension, predating the forced alliance with the spirit, is revealed in the couple's narrative—their relationship was already very difficult because Moacyr was pathologically jealous:

> Pombagira Menina still helps us. She often punished me, but she also helped me a lot. She helped me here at home and she helped me at work. Thanks to her, I began to trust my wife more, because I was terribly jealous. She couldn't talk to anyone, even a woman, because I was really,

pathologically jealous. Even before we got married, I felt this terrible distrust—I thought that any man who came near her wanted to steal her from me! But this was already the Pombagira intervening because she didn't want us to marry. But after I made a pact with her, my jealousy disappeared. Edí hated my fits of jealousy—she even wanted to go back to her mother's and leave me, but then the Pombagira managed to calm me down! Now, if Edí tells me she's going somewhere, there's no problem because I trust them [the spirits]. I think there's no one better to look out for her, because they see everything. People say that Exu is dangerous, that he kills people . . . but in fact he doesn't kill or hurt anyone. It is we [human beings] who are evil and offer him many things to cause problems in other people's lives!

Moacyr's jealousy was also one of the main reasons for his arguments with his wife's spirit. He felt that Pombagira enjoyed being among men too much, adopting provocative poses (her skirt hitched up, legs showing). At the same time, the mystic war between the spirit and the man was often translated, for the latter, by difficulties on a sexual level:

Pombagira made me nervous; she made me argue with Edí, who rejected me in bed. It was always a sacrifice. We argued a lot over this. This is how Pombagira punished me: we'd be in bed, and suddenly, it triggered something—I couldn't concentrate any more, and it was over. Afterwards we found out that it was she who provoked it, and so we had to accept it.

There were sexual problems, then, but also problems within the couple, for Moacyr was not faithful to his wife. Over time, Pombagira took on the role of guardian of their marriage, preventing the husband's infidelities, as Edí relates:

Pombagira lets me know immediately when something is going to happen. One day, when I had just had an operation, I was with my mãe-de-santo. My husband had arranged to meet a woman. He said that he was going somewhere and that I shouldn't go with him because I was ill. He didn't tell me that he was going to see another woman, of course, because he was frightened. But later, he told me that near his mistress's house, he had seen a woman on the street corner who was roaring with laughter [a sign of Pombagira's presence]. Terrified, he tried to run away, but at each street corner he met the same laughing woman. When he got to his mistress's house, she was burning with fever. He came back home to me, trembling with fear, staring wide-eyed. He told me everything that had happened and said that it was my Pombagira who'd followed him, and that he was terrorized and preferred to come home. I told him, "You deserve it!" From that moment on, he calmed down [with women], because my Pombagira is very vigilant—she takes good care of me!

Pombagira Menina is, then, the woman's protector in marriage. She solved the problem of Moacyr's excessive jealousy in the same way that she solved the problem of his infidelity: by asserting her mystic power. She is also the protective spirit of the whole family group. In Moacyr's eyes, she is the best guarantee of his wife's fidelity because she protects her from any dangerous influence that other men might exercise. At the same time, she prevents any infidelity by the husband, thus keeping the peace within the couple.

Most mediums' narratives revolve around the relationship between the sexes; sexual relations, sexual power, jealousy, and betrayal are the battleground where spirits and men fight. In fact, sex—above all, the absence of a normal sex life—is always used as a sign of inadequacy in men's relations with spirits. Women cannot have normal sexual relations with their husbands if they have not first accepted the relation which, as a priority, binds them to their spirits, as the story of Edí and Moacyr shows us. In the same way, for Rosinha de Mulambo, the lack of a normal sex life—her husband preferred masturbating to having intercourse with her—is the explicit sign of her spiritual mission. However, the drama's outcome is different in the two stories, which are exemplar: in Rosinha's case, her husband does not respect the pact with the spirit, which results in his separating from his wife and losing all his material possessions; in Edí's case, Moacyr accepts and respects the pact made with the spirit, who helps him on a material level (especially with his work) and saves his marriage. In both cases, the suffering of the medium and those close to her stops as soon as the alliance with the spiritual protector is accepted.

The spirit, then, becomes the woman's ally in negotiating her freedom's limits, which the man must not cross. Questioned about the conflict which had set her against the husband of her horse, this is how Pombagira Menina replied: "These days, things are better between him and me, but not completely, because I have to look after what is mine, in order to remain forever beautiful and gorgeous. All this [she indicates her horse's body] is mine . . . he [Moacyr] cannot cross this limit!"

In Edí's story, as in Rosinha's, the conflict between the spirit and the husband reveals the woman's great ambivalence with regard to her role as a wife. It is always a short time before the wedding that spirits manifest themselves to show their disapproval. In both narratives, the Pombagira possesses her horse in a violent manner, punishing her until she accepts her true master. The spirits' interest is also expressed in the form of sexual harassment, as in Rosinha's case, when she was visited by a tall, black man who wanted to "possess" her, or in Edí's case when she is visited by her Exu (Tranca-Rua) who substitutes himself for her husband:

> I am a clairvoyant medium, and I see spirits. I asked the pai-de-santo to take some of this clairvoyance from me, for I was afraid. I saw Tranca-Rua who came into the house; I was in the bedroom, and he stayed outside, only coming in when my husband had gone out. When he was alive, Tranca-Rua was a priest. He speaks well and always wears a black cassock and a red hat. He's big and strong and very handsome. But he wouldn't let me see his face and turned away each time I tried to look at him. He was killed because a woman had been raped in his church, and people held him responsible and hanged him at the church door. Tranca-Rua used to come and see me, even before I got married. He used to come into my bedroom and get into my single bed . . . he used to come up the stairs . . . everyone could see him!

Edí's bed was, therefore, inhabited by spirits, both before and after her marriage to Moacyr. In order for him to fulfill his role of husband, he had to accept the conditions imposed by the spirits and establish a pact with them. To do this, the husband's knowledge of the religion is revealed as being crucial. Rosinha's husband, who knew little of spiritism, did not possess the knowledge to decipher the drama and had to separate from his wife. Moacyr's knowledge of the spirit world, however, enabled him to understand what was happening, and to establish a lasting pact with his wife's protector.

In reality, the conflict between the man and the woman always revolves around maintaining a space of freedom for the woman, linked to the practice of religion and the development of her symbolic capital. The woman reaches a position superior to that of her husband, who does not benefit from the same spiritual alliances. He must, therefore, bow to his wife's mediation for any contact with that which is sacred. The acceptance of what Boyer-Araujo (1993) calls the invisible companions becomes indispensable for the smooth running of the relationship between men and women. Accepting them also means accepting the power held by the woman and thus her exceptional position: she is not a woman like any other, for she has spiritual protectors. The elevation of the woman's social status, determined by the accumulation of a symbolic capital which makes her a sacred being, very often justifies the woman's rejection of the man and the assertion of her own independence: she no longer needs a man's protection because the spirits protect her. Once her alliance with the spirits is accepted, the woman becomes the central figure of the household. As in Edí's case, the husband occupies a secondary position within the religious group centered on his wife.

The stereotype of the pombagiras rests upon a fundamental ambiguity. Their powers are connected with feminine attributes such as seduction, sensuality, and vanity—attributes which may become dangerous, for they are no longer controlled socially. In this way, the image of Pombagira is the negation of the dominant female model of Brazilian society: she is the prostitute, the woman of low morals. She does not define herself in relation to men: Pombagira abandons her husband, kills her children, and uses men for her pleasure. Her sexuality is not at the service of reproduction, and she contradicts the ideal feminine role.[10]

Pombagira's principal field of action is sexuality, but a sexuality which is not defined with regard to men and their pleasure. On the contrary, she directly controls the sexual potency of men, who, if they wish to keep their role in the couple, must submit to the spirit. The alliance with Pombagira does not lead to the woman's submission to a dominant masculine model, but the assertion of a space of freedom and power which is exclusively feminine. Thanks to her spiritual protectors, the woman may therefore go from being dominated to being the dominant partner, as much in her professional life as in her personal life.

PART III

THE CONSTRUCTION OF TRADITION

⚜ 6 ⚜

EXU AND THE ANTHROPOLOGISTS

We have seen how today Exu still has most of his African characteristics in Candomblé. However, these characteristics have not
been emphasized with the same intensity in Afro-Brazilian studies since the beginning of the twentieth century. On the contrary,
as in the reinterpretation of Exu from Umbanda to Candomblé,
they seem to have been the object of an intense negotiation
process with the dominant values of Brazilian society. In this
way, we go from an Exu denied, identified with the Christian
devil, and dangerously bound to the practice of black magic to an
Exu who is a mediator between men and gods, a key element in
the religious construction of the true African tradition.

This semantic shift in the figure of Exu is linked to the adaptation strategies put in place by believers in religions of African
origin, according to the perception that Brazilian society had of
them. Anthropologists' writings record this variation over time,
seldom connecting it to the changes in Brazilian society regarding the imaginary associated with black culture and religion. At
pains to make a link between Africa and Brazil, researchers have
too often kept the image of Candomblé as an island without
a history, where the sole preoccupation consists of remaining
faithful to a past that wishes to be immutable. However, when
we undertake a critical reading of their writings, we can see an
evolution of the significance given to the figure of Exu which
does not exactly match the supposed opposition between pure

religions and degenerate cults.[1] The differing perceptions of the role played by Exu seem to be one of the principal issues in the symbolic struggle among the terreiros in the Afro-Brazilian religious field.

The continual adaptation of religious categories shows their capacity to integrate into the values of the surrounding society, making Nagô Candomblé the paradigm of pure African religion even when it manipulates tradition in order to deny its less presentable aspects. The bond between researchers and members of the terreiros considered the most traditional is, then, less a sign of the resistance of African culture, as Bastide claimed, than the result of a strategy, a political practice of accommodation to the dominant values of Brazilian society.[2] My analysis of the modifications of Exu's image in researchers' writings, with regard to the social and cultural context in which they appear, aims to show how an African tradition has been constructed—on a political level—in a quest for legitimacy.

Blacks as Scientific Subjects

Afro-Brazilian studies were born at the moment when blacks became part of the nation, after their long journey toward freedom. The abolition of the slave trade in Brazil in 1850 was the result of pressure exerted by England, which had prohibited the trade on March 25, 1807. The Final Act of the Congress of Vienna in 1815, signed by the king of Portugal, banned the slave trade from all the ports of the African coast north of the equator. However, in contrast to England, where emerging industrialization led to a search for new markets for English merchandise, in Brazil the economy depended directly on the work of slaves, and the country had every interest in continuing the slave trade with Africa.

Brazil's independence, proclaimed on September 7, 1822, was not immediately recognized by England, which imposed total abolition of the slave trade as a prerequisite. In 1825, the Portuguese and English governments finally recognized Brazilian independence, and shortly afterward a treaty was signed between Brazil and England, declaring the abolition of the trade. However, the resistance of slave merchants and big landowners made it difficult to put this treaty into practice. From 1807 to 1835, Brazil, especially Bahia, experienced a series of slaves' rebellions which began to undermine the system of slavery.[3] It was not until 1850, with the Euzébio de Queiroz

Law, that the slave trade with Africa was definitively abolished. The first law in favor of slaves—the Law of the Free Womb—was promulgated in 1871, granting freedom to any child of an enslaved mother born after this date. The abolition was to mark the political and economic decline of the *fazendeiros* (big landowners) of the Northeast, who were irredeemably dependent on the slave mode of production, and whose influence was being replaced by the emerging power of the big landowners of the Southeast. The abolition of slavery was decreed in May 1888, with the *Lei Aurea* (Golden Law), one of the monarchy's last acts before the republic was proclaimed on November 15, 1889.

Among the intellectual elite, these great changes were accompanied by a debate about Brazilian society and its human components: whites, blacks, and Indians. In 1838, the emperor Dom Pedro II had created the Historical and Geographical Institute, whose mission was to rethink Brazilian history in order to consolidate the state. In 1840, the Bavarian naturalist Carl Friederich von Martius won the competition for the best historiographic project on Brazil; according to him, Brazil's mission was to carry out the blending of races, under the watchful supervision of the state. However, this interbreeding also led to the inevitable degeneracy of the Brazilian people, obliged to mix races from different levels on the evolutionary scale.[4] It therefore became necessary to study all that had contributed to the nation's uniqueness, setting aside the valorization of the Indians, a characteristic of the romantic movement, to focus on the analysis of black culture, as Silvio Romero claimed (1888, 10–11):

> It is a disgrace for science in Brazil that none of our work has been dedicated to the study of African languages and religions. When we see men such as Bleek spend decades and decades in the heart of Africa with the sole purpose of studying a single language and recording myths, we, who have material in our homes, who have Africa in our kitchens just as we have America in our forests and Europe in our drawing rooms, we have achieved nothing in this field! It is a disaster! . . . Blacks are not only economic machines; they are, above all, and despite their ignorance, scientific subjects.

Anthropology became, therefore, an indispensable element in the conception of Brazil: the Other was not exterior to the nation, he was an integral part of it. In 1888, when the abolition of slavery was proclaimed, the imaginary linked to the blacks had shifted from captivity—necessary because it was civilizing—to a black danger associated with slaves' liberation, which threatened the civilization and the very survival of the state. The rebellions of the first half of the nineteenth century had left deep scars in the imaginary of the white elite. Everything pointed to blacks' inferiority; they were vagabonds on the margins of society who did not want to work, alcoholics, and dangerous elements.

It was in this cultural and political climate that the first "Africanist" studies developed in Brazil, pioneered by Raymundo Nina Rodrigues. This coroner defended the evolutionary theories dominant in his time: blacks were culturally inferior, and their presence in Brazilian society represented a danger for the nation as a whole. So, having stated the "psychological inaptitude of the inferior races in the search for higher abstractions of monotheism," he underlined the danger that blacks represented for the other components of the Brazilian people: "one should not believe, however, that [fetishistic] practices are limited and their influence circumscribed to simple, ignorant Negroes . . . in Bahia, all the so-called upper classes are apt, perfectly apt, to *become Negroes*" (1900, 146–47).

Nina Rodrigues developed a discourse in Brazil which conferred upon the recently freed blacks a new inferiority, this time in the name of science. In fact, despite the evident interest expressed in the culture of the Africans of Bahia, his work was driven by a normative project aiming to regulate relations between the races. Thus, in a work (1938) dedicated to the relations between races and the penal code in Brazil—originally published in 1894, before his studies on Afro-Brazilian religions—he proposed that Brazilian penal legislation be divided into different codes, for each race presented a different degree of evolution. He also proposed that the civil responsibility of blacks and Indians, like people of mixed race, be diminished, as is the case for children and the insane.

In Nina Rodrigues's study (1988, 268) the concept of blacks resisting civilization was qualified by the assertion of a "difference in capabilities and cultural levels" among the African people who had been brought to Brazil. Nina Rodrigues took up the hierarchy among the races established by Romero, according to which blacks were superior to Indians but inferior to whites, who were divided between the Aryan race, the most inclined to progress, and

32. Xangô's assento. PHOTO BY AUTHOR.

other races—such as the Latin race, which showed obvious signs of decline.[5] It was not the reality of the blacks' social inferiority that was being questioned, for their inability to adapt to civilization was "organic and morphological," but the degree of inferiority the Africans' presence led to, through crossbreeding, in the process of the formation of the Brazilian people:

> However, our studies show that, contrary to what is usually supposed, black slaves brought to Brazil do not belong exclusively to the most degraded, the most brutal or the most savage of African peoples. Here, the trade has introduced several blacks from among the most evolved and also Hamitic half-castes converted to Islam and coming from African States that are, of course, barbaric, but among the most evolved. (Ibid., 268–69)

The Africans less barbaric than the others were the Nagôs, most of whom lived in Salvador de Bahia, and formed the aristocracy of the blacks brought to Brazil. A state religion in Africa, their religion in Brazil was reduced to the simple practice of sorcery, "condemned by the dominant religion and by the scorn, often barely apparent, of the influential classes who, in spite of everything, feared them" (ibid., 238–39).

Nina Rodrigues, therefore, protested against the abuses perpetrated by the authorities in the repression of Afro-Brazilian religions. Indeed, Article 157 of the penal code of 1890 condemned the practice of "spiritism, magic, and sorcery," as well as the illegal practice of medicine and cartomancy—i.e., all that was used "to fascinate and subjugate public credulity" (ibid., 252). These regulations, targeting fetishists who practiced magic and sorcery, were absent from the penal code of 1830, when slavery was still in force. The anxiety aroused by black sorcerers became apparent when they were granted equality—theoretically—with other Brazilian citizens.[6]

Nina Rodrigues denounced police repression—very heavy at the time, as shown by the extracts from the newspapers that he quotes—and the recourse to "violent, arbitrary and illegal acts" carried out against Jeje-Nagô Candomblé,[7] which he considered a "veritable religion":

> As shown in our current study, corroborated by studies carried out in Africa, the Jeje-Nagô cult involves a veritable religion, whose purely fetishistic period is practically over, and which is close to polytheism. Our Candomblés, the religious practices of our Negroes, may therefore be a mistake from a theological point of view, and for this reason we may hope for the conversion of its adepts. But, in the absolute, they are not a crime and do not justify the police's brutal aggressions, of which they are victims. (1988, 246)

Nina Rodrigues saw, in the heritage of the inferior races which had colonized Brazil, the origin of the "idiot terror of bewitchment and cabalistic practices" (ibid., 247). He added that such well-organized sorcery assumed the same social—and therefore legal—responsibility on the part of the sorcerers and their clients, who were often from the upper classes.[8] Nina Rodrigues had carried out his research in the Gantois terreiro, which had just been created in 1896, following a split from the Casa Branca, the first Candomblé terreiro. His informant and principal guide in the world of Afro-Brazilian religions was Martiniano Eliseu do Bonfim, who played a central role in the affirmation of the traditionalism of Nagô Candomblé. A highly-respected diviner (*babalaô*) in the black community of Bahia, he was Nina Rodrigues's interpreter of the Afro-Brazilian world, and the coauthor of the theory of Nagô superiority.

From 1900 until his death in 1906, Nina Rodrigues's concern about the repression of cults began to occupy an increasingly central place in his work. If in the beginning he recognized the coexistence in the same individual (the pai-de-santo) of the roles of "sorcerer, diviner, priest, doctor and sage" (1900, 92), a few years later he drew a clear boundary between the Jeje-Nagô Candomblé religion and the practice of sorcery, relegating the latter to the category of less pure cults. Furthermore, in his first work he discussed *feitiço* (negative magic act, bewitchment), which rendered the sorcerer much in demand, even by the upper classes, and whose aim was to harm the person against whom it was directed; but in his work on Africans in Brazil, the practice of sorcery became a way to criticize the repression used against terreiros practicing the true African religion. In 1900, Nina Rodrigues wrote that Exu's identification with the devil was "the product of the influence of Catholic teaching" and that Exu was an orixá like the others, with his brotherhood and his worshipers (ibid., 25). Some years later (1988, 228), in his eyes Exu became the incarnation of evil, the lord of black magic, and his role in the ritual practices of traditional houses had to be denied.

Nina Rodrigues died in 1906 in Paris, and for almost twenty years his studies on the cultural contributions of blacks had no one to continue them—with one exception: Manuel Querino, also connected to the Nagô terreiro of the Gantois. In 1916, during the Fifth Brazilian Congress of Geography, Querino gave a talk on African customs in Bahia (1988), which was published in 1938 after his death. A republican, liberal, and abolitionist, Querino dedicated himself to research among elderly Africans who frequented the Gantois, in order to reconstruct the rituals connected with Candomblé.

Following his informants' indications, Querino distinguished between two types of magic act according to whether they were positive (*ebó*) or negative (*feitiço*). The ebó (sacrifice, in Yoruba) is placed at a crossroad. Doing so satisfies aims as varied as fulfilling a promise, concluding a transaction, or warding off an enemy, to whom it may also cause moral harm. The aim of the feitiço, on the other hand, is to "cause death, to handicap, to offend someone, to make him insane, to make him sink into alcoholism, etc." (1988, 54). And, like Nina Rodrigues, he identified Exu as "Man's enemy."

It was not until the 1930s, however, that Ramos took up Nina Rodrigues's work and updated it. The notion of race was replaced with that of culture; Tylor's theory on animism was replaced by Lévy-Bruhl's law of participation; the psychoanalytic perspective was applied to the study of syncretism and to the correspondences between African divinities and Catholic saints. Under the direction of Arthur Ramos, a psychiatrist and social scientist who at that time was forensic examiner at the Nina Rodrigues Institute of Bahia, Nina Rodrigues's works were republished, and Afro-Brazilian studies aroused new interest. Ramos himself also carried out research in the Gantois terreiro, which he joined, submitting himself "for the sake of scientific research" to the confirmation ceremony of the ogans with his friend Hosannah de Oliveira, a professor of medicine at Bahia (Ramos 1951b, 70).

In 1934, Ramos dedicated his studies to the Bantus' religious contributions, but he did not question Nina Rodrigues's declaration that he had found no Bantu influence in Salvador, because of the Sudanese predominance in this region. In contrast, in the Southeast of the country, notably in Rio de Janeiro, the presence of religions of Bantu origin was still very strong, despite their "deterioration" due to an extreme syncretism which made it difficult to recognize the original elements (1951b, 100). This was, however, a generalized tendency because, according to Ramos, "in Brazil, African religions with pure origins" had already disappeared, and even in Bahia it was impossible to stop "the avalanche of syncretism" (ibid., 168).

Ramos established for the first time a clear distinction between religious practices and magical practices. In fact, while primitive religion was closely linked to magic and could not be conceived of separately, in the passage from Africa to Brazil, magical practices were divided little by little into "those belonging to the religion itself and those which, later, would constitute sorcery," the babalaô and the pai-de-santo being opposed to the sorcerer and the *curandeiro* (healer) (ibid., 61). Faced with a law accusing them of antisocial practices and charlatanism, Ramos sought to defend Afro-Brazilian religions, claiming that curandeirismo, repressed by the law, was a phenomenon distinct from charlatanism, for which it was mistaken: the charlatan "is a voluntary, conscious and responsible transgressor of a class code, while the curandeiro is an uncultivated individual, an avatar of the black fetishist, who believes in the spiritual virtues of his practices" (ibid., 215). The beliefs of black people were not, then, the domain of the police, but a question of culture: with time and under the action of acculturation, the Africans' de-scendants would naturally abandon these practices.

For the first time, Ramos underlined ambivalence about Afro-Catholic syncretism: while "Afro-Bahians" identified Exu with the Catholic devil and feared him, they "also respected him, making him an object of worship" (1951b, 45). In 1943, the recognition of this ambivalence led Ramos to claim that "for his adepts, Exu is not malevolent" (1961, 341). Exu slowly began to regain his place in the world of religion.

The Renaissance of Afro-Brazilian Studies

In Brazil, the period from 1910 to 1930, the date of the end of the oligarchic republic, saw political and economic power pass from the agrarian elites of the Northeast to the urban elites of the Southeast. The São Paulo bour-geoisie, connected with the production of coffee, which had become the country's principal source of riches, became synonymous with modernity. It was during this period that what Nelson Werneck Sodré (1974, 50) called the "two Brazils" took shape: a "cosmopolitan" Brazil, concentrated on the coast, which looked toward Europe and was receptive to its influences; and an "authentic" Brazil, linked to the hinterland, where ancient roots had conserved their original purity.

The 1920s were heavily marked by change. It was the time of the *tenen-tismo* (the army lieutenants' rebellion), the beginning of urbanization and industrialization, and the commercialization of popular art, with the diffu-sion of records and radio broadcasts which made the samba, a product of black culture, one of the symbols of Brazilian culture. In 1922, in São Paulo, the group led by Oswald de Andrade, Mário de Andrade, and Menotti del Picchio organized the Week of Modern Art. Brazilian Modernism was in-fluenced by the European avant-garde, who had just discovered primitive art and culture. So exoticism returned to Brazil via the European perception of the Other, with ethnological descriptions and anthropological interpreta-tions from Frobenius and Lévy-Bruhl as vehicles. The discovery of the sav-age led to the writing of texts as important as Mario de Andrade's *Macu-naíma* and Oswald de Andrade's *Manifesto da poesia Pau-Brasil.* For the latter, the mythical noble savage metamorphosed into an evil savage, a devourer of white men; Brazil thus became the incarnation of an anthro-pophagous civilization, the product of the ingestion of elements of diverse provenance.

Reacting to the 1922 Week of Modern Art, Gilberto Freyre drafted a manifesto in 1926, in which he placed value upon the strength of tradition, popular taste, and Brazilian culinary art, all elements characterizing tradi-tional Brazil (1967). In 1933, he published *The Masters and the Slaves* (1946), an analysis of the formation of Brazilian society from the meeting of the three races, which gave birth to the ideology of the melting pot, the founding myth of the modern Brazilian state.

Freyre, a pupil of Franz Boas, replaced the notion of race with that of culture and contested the theory of the racial inferiority of black people, claiming, on the contrary, the extreme importance of their contribution to the creation of Brazilian society. Freyre did not glorify African purity; to him, it was racial mixing that gave birth to Brazil. However, the conflict between the past and the present was a key issue in his work, with the past being idealized and the present seen as a kind of decadence and deteriora-tion of pure and authentic forms of the past. While previously racial mixing played a central role in the forming of Brazilian culture, it was now a nega-tive element, "capable of corrupting and degrading the authenticity of the cultural product" (ibid.). Freyre set tradition against modernity, with the latter as the symbol of the degenerated culture of the urban bourgeoisie of the Southeast. Thus, if modernism was linked to the political and economic assertion of the new urban elites, Freyre's theses were the expression of aristocratic rural power, which saw its hegemony irredeemably threatened.[9]

The 1930s were a period of great upheaval in Brazilian society, on a cultural level as well as a political one. The Communist Party had just been founded, and unionism proved to be very active in the large urban centers of the Southeast. From 1935 onward, there were repeated uprisings (popular and military), and police repression was very heavy. From then on, Bra-zilians lived in a state of permanent siege. In 1937, President Getúlio Vargas proclaimed a new constitution on the model of the fascist constitution in Italy, and established the so-called New State (*Estado Novo*). Parliament was dissolved, a state of emergency was declared, and social and union organizations were controlled by a strong and authoritarian state. Vargas's dictatorship was to last until 1945.

It was also a period of strong oppression of minorities. In São Paulo, as well as in the schools of Rio Grande do Sul, a state with many immigrants, there were frequent inspections to prevent the use of foreign languages; anti-Semitism was rife. At the same time, Afro-Brazilian houses of worship were raided by the police, and accused of being hotbeds of communist propaganda (see Dantas 1984). It was in this setting that a new wave of Afro-Brazilian studies developed in Brazil.

Arthur Ramos, a disciple of Nina Rodrigues, adopted a medical and psychological approach not unlike that of his master, seeking to prove the possibility of improving the blacks' prelogical mentality through education and "contact with a more evolved form of religion"—obviously Catholicism (Ramos 1951b). In 1934 he took over the direction of the Department of Mental Hygiene in Rio de Janeiro and carried out research in local Macumba houses of worship in order to test his theory.

The same type of approach led to the foundation of the Department of Mental Hygiene in the city of Recife in Pernambuco, in the Northeast, under the direction of the psychiatrist Ulysses Pernambucano, another of Nina Rodrigues's disciples. In this way, intellectuals tried to free religions from police control by putting them under scientific control. The primary preoccupation of these teams of psychiatric doctors was to analyze the causes of certain forms of "religious delirium" linked to ritual possession, which was considered at the time as a psychopathological phenomenon. The Department of Mental Hygiene was, in fact, a division of Pernambuco's Assistance for Psychopaths (as it was then called). Apart from biological factors, the department's founder and his disciples (Gonçalves Fernandes, René Ribeiro, and Waldemar Valente, among others) researched the social factors which produced this pathological behavior. Enrollment on the registers of this service, with the legitimation brought by the scientific analyses that this implied, enabled the Xangô houses of Recife to obtain permits from the police and be able to function in peace. Therefore, the pais-de-santo cooperated fully, for their centers depended upon this legitimation as places where the true African religion was practiced.[10]

Thus, as happened in Bahia, centers seen as unorthodox became the incarnation of sorcery, which was constantly denied in the traditional Nagô houses of worship. Gonçalves Fernandes (1937) established the boundary between licit and illicit by distinguishing between magic and religion: traditional pais-de-santo practiced religion for they preserved African wisdom, while unorthodox pais-de-santo, who did not possess this knowledge, were doing evil and exploiting popular credulity. The former were not acting against society, threatening neither its order nor its dominant values; the others, on the contrary, were antisocial and could be repressed in the name of the law. The separation between priest and sorcerer, as shown by Ramos, thus became a prime way to distinguish pure religions from degenerate cults.

In this context, the work of Édison Carneiro appeared emblematic of the assertion of the hegemony of the Nagô religion over other cult modalities. In fact, while Carneiro took an interest in Bantu Candomblé at the end of the 1930s, it was only to confirm its nontraditionalism: syncretism was much stronger there than with the "Jeje-Nagôs," for the Bantus were far more open to external influence. And it was in Caboclo Candomblé, "the lowest rung on the ladder of Candomblés, a kind of bridge between the complete adherence of the black Bantu to *baixo espiritismo* [low spiritism]"[11] (Carneiro 1991, 235), that the degradation of the original purity was expressed in the most flagrant manner.

Differentiating between degenerate Bantus and pure Nagôs also revolved around the relation between magic and religion, one of the main preoccupations in the normalization of cults. While in previous times bewitchment occurred in Nagô religions, it was now used "exclusively in Caboclo Candomblés" (ibid., 86). This reference to a time when Africans practiced sorcery in Bahia reveals a very selective conception of the past: if the traditionalism of the Nagôs is legitimized by the past, the negation of this same past, through the strategic covering up of magical practices as a reaction to dominant values, would appear to be another sign of the purity of a religious group, as opposed to the degeneration of others.

This process is repeated when it comes to analyzing the figure of Exu, who embodies the forces of man's enemies. Carneiro gives us a list of despachos or ebós (magical works) in which Exu uses his diabolical influence (ibid., 169). However, Exu's negative action remains limited to Bantu Candomblés: "There are even some people who claim that Exu has a benevolent nature. However, sorcerers naturally venerate him, which terrifies the lower classes of the population" (ibid., 145). The other cults limit themselves to the respect due to "him who may dispose of men's lives at will" and

33. *Alabés*, the drummers of the terreiro. PHOTO BY AUTHOR.

ward off Exu with the despacho ceremony, so that he cannot cause them harm (ibid., 144).

This negation of the cult of Exu in the Nagô terreiros is questioned by Ruth Landes, who carried out her research in Bahia in 1938 and 1939. She was introduced to the world of Candomblé by Carneiro. Her work, on the origin of the myth of matriarchy in Candomblé (a theory which became, despite repeated criticism, a new sign of the purity of the Nagôs), constitutes an incredible reservoir of information about the life of Candomblé in the 1930s, especially the political mechanisms of legitimation at work within the cults.

Unlike Carneiro, who carried out his research in the Casa Branca and who had close links with the Axé Opô Afonjá, Landes found a valuable key informant in the Gantois terreiro: Zezé de Yansan, the daughter-of-saint of Menininha do Gantois and the wife of the ogan Manuel (Amor), whom she paid for information (Landes 1967, 159). In one article, Landes defines Exu as "a goblin-creature involved in evil magic [but] indispensable to cult practice" (1940a, 263). And according to information she received from a priestess, she adds: "He is really of more value than the gods because he gets things done and has no vanity. He never castigates people with illness or loss of wealth. He is ready for service anytime, resting at the crossroads.

There are different types of Eshu but all are regarded in this ambivalent way" (ibid.). She even mentions the existence of female Exus, linked to Yansan, who happened to be her Nagô informant's orixá: "Every god appears to have one or more Eshu-lackeys doing his dirty work for him; the warrior goddess Yansan has a 'gang' of at least seven of the 'wildest' and they are all female" (ibid.). In fact, Landes, the sole exception among anthropologists of the time, suggests that denying practicing sorcery is, in reality, a strategy of legitimation in traditional houses of worship:

> "Mothers" of the renowned fetish temples deny employing Eshu, indicting that they consider themselves above petty interests, but they all know what formulas to use with him and they undoubtedly resort to him privately. Inasmuch as the Catholic Church stigmatizes Eshu as diabolic, priestesses are constrained to favor the gods, which are identified with the great Catholic saints. (Ibid., 264)

The 1930s were also marked by the organization of Afro-Brazilian congresses. The first, held in Recife in 1934, was inspired by Ulysses Pernambucano and Gilberto Freyre, following the great success the latter obtained in 1933 with his work *The Masters and the Slaves* (1946). Freyre's popularity resulted in the participation of a great number of intellectuals along with, thanks to Pernambucano's work in the Department of Mental Hygiene, several babalorixás and iyalorixás from Recife. In a talk he gave about Pernambucano in 1944 in Maceió, in Alagoas, Freyre explained how the idea of organizing an Afro-Brazilian conference came to him:

> Originally, I planned to organize . . . a congress of the "cults" or "religions" of African origin, which would have reunited delegates of the main so-called African cults existing in Brazil. However, the taste for orthodoxy was so strong in some heads of religions that it seemed impossible to unite the imagined conclave. (*Estudos afro-brasileiros* 1988, 12)

The best-known Brazilian intellectuals of the time (Ramos, Edgar Roquette-Pinto, Mário de Andrade, and Carneiro, among others), as well as Herskovits, who was beginning to take an interest in the study of black cultures in Brazil, participated in this conference. The talks were followed by a dinner composed of Afro-Brazilian ritual dishes and a recital of sacred music from Xangô.

In 1937, Carneiro organized the second Afro-Brazilian congress in Bahia along the same lines, gathering intellectuals and heads of religions. Carneiro persuaded Aninha, the mãe-de-santo of the Axé Opô Afonjá, and Martiniano Eliseu do Bonfim (the key informant of the time for any anthropologist interested in Candomblé) to participate. This is how Carneiro describes Aninha, whom he had met for the first time shortly before the congress: "instead of a simple mãe-de-santo who showed herself to be favorable to the congress, we met an intelligent woman who followed and understood our discourse, who read our studies and who liked our work" (quoted in Oliveira and Costa Lima 1987, 59). Aninha seemed immediately to understand the importance of this alliance between religious leaders and intellectuals. She wrote an essay on ritual cooking in Candomblé, which she presented at the congress, and she organized a big celebration for the participants in her terreiro. Oliveira and Costa Lima evoke, with reason, the tactical nature of her decision: "Fifty years on, we still talk about the moment when a traditionalist and rigorous mãe-de-santo did not hesitate to organize in her terreiro a celebration which was not part of the ritual calendar, for an end she considered necessary (and the Xangô of the house must have given his permission!)" (ibid., 59).

The organization of the Bahia conference was difficult because it lacked a personality of national renown, as Freyre had been for the conference in Recife.[12] It was, nevertheless, a success due to the presence of heads of terreiros, "who conferred [upon the meeting] a high level of authenticity and guaranteed it huge popular approval" (ibid., 28). Martiniano do Bonfim was chosen as the honorary president of the congress, for at the time he was the most respected figure from the Afro-Brazilian religions and the one who had the closest relations with the anthropologists. He presented a talk on "The Ministers of Xangô," an African institution which had just been introduced in the Axé Opô Afonjá and which is often regarded as the first example of Candomblé's re-Africanization.[13]

Martiniano then became the honorary president of the Union of Afro-Brazilian Cults, of which Carneiro was the general secretary. The Union, which was originally called the African Council of Bahia, aimed to obtain religious freedom, proposing, as Carneiro wrote to Ramos, to "replace the police in the directing of African cults" (quoted in Ramos 1971, 152). Along with pais and mães-de-santo, it included among its members several intellectuals, such as Aydano do Couto Ferraz; Álvaro Dória, the director at the time of the Nina Rodrigues Institute; and Ramos, who was admitted as an honorary member. These scholars collaborated in the assertion of the Jeje-Nagô model as synonymous with purity and traditionalism, and therefore the only one to be taken as legitimate by society as a whole. In a document addressed to the governor of the state of Bahia after the congress, Carneiro wrote: "As has been sufficiently proved by the most perspicacious observers, notably Nina Rodrigues and Arthur Ramos, and the Afro-Brazilian congresses already held in Recife (1934) and Bahia (1937), there is nothing in the African cults to threaten morale or public order" (quoted in Ramos 1971, 199–200). Thus, anthropologists became the guarantors of the Africanity of the cults and, consequently, of their legitimacy.

Magic and Religion

In 1942, Melville J. Herskovits gave an historic talk at the Faculty of Philosophy of the University of Bahia. It was an analysis of the main issues addressed in anthropological research in Bahia. Herskovits, one of the pioneers of studies on the processes of acculturation, saw in the descendants of Africans in the Americas fertile ground for the study of the interpenetrations of civilizations. In his talk, he emphasized the fact that, with the exception of Freyre's and Pierson's studies,[14] all other research had been dedicated to the analysis of the "Afro-Bahians'" religious practices.

Herskovits therefore proposed a research program which took into consideration all elements of the "Afro-Bahians'" life, with the aim of describing their "civilization" as completely as possible (Herskovits 1967, 94). He insisted on the importance of recording variations in the study of religion, and on the need to study lesser-known houses of worship because the more important ones had already been described (ibid., 98). Among other things, he asserted the normality of the phenomenon of possession, produced by a psychological process which he defined as a conditioned reflex.[15] Herskovits also underlined the necessity of carrying out research into the contributions of the Bantus to black Bahian culture, stating that "no exclusivity can be justified in the analysis of origins":

> It is difficult to accept the response usually given that the mythology and social organization of the Bantu people being "weaker," "less elaborate" and "less evolved" than those of the Sudanese, their traditions gave way before the beliefs of the latter, which were more closely unified and better functioning. In the Congo region are to be found some of the most complex cultures of Africa, and there is nothing to indicate that they were constructed with fabric so fragile that they would automatically yield on contact with systems [of belief] from Western Africa. (Ibid., 99–100)

However, it seems that not many people emulated Herskovits. In fact, the only study dedicated to this subject was that of Luis Viana Filho (1988), who published an essay in 1946 on slavery in Bahia. He showed that the Bantus were very important, both numerically and culturally, among the black population of Bahia. This fact was certainly indisputable, as Freyre recognized in his preface to Viana Filho's work, but it was not enough to overcome the superiority of the Sudanese.[16] According to Freyre, Bantus were "gentler and more accommodating" than the Sudanese, who were "more conscious than anyone else of the values of their culture and, for that reason, more rebellious and animated by a sentiment of African and even human dignity, making them the Castilians or Catalans of black Africa" (Freyre, preface to Viana Filho 1988, 8). The Sudanese—and therefore the Nagôs—represented the "aristocratic element" of Bahia's slave population, examples of initiative and resistance among the other blacks.

In 1944, Roger Bastide, who had come to Brazil in 1938 to take the chair of sociology at the University of São Paulo, vacated by Claude Lévi-Strauss, undertook a trip of about a month to the Northeast. This introduction into the world of Candomblés seems to have fascinated Bastide, who wrote a book about this brief experience (1945). Encouraged by Bastide, Pierre Verger, another Frenchman who was to make a profound mark on Afro-Brazilian studies, arrived in Bahia on August 5, 1946, where he lived until his death in February 1996.

In 1948, Carneiro published a work (1986) which became a classic, based on the research he carried out in the Nagô terreiro of the Casa Branca. For the first time, the cult of Exu, which had always been denied in everything to do with "Sudanese" religions, found its place in the Nagôs' ritual. To do so, however, it had to change its image. Therefore, the despacho ritual, which had always been justified as necessary for warding off a negative and diabolical divinity, became an invocation to Exu for him to perform his role of man's ambassador to the gods (ibid., 69). Exu had thus been the subject of an erroneous interpretation, for his identification with the Christian devil stemmed from the fact that sorcerers invoked Exu to harm their victims. However, in Nagô Candomblés, Exu was the comrade, the protector and messenger. His presence was legitimate, for it had been scientifically attested that magic was not practiced there, but confined to Bantu terreiros.[17] Therefore, once the legitimacy of the houses of worship had been established by scientific congresses, Exu was able to become a new entity, neither good nor evil.

Gradually, this recognition of Exu's presence in traditional Nagô terreiros became widespread in anthropologists' writing. René Ribeiro, directed by Herskovits, developed a thesis on the Afro-Brazilian cults of Recife in which he claimed that all the houses of worship had one or more "seated" (assentados) Exus. However, Exu being a difficult saint to "treat," "known by all, and always present in believers' conversations," informants were very reticent when questioned about his characteristics and functions (René Ribeiro 1978, 56), especially when it came to evoking magic rituals in the cult:

> Magic is so closely linked to sacrifices and offerings, for example, that few priests allow strangers [to the cult] to witness more than one stage of the rituals, which they direct at determined occasions. Often, when the researcher brings up the question of the details of these ceremonies, the priests cleverly but politely avoid his questions, or, if he shows a particular interest in magical practices, they accuse him jokingly of being an "ebó researcher," meaning that he wants to verify the practice of curandeirismo and harmful magic. (Ibid., 67)

Exu, harmful magic, and curandeirismo were inextricably linked; silence about Exu's role thus signified wanting to protect oneself from accusations of sorcery or of the illegal practice of medicine, punishable by Brazilian law.[18] However, while Exu's presence was no longer denied, even in the most traditional houses, the latter nevertheless distinguished themselves from untraditional houses of worship in that their members were not possessed by Exu, that possession being a sign of the cult's degeneration. The negation of Exu continued, then, on another level: one ought not to be possessed by an orixá associated with the devil.[19]

Constrained by their informants, who took great pains to avoid everything that could lead to accusations of sorcery, anthropologists limited their analyses to the "presentable" aspects of religions:

> Confronted with a system made up of elements of religiosity (harmony, solidarity, etc.) and the attributes of magic (internal dissidence, individualism and political quarrels), intellectuals fixed their attention upon religion, public ritual, the collective and all that constituted what might be called 'onstage' activity, while omitting private ritual, the individual and magic, which integrated the activities taking place backstage. The rupture between the backstage interdependent magico-religious activities and those onstage was the result of the intellectuals' attempt to "cleanse" certain *terreiros* from aspects regarded as negative, and so have them declared legal, even if that resulted in creating a romantic vision of the dominated. (Dantas 1984, 111)

The 1950s marked an important change in the perspective of Afro-Brazilian studies. At the time, Africa no longer seemed to have the same epistemological importance as it had had previously. The reconstruction of blacks' history in Brazil, and their passing from slavery into the class structure, was central and led to a sociological phase of black studies in Brazil.

Brazil had radically changed under the developmentalist politics of the government of President Juscelino Kubitschek. The country's development and modernization efforts provoked a huge increase in economic activity, due to its opening up to foreign capital, which also resulted in heavy political dependence. The role of national culture was then analyzed by Brazilian intellectuals in a new way: culture became a central element in the quest for a national identity. Thanks to the myth of racial democracy, a pessimistic vision of the national reality—which had marked the cultural debate at the beginning of the twentieth century—was replaced by an exaltation of Brazilian society, the harmonious product of three races which was becoming an example for the rest of the world.

34. Logunedé's assento. PHOTO BY AUTHOR.

In 1951, UNESCO, whose Department of Social Sciences was run by Arthur Ramos, commissioned a series of studies with the aim of analyzing the model of "harmonious" race relations in Brazil. The results were varied, depending on the location of the research: for example, René Ribeiro, analyzing the role of religion in race relations, defended the founding myth of racial democracy in Recife, in contrast to the sociological school of São Paulo, which denounced its role of social control. It underlined the polarization between the Northeast (notably Bahia and Recife), a region of racial democracy, and the Southeast, an area of class conflict and white racism.[20]

Bastide, who, with Florestan Fernandes studied race relations between blacks and whites in São Paulo, warned Alfred Métraux, at the time a member of the Department of Social Sciences at UNESCO, that he would be "obliged to demystify the myth of racial democracy in Brazil by showing that it was only another name to designate a system just as discriminating, albeit in a different form: paternalism" (quoted in Françoise Morin 1994, 30). However, although Bastide denounced the unreality of this paradise of race relations of which Brazil was the champion, he did not have the same critical view of Afro-Brazilian religions. In 1953, he published a study on the Macumba of São Paulo, which was reprinted in *Estudos Afro-Brasileiros* (1973). In the article, Bastide reiterated the contrast between authentic Nagô Candomblé and degraded Macumba, owing to the mythological poverty of the Bantus.

However, it was above all in his works of 1958 and 1960 that Bastide, back in France, gave shape to this ideal of a pure and authentic Candomblé (1958, 1978). Bastide had become an adept of the god Xangô and was, like Verger, linked to the terreiro of the Axé Opô Afonjá of Mãe Senhora. As many authors point out, in Bastide's work, it is hard to distinguish between the intellectual and the initiate. Like Verger, his friend and guide in the world of Candomblé, Bastide finished by substituting one ethnocentrism by another, placing even more value on the Nagô tradition, of which the Axé Opô Afonjá became the model.

In 1958 Bastide reaffirmed the opposition between two types of religion, linked to two types of magic, black and white. If the first "tends to take the shape of the cult of Exu," the second merely "tends to take the shape of amulets and charms" (1958, 151). However, quoting Carneiro, he underlined the fact that this diabolical use of Exu was limited to Bantu Candomblé: "Their religious leaders are often specialized in the fabrication of statuettes of Exu which become their zealous servants, blindly obeying orders; under their command, they come out at night from their *pegi* [shrines], in order to spread misery and death" (ibid.). On the other hand, traditional—i.e., Nagô—Candomblé, refusing to practice black magic, made sure not to confuse Exu with the devil. There, one could find "the true face of this much maligned divinity" (ibid., 152). Possession by Exu, far more frequent in Bantu Candomblé, was very limited in traditional Candomblé and had a different nature, becoming a kind of divine punishment (ibid., 153).

This negation of possession by Exu obeyed the same logic that determined the negation of the cult of Exu since the end of the previous century in traditional terreiros: the goal was to avoid entering into conflict with the dominant values of Brazilian society. In this way, Exu was freed from his negative aspects, while possession, which could be interpreted as diabolical, was denied. Therefore it was not Exu who was "seated" in the head of his son, but Ogun, a more acceptable god. This change of attitude became even more obvious when Bastide analyzed Exu's function in African tradition: he was the "god of order," who "opens the doors between different compartments of the real" (ibid., 170), "meaning that it is he, and he alone, who represents the principle of dialectics and intercommunication" (ibid., 171). His role was central: "he is everywhere along the line which goes from orixás to mortals or from mortals to orixás" (ibid., 172).

However, it was in *The African Religions of Brazil* (1978) that Bastide, speaking of Exu, naturalized the opposition between the Nagôs (or Ketu), who practiced religion, and the Bantus, who practiced magic:

> The Ketu have faithfully preserved the African image of Exu, the intermediary who speaks through the shells in the name of the *orixás*, the god of orientation, a young boy, mischievous rather than spiteful, who takes good care of his "people." On the other hand, in the Bantu "nations," where the mythology of Exu was (for good reason) unknown and where magic always played a bigger role than in the other "nations," this demoniac element is continually growing. In the *carioca macumba* it will finally predominate. (Ibid., 253)

Exu's identification with the Christian devil was inherited from the colonial period and could be found in the police's persecution of cults:

> All these [African] characteristics and many of the myths that illustrate them were carried over to Brazil, but some of them developed more fully than others. Because of slavery the blacks used Exu in his capacity as patron of witchcraft in their struggle against the whites, so that his sinister side was emphasized at the expense of his function as a messenger. The mischievous god became the cruel god who kills, poisons, or drives men mad. But Exu's was a one-way cruelty; to his black worshipers he was a savior and compassionate friend. The abolition of slavery and the proclamation of the equality of all Brazilians before the law might have been expected to check this evolution toward the diabolical since it put an end to caste conflict, but police persecution of the African re-

ligious sects and party political struggles accentuated the tendency of the colonial period. For this reason the *ebó* sacrifice of today is still the magic *ebó* it became in the time of slavery. The black chicken that used to be sacrificed to Exu and thrown into the uninhabited bush is now stuffed with tobacco, roasted corn, and other ingredients and placed in the path of the intended victim. (Ibid., 252–53)

It would seem logical to infer that the role of protector of blacks, which Exu fulfilled during slavery, would become a characteristic exclusive to Bantu cults, because Nagôs did not practice offensive magic. But how could the Bantus, always regarded as more accommodating and weaker than the Nagôs, have embodied the blacks' noble struggle against oppression? Their use of Exu and ebós must then have been limited to evil and black magic, which the Nagô Exu "naturally" lacked. Thus the ambivalent nature of any Yoruba divinity was polarized; in the case of Exu, between good, associated with the Nagôs, and evil, the monopoly of the Bantus.

Bastide drew a clear border between religion and magic, present in practitioners' discourse as simple patterns of accusation,[21] as much within as outside the religious group. With Bastide, the opposition between Nagô Candomblé, synonymous with religion, and Bantu Candomblé (or Macumba), synonymous with magic, was reinterpreted in the light of the opposition between magic and religion in anthropological discourse. Émile Durkheim (1912) had established a distinction between magic and religion which was not absolute, its limits remaining fundamentally undefined. The same goes for Henri Hubert and Marcel Mauss (1902), who attempted to draw a boundary between religion, characterized by sacrifice and associated with solemn, public activities, and magic, associated with malevolence and linked to private, secret activities, but were obliged to recognize that this boundary was blurred and that a great number of practices could not be the exclusive product of one or other of these two poles.

However, in Candomblé, magic is intrinsically linked to religion, for believing in divinities implies belief in their capacity to manipulate the universe in favor of their protégés. The opposition between magic and religion, a component of anthropological discourse, offered a theoretical framework for the accusations of sorcery, which was then used as a political instrument to define religious identity. Bastide—and others after him—

interpreted what was part of a typically African political discourse (accusations of sorcery) as proof of the existence of a clear distinction between those who practiced religion (the Nagôs) and those who resorted to sorcery (the Bantus).

In 1970, Bastide reaffirmed this opposition between the positive Exu of the Nagôs, "the obligatory intermediary between men and gods," and the negative Exu, the malevolent divinity of the Bantus. It is in Macumba, however, that the fusion between Exu and the devil becomes complete and "the dualism between good and evil triumphs" (Bastide 1970a, 223). The same opposition, used to demarcate the boundaries between Nagô and Bantu Candomblé, enabled him to trace the limits between Candomblé, the seat of tradition, and Macumba, the seat of disintegration caused by modernity: "Exu is one of the rare African gods whose name has been conserved in the very disintegrated Macumba of São Paulo. Why? Because in São Paulo Macumba has ceased to be a religion and has become a form of magic; the *macumbeiro* is the sorcerer who performs black magic, and he uses Exu's power to do this" (ibid.).

The dualism between good, associated with Oxalá, and evil, associated with Exu, as outlined by Nina Rodrigues in 1900, was transformed into a dualism between a social Exu and an antisocial Exu, thus becoming one of the pivots of the internal differentiation of Afro-Brazilian religions.

From the Brazilian to the African Exu

After the 1950s, black studies in Brazil was divided between a sociological school, connected to the so-called school of São Paulo, which analyzed race relations in Brazil, and a culturalist school, attached to the Centro de Estudos Afro-Orientais, which began to develop the field of Africanist studies. The center, founded in 1959 as part of the Universidade Federal da Bahia, soon became, according to one of its directors, "the most active study center for Africanists in Brazil" (Oliveira 1976, 115).

In the 1960s, the process of decolonization in Africa had aroused the interest of the Brazilian government, which was seeking to create new markets. The time was propitious, then, to emphasize what part of Brazil, at least, had conserved from its African cultural heritage: the Yoruba heritage. This is how Waldir Freitas Oliveira explains the development, starting in the

1960s, of comparative studies in black culture: "We started from the principle that it was impossible to have an exact comprehension of the cultural importance of black Brazilians without knowing the roots of this culture so alive and so present here. And, thanks to a bold and ambitious program, Pierre Verger and Vivaldo da Costa Lima were immediately sent to Africa at the University of Bahia's expense" (ibid.). Obviously, "this culture so alive and so present" was the Nagô culture. Verger and Costa Lima were therefore sent to Benin and Nigeria, like many other researchers after them.[22]

The 1960s were marked by great changes in Brazilian political and cultural life. Artists actively participated through theatrical productions (Nelson Rodrigues and Dias Gomes) and politically engaged cinema (Glauber Rocha's *cinema novo*). In 1964, the military dictatorship was established and all constitutional guarantees were suspended. The years that followed were ones of oppression and armed struggle, but also of the so-called Brazilian miracle, impressive economic growth. In 1968, the tropicalism movement exploded, touching popular music as well as cinema and theater. The movement's founders—Caetano Veloso, Gilberto Gil, Torquato Neto, and José Carlos Capinam—were inspired by modernism to critically revise Brazilian culture through the anthropophagous metaphors of Oswald de Andrade. The reappropriation of elements from popular culture, present in the Northeast since the 1930s, became more dynamic. Black culture, with Candomblé, began to occupy a central position in artistic production.

It was also the era of the counterculture, which chose Macumba as its symbol of rebellion against conformism and the repression exercised by the dictatorship. Luz and Lapassade's book (1972, xiv) made a great impression in this field: "We have to put an end to this cult of Africa, 'African origins' and this Africanist devotion. We ought, on the contrary, to mark the breaking away from Africa, asserting and showing the specificity and originality of the Brazilian black."

Thus Macumba became the scene for the expression of libertarian aspirations. It told the story of the "struggle for the freedom of political and social desires," embodied in Quimbanda, and of its repression, embodied in Umbanda. Exu and Pombagira were converted into "symbols of a libertarian proposal" (ibid., xvi). Quimbanda was no longer the incarnation of evil; it became a "project of sexual liberation," where free love, bisexuality, and the "dramatization of all homosexual and heterosexual desires" could flourish (ibid., xxi). "Macumba is rejected by the institutions because it is a counter-institution and a counterculture in which a countersociety expresses itself" (ibid.).

Macumba Exu, rebellious and not submissive, incarnated Brazilian society's desire for freedom.[23] The echo of this reinterpretation of Exu, clearly opposed to the current of Africanist studies, made itself felt in Bastide's posthumously published writing:

> But Macumba, . . . by emphasizing Eshu while transforming the signifi-cance of the intermediary god into an angel of rebellion, allowed the revolt of the sub-proletariat to discover a path where the desire of an "other" society, impossible to achieve politically because it was not con-ceptually structured nor thought out, could nevertheless express itself, if not in a coherent or constructive way, at least in inarticulate cries and gestures without significance—in short, in a pure explosion of savagery. (Bastide 1975, 224)

Of all Bastide's pupils, it was Renato Ortiz who most faithfully repro-duced his master's vision of Exu. He saw in "religious survivals" such as the figure of Exu, the persistence of the traditional in urban life. Eliminating Exu, the personification of evil in Umbanda, would be equivalent to sever-ing links with tradition: "Exu's primary significance may be inferred: he is what remains of the black people, of Afro-Brazilians, what remains of tradi-tion in modern Brazilian society. Eliminating evil may then be reduced to ridding ourselves of the ancient Afro-Brazilian values in order to better integrate into a class society" (Ortiz 1988, 134). However, Exu, "the only divinity in Umbanda to keep the characteristics of his black past" (ibid., 133), must submit to Umbandist beings of light, in order to control his power of rebellion.

It was Juana Elbein dos Santos, another of Bastide's pupils, who defini-tively altered Exu's image in Afro-Brazilian studies and also within the cults. An Argentinean anthropologist initiated in the terreiro of the Axé Opô Afonjá and married to Deoscóredes dos Santos (Mestre Didi), a high digni-tary of the Nagô cult, she instituted a methodology which consisted of analyzing Candomblé "from within" (Juana E. dos Santos 1976, 18). Being both an anthropologist and an initiate became one of the essential condi-tions for a true understanding of the culture studied.

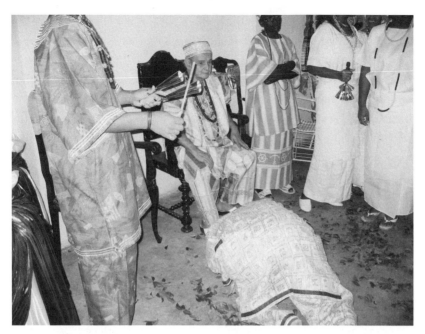

35. Alvinho de Omolu during the celebration of the fiftieth anniversary of his initiation.
PHOTO BY AUTHOR.

The time was ripe, as much on a social level as on a political one, for the valorization of Afro-Brazilian religions. Nagô Candomblé—especially the three traditional houses of the Casa Branca, the Gantois, and the Axé Opô Afonjá—had become synonymous with Bahian tradition and culture. Being initiated in one of these three terreiros was—and still is today—an attestation of traditionalism. Furthermore, on January 15, 1976, Roberto Figueira Santos, the governor of the state of Bahia, approved a decree that exempted the Bahian terreiros from the obligation of registering with the police. The final stigma was removed.

Juana Elbein dos Santos, in *Os Nagô e a morte* (1976)—a work which had considerable success in the field of Afro-Brazilian religions, even becoming a kind of Nagô Candomblé bible—analyzed the role of Exu through the "African tradition" of the Nagôs. Exu (or Èṣù, as the author prefers to write it, following Yoruba spelling) became "the most important entity of the Nagô system" (ibid., 171), "the dynamic principle of communication and expansion, the dynamic element, not only of all the spiritual beings, but also of all that exists" (ibid., 130).

Exu is now closely linked to the notion of axé, which Bastide thought of as being a vital energy, a kind of *mana*.[24] Juana Elbein dos Santos developed this notion, making it the central element of the religion: "The àṣẹ provides impulsion to liturgical practice which, in return, restores it, thus setting the whole system in motion" (ibid., 37). It is Exu who sets in motion the force of the àṣẹ, through which is established the relation between the aiyé (the earthly world) and the òrun (the world of the gods) (ibid.). The àṣẹ—"principle and force," "power of realization"—is also the basis of the perpetuation of the terreiros: "The transmission of the àṣẹ, through initiation and liturgy, involves the continuation of a practice, the absorption of an order, of structures, of the history and future of the group (terreiro) as a whole" (ibid., 46).

If it is Exu who transmits the àṣẹ, he then becomes, rightfully, the most important entity of Nagô Candomblé. Because he is the ẹlẹ́bọ, the transporter of the ebó, now limited to religious sacrifice, it is he who controls the restorative process of the vital force, the àṣẹ: "Sacrifice, in its wide range of purposes and modalities, restituting and redistributing the àṣẹ, is the only way to conserve the harmony between the different components of the system, between the two planes of existence, and to guarantee the continuation of this harmony" (ibid., 161).

Any trace of the malevolent ebó was definitively erased: in Nagô tradition, Exu does nothing but good and is at the center of the religious system. Juana Elbein dos Santos thus took up and amplified Bastide's interpretation (1958) of Exu as the great communicator between the different compartments of the universe. For her, Exu could not be categorized: "he is a principle, and, like the àṣẹ he represents and transports, he inevitably participates in everything that exists" (Juana E. dos Santos 1976, 131). Consequently, interpreting the padê ceremony as a way of conjuring the nefarious presence of Exu contradicts Exu's function as "the guardian and sole guarantor of any ritual activity's smooth running" (ibid., 198).

This interpretation of Exu's role unleashed a fierce controversy between Pierre Verger and Juana Elbein dos Santos. In 1982, Verger contested—very violently—J. E. dos Santos's scientific probity, accusing her of having manipulated data with the aim of edifying systems "of impeccable logic, very well received, incidentally, in international scientific congresses, but which, on closer examination, are a tissue of suppositions and intelligently presented hypotheses, but which have nothing to do with the culture of the Nagôs-Yorubas, and thus running the risk of contaminating orally transmitted traditions which are still preserved in nonerudite circles" (Verger 1982b, 10). Indeed, in 1966, Verger had published an article in Nigeria (reprinted in Brazil in 1992) in which he identified the axé as a nonanthropomorphic form of theism, referring to the cult of Sé, a supreme being for the Anago of ancient Dahomey. Exu's identification with the axé, proposed by Juana Elbein dos Santos, would then equate Exu with a kind of supreme god, for the propagation of the axé depended upon him. Santos's response (1982, 12) was no less violent, accusing Verger of being nothing but "the residual expression of colonialism." We can hear in this debate the echoes of the struggle, in this case between initiated researchers, for the recognition of their sole authority on the subject of African tradition.

IN SEARCH OF LOST ORIGINS

Talking about a pure African tradition, one is obliged to ponder a subject whose contours are not always well defined. What actually are traditions? What purpose do they serve? Why do people preserve them? Does being traditional signify keeping an original purity, as some would claim, or reinterpreting this purity when faced with new situations, according to a cultural core which reasserts the distinctive signs of that same tradition?

Eric Hobsbawm and Terence Ranger (1983) highlighted the act of construction involved in any tradition. Invented traditions are the response to new situations in the form of references to old situations, establishing "their own past by a quasi-obligatory repetition" (2). The authors also underline the political nature of these traditions, which often assert the historical continuity of a cultural and social identity.

But under what circumstances is one driven to try to re-establish tradition? This usually happens when the tradition is perceived as an ideal that has been lost in the face of advancing modernity. As Hobsbawm and Ranger point out, there is no need to revive or invent traditions when old customs are still preserved. The loss of tradition is the driving force for this seeking of origins, then, and the aim is always to reconstruct an original state. This movement toward the past very often becomes a political instrument to legitimize the position occupied by a group that asserts its traditionalism within a hierarchical society. Those possessing a tradition possess a past, a historic continuity which transforms them into the subject of their own history; asserting one's traditionalism, then, implies distinguishing oneself from others, who no longer have a defined identity. Constructing one's own representation of the past—tradition—thus becomes a means of negotiating one's future.

This longing for tradition is not limited to native discourse in search of cultural roots; it also drives anthropological discourse, long confronted with the urgency of gathering cultural traditions threatened by the advance of modernity. The opposition between tradition and modernity has never been symmetrical: modernity is often identified with a type of rational thinking that is only rarely relativized, while tradition is identified with a vague idea of continuity with the past. The passage from one to the other is marked by the loss of tradition and the birth of a modern culture, when "naturally traditionalist" people are obliged, by the pressure of extraordinary circumstances, to abandon their "natural" attachment to the beliefs of past generations (Boyer 1990). Furthermore, the use of the term "traditional" in anthropology only consolidates a framework of intellectual reference organized around a whole series of dichotomies, like tradition and change, or traditional society and modern society.

However, the pertinence of this system of binary oppositions reveals itself to be particularly problematical. In reality, change is always present in so-called traditional events. It would seem, therefore, that to talk about tradition obliges one to refer to this blend of the present and the past upon which it is founded: "in reality, what is unconscious in a tradition is that it is precisely the work of the present seeking support from the past" (Pouillon 1974, 159). In this way, tradition becomes the issue at stake between some houses of Nagô Candomblé, which assert their traditional behavior as a political instrument in order to express their differences and rivalries in the religious field, and anthropologists who make this native category an analytical category, contributing to the crystallization of a supreme ideal of Africanity. We shall see elsewhere how anthropologists, perhaps more so in Brazil than anywhere else, have very often designated as traditional some phenomena "which they know pertinently are not reproducing an original model, which they also know does not really exist" (Lenclud 1987, 113).

Tradition—which is, above all, a model of social interaction—becomes one of the principal instruments in constructing an identity through the selection of a determined number of characteristics which help to establish boundaries between ourselves and the Other. The interacting nature of tradition, and its strategic use in asserting the identity of the group which claims it, contribute to marking its specificity as something which is not fixed but continually reinvented, and always invested with new significance. I shall therefore analyze Nagô tradition according to these three characteristics: it is, like all traditions, interacting, constructed, and political.

The Memory of Tradition

We have seen how the evolution of Exu's image and his role in the religion accompany the construction of an identity linked to Nagô Candomblé, marked by tradition and purity in opposition to the mixing and degradation present in other cult modalities (Angola or Caboclo Candomblé). In the same way, the opposition between magic and religion, one of the foundations of anthropological theory, is also found in practitioners' discourse (accusations of sorcery), the state's normative discourse (the repression of cults), and anthropologists' discourse (their systemization of Afro-Brazilian religious practices).

This convergence is expressed most completely in Bastide's work. In his classification of African religions in Brazil, he uses the opposition between magic and religion as the equivalent of an opposition between tradition and modernity. Nagô Candomblé therefore personifies an ideal world where conflicts do not exist and original African values are faithfully conserved:

The *candomblé* is more than a mystic sect; it is a genuine bit of Africa transplanted. Among banana plants, bougainvilleas, breadfruit trees and [a] gigantic fig tree from whose branches trail the veils of the *orixás*, or beside golden sandy beaches edged with coconut palms, stands the *candomblé*, with the huts for the gods, the living quarters, the roofed shelter where at night the beating of drums summons the ancestral deities. Women, girls, and men bustle about their work—cooking, having their hair dressed by the deft hands of old women. Half-naked children frolic under the fond eyes of mothers adorned with liturgical necklaces. It is as if one had taken a cutting of Africa and rooted it in Brazilian soil, where it bloomed again. Here sexual, economic and religious behaviour fuse in a harmonious unity. (Bastide 1978, 224)

It is these three areas of behavior which oppose traditional religions to syncretic cults. Traditional Candomblé, synonymous with Nagô for Bastide, thus constitutes a coherent and functional whole, for the individual submits his passions and desires to preserve the group: "anything that might separate individuals and thus disrupt the group—eroticism, ruthless ambition, avarice—is controlled, not in order to suppress it but to make it compatible with the impulses of the other members" (ibid., 225). So, while "traditional" terreiros may resort to magic, its real function would be integration, "since all problems can be resolved through the authority of the priests and the discipline they impose upon the members" (ibid., 227).[1] The same goes for "economic behavior" which, according to Bastide, is more closely linked to the notion of prestige than to profit in Nagô Candomblé. "The shameless exploitation of the credulity of the lower classes" (ibid., 300) is, then, the result of the loss of African values:

> Admittedly the capitalist economic system and the profit motive have been introduced into the *macumbas* and into some *candomblés* and *xangôs*, thus commercializing them. But we must not judge the traditional sects by modern caricatures. In the first place, the priests in charge of these "tourist *macumbas*" are not "made"—i.e., they have not undergone the long process of initiation and have only an indirect, incomplete knowledge of the "secrets" of the African religions. (Ibid., 228)[2]

The introduction of capitalist economy is, then, the factor which led to the degradation of Afro-Brazilian religions. Basing his theory on the Marxist theory of the relations between infrastructure and superstructure, Bastide opposes traditional religions and degraded cults, in the passage from a world of solidarity and communion to a world in which there is no place for African values. Under "the erosive effect of the big city" (ibid., 295), which leads them to incorporate themselves into a class society, descendants of Africans belong to two worlds, "different if not opposed"—that of Candomblé, which recreates Africa in Brazil, and that of Brazilian society. In each of these two worlds, the relations between infrastructure and superstructure are reversed: "Where the man of African descent has succeeded in carving out a niche in which the religious values he brought with him across the ocean can flourish, those values secrete the structures. Conversely, where he occupies a position in the structures of the national society, those structures will modify the traditional values" (ibid., 375).

Thus Macumba leads to the loss of traditional values transmitted by "African religions," while "Umbanda spiritism" is the reflection of the reorganization of what remains of this "African homeland," "on new foundations and in accordance with the new attitudes of proletarianized blacks" (ibid., 295). In large, industrialized cities, "*macumba*, no longer anchored in a structured collective memory, is individualized, although it still remains a [religious] group" (ibid., 296). However, in passing from the collective form to the individual form, it degenerates, and religion becomes magic, practiced by "the lone, sinister *macumbeiro*" (ibid., 299). If Candomblé—at least, a certain type of Candomblé—is seen as a means of social control and an instrument of solidarity and communion, Macumba, on the other hand, "leads to social parasitism, to the shameless exploitation of the credulity of the lower classes, or to the unleashing of immoral tendencies that may range from rape to murder" (ibid., 300).

By basing his work on this opposition between (Nagô) Candomblé, a supportive community, and Macumba (and with it, the Bantu cults from which it originates), the seat of the degradation of African values, Bastide constructs a theory of the interpenetration of civilizations and questions the relations which exist between social structures and religious values. He takes into account the cultural change—an expression he prefers to the overly general concept of acculturation (ibid., 382)—taking place in the "Afro-Brazilian sects," while respecting the idea (which has become commonplace in anthropological literature) of the traditionalism of Nagô Candomblé.[3] Bastide identifies the world of traditional Candomblé as a place where collective values and representations dominate social structures. On the other hand, in Macumba and the "syncretic sects" of the Southeast, the loss of traditional values leads to the dissolution of the original solidarity. This degradation is also expressed in an opposition between the group and the individual: while in the most traditional Candomblé, the group predominates, thus culturally determining "the content and the expression of African mysticism," in Macumba, especially Paulist Macumba, "individual complexes tend to play a more important role than tradition" (ibid., 379).

In this manner, Bastide establishes a kind of law, according to which each time control of the group is relaxed, mysticism passes from the expression of collective models to the individual experience of social change, resulting in modifications in trances: "to use psychoanalytical terms, the trance of the *candomblé* still represents the triumph of the superego, i.e., of the collective norms, while the trance of syncretistic or improvised sects is the triumph of the self" (ibid., 380).

Traditional Candomblé is a closed society, barely coming into contact with "the erosive effect" of class society, while "Umbanda Spiritism," born from the new way of life in the Southeast, made mystic trance "a channel of upward social mobility or a symbolic expression of the class struggle" (ibid., 389). Traditional terreiros are, then, "axiological communities" reproducing the religious values and standards of behavior to which they are linked. Around the maintaining of these religious values, or what Bastide calls the "restoration" of African civilization, is played out the differentiation between sacred and ideological: acculturation favors the distortion of sacred values into ideologies or, in other words, the linking of these values "to different group interests" (ibid., 404).

If, however, "Umbanda Spiritism" incarnates what Bastide defines as an ideology, traditional Candomblé, as a "community niche," becomes the symbol of "cultural encystment" against the dominant society: "the more closely integration adheres to the community type, or the greater the social or cultural encystment within which it occurs, the less profound the syncretism" (ibid., 283). Nevertheless, this does not prevent the social integration of the members of these "axiological communities," for the principle of compartmentalization (*principe de coupure*) enables them to live "in two different worlds and to avoid the tensions and discords, the clash of values and the conflicting demands of the two societies" (ibid., 377).

Bastide had already used this notion to support his interpretation of the "cosmos philosophy" which organized the Nagô religion (1958, 237). In order to combine Lévy-Bruhl's law of mystical participations with Durkheim and Mauss's law of classifications, he needed to postulate the existence of "compartmentalized thinking" (*pensée coupante*), separating and demarcating the concepts. In this way, the principle of compartmentalization becomes "a hinge between the principle of participation and the principle of symbolism" (ibid., 243).

In his thesis of 1960, however, the principle of compartmentalization is no longer limited to the organization of the "subtle metaphysics" of Candomblé; it also applies to the relations which Candomblé has with mainstream society, thus becoming "an instinctive or automatic reaction, a defensive posture against anything that might disturb one's peace of mind" (1978, 386). But this ability to live in two worlds in spite of their contradictions proves to be the monopoly of "families having traditional connections with the *Candomblé*," "in communities where color prejudice is at a minimum" (ibid., 387); in the Southeast, the class struggle, the degradation of religion, and racism prevent what ought to be one of the characteristics of African thought from being maintained.

Because of the principle of compartmentalization, Bastide makes a claim for an internal difference in "Afro-Brazilian sects," established by the responses they make when faced with external changes. Thus, although in 1958 Bastide does not exclude the influence of groups' or "dominant families'" interests on cults as a whole,[4] in 1960, he definitively presents Candomblé as an island without history and without tension, the supreme example of a communal world threatened by capitalist society. The theory of cultural encystment would seem, then, to reproduce the myth of paradise lost.

In reality, religious changes brought about by the need to adapt to new events are present in both traditional Candomblé and "syncretic sects": "The changes which may affect the religious systems are therefore only . . . phenomena of adaptation and re-tuning with regard to a reality which is not of a religious nature. They are the effects of 'return' or 'repercussion' or a 'chain reaction in a *gestalt*'" (Bastide 1969, 9). It is by following an internal logic that religious mutations occur, always within a certain gestalt, a configuration or pattern "given by the previous state of the sacred" (ibid., 12). For Bastide, the words "mutation" and "change" are contradictory to the very idea of religion; in his eyes, all religion tries to commemorate origins which are updated through rites. Therefore, for traditional religions, he prefers to talk of emergence rather than mutation, as though each mutation was already present, in latent form, in the "archaic nucleus of the sacred" (ibid., 9). The function of this notion of emergence is to conceal discontinuities under the idea of continuity.

To justify the emergence of new elements which preexisted in the gestalt of traditional religion, Bastide uses Halbwachs's notion of collective memory. Memory is thought to be inscribed in a determined place and to be linked to a social group, as "memories are always articulated in respect to interrelationships within an organized collectivity" (Bastide 1978, 382–83). The collective memory can be activated only if the ancestral institutions have been preserved. Building on Halbwachs, Bastide sees an analogy for collective memory in the physiologist's view of the brain: "Africans' transplantation to the New World poses a similar problem to that of cerebral lesions; and, of course, because amnesia may be only temporary, of the subsequent formation of new mnemonic centers in the brain" (1970b, 85). If everything is preserved in the collective memory, it is possible to reconstitute the past by recreating the severed links with the original culture. It is a question of filling the gaps left by the uprooting of slavery and by the structure of secrecy at the origin of Candomblé's hierarchy. However, not all the images of tradition can be reactivated, only those which are in accordance with the present (Halbwachs 1925, 401).

Bastide uses the selection of revived memories in another opposition which distinguishes Nagô Candomblé from syncretic cults. The latter opt for purging, "in eliminating from the social heritage whatever is too incompatible with modern society, whatever shocks people by reminding them too brutally of barbarism"; Nagô Candomblé, on the other hand, opts for purification, which "will necessarily take the form of a return to the true original tradition behind these decadent forms" (Bastide 1978, 340). It is, therefore, to resist the subtle influence of the white people's world that "traditional sects" have become stricter, aiming to remain true to their original values:

> This "return to Africa," to use the expression of Couto Ferraz, has been translated into action by uniting all the traditional sects into one federation, which then excommunicates "syncretized" sects. Today a movement is under way to purify the *candomblés* in reaction against the debasement of the *macumba* and to deepen the religious faith of their members. (Ibid., 169)

This return to Africa, which has always been present in Candomblé, is the reactivation, symbolic rather than real, of a pure tradition which must be reconstituted on Brazilian soil. The need to do so becomes more urgent

36. A caboclo's
manifestation.
PHOTO BY AUTHOR.

with the increase of the nefarious effects of tourism and of whites' and
mulattos' participation in Candomblé, which create an ever-widening gap
between "traditional" terreiros and those which "seek esthetics as much as
religion":

> This movement of disintegration has been compensated for by a ten-
> dency to the contrary, where new means of communication play a very
> important role—the reinforcement of roots in Africa, fed by the comings
> and goings between Brazil and Nigeria of men, merchandise and ideas.
> We are faced with two tendencies: one tending toward an "Americaniza-
> tion," which encompasses the huge expansion of Caboclo Candomblé or
> wild trances, a tendency which is opposed to the other, founded upon the
> search for a re-Africanization and Afro-Americans' awareness of their
> intrinsic condition [as African descendants]. (Bastide 1973, xv)

The "initiatory" journey to Africa became more and more important in the process of reinforcing roots, leading to a re-Africanization at any price, through courses in divination and in Yoruba language and civilization.

From Brazil to a Mythical Africa

Descendants of Africans first traveled back and forth between Brazil and Africa during the second half of the nineteenth century, when the movement of returning to the west coast of Africa intensified among freed slaves. The movement, which began in 1835 with the failure of rebellions in Bahia and the expulsion of the condemned rebels, soon took on, for members of Candomblé, the nature of a symbolic journey toward the land of their origins: going to Africa signified making contact with the source of religious knowledge and of tradition which had been broken up by slavery. By 1868, a large Brazilian colony was present on Nigerian soil. The former slaves, known as "Brazilians" in Africa, were concentrated in Lagos, where they formed a community which distinguished itself from the local Africans by its dress, Catholic faith, and the reproduction of Brazilian folklore. The "Brazilians" were—and felt—different from the Africans, for they saw themselves as agents of progress and civilization in an Africa still plunged in barbarism. Brazil, on the other hand, was a paradise where men were happy, masters benevolent, and nature generous. From being a collective tragedy, slavery thus metamorphosed into a civilizing myth (Cunha 1985, 145).

This "Brazilian" community, whose dimensions vary in different reports,[5] became the reference point for former slaves who came back to Africa, especially to Lagos (Nigeria). Paradoxically, beginning in the last decade of the nineteenth century, the community, which had made Catholicism the symbol of its identity, became the inspiration for a return to the roots of Yoruba culture. By adopting traditional names and clothing, and through their interest in Yoruba traditions and history, the "Brazilians," regarded as foreigners in Africa, opened the way toward what Cunha (ibid., 13) calls a "metatraditionalism" which was to mark the emergence of the concept of nation in Nigeria (see Peel 2000). In parallel, in Brazil, the journeys to Africa were transformed—in oral tradition—into initiatory voyages, erasing the ignominious scars of slavery. While for the "Brazilian" residents of Lagos, slavery was transformed into a civilizing myth, the journey to the land of origins became a source of prestige for members of Candomblé, through the direct contact with their roots, transforming former slaves or their descendants into "Africans."

Several stories remain about the most renowned characters of Bahian Candomblé's travels between Brazil and Africa. Their prestige seems to arise, for the most part, directly from the fact of having accomplished the journey, proving their traditionalism. These stories are the founding myths of Nagô purity and tradition.

The first of these mythical journeys was made by Iyá Nassô, the founder of the Casa Branca terreiro. Versions of this story differ from one author to another.[6] This terreiro—which, according to Carneiro, was founded in 1830 by three African women (Iyá Adêtá, Iyá Kalá, and Iyá Nassô)—gave birth to two other terreiros regarded as the birthplace of the Nagô tradition—the Gantois and the Axé Opô Afonjá. According to Verger (1981, 28), the names of the founders, "originally from Ketu,"[7] were Iyalussô Danadana, who went back to Africa to die there, and Iyanassô Akalá or Iyanassô Oká, who was helped by Babá Assiká. Iyanassô made the journey to Ketu in the company of Marcelina da Silva (Obá Tossi), her spiritual daughter, or, according to other versions, her biological daughter.[8] Iyanassô, Obá Tossi, and her daughter Magdalena spent seven years in Ketu, where Obá Tossi's daughter had three more children, the youngest of whom, Claudiana, was the mother of Maria Bibiana do Espírito Santo, Mãe Senhora, of whom Verger was the "spiritual son" (ibid., 29). The group then returned to Bahia, accompanied by an African, Rodolfo Martins de Andrade (Bamboxé). Obá Tossi was to become the second mãe-de-santo of the Casa Branca upon the death of Iyanassô and was to initiate Aninha, the founder of the Axé Opô Afonjá.

Bastide (1978, 165) accepts Carneiro's version, but he quotes only Iyá Nassô. He underlines the fact that "Carneiro makes no mention of a point of great interest to us, namely that even though Iyá Nassô was connected with Bahia through her mother (who was a slave there before she returned to Africa to enter the priesthood), she was born in Nigeria and went to Bahia of her own accord, as a free woman, accompanied by a *wassa* (a member of the priesthood), to found a *candomblé*—the one at Engenho Velho."[9] Obá Tossi, who had also come from Africa "of her own free will," returned to her country later, "no doubt to perfect her knowledge of the cult and initiate herself more deeply into its secrets" (ibid.), returning to Brazil after seven years to replace Iyá Nassô as the mãe-de-santo of Casa Branca.

In Verger's version, the three founders were freed slaves, members of the brotherhood of Our Lady of the Good Death. Iyá Nassô's journey to Africa proves the "purity" of Senhora's family, whose mother was born on African soil—what's more, at Ketu, the birthplace of the tradition—according to Verger. Bastide's version (1978, 165) describes Iyá Nassô as an African "free woman," "born in Nigeria," whose mother had been a slave in Brazil before returning to Africa "to enter the priesthood." The founder of the first Brazilian Candomblé is thus legitimized twice over, for she was born in the ancestors' land and was the daughter of a priestess of the cult, becoming the incarnation of the African tradition. Obá Tossi, also having come freely from Africa, returned to the land of her birth in a quest for knowledge before becoming the new mãe-de-santo of the Casa Branca.

However, this second version is even more problematic than the first. It is hard to imagine that the spiritual daughter of the first mãe-de-santo of Brazil would need to return to Africa "to perfect her knowledge of the cult," as she had been initiated by an African priestess, herself the daughter of another African priestess. The founding myth of Candomblé in Brazil seems to be built upon a lack of full knowledge and the perpetual search for forgotten secrets. Africa thus becomes the place of the symbolic erasure of the infamous mark left by slavery and, at the same time, the locus of incomplete knowledge, forcing the cult members into an incessant quest for lost ritual knowledge.

The third journey to Africa, which also appears as a founding myth, is that of Martiniano Eliseu do Bonfim, Nina Rodrigues's informant and collaborator, and a legendary figure of Bahia Candomblé.[10] His father—a member of the Egba, one of the Yoruba subgroups—had been brought to Brazil as a slave in 1820 and liberated there in 1842 (Oliveira and Costa Lima 1987, 50). Martiniano, born around 1859, went with his father to Nigeria for the first time in 1875, staying in Lagos until 1886. This first journey earned Martiniano great prestige among the practitioners of Candomblé, and very soon he became a much sought-after babalaô (diviner) (Verger 1981, 32).[11] In 1910, Martiniano helped Aninha (Eugenia Ana dos Santos), who had been initiated by Obá Tossi and had then distanced herself from the Casa

Branca, to found the Axé Opô Afonjá. During her long trips to Rio de Janeiro, Aninha conferred the leadership of the terreiro upon Senhora de Oxum (who became the second mãe-de-santo of the Axé Opô Afonjá).[12] In 1935, when she returned definitively to Bahia, Aninha began, once again, to collaborate with Martiniano, who introduced into his terreiro the African institution of the obás of Xangô, discussed later in the chapter.

Landes (1994) offers us an extremely vivid portrait of cult life, in which we find the best-known figures of traditional Candomblé in Bahia. The author appears to have assimilated perfectly the cults' internal logic, which relies on gossip, a powerful communication tool in Candomblé, used as much for individual power strategies as for circulating information. In fact, most of the information transmitted by the oral tradition arises from the "mechanisms of gossip at work in the political structures of the terreiros" and so should be analyzed as instruments of "the ideology of prestige" (Oliveira and Costa Lima 1987, 154). Around this gossiping, extremely important in the world of Candomblé, interest groups confront one another and assert their power. Gossip seems to be a catalyst of the social process (Paine 1967).

Even if Landes is not always conscious of the political use made of this information or the underlying logic of accusation between terreiros, her text clearly reveals an elaborated and purified tradition which does not always correspond to reality. Landes met Martiniano when he was eighty years old. He was regarded as "an institution in Bahia, indeed throughout Brazil," because he studied "the tribal lore of his ancestors in the bush itself, and also [learned] English at the mission school" (Landes 1994, 22). Since Aninha's death in 1938, the old man no longer visited the terreiros because he felt that the tradition had already been lost, and that young people did not want to know the truth. Landes wrote about how the reputation of being a sorcerer weighed upon him:

> Temple followers thought that he had performed magic for Aninha during his long service at her temple, magic which she needed to have done, but which her priestly vows would not allow her to perform. He was in fact indispensable to her, unlike any other *ogan*, and her success grew with the association. She was the priestess, he was the sorcerer. (Ibid., 209)

The author had obviously heard these accusations in other terreiros, especially in the Gantois, where she carried out her research. The accusations are an example of gossip, whose aim is to contest adversaries' legitimacy. Nevertheless, Landes tried to discover whether or not Martiniano practiced magic. She went to his house, accompanied by a hairdresser who had been instructed to ask for a despacho, considered at the time to be a work of black magic. Martiniano agreed, but during the divination, he demanded a large sum of money: "the first question I gave you free; but after that you must pay" (ibid., 215). Landes was left with an image of him as an "old sorcerer at bay" (ibid., 216). She never met him again.

During the 1930s, journeys to Africa, which had become no longer founding myths but mechanisms of legitimation, continued to be a means of improving religious status for members of Afro-Brazilian religions. This was the case for Pai Adão in Recife, who undertook such a voyage "to undergo initiation rites" (Bastide 1978, 165). The prestige that he gained from this enabled him to claim power within his house of worship: "on his return, having succeeded in taking control of the religious group into which he had been initiated, thanks to the prestige acquired because of his journey and in spite of the normal rules of succession, he introduced a series of innovations in the group's practices which considerably changed the rituals followed until this time; the contra-acculturative influence of this character deserves in-depth study" (René Ribeiro 1978, 108).[13]

However, the initiatory journey to Africa did not signify a desire to become African, for—as Freyre points out (quoted in Lody 1979, 14), talking of Pai Adão—Candomblé members who traveled to Africa kept their Brazilian identity: "he himself once told me that he always felt like a foreigner among Africans . . . as someone who longed to return to Brazil." These journeys, then, were undertaken with the view of acquiring knowledge, which would lead to prestige on returning to Brazil. They were, and still are, formidable political instruments.

Pierre Verger, or the Messenger's Role

The most emblematic figure of this quest for African roots was Verger. He arrived in Brazil in 1946, after a long period of travel through Latin America. In São Paulo, he met Bastide, who advised him to go to Bahia to rediscover

Africa, which he already knew, having worked as a photographer there. Verger arrived in Salvador on August 5, 1946. He was charmed by the city and its religious cults, and he decided to establish himself there.

As Bastide says (1958, 9), Verger tried, in comparing Africa and Bahia, to bring out "the Bahian Negroes' fidelity to Africa." The spiritual son of the mãe-de-santo of the Axé Opô Afonjá, Senhora de Oxum, who had succeeded Aninha, Verger was not particularly interested in anthropology at the time; during his successive travels in Africa, he took notes only in order to "fulfill his role of messenger" and so be able to "describe Africa" to his Bahian friends (Métraux and Verger 1994, 62).

In 1952, he set off for Porto Novo in Benin, from where he made brief trips to Nigeria. It was during one of these excursions that he obtained a letter from the king of Oshogbo for Senhora. He mentions it to Métraux in a letter dated January 27, 1953: "I returned from Nigeria yesterday, rich with several new forms of salutation to the orishas, six pebbles from the river Oshun, some divine knick-knacks and a letter of a king's compliments to Senhora, my Bahian mother" (ibid., 158).[14] However, the greatest sign of recognition that Verger brought back from Africa for his Bahian mãe-de-santo was a letter from the Aláàfin of Oyó addressed to Senhora, granting her the title of Ìyá Nasó, which, as we have seen, was the oyè (title) of the woman in charge of the cult of Xangô in the royal palace of Oyó, in Nigeria, but also the name of the founder of the Casa Branca. Senhora's son, Deoscóredes dos Santos (1988, 18–19), remembers the event:

In August 1952, Pierre Verger arrived from Africa with a xeré [ritual bell] and an edu ara [sacred stone of Xangô], which had been entrusted to him by the Ona Mogba [Xangô priest], on the instructions of the Obá Adeniran Adeyemi, Alafin Oyo, to be delivered to Maria Bibiana do Espirito Santo, Senhora. These gifts were accompanied by a letter, granting her the title of Iyanassô, which was confirmed in the Axé Opô Afonjá terreiro on August 9, 1953, in the presence of all the "sons" of the House, representatives of several terreiros, intellectuals, friends of the cult, writers, journalists, etc. This event marked the renewal of the former religious ties between Africa and Bahia, which became even closer afterward, as Mãe Senhora maintained a constant exchange of gifts and messages with kings and other important people from the cult in Africa.

The symbolic value of this missive, which the direct descendant of the god Xangô in Africa[15] addressed to Senhora, was essential for her to assert her authority, for she was mãe-de-santo of a terreiro of whom Xangô was the protecting orixá. Furthermore, with this title, Senhora became the legitimate custodian of the true tradition of the Nagôs: "by erasing the time passed, because of this distinction, Senhora spiritually became the founder of this family of Candomblé of the Ketu nation in Bahia, all originally from the Engenho Velho" (Verger 1981, 30).

Senhora's consecration was completed during the celebration of her fifty years of initiation to the goddess Oxum in November 1958, when an impressive number of influential people from Bahia, Rio, and São Paulo, as well as the president of the republic, Juscelino Kubitschek, and the minister for education, participated in the commemoration. Zora Seljan, a journalist and "friend of the terreiro" presented Senhora as the "Dame of the Ketu nation," adding that "the heritage of the Nagô culture is religiously preserved in her hands, because the history of Candomblé in Brazil coincides with the history of her family" (quoted in Deoscóredes dos Santos 1988, 20). In the reconstruction of the direct lineage of Mãe Senhora from Iyá Nassô, founder of Nagô (Ketu) Candomblé in Bahia, Marcelina da Silva (Obá Tossi), her great-grandmother, becomes the biological, rather than spiritual, daughter of Iyá Nassô: "and so Senhora is related by birth to African princes and kings, who correspond with her and send her gifts" (ibid.).

In 1965, Senhora was elected "Black Mother of the Year" during a solemn ceremony which took place in the Maracanã stadium in Rio de Janeiro. In 1966, the Senegalese government awarded her the Knights' Order of Merit "for her ceaseless activity in favor of the preservation of African culture" (Santos and Santos 1993a, 161). When she died, on February 22, 1967, huge crowds attended her funeral. Her son, Deoscóredes dos Santos (also known as Mestre Didi), did not attend the ceremonies, for, like others before him, he had left for Africa, accompanied by his wife, Juana Elbein dos Santos, and Pierre Verger.

Verger had spent many years between Brazil and Africa, where, in 1953, he had been initiated to the cult of Ifá and had become a babalawo, under the ritual name of Fatumbi (Ifá has put me back into the world). Through his travels, he was a vehicle for the flow of information which symbolically bound Brazil to Africa.[16] Following the creation in 1959 of the Centro de

37. Omolu's assento.
PHOTO BY AUTHOR.

Estudos Afro-Orientais, anthropologists began to replace initiates in trips
to Africa, in a similar quest for the "secrets" of African religions.

By 1959, the date of the fourth Luso-Brazilian Symposium in Bahia, it
had already been decided to create a chair for the teaching of the Yoruba
language at the University of Bahia. The chair was filled for two years by the
Nigerian Ebenezer Latunde Lashebikan. Thus Africa was transported to
Brazil to "purify" the religion, as Verger indicates in a letter to Métraux
dated October 1, 1960:

> We have a course in Yoruba at the University of Bahia, given by Ebenezer
> Lashebikan, a native of Nigeria, who has come especially for this pur-
> pose, called by the University Rector. We are at the sixth lesson, and
> there has been a flood of descendants of Nigerians to re-learn to speak a
> language that they still know how to chant. All the Gotha [elite] of the

Afro-Brazilian Sect are there. But there is nothing but anger to be expected from Melville J. Herskovits and Frances, his wife, when they learn that the field of cultural experience that this good city once was has thus been so savagely "damaged." (Métraux and Verger 1994, 294)[17]

During the 1960s, researchers from the Centro de Estudos Afro-Orientais traveled mostly to West Africa, as in 1967 did Deoscóredes dos Santos, who received a grant from UNESCO "with the aim of acquiring, through his observations, a more profound and exact vision of the evolution and acculturation process of Brazilian blacks, essentially on a religious level" (Oliveira 1976, 116). Deoscóredes dos Santos and his wife—the anthropologist Juana Elbein dos Santos, who had been initiated by Senhora in 1964 (Juana E. dos Santos 1976, 15)—set off for Dahomey (now Benin) with the aim of visiting the king of Ketu, accompanied by Verger, "known to everyone as babalaô Fatumbi and the king's friend" (Deoscóredes dos Santos 1988, 35). On being presented to the king by Verger, Deoscóredes recited the oríkì of his African lineage: Asipá Borogun Elesé Kan Gongôô. He was then recognized as the descendant of the Aṣipá family, "one of the seven principal founding families of the kingdom of Ketu" (ibid., 36).

This oríkì, in fact, refers to aṣípa, an honorary title very widely used in Yorubaland. Originally it was the title of one of the seven members of the Ọ̀yọ́-Mèsì, the council formed by the dominant nonroyal lineages of the city of Oyó. Samuel Johnson (1957, 72), who wrote a monumental history of Oyó, defined it as follows: "He performs the duties of the junior. He is called the 'Ojùwá,' i.e. the one who distributes whatever presents are given to the Ọ̀yọ́-Mèsì." But the title spread through most of the Yoruba kingdoms, which, at the time of the Oyó empire, modeled their political and military organization after the metropolis: "the Aṣípa is a title borrowed from Ọ̀yọ́ to satisfy any war-chief who, being equal by merit to the Ọ̀tun and Òsì, yet just missed becoming either" (ibid., 133). Aṣípa, then, was an honorary title rather than a hereditary one, belonging to a war chief, fourth in the hierarchy after the balógun (lord in war), and the ọ̀tun and the òsì balógun, his substitutes "on the right" and "on the left." Robert Smith (1988, 74) writes of a war chief who was named governor of Lagos at the beginning of the seventeenth century, when the city was only a military camp. He had to represent the interests of the ọba (king) of Benin (a large kingdom to the east of Yorubaland, not to be confused with present-day Benin): "the man chosen is named in both Lagos and Benin tradition as Ashipa" (ibid.). Similarly, Chief J. B. Akinyele, in his *History of Ibadan*, cites *aṣípa kakanfò* (the title of the head of the army) as one of the very common names in Ibadan which, when it was founded at the beginning of the nineteenth century, was a military camp (quoted in Costa Lima 1966, 31). Samuel Johnson also mentions an Aṣípa who was army chief during the war between the Ibadan and the Ijesha in 1869, and another Aṣípa of the Ekitiparapo, who was a hostage in the hands of the Ibadan in 1886 (1957, 379 and 551). Abraham (1958, 176) also quotes the aṣípa of Owu when referring to the tribal wars of the Egba.

Therefore, the oríkì that Deoscóredes dos Santos recited could easily be understood in any Yoruba kingdom as the praise name of an army chief (the rest of the oríkì is difficult to translate owing to the absence of tones, but Borogun seems to refer to war, *ogun*). If it were a hereditary title, it would be connected to the city of Oyó (the nonroyal lineages of the Òyọ-Mèsì) and not to that of Ketu. Among other things, in his *The Story of Ketu* (1956), Parrinder talks of only five royal lineages in this city. It would seem, then, that the founding myth of this Candomblé family is the result of a bricolage of the history of Yoruba kingdoms, which aims to eliminate the less traditional elements. In fact, the oríkì recited in front of the king of Ketu was that of Obá Tossi, the great-grandmother of Deoscóredes dos Santos's mother Senhora, purified of any traces of less traditional origins.[18]

Three years later, in 1970, Santos returned to Nigeria and was confirmed as Balé Xangô (head of the Xangô cult) in the principal temple of Oyó, at a ceremony organized for him by Wande Abimbola. On his return to Brazil, he became the "continuator of Senhora's work to preserve and valorize Afro-Brazilian culture" (Deoscóredes dos Santos 1988, 36). More recent were the equally prestigious visits of the fourth and current mãe-de-santo of the Axé Opô Afonjá, Mãe Stella (Stella de Azevedo Santos), known by her African name Odekayodé (Oxossi brings the arrival of joy); Olga de Alaketu (Olga Francisca Regis), "descendant of the royal family of Ketu" (Costa Lima 1977, 28); and Obarain (Balbino Daniel de Paula) of the Axé Opô Aganjú terreiro.

The logic which sees a journey to Africa more as a means of acquiring lost knowledge than as a means of increasing one's prestige in the religious world becomes central to the re-Africanization movement in São Paulo, inciting several pais and mães-de-santo to make the pilgrimage to the mythical land. With these journeys, the re-Africanized terreiros of São Paulo distanced themselves from Brazilian Candomblé—even the most traditional—as they created direct links with the original culture. This is what occurred in the terreiro of Sandra de Xangô (Sandra Medeiros), who, in 1983, affiliated herself to a Nigerian babalawo, Donald Epega, with whom she created a re-Africanized Ketu rite: "in trying to eliminate from their practices any kind of syncretism or development regarded as inappropriate for the cult of the orixás, and in using as a model what is currently practiced in Africa, these priests have 'reconstituted' the Ketu nation and have distanced themselves from the transformations which were the result of its installation in Brazil" (Vagner Gonçalves da Silva 1992, 89).

The effects of these priests' return to "African purity"—including the honorary titles as well as anthropologists' recognition of their legitimacy—are directly reflected in the success of their houses of worship, often honored by what Vagner Gonçalves da Silva calls "attestations of competence bestowed by erudite works." The growing demand for trips to Nigeria—and to a lesser extent Benin—led travel agents in Rio de Janeiro and São Paulo to promote organized trips for Candomblé initiates (ibid., 243). And so, as during Martiniano do Bonfim's day, Lagos became the Mecca of Afro-Brazilian religions.

The Obás of Xangô: The First Example of Re-Africanization

The modification of rituals introduced by re-Africanized pais and mães-de-santo are one of the most obvious consequences of these journeys to Africa in search of a lost tradition. The innovations are not made without creating certain tensions with the mother terreiros, which do not always accept them willingly. After all, which traditions should be respected and perpetuated—one passed on by "traditional" terreiros, or one sought directly on African soil? The very legitimacy of the mediation of the great religious centers of Bahia is at stake here.

Thanks to anthropologists and initiates visiting Africa, we have seen that the "pure African tradition" is constructed around a common religious syllabus which, from the Casa Branca, passing through the Gantois, is

38. *Olubajé*, the annual festival for Omolu. PHOTO BY AUTHOR.

crystallized in the Axé Opô Afonjá. Nonetheless, it is this very house of worship which has modified its ritual, for the first time, by introducing the institution known as the obás (ministers) of Xangô. It involves a group of *olóyè* (cult dignitaries, holders of honorary titles) connected with the cult of Xangô, the patron divinity of the Axé Opô Afonjá. The institution was brought back from Africa by Martiniano do Bonfim, Aninha's closest collaborator. Martiniano's many trips to Nigeria had earned him such prestige that he had become, in the eyes of the cult's initiates as well as scholars, the interpreter of Africa on Brazilian soil.

It was during the second Afro-Brazilian Congress in 1937, even before the obás were officially introduced in the Axé Opô Afonjá (Costa Lima 1966, 6),[19] that Martiniano revealed the existence in the terreiro of the "African institution" of the obás of Xangô. He related the Yoruba oral tradition about the death and deification of Xangô, the third Aláàfin of Oyó: Xangô was the powerful master of a large kingdom, but two of his vassals, Timi and Gbonka, threatened his power. Xangô tried to get them killed by setting them against each other, but they escaped from their trials unscathed. Xangô then fled his palace with one of his wives, Yansan (Oyá), and hanged himself from a tree in the forest. A storm of such violence as had never been seen before raged over the city of Oyó, with blasts of thunder and lightning: it was a sign that Xangô had become a divinity. His cult was instituted in the city, and thunder became the god's symbol.

According to Martiniano do Bonfim's version (1950, 347), the ministers of Xangô, the *mangbas*,[20] formed a council responsible for maintaining his cult, "organized just as the twelve ministers on earth had accompanied him, six on the right side, and six on the left." This, then, is an African institution, faithfully reproduced in Bahia: "These ministers, former kings, princes or governors of territories conquered by Shango's bravery, did not allow the hero's memory to fade in future generations. This is why, in a Bahian terreiro dedicated to Shango Afonja, twelve *ogan*s, protectors of the temple, bear the title of ministers of Shango" (Verger 1957, 314).

The list that Martiniano presented at the 1937 congress was somewhat different from the one we know today. According to Costa Lima (1966, 34), himself an obá of Xangô of the Axé Opô Afonjá, the modification of the names of the ministers of Xangô was due to the fact that Martiniano had been "hurried by the organizers [of the congress] to present a communication" and it was only later that he elaborated the partition of the obás into two groups, right and left.

The polarization between the right (òtun) and left (òsì) can be found in the religious and political organization of the Yoruba. In the Axé Opô Afonjá terreiro, the names of the obás on the right are Obá Abiodun, Obá Aré, Obá Arolu, Obá Telá, Obá Odofin, and Obá Cancanfó; those on the left are called Obá Onanxocun, Obá Areçá, Obá Elerin, Obá Onicoí, Obá Olugbon, and Obá Xorun (ibid., 7).[21] All these names are also found in Samuel Johnson's *The History of the Yorubas* (1957), published for the first time in 1921 in Nigeria. Later, Costa Lima (1966) traced the origin of each of these terms, which form a group of names and honorary titles (oyè) reproducing the history of Oyó in Brazil. Thus, Abiodun is the name of the twenty-ninth Aláàfin of Oyó, who reigned from 1789 to 1796; Aré and Cancanfó refer to the chief of the armies;[22] Arolu is a title from the Ogboni society;[23] Telá means a member of the royal line of Oyó; Odofin is a title from the Ibolo, who lived in one of the provinces of the Oyó empire; Onanxocun is derived from ọnọ̀n-ìṣokùn, one of the king's "three fathers," who was chosen from the same branch of the royal lineage as that of the new king; Aresa (or Areça) is the chief of Iresa, part of the metropolitan province of Oyó (Ẹ̀kún Òsì), just as Onicoí is the chief of Ikoyi, and Olugbon the chief of Igbon; Elerin signifies the chief of the city of Erin. The last of the obás of the left is Obá Xorun, whose name refers to Baṣorun, the chief of the Ọ̀yọ́-Mèsì, the council of Oyó. A kind of prime minister, he held great power and was linked to the dominant lineages of the city. He performed very important ritual and political functions, and it was he who ratified the choice of the new Aláàfin; it was also he who, if the king's conduct was not satisfactory, presented him with parrot's eggs, which was a sign of his obligation to commit suicide. This was, then, one of the biggest responsibilities in the Oyó empire.

It is clear that the titles in Martiniano's list are the result of a bricolage of Yoruba history.[24] All the titles of the obás of Xangô are collected in Johnson (1957), written before 1887 and published in 1921, which constituted a reference for Yoruba history studied in the mission schools in Nigeria. The influence of Martiniano's trips to Nigeria is very clear: "Martiniano's lectures on Yoruba traditions in Lagos, and the large body of oral traditions with which he was no doubt familiar, enabled him to recreate with Aninha the titles of the obás of the Axé Opô Afonjá, evoking the names and oyè of 'kings, princes and governors' of the Yoruba nation" (Costa Lima 1966, 9).

The obás of Xangô, the fruit of a reconstruction of the past destined to reinforce the Yoruba (Nagô) origins of the terreiro, became for Aninha, its founder, a sign of her close ties to the land of origins, and thus of her great traditionalism, as she declared to Pierson: "My terreiro is purely Nagô, like the Engenho Velho [Casa Branca]. But I have resuscitated a large part of the African tradition that even the Engenho Velho had forgotten. Do they have a ceremony in honor of the twelve ministers of Xangô? No! But I do!" (quoted in Costa Lima 1977, 20).

Aninha's pride in this resuscitated tradition reveals its importance in the politics of the terreiros, as it enables her to emphasize her Nagô purity. She founded her terreiro, the Axé Opô Afonjá, after a split with the Casa Branca.

It was, therefore, necessary to distinguish the new terreiro from the mother-house, through a surplus of traditionalism. The second Afro-Brazilian Congress of 1937 was the perfect occasion to establish this difference, with the benediction of the intellectuals present. Most authors who criticize the valorization of the Nagô model attribute the imposition of a model of purity to the conscious action of intellectuals, in order to better control the cults (Dantas 1988; see also Matory 2005). The example analyzed here, on the other hand, allows us to see the agency of the Bahian Candomblé leaders, notably those connected to the terreiro in question, who succeeded in imposing their own vision of tradition upon the intellectuals.

Upon analysis, the political nature of the institution of the obás of Xangô becomes evident. The obás can be defined as the elite ogans, an honorary title for men. Like the ogans, they are the terreiro's protectors and its primary source of prestige: "Aninha chose her obás from among the ogans and 'friends of the house,' people whose behavior she appreciated and whose social position and prestige rebounded upon the terreiro. The first obás were chosen, then, from among the most enlightened ogans, of the highest position in the group, who were stable and prosperous in their businesses and professions, respected and well connected" (Costa Lima 1966, 9).[25]

Aninha's death in 1938 sparked a "period of tension caused by the more or less flagrant struggle for succession in the terreiro" (ibid.). Senhora, the new mãe-de-santo, had difficulty in imposing her authority because, for a long time, most positions in the religious hierarchy of the terreiro were occupied by ebomis (priestesses initiated for longer than seven years), theoretically all candidates to succeed Aninha—such as Ondina Pimentel, who was to be the third mãe-de-santo of the Axé Opô Afonjá. Senhora was under forty years old when she was chosen, even though she was one of the terreiro's most senior daughters-of-saint, having been initiated at the age of eight. She had close religious ties with Aninha, for her great-grandmother (Obá Tossi) had been Aninha's mãe-de-santo. This complicated choice also affected the institution of the obás of Xangô: "Because of this, several obás, former ogans of the house of worship to which they were connected through ties of friendship or family, distanced themselves either gradually or brusquely from the Axé [terreiro], for they refused precisely the ritual supremacy of a new iyalorixá with such a strong personality as Senhora de Oxum" (ibid.).

Because the obás were life members, their distancing themselves caused problems, and so Senhora decided to appoint replacements for them and also to modify their number. Each of the obás, who were already divided into those on the right and those on the left, gained an *otun* obá and an *ossi* obá—i.e., a replacement on the right and another on the left. Thus the original twelve members became thirty-six. It was due to this alteration within an institution which she conceived of as profoundly political that Senhora managed to assert her power in the terreiro: "The first otuns continued to be 'friends of the house,' ogans of the terreiro who had been there since the 'time of the late Aninha,' but there were also friends of the [new] iyalorixá or who had supported her during the period of stabilization of the terreiro's succession" (ibid.).

Gossip arose from the tension thus created, in which the "orthodoxy of the olden days"[26] was constantly regretted. The new obás were selected from friends of the terreiro—"and its visitors"—all belonging to the upper classes, but not always connected to the cult by real religious commitment: "the group of obás gradually turned, from an auxiliary group of the house [of worship] on a ritual and socio-economic level, into a terreiro's support on a purely socio-economic level" (ibid., 23).[27] For the senior obás, this was an unacceptable innovation, as they believed in the true African origins of this tradition, which proved to be a political instrument to establish Senhora's religious power. The recruitment of obás and their replacements among the most important intellectuals in Bahia (but also among some foreigners) allowed her to legitimize her position.[28]

As we have seen, Verger's arrival and his various travels in Africa represented a formidable support for Senhora. The African titles she received through Verger endowed her with such prestige that, long after her death, her son was able to write in the history of the Axé Opô Afonjá terreiro that Senhora became the terreiro's iyalorixá "as was her right, for she came from a traditional family of the Ketu nation" (Deoscóredes dos Santos 1988, 16). Senhora's power reflected upon the entire terreiro, thus serving as an example of what Hobsbawm and Ranger (1983) call an invented tradition, where history is exploited with the aim of consolidating the cohesion of the group and legitimizing its actions.

The recreation of a tradition from historical data is always presented, especially in the case of the obás of Xangô, as the updating of a past or

39. Logunedé, Alvinho de Omolu's second *orixá* manifestation. PHOTO BY AUTHOR.

original tradition which has been momentarily lost. In reality, as Robin Horton states (1990, 86), even members of the most traditionalist communities rework to their own ends the worldview they have inherited, "up until they apply it to everyday life, according to their own self-interest." However, this adaptation must always be hidden under the cover of faithfulness to one's origins. Thus, the ritual modification made by Senhora (the otun and ossi obás) became a "logical complement" (Costa Lima 1966, 13), because it reproduced an originally Yoruba ritual logic. This reinterpretation of ritual logic—sustained, as Bastide would say, by a clearly African gestalt—aimed to highlight a limited group of elements (for example, the polarization between otun and ossi) as distinctive marks of the African tradition. But, as we have seen, the innovations to the ritual, inevitably presented as a rediscovery of part of a forgotten tradition, are used for clearly political ends, both within and outside the religious group.

The political strategies used in the world of Candomblé were kept quiet for a long time, mainly because of the ties binding anthropologists to terreiros: anthropologists, usually linked to the terreiros they study by religious ties, have at their disposal all the necessary information, but they cannot use it if they want to preserve a good relationship with their informants. They have to respect a code of conduct which obliges them to keep silent about any events which could destroy the romantic vision of a traditional Candomblé, where harmony reigns. In reality—as any researcher who is interested in Afro-Brazilian religions well knows—power and prestige are at the center of the Candomblé universe. This prestige depends upon the individual's social, economic, and political status, and the position, either inherited or acquired, that he holds in the cult's hierarchy. The accumulation of prestige (which results, for example, from legitimation by anthropologists) enables a "traditional" family-of-saint to reinforce its power, or even to found a new tradition.[29] In order to assert one's superiority, however, it is necessary to prove the inferiority of the others, since there is no power without asymmetry in social relations. The construction of a "pure African tradition," incarnated by certain terreiros, thus becomes a sign of difference—a surplus of traditionalism, and hence prestige—in comparison with the other terreiros.

Travels in Africa and the ensuing ritual modifications are, then, a powerful instrument of prestige for the individuals and terreiros concerned. These journeys would seem to be motivated by a loss of tradition in the place in which they start (Brazil), which obliges the members most concerned about lost purity to seek it in the original land (Africa). One of the fundamental reasons for this loss seems to be the structure of secrecy, linked to the difficult and incomplete transmission of knowledge from the initiators to the initiated. But what is most important in initiation, which marks the individual's entry into the religious group, is not the transmitted skills or ritual knowledge, but the formalization of the contact with spiritual entities according to the rules of an ideal model of orthodoxy which has become prescriptive. The compulsory nature of initiation seems to have the same function as travels in Africa—a source of legitimation and prestige more than the discovery of a body of knowledge to be fully acquired later. Knowledge is acquired over the years, during a long process which depends upon the good will of the initiator. Subject to the law of secrecy, knowledge is not dispensed in equal measure to all initiates; it, too, is an instrument of power in the terreiros.

Furthermore, the lack of initiation does not necessarily imply ignorance of ritual knowledge: this is true of pais and mães-de-santo from Umbanda who, once initiated into Candomblé, immediately take up their previous positions of command in their houses of worship. As Costa Lima writes (1977, 137):

> In the ideology of these pais and mães-de-santo, there is nothing that can include their groups in the category of cults which diverge totally or partially from the religious system in which they hope to participate. It is completely the opposite, for these leaders try to preserve, with a zeal equal to the most fervent of converts, the ritual models they have chosen as prescriptive, and to concretize the essential postulates of the doctrine.

Initiation is used, then, to acquire authority, which distinguishes those who know from those who do not. The experience of initiation confers a status of veracity to the words and deeds of the initiate; simple mediumship is not sufficient. During initiation, the axé (or àṣẹ, to use Yoruba spelling, as Juana Elbein dos Santos does as a sign of Africanity) is transmitted directly "from the hands and the breath of the most senior [initiates]." Words, then, become central, for they "exceed their rational semantic content to be a conductor of àṣẹ, in other words, a conductor of the power of realization" (Juana E. dos Santos 1976, 46). Knowledge is of value only to the extent that it is lived through ritual experience, when it is incorporated in an active manner.

If it is the word that transports the axé, the basis of the whole religious construction of Candomblé, the only way to have access to ritual knowledge is to find it where the axé is concentrated: in the three houses of worship considered traditional in Bahia or directly in Africa, as cult founders did. However, this same Africa which legitimized the Nagô tradition has now metamorphosed, according to the current mãe-de-santo of the Axé Opô Afonjá, Mãe Stella, into a mere object of curiosity:

> Roots exist, but they are so old! . . . I have been to Africa twice, to Lagos and Benin, but it wasn't to go and find the roots [of the cult], because I'm the descendant of Africans, not an Africanist; so I think that it is fanaticism to go seeking roots, there's no reason for it. You can go there to see if it's still possible to learn something, for it's always good to learn, but the roots are with us—we are the branches of those roots. If the roots die, the

branches cannot resist. And so our roots are here. Going to Africa is just a trend. (Quoted in Vagner Gonçalves da Silva 1992, 247).

It is, then, those who have no roots who go and seek them elsewhere—in Africa or Bahia. However, in the words of the Axé Opô Afonjá's leaders, if one really wants to understand Africa, one has to look at Brazil, where the true African tradition has been conserved. It is Brazil—that of traditional Nagô terreiros—which today can restitute the traditions lost by the Africans, as in Marianno Carneiro da Cunha's (1984, 11) description of an inverted re-Africanization:

> When I arrived in Ifé, in 1974, no-one knew the *paxorô* [ritual tool of Oxalufan] anymore. The king said to me, "Ah, it does exist; my father used to say that Oxalufan had an emblem called paxorô, which is like this and like that, but we no longer knew how to make it" . . . During my vacation in Brazil, I went to Bahia and, with Pierre Verger, we bought a paxorô which I kept with me until he arrived in Nigeria. Together we offered it as a present to the king of Ifé, the center of the cult to Oxalufan.

African tradition has been preserved in Brazil. It is incarnated in the champions of tradition, whether heads of terreiros or anthropologists. The debate about the locus of the "true" tradition is then at the center of the re-Africanization movement, shared between the direct search for tradition on African soil and the mediation of Africans who bring it to Brazil. It is the monopoly of this mythical Africa that is at stake here.

WHICH AFRICA? WHICH TRADITION?

Journeys to Africa, Yoruba language and civilization courses, the struggle against syncretism, the reappropriation of the forgotten technique of divination using odùs, and the rediscovery of an "African cultural complex" which unites different religious practices of African origin are various reactions to the same problem: how to renew the severed links with the original African culture and thus assert one's traditionalism. While in the Southeast the re-Africanization movement occurs principally through courses in Yoruba language and practices of divination, in the Northeast the debate about syncretism in Candomblé prevails. Ever since the end of the 1970s and the definitive recognition of Candomblé as a religion, the spirit which inspired the first Afro-Brazilian congresses in the 1930s has reemerged on an international level. In 1981, the first International Congress of Orisha Tradition and Culture was organized in Ilé-Ifé, in Nigeria. The congresses are referred to in Brazil as the COMTOCS and internationally as Orisa World.[1] According to *Siwaju*, the newsletter of the National Institute of Afro-Brazilian Culture and Tradition (INTECAB), which helped organize the congresses, the COMTOCS' aim was to bring together religious leaders from Africa, the Americas, and the Caribbean with the same aim in mind: to unify the tradition of the orixás through the "struggle against the fragmentation of African religion in the world" (Juana E. dos Santos 2007, 3).

With the renewed interest in black religions, anthropologists began to re-discover the old formula of Afro-Brazilian congresses, which symbolically reunited "anthropologists, artists, black leaders and pais-de-santo" (Motta 1985).

In 1983, the second COMTOC was held in Salvador, in Brazil. Among the participants was the king of Ejibo, a Yoruba city consecrated to the cult of Oxaguian, and according to Luz (1993, 84), his visit constituted "a signifi-cant moment in the transatlantic continuity of the values of the tradition of the orixás in the Americas." In 1986, following internal differences, two versions of the third COMTOC were organized, one in Ilé-Ifé (Nigeria) and the other in New York, where the fourth congress was also held, in 1988. In 1990, it was São Paulo's turn. At the same time, Yoruba language courses spread in the Southeast. Learning the language has become a way of culti-vating African roots.

The Yoruba Language in Brazil

In the beginning of the twentieth century, Nina Rodrigues (1988, 129) was already stressing the role of lingua franca which Yoruba played among the slave population in Bahia. He criticized the fact that Bantu languages were the only ones considered worthy of linguists' attention in Brazil. He added that while Kimbundu predominated in the north and southeast of the coun-try, it was Nagô (Yoruba) that prevailed in Bahia. However, he recognized that depending totally upon the memory of slaves' descendants could some-times lead to error:

> The importance of the Nagô language in Bahia is so well known that it is sometimes exaggerated. In 1899, when they arrived in this city [Sal-vador], the Catholic missionaries who traveled around Brazil in an at-tempt to collect donations for the catechesis in Africa were advised to address the city's colored population in Nagô. Father Coquard's sermon in the cathedral on January 4th was a complete fiasco . . . it was a mistake to suppose that our Creole population has maintained such a pure Nagô language that it would be able to understand the missionaries; those who spoke the language used a patois, a debased mixture of Portuguese and various African languages. (Ibid., 132)[2]

Nevertheless, this did not prevent Nina Rodrigues (who worked very closely with his key informant, Martiniano do Bonfim), from emphasizing the superiority of the Yoruba language: "it has, here, a certain literary quality which, it seems to me, no other African language in Brazil has ever had, except, perhaps, Hausa written in the Arabic alphabet by the black Muslims" (ibid.). Thirty yeas later, Carneiro (1991, 110) reaffirmed the need to study the Nagô language, which is "the Latin of Sudanese languages." In 1933, Carneiro began to learn Nagô, with Martiniano as his teacher and with the help of a guide to the language published by the African Missions Society of Lyon, in France (ibid., 113).

Learning the original language is a dream that has persisted ever since. As we have seen, in 1959, the fifth Luso-Brazilian Symposium gave rise to the creation of a professorship in Yoruba at the Centro de Estudos Orientais (CEAO) of the Federal University of Bahia. This chair was filled by Ebenezer Latunde Lashebikan, a professor who had come especially from Nigeria.[3] Afro-Brazilian religious elites attended the course, which, from 1961 onward, was taught regularly at the CEAO (Oliveira 1976, 115). In 1974, an agreement was signed by the Brazilian government, the Federal University of Bahia, and the city council of Salvador, in order to launch a program of cultural cooperation between Brazil and African countries and develop Afro-Brazilian studies (ibid., 117).

The agreement made it easier for many Nigerians to come to Brazil, either as students or as professors. This was so, in 1976, for Olabiyi Babalola Yai, "a lecturer in the Department of African Languages and Literatures, University of Ife, who was in Brazil . . . as the Yoruba language teacher in Bahia" (Abimbola 1976b, 619). The importance given to Yoruba language courses by Candomblé initiates was a reaction to what Abimbola defined as a linguistic problem: "the situation is a painful one to many of the orisa devotees who would pay any price to acquire the linguistic ability necessary for an understanding of their own repertoire" (ibid., 634). The University of Ifé decided to send Yoruba professors to the CEAO, with the aim of giving Candomblé initiates linguistic competence so that they could, at last, understand the meaning of their sacred texts. However, according to Abimbola, the orixás' worshipers in Brazil had been separated from their African counterparts for too long: the spatial distance exacerbated the "linguistic problem." He therefore suggested coordinating regular exchanges, through private or public means, to facilitate contact between initiates from America and Africa (ibid., 635).[4]

In 1977, the University of São Paulo and its Center of African Studies organized their first course in Yoruba language and culture, in the social science department. Over the next decade, more than six hundred students, mostly Candomblé pais and mães-de-santo, took this course. The Nigerian students responsible for the course soon realized that their pupils were more interested in the secrets of the religion than in the language itself: "over time, learning the language took second place, superseded by the teaching of the myths and rites of the Yoruba divinities" (Prandi and Silva 1989, 235).

At the same time as officially teaching Yoruba, these Nigerian students began giving lessons on orixá rituals. To do so, they relied on the works of the Africanists, which their knowledge of English enabled them to translate for their Brazilian public. Thus, the oral transmission, which had been the basis of learning in Candomblé, was in part replaced by the study of a collection of "sacred" works, written mostly by white anthropologists.

Vagner Gonçalves da Silva, who took part in the course, describes the consternation caused by this new source of knowledge among the initiates most attached to Brazilian tradition:

> During the course, the discovery of the existence of books revealing information usually regarded as taboo in the terreiros was greeted with great enthusiasm. The lessons and contact with Africans, as well as providing rudimentary Yoruba (which can be used to translate chants and the names of the orixás), enable us to relativize questions which, up until now, were presented as dogma, or to reconsider knowledge reputed to be "certain." I saw disappointment among many of my friends, especially those who were initiated, when they realized the difference that existed between the Brazilian orixá worship (at least as it was practised in their terreiros, mixed with other "nations" such as Angola, or subject to Catholic influence) and the cult practiced in Africa, as described by the Nigerians. Confronted with the impossibility of harmonizing the teaching received in the terreiro with that received in the course, these students then abandoned the course. However, the younger ones (in terms

of initiation age), or those who were to a greater or lesser extent in disagreement with certain Brazilian practices such as syncretism, were able to redefine some of their religious notions, and thus legitimize them "academically." (1992, 237–38)

Another example of this contradiction between a Brazilian and an African tradition is given by Márcio Pereira, a pai-de-santo from Rio de Janeiro: "What happens is that certain things we offer orixás in Africa are not accepted by the same orixá here in Brazil. I think that he has got used to it all. After four hundred years here in Brazil, wouldn't he have learnt to speak Brazilian?"

Despite these legitimate concerns, taking Yoruba language and civilization courses, as well as parallel courses on the ritual practices became synonymous with culture and proficiency in a sacerdotal career. The old pais-de-santo were almost all illiterate and without education; today, the new initiates are well-educated, go to college, and can speak other languages. The classic division between researcher and initiate is gradually fading—one has to carry out thorough research to understand one's religion, rediscovering the "true" Africa through bibliographic sources. In this way, the combination of initiation and research becomes obvious in the most re-Africanized terreiros, such as Sandra de Xangô's in São Paulo. Vagner Gonçalves da Silva (ibid., 14) explains that in this house of worship, an "intellectualized" Candomblé is practiced, as its adepts, starting with the mãe-de-santo, all have a university education: "In the *terreiro*, we use copious bibliographical sources, and research is valued as it is considered as a way of increasing religious knowledge and discovering the fundamentals of certain ritual practices."

Parallel courses developed in the most re-Africanized terreiros or in institutions created especially for this purpose, as was the case in São Paulo at the Association of the House of Afro-Brazilian Culture (ACACAB), whose aim is to promote aspects of black culture and identity, and the Foundation for the Yoruba Religion and Tradition in Brazil (FUNACULTY)—founded by Aulo Barretti, a former student at ACACAB—which offers its students a library specializing in the history, religion, and culture of the Yoruba.

The most interesting example, however, is probably that of the Oduduwa Cultural Center, founded in São Paulo by Sikiru Salami. Born in Abeokuta,

40. House of Oxalá.
PHOTO BY AUTHOR.

Nigeria, he came to Brazil in 1982; in 1990, he was in his third year as a student of social sciences at the University of São Paulo, where he concurrently taught Yoruba language and culture. The Oduduwa Cultural Center runs Yoruba language courses and also courses on divination, ebó, and magic, illustrated with videos. Oduduwa Editions also publishes books written by Nigerians on these topics. In the introduction to his study of orixá mythology, Sikiru Salami (1990, 18) writes that he does not consider himself merely a researcher, for his mission is "to rediscover the culture of the Yoruba": "Brazilians' faith and interest are among the main reasons which led to my writing a series of books on the orixás." The great demand from the religious market—this thirst for further knowledge about religion—has made the course and its publishing house a success.

Studying Odùs, or Re-Africanization in Rio de Janeiro

The first course in Afro-Brazilian culture was organized in Rio de Janeiro in 1976 by a Carioca babalorixá, Ornato José da Silva, an author of books on orixás. He worked closely with a young Nigerian, Benjamin Durojaiye Ainde Kayodé Komolafe (Benji Kayodé), a medical student at the University of the state of Rio de Janeiro (UERJ). Kayodé presented himself as an awo[5] who had just arrived from Nigeria. This "first basic training course for seminarists in Afro-Brazilian religions" was held at the Umbandist Spiritual Congregation of Brazil, directed at the time by Tancredo da Silva Pinto.[6] Among the first group of pupils (all initiates) were two great figures who worked extremely hard to make this type of course widely available in Rio de Janeiro: Ruth Moreira da Silva and José Beniste.

It was also in 1976 that the Yoruba Theological Society of Afro-Brazilian Culture was founded, directed by Eduardo Fonseca, Jr. In that same year, he organized the first Afro-Brazilian Culture Week, which took place November 9–11 in the auditorium of the Brazilian Press Association. Nigeria's ambassador, Olajide Alo, gave the closing speech, emphasizing the importance of such initiatives in developing ties between Africa and Brazil.

In 1977, the Society employed as a Yoruba professor another young Nigerian, Joseph Olatundi Aridemi Osho, a student from the Polytechnic School of the Federal University of Rio de Janeiro. This appointment lasted until the beginning of 1979, when he started giving lessons at the Yoruba Culture Research and Study Center, founded in 1977 by Fernandes Portugal. The Center had an ambitious project: to put in contact with one another religious adepts and social-science researchers specializing in the study of Afro-Brazilian culture. To do this, conferences were given in terreiros and associations, as well as at a private university in Rio de Janeiro, the Estácio de Sá, and Yoruba courses were held in the Center itself. Members of the public who took these courses were religious adepts seeking to further their knowledge of Yoruba culture. They complained of being held back by the fact that the elders had not passed all the knowledge at their disposal on to the younger generation.

One of the ritual practices which had been forgotten in Brazil was divination by odùs, the configurations (signs) which form the basis of the Ifá divinatory system. Two hundred and fifty-six combinations of the sixteen principal odùs are possible, each linked to a story (*itan*) from the corpus of Ifá. The aim of divination is to reveal the sacrifices men must make, via the identification of the odù and itan corresponding to each particular situation, in order to restore harmony between the material world and the spiritual world.[7] The first divination courses included teaching the Ifá literature, which was then combined with studying the Yoruba language. However, the creation of these new courses inevitably caused conflict with the organizers of official language courses. It was for this reason that Fernandes Portugal (Babaláwo Sàngótola) soon questioned the legitimacy of the Nigerian professors: "There is a rumor which claims that some of these Nigerians were not initiated, and this is absolutely true. They were Anglicans, and others were Muslims, and they knew nothing [about the cult of the orixás]. They nevertheless initiated people [to Ifá]." Similarly, he said about the Africans' disciples, who were former students of the courses run by his establishment: "Unenlightened Brazilians approached these people [the Nigerians] dumbfounded, and they cast doubt upon their entire history and all their knowledge, accusing the Brazilian babalorixás of knowing nothing. There were those who left their houses of worship in order to perform ritual ceremonies with these Africans."[8]

On January 14, 1978, Kayodé and Richard Yinka Alabi Ajagunna, another Nigerian student from Rio de Janeiro's School of Medicine, held the closing ceremony of the first African divination course, granting the title of *omo* (son of) Ifá to their pupils. Becoming omo Ifá was equivalent to having received the first confirmation of the hand of Orunmilá (or *awo fakan*), the first step in the initiation process of a new babalawo, the priest who practices the divinatory art. Among the fourteen students who took part in this final ceremony was José Nilton Vianna Reis, better known as Torodê de Ogun, who received the name of Ifasaiyo (Kayodé and Silva 1978).

Torodê had been initiated in 1957 at the age of fourteen by Joãozinho da Goméia, one of Brazil's most famous pais-de-santo. As we have already seen, the latter had changed his axé, his original tradition—he had changed waters, to use the Candomblé expression—performing ritual ceremonies with Mãe Menininha do Gantois, Brazil's best-known mãe-de-santo and a representative of traditional Nagô Candomblé. In reality, Torodê saw this passage from Angola tradition to that of the supposedly purer Nagô as a loss of purity: "It happened in 1958 or 1960, I don't remember exactly. We changed to Ketu (Nagô), but we continued to organize ceremonies according to Angola rituals, especially during initiations. And so we became a 'mixed' terreiro. Joãozinho respected the Angola ritual for those that liked it, but for those who were Ketu, he followed the Yoruba ritual."

Upon the death of his initiator in 1971, Torodê went to Nigeria "to see things from close up." From then on he returned to Africa periodically: "After performing ritual ceremonies in Africa, I severed my ties with the Brazilian pais-de-santo. I became independent, because my pai-de-santo was dead and I had already opened my own house of worship. I wasn't going to depend on a pai-de-santo my whole life!" Referring to a purer tradition— the African tradition—thus enabled him to assert his independence and his supremacy over the priests who had remained linked to Brazilian "mixed" practices.

In 1977, Torodê organized courses in Yoruba language and orixá mythology in his house of worship, the Ilé Axé Ogun Torodê, in Rio de Janeiro. Lessons were given by Kayodé and Ajagunna. The emphasis was on the Ifá corpus, the divinatory method, and above all on the study of the odùs. This is how Torodê expressed the difficulty experienced by several students in adapting to the Africans' teaching:

> At the time our group was composed of fourteen people, but most of them didn't learn and didn't understand. They preferred to content themselves with the method, known in Brazil, which consists of interpreting intuitively the different combinations of the cowries. I, myself, would never allow such a thing. If a method exists, you have to learn it and practice it, not just guess. If you're just going to guess, you may as well use anything—matches, beans, or grains of corn!

After being confirmed as omo Ifá in 1978, Torodê continued his studies in order to become a babalawo, carrying out annual ceremonies with the Nigerians. The rest of the group dispersed. After nine years, Torodê received the title of babalawo from Kayodé. In 1984, Torodê began to teach Ifá divinatory practice himself, as well as Yoruba culture and ritual in his own terreiro. Every year he organized one or two study groups of forty to fifty people each, who were usually initiates interested in African tradition. But according to Torodê, being initiated was not a decisive factor for being accepted in the course, "for one can be a priest of Ifá without being initiated into the cult of the orixás."[9]

Yoruba culture and language teaching was based on texts from Nigerian literature and anthropological studies such as Bascom's *Sixteen Cowries* (1980). As these works were not translated into Portuguese and were somewhat inaccessible for initiates, the young Nigerian students translated extracts; in this way, the texts were gradually divulged. Torodê talks here of the consequences that the courses had in Candomblé circles:

> They caused quite a stir because Brazilian customs were entwined with Catholic beliefs. What's more, when the Africans tried to separate the two, the most radical [people], who believed that Saint Barbe was Yansan and Ogun was Saint George, did not accept it . . . Personally, I found it all absurd. I could not understand why, for a Bahian, Ogun should be Saint Anthony, who was Portuguese, or Saint George, who was George of Cappadocia, a Syrian from the Roman army. This is why, when my pai-de-santo died in 1971, I wanted to return to the religion's roots in Africa.

While, on the one hand, Torodê admits the importance of this direct contact with sources, on the other hand, he recognizes that setting off in search of lost purity can be a trap. Thus, when talking of the young Nigerians who gave lessons in Brazil and who were his initiators, he says:

> The advantage was that they knew the language [English and Yoruba]. I already had quite a few books, and so together we did some interesting work. They translated and with my knowledge of rituals we organized everything . . . My sister-of-saint, Gisèle [Binon-Cossard] said to me: "Listen, don't delude yourself with the Africans—they're just kids; they're young and don't know the rites. It was their fathers, mothers and grandparents who knew." But it isn't important. Thanks to them, at least we understood the language . . . in fact, many of them did not even know the [orixá] initiation process. They saw all this in Brazil.

The end of the 1970s saw a change in the nature of Yoruba language courses. The initiates who took the courses were not really interested in learning the language, but rather in learning secret knowledge. This was expressed by a growing demand for information about the *fundamentos*. In 1980, José Beniste, a historian and author of books on Afro-Brazilian

41. Ogans in Alvinho de Omolu's terreiro. PHOTO BY AUTHOR.

religion, launched an Afro-Brazilian cultural program on Radio Roquette Pinto. At the time, he was already a regular visitor to the Axé Opô Afonjá of Rio de Janciro, in Coelho da Rocha, where he received the title of ogan in 1983. Beniste began to teach courses with Ajagunna in an Umbanda center situated in the north area of Rio de Janeiro. Initially he collaborated with Ruth Moreira da Silva, who also ran a course with him at the Brazil-Nigeria Institute.

Since 1990, another course in divinatory practice has been given by Adilson Antonio Martins, who was initiated in 1968 by the pai-de-santo Zezinho da Boa Viagem, himself initiated by the babalorixá Tata Fomotinho, of Jeje lineage from São Felix in Cachoeira, Bahia. Martins had begun to take an interest in the cult of Orunmilá (Ifá) when the African students arrived. He became friends with Kayodé and the other Nigerians, and together they worked on bibliographical research. However, he felt the need to delve deeper and was initiated as *awo fakan* by a Cuban babalawo, Rafaél Zamora Díaz, who established himself in 1991 in Rio de Janeiro. According to Fernandes Portugal and Adilson Martins, at the beginning of the 1990s there were only two babalawos in Rio de Janeiro: Rafaél Zamora (Ogunda Keté) and Alberto Chamarelli Filho, initiated by Zamora in Cuba in 1992.

Torodê de Ogun and Fernandes Portugal are two of the representatives of re-Africanized Candomblé in Rio de Janeiro. Portugal defines his terreiro as "re-Africanized Ijexá." In fact, Portugal was initiated in 1970 into the Ijexá nation by Zezito de Oxum, the son-of-saint of Eduardo de Ijexá, a very well known pai-de-santo in Bahia. In Portugal's terreiro, which was re-Africanized after his trips to Africa, there are no longer ceremonies (obrigações) after seven years of initiation, but annual ceremonies: depending on each initiate's learning abilities, the babalorixá may proclaim him or her an ebomi (initiate of more than seven years) even before the end of this period. In the same way, the large skirts with starched underskirts, habitually used in Candomblé, have been replaced with African clothes. The use of loincloths and African turbans is today more widespread in Candomblé circles. Torodê justifies the changes in the sacred clothing by his journeys to Africa, but these modifications can give rise to criticism, for the African tradition enters into conflict with another tradition—Afro-Brazilian tradition.

Unity in Diversity

The proliferation of language courses and their gradual transformation into lessons in divination or ritual practices raise the question of who is authorized to speak in the name of tradition. The presence of the Nigerian students—who, by the sole fact of being African, focused the interest and hopes of a large part of the community of initiates—did not pass unnoticed among the Nagô Candomblé elites.

In INTECAB's journal, Juana Elbein dos Santos (1991–92, 2) published an article, dated October 1990, in which she criticized the Africans who come to Brazil to teach African tradition:

> A large part of the black population of Bahia . . . makes Africa and Africans idealized paradigms of knowledge and extraordinary powers . . . any student from Nigeria, Benin or any other region [of West Africa] will be transformed into a revered idol, a source of values and knowledge, which will enable [hierarchical] positions within the community to be enhanced. The Brazilians open their houses of worship and their

wallets—usually [paying] in dollars—for these "connoisseurs," thus casting doubt upon their own heritage and their own knowledge, handed down from generation to generation . . . It will not be these "new connoisseurs," who arrived during the last decade on our beaches, themselves the product of another historical colonial experience . . . , who can interfere with our tradition, pointing out, correcting, publishing profane books, performing spectacular divining practices and inventing traditions. Our tradition was created and continually recreates itself from inaugural principles, but with its own dynamic, participating dialectically in the Brazilian social reality.

This is a remarkable vision of an Africa which simultaneously legitimizes some (anthropologists who have carried out research in Africa, and members of traditional Candomblé terreiros) and calls into question the legitimacy of others (Yoruba teachers): "in fact, our Brazilian brothers do not understand that sub-Saharan Africa suffered a terrible colonization process, and the destructuring of its most significant traditional values" (ibid.). All the same, Juana Elbein dos Santos does not contest the existence of "pockets of resistance and continuity," authenticated by the various travels she and her predecessors undertook in Africa. The question is to know which are the pockets of resistance. Therefore, re-Africanization no longer has to come from Africa; it is no longer a return to African roots: it arises from the search for the "inaugural principles" of the religion, which, "on a religious level, are equivalent to the *axé*, and on a philosophical level, to the *arkhé*" (ibid.).

The notion of arkhé has been amply used in the works of Muniz Sodré, Juana Elbein dos Santos, and her husband, Deoscóredes dos Santos. According to the latter two, arkhé signifies both "principle of beginning and origin" and "principle of power and command." The notion of arkhé, in initiatory communities, evokes the idea of an inaugural principle, "recreator of all experience" (Santos and Santos 1993b, 46). For Marco Aurélio Luz (1992, 67),[10] "*arkhé* is not limited to an historical, social and cultural inaugural principle, but it encompasses the mystical energy which is constitutive of the ancestrality and cosmic forces which govern the universe in the dynamic interaction of the restitution of the axé from the aiyê (the material world) to the orun (the spiritual world)."

The axé, then, becomes the materialization, on a religious level, of the arkhé, a kind of archaic nucleus of the sacred at the origin of what they call the "African civilizing complex" (Luz 1993, 61). But talking of an "African civilizing complex" implies the existence of a common ground of black culture since in Brazil this is a plural culture, born of the contributions of different ethnic groups. The contributions of each of them are linked by what the Santos call a "semantic pact," which "has to take into account the contradictions and controversies with regard to the other sectors of society, while creating from its identity strategies for contact and relations" (Santos and Santos 1993b, 42). And so a "decolonizing action" must be set up, in order to "recompose and make conscious this complex semantic pact, both its memory and its continuity" (ibid.).

But what do we mean when we talk of "decolonizing action"? Here, it is a question of syncretism, which has been the center of debate within Candomblé since the end of the 1970s, when the "theory of the mask" became predominant: Africans acted as though they accepted Catholic values in order to escape from colonial oppression. This was Bastide's theory, which, through his principle of compartmentalization, saw the Western world and the African world as incompatible and incapable of mixing with one another. Where the African world has been preserved, contact with the Western world has led to only a simple juxtaposition of cultural elements. Syncretism is, then, negligible in communities which are symbols of cultural encystment with regard to the dominant society (Bastide 1978). In Brazil these "community niches" are represented by the traditional terreiros of Bahia.

To claim that the African world and the Western world cannot mix is equivalent to claiming the unreality of syncretism, at least as regards traditional houses of worship, where the purity of the African world has been preserved (Capone 2007). The resulting desyncretization movement aims to eliminate all elements of Catholic origin which no longer have reason to exist, for the historical context today is very different: "We are in a democracy and we have a constitution which guarantees our freedom of religion. The time has come for all the terreiros' leaders of different nations here in Brazil to reach a decision and decide once and for all to do away with this syncretism which Catholics say exists in Afro-Brazilian religions" (Deoscóredes dos Santos 1990).

All that needs to be done, then, is to remove "the mask," and the primordial Africa in all its purity will be revealed. At the head of the desyncretization movement, we find the iyalorixá of the Axé Opô Afonjá, Mãe Stella, who undertook, with other Bahian iyalorixás, a crusade against syncretism during the second COMTOC, held in Salvador in 1983. It was not by chance that this declaration was made during the first COMTOC held in Brazil, which the Santos and their Society of Studies of Black Culture in Brazil (SECNEB) helped to organize. This is the circle within which a new anthropological interpretation of Afro-Brazilian religions was defined, which had intense repercussions in the terreiros. The directors of SECNEB, who maintained good relations with the political authorities and traditional priests of Nigeria, then moved to create an international association to preserve the orixás' rites and traditions, and to build an "ecumenical" organization of Afro-Brazilian religions. However, to do so, it was necessary to postulate a basic unity of the black world, including the different African peoples and blacks from the diaspora.

An example of this change in perspective is given by Luz (1983), who underlines the unity of what he calls "black religion" through the common worship of a supreme god. His main concern is to prove that continuity exists between African and Afro-Brazilian religions. Luz classifies the "black religions" according to their "vocation" of updating their African origins in Brazil and of "giving continuity to the black civilizing process." However, this vocation may be embodied only in religious communities which have preserved very strictly "the symbolic and ritual systems which they have inherited"—i.e., the traditional Nagô terreiros of Bahia. As for the other terreiros, the closer they are to traditional houses of worship, the more "the complexity of the original religious system is preserved in its entirety, with few gaps and therefore few or no symbolic and ritual variations exogenic to the original context" (ibid., 31). Traditional Nagô terreiros are thus classic examples of centers where this new culture of resistance expresses itself, becoming the symbols of an African identity, actively sought by the black movement.[11]

African descendants, then, have once again become the protagonists of their own history, capable of setting up strategies which enable them to "act within the interstices of the system." Conversion to Catholicism, far from being a simple strategy by slaves, is seen as a strategic way to play

with "the ambiguities of the system": "the black originality consists of having lived a double structure,[12] of having played with the ambiguities of
power and, in this way, of having been able to implant parallel institutions"
(Sodré 1988, 132). Therefore, if African descendants can use their agency
to find their place in the system, syncretism, which has always been a
problem in the search for religious purity, must necessarily change its image: it becomes, then, a "dialectic response to the long process of resistance-
accommodation" (Juana E. dos Santos 1976, 23).

However, because blacks in Brazil are obviously of mixed ancestry, and
their culture is the product of different cultural contacts, it becomes imper-
ative to search for the common elements in the different religious cults of
African origin. From this perspective, syncretisms became "mechanisms at
the service of variables" and expressions of the continuity and expansion of
the "black civilizing process." But where is this process concentrated? In
religion, which plays a "historic role" in the creation of community groups
defined as "organizational centers of cultural resistance." Juana Elbein dos
Santos (1977, 26) makes Bastide the guarantor of the hegemonic mission of
the traditional leaders: Bastide would have recognized, through "intellectual honesty," that "the law of seniority," fundamental to any initiatory religion, relegated him, a French researcher, to a subaltern position. "True
negritude" was defined by Bastide as an "existential assertion" and the "expression of the ethos of the black community." It is embodied in religion,
which "transmits most powerfully the essential values of this negritude"
(ibid.), having survived all kinds of pressure, thanks to the "dialectic process
of resistance-accommodation" which gave rise to different religious practices. According to Santos, this process embodies the "discontinuity within
continuity" (ibid.). Syncretism then becomes a form of resistance, for paradoxically it expresses the unity of the black community.[13]

Laid out here are the basic concepts of the future discourse of INTECAB,
founded in 1987 after a split during the COMTOC of 1986. INTECAB[14] presents itself as "representative of different traditions which perpetuate the
African ancestors' heritage in the New World." It gathers together the Afro-
Brazilian houses of worship which seek to unify a religious field which has
always been highly fragmented.[15] Its aim is to "preserve and spread the
African ancestors' spiritual heritage which constitutes the nucleus of our
identity and our existence," and to gain recognition for "the right to a

specific identity for the most significant contingent of the Brazilian population." For INTECAB, this identity is founded upon tradition, "understood as the continual and dynamic renewal of the inaugural principles of the black civilizing process."

In these words we can see the traces of a debate which arose within SECNEB (see Juana E. dos Santos 1976 and Luz 1983) and was then formalized in the writings of Muniz Sodré (1988), Luz (1992, 1993) and Santos and Santos (1993a and b). The idea of a "discontinuity within continuity" finds its echo in INTECAB's motto: "unity in diversity." Candomblé and Umbanda, then, are simply variants caused by "resistance-accommodation" strategies, which are, in fact, merely the instruments of continuity of the same "cultural complex." Candomblé and Umbanda distinguish themselves by the variables that these religions have incorporated: homogenous variables which have given rise to an "intertribal syncretism" for Candomblé, and heterogeneous variables from other cultural complexes for Umbanda.

This idea of a discontinuity within continuity was developed by Bastide during a symposium held in 1970 in Jamaica by the Committee of Afro-American Societies and Cultures of the Social Science Research Council, where he took up Georges Gurvitch's notion of "discontinued continuity," or "discontinuity continued":

> But Gurvitch contented himself with noting the existence of a double dialectic movement between continuity and discontinuity; we would like to go beyond that here, and see if the example of the Afro-Americans allows us to discover an explicative (and not simply descriptive) model of this interpenetration of continuity within breaks, such as discontinuity in what appears to be pure maintenance of the past. (Bastide 1996a, 77)

However, while Bastide does not fail to underline the ideological dimension of this continuity[16] and how it is culturally constructed,[17] he nevertheless asserts the existence of "cultural preserves" in the Brazilian Northeast, which, he claims, impose cultural continuity as a response to social discontinuity. It is in these pockets of resistance that "true negritude" finds its expression: a negritude which no longer depends on political ideology but is an "existential assertion." The members of traditional terreiros, whose mission is to renew the ties with the "black civilizing process" through religious initiation, embody this "true negritude." In order to highlight this civilizing process, common to all the different cults claiming African origins, it is necessary for the "less pure" religions, such as Umbanda, to undergo a re-Africanization, using as a model the "purer" religion of Nagô Candomblé:

> Umbanda cults profess a profound and veritable respect for the terreiros which perpetuate traditional religions. Despite liturgical differences, variants and elements from other cultural systems, by their structure and way of life, Umbanda religion is part of and derives directly from the African heritage. This is how the most enlightened leaders of the Umbanda Federation understand it, who attempt to maintain good relations with traditional religions and work to establish a unified Umbandist liturgy reinforcing the elements of African tradition within it. (Santos and Santos 1993a, 162–63)

Therefore, Umbanda must draw closer to the "purer" forms of Afro-Brazilian religions in order to become stronger and more African." About the syncretism between Umbanda and Candomblé, known as Umbandomblé, Luz (1993, 106) writes: "in this way, Umbanda seeks to strengthen itself through the cosmogony of sister religions which belong to the same Negro-African civilizing process in Brazil." Thus, while syncretism with Catholicism is merely the product of the colonial experience, and for this reason should be denounced as an unsuitable solution for Afro-Brazilians, syncretism between "sister religions," taking as a model the most highly valued form, becomes completely desirable.

What, then, is the common ground for this basic cultural complex linked to the black civilizing process? According to Francisco Dalmir (1992, 183), this is the cults of cosmic forces (orixá, baculo, inkice, vodun) and ancestors (egun, preto-velho, caboclo), as well as the founding principle of any Afro-Brazilian religion—namely, "the axé for the Nagôs and the *muntu* for the Bantus." The core of black culture is not only the ethos specific to the terreiro communities, but also and above all its *eidos*, "its transcendental dimension" updated in religious communities (Luz 1992, 68). This culture is fundamentally different from Western culture; it is, according to Sodré (1988, 136), a culture which does not refer to a space directed toward an "irreversible linearity," but a "curved space, which contains operations of reversibility, in other words, of symbolic return." The notion of axé and the structure of secrecy, then, play a central role in black culture:

When the secret is institutionalized—as is the case of the *awo* in black culture—communication is made possible by the initiatory process . . . , through which the secret contents are gradually passed down over time. Tension within the group is fed by the appearance of the secret, exhibited either via the signs of secret rites, or via the terreiro's public ceremonies enacting the mythical vicissitudes of the orixás or ancestors. (Ibid., 138)

The secret is void, however, and exists only for the purpose of redistributing the axé:

In the awo, the Nagô secret, there is no mystery to reveal—therein lies its strength. The purpose of the secret cannot be reduced to the revelation of mere knowledge. The secret is a dynamic of communication, of redistribution of axé, of existence and vigor of the rules of the cosmic game. It circulates as such, like awo, without being "revealed," for it proves that the Truth exists and that it must be brought to light. (Ibid., 142–43)

The association of the notion of axé (on a religious level) with that of arkhé (on a philosophical level) includes, then, a third term: the void secret.[18] Thus, according to Sodré, the arkhé becomes "the void which escapes purely rational attempts of being apprehended" (quoted in Santos and Santos 1993b, 44). In order to know the arkhé, the inaugural principles of the "black civilizing process," contact must be reestablished with those who have kept and preserved its transcendental principle, which is the axé. Consequently, if religion is the main expression of negritude, the repositories of the axé become, rightly, the legitimate representatives of this negritude. In this way, the high priests of the cult are transformed into leaders of the blacks' new political struggle. It is all a question of knowledge of the true tradition: "the deeper the knowledge of dogma and liturgy, the more the *axé* is developed and tradition preserved" (Santos and Santos 1993a, 172).

This is the first evocation of dogma, a fixed, established doctrine and a ready-to-impose orthodoxy, which Afro-Brazilian religions, through their freedom and dynamic, seem to ignore. Thus the founders of INTECAB preach respect for dogma in order to be able to develop the axé, the basis of the black civilizing process. It remains to be determined which tradition should be preserved.

Exu: Between Re-Africanization and Religious Unification

Once again, Exu offers us a good example of the multiplicity of traditions. As we have seen, this god has experienced a series of modifications which, throughout the history of Afro-Brazilian religions, have transformed him from a demonic entity into a central element of African metaphysics. The re-Africanization movement, mainly through language courses, seeks to reestablish real communication between man and the gods, among whom Exu, as messenger, plays a major role.

However, while in Brazilian terreiros Exu's importance is never questioned, this is not the case in re-Africanized circles, where he seems once again to be demonized—for example, in Ade Dopamu's work (1990), published by Oduduwa, a small publishing house in São Paulo whose goal is to spread the "true" African tradition. According to the book's front cover, the author, "born and living in Nigeria," is head of the Religion Department at the University of Ilorin, in Nigeria, where he lectures on "African religion and religious comparative studies." This book, intended for all initiates of Afro-Brazilian religions, seeks to establish the veritable nature of Exu "in the light of African tradition": "The controversy around this being results mainly from the ignorance in which all those with no access to authentic African traditions find themselves. Knowledge of their origins is necessary for our practices and discourse to be coherent and well founded. It is from the roots that the nourishing sap must rise."

Dopamu wishes to encourage the reader to reflect upon the real nature of this god through a comparative study of the Exu of traditional Yoruba religion and the devil of Christian and Muslim traditions. He claims to prove the legitimacy of the translation of the word "devil" by "Exu" in the Bible and Koran in Nigeria: "this method has inevitably led me to discover that Exu is the invisible enemy, the spiritual enemy of man" (Dopamu 1990, 11). Despite the great number of contemporary Yoruba authors who define Exu as an entity neither completely good nor completely bad, Dopamu sees in him the incarnation of evil: "to characterize him as entirely evil is our greatest concern" (ibid., 34). Thus, if one of Exu's characteristics remains knowledge, this is, according to Dopamu, always misused; and if Exu agrees to deliver sacrifices, it is only to keep men and divinities perpetually under his control.

42. Ogun's assento.
PHOTO BY AUTHOR.

It goes without saying that this negative vision of Exu is in complete contrast to the one championed in the works of Bastide (1958) and Juana Elbein dos Santos (1976). Indeed, the influence of anthropological writing upon adepts of Afro-Brazilian religions should not be underestimated. It is rare for initiates, and even more so pais and mães-de-santo, not to possess several copies of the best known books about Afro-Brazilian religions. The most widely read is without doubt that of Juana Elbein dos Santos, *Os Nagô e a morte*, as it is supposed to express the tradition of the Axé Opô Afonjá.[19] How can this vision of an Exu identified with the devil, the product of the true African tradition, be accepted when Exu constitutes the nucleus, the dynamizing element, of the religious practice in traditional terreiros? In fact, Exu not only delivers sacrifices; he also propagates the axé, which, according to INTECAB's theoreticians, is linked on a religious level to the arkhé, the inaugural principle of the "black civilizing process."

Exu is, then, metamorphosed into an element of resistance to "neo-colonial oppression," whose agents ("the missionary fathers") understood the central role of Exu as "an entity who dynamizes the black religious and cosmogonic system" (Luz 1993, 96). In an article on religious offerings, Tateto Nogueira, INTECAB's coordinator in the state of Minas Gerais, writes on the subject of Exu:

> At crossroads, as with any other place, the offering requires the convocation of the dynamizing agent of all relations and all nature, which is Exu, who, let me say once again, has nothing to do with the devil or any other mythical being "representative of Evil." Exu's invocation is necessary, for he is the deliverer of everything, both homage and prayer. (1991–92, 8)

Furthermore, communication between Afro-Brazilian religions hinges on Exu because he is the only divinity present in all cult modalities. Therefore the less pure religions should look to their "sister religions" that are closer to the true African tradition, in order to correct the mistakes of syncretism. Through INTECAB, and its efforts to unify religious practices, a version of the African tradition is thus placed in the forefront, a version that other Afro-Brazilian religions must use as a model (at the price of a religious homogenization) in order finally to be legitimized by this Africa reconstructed in Brazil.

CONCLUSION

Two major questions have risen up from our journey into the world of Afro-Brazilian religions. What mechanisms are at work in the construction of tradition? How do power relationships affect the internal organization of the Afro-Brazilian religious field?

It seems impossible to label one or another religious modality as traditional, when, as we have seen, there are constant shifts between tradition and change, even in what are regarded as the purest Candomblé nations. In this way, an invented institution such as the obás of Xangô becomes the symbol of a rediscovered tradition in the Axé Opô Afonjá, and its modification—unacceptable to traditionalists—is reinterpreted (and legitimized) within the framework of an African logic. It is in the name of greater proximity to a mythical Africa that one religious group claims hegemony over the others. Anthropologists, by recognizing a religious family's traditionalism, justify its position, and become in some way the guarantors of orthodoxy.

It is therefore definitively impossible to talk of Candomblé as a religious practice which clearly distinguishes between those who practice the "African religion" and those who allow themselves to be contaminated by external influences. What was presented for a long time as a monolithic unit from which emanated the essence of an immutable past is now to be seen as a complex entity whose boundaries can be negotiated. In fact, despite the elaboration of an orthodox model thanks to the convergence of discourses of anthropologists and religious leaders, our analysis has highlighted a reality that is extremely different, in which the ideal orthodoxy conflicts with the countless ritual rearrangements performed in ritual practice.

We have thus moved on from an essentialistic vision of culture, at work in the "back to the roots" movement, to a culture perceived as constantly reinvented, recreated, and recomposed around new meanings. Our analysis of Afro-Brazilian religions concludes with this paradox: what anthropologists used to present as apparently well-defined, clearly demarcated realities (traditional religions and syncretic cults) collide with cult members' constant negotiation of their religious identity. The differences seem to be instituted by the religious leaders' discourse rather than by a real opposition in ritual practice. Religious designations—and the hierarchizing dichotomies they imply—are the product of a political discourse, where the differences in terms of purity serve to confirm the position occupied by each terreiro in the religious market. Any change or religious mutation is not necessarily a sign of degeneration but can be reinstated, as we have seen, in a system of transformation within the same *gestalt* (to use a term dear to Bastide). Exu, the "builder of bridges," the personification of the "thought in motion" (Bastide, 1970c), becomes then the archetypal avatar of this reality: his various metamorphoses show us how religious categories are constantly reformulated in ritual practice.

An analysis of the figure of Exu in different religious modalities offers a very different image of them from the one usually given in Afro-Brazilian studies: instead of a world where harmony reigns and change does not, and cannot, have a place, we discover a universe founded on political strategies, a universe left unexplored for too long because the ties that bound anthropologists with the religious groups made impossible any analysis of this kind. However, if one model of tradition has been given more credence than the others, this is not due to the intellectuals alone, as Dantas claims (1988); on the contrary, in this book I wanted to show the agency of Candomblé members, whose political strategies have been rarely emphasized. As Sodré (1988, 169–70) explains: "In Bahia, slaves' descendants, heads of terreiros, still say: 'The white man is educated, the black man is cunning (*O branco faz letra, o negro faz treta*).'" *Treta* means stratagem, trick or cunning ploy in a struggle. For black Brazilians, this signifies acting within the interstices of social relations."

Thanks to the political ability, they manage to transform change into continuity. By rethinking tradition, it becomes possible to disclose an archaic nucleus, a founding cultural complex, toward which it is necessary to return in order to find the purity of a lost past. Therefore, the problem is no longer to purify religious practices from syncretism, as if by eliminating the weight of the colonial past and the ignominious experience of slavery, a pure Africa could liberate itself at last, but to unveil the common basis—the black civilizing process—which would unify all the Afro-Brazilian religions. However, while the existence of a common ground may seem obvious, especially in what I call the religious continuum of Afro-Brazilian religions, it would seem in reality to be far more mixed than the theorists of "unity in diversity" would admit. Claiming a greater proximity with Africa can be, now more than ever, a political instrument in the hands of those who enhance one tradition over the others.

With this in mind, analysis of the transnational networks between initiates from Brazil, Cuba, and North America and representatives of the African tradition in Nigeria, whose importance in the Brazilian context is evident, becomes a new laboratory that allows us to test our hypothesis. The movement of Orisha World and its International Congresses of Orisha Tradition and Culture (COMTOCs) have led to two different trends in Brazil: one which claims its legitimacy by referring to the original land (Yorubaland, especially Ilé-Ifé, the mythical cradle of the Yoruba) and one which seeks to perpetuate a ritual supremacy historically established by this convergence between religious leaders and anthropologists.

In 1990, the fourth COMTOC was organized in São Paulo by the representatives of the most re-Africanized terreiros. It is in this city that discontent about the preeminence of Bahian houses of worship was strongest. In reality, the re-Africanization movement, which cultivates ritual and political alliances with the Yoruba, concealed the desire for legitimation of certain religious groups regarded as newly converted in the traditional Afro-Brazilian circles. The city of São Paulo, perceived as the land of Umbanda and Macumba and therefore associated with the syncretic cults, was presented during the conference as a new traditional center. This is why, during the fifth COMTOC, held in San Francisco in August 1997, a representative of the re-Africanization movement in São Paulo, emphasizing his connections with Nigeria, publicly claimed the role of defender of the African tradition in Brazil, in open opposition to the Salvador houses of worship.

The same opposition between a tradition linked to Africa and another modeled within the diaspora is found in the United States, where adepts of the orishas' religion criticize what they call the Cuban *santeros*[1] misrepresentations. In fact, since the 1960s, following the migration of a large number of Cubans fleeing Castro's revolution, Afro-Cuban religions have been spreading all over the United States. The encounter of Lucumí practitioners, black nationalists, and Yoruba babalawos from Nigeria have set up the basis of a re-Africanization movement in the United States, which reproduces the same issues as those in Brazil. Thanks to the "back to the roots" movement, the incessant reinterpretation of the cultural heritage of Afro-Cuban origin has enabled the diffusion of religions of African origin on American soil. While Cuba continues to be the reference for a great number of American practitioners of Santería (or Lucumí religion), criticism of Afro-Catholic syncretism and the search for religious purity lead an ever greater number of new initiates to look toward Africa, which becomes the key symbol in the process of religious identity construction in the United States as in Brazil.

In both countries, initiates follow the same religious path, which goes from cults considered the least African toward those which are identified with the "true African tradition." Thus, Puerto Rican practitioners of Spiritism did not hesitate to combine different ritual practices in order to move closer to the ideal of Africanity embodied by Cuban Santería. As with the passage from Umbanda to Candomblé in Brazil, that from Spiritism to Santería was considered by practitioners as the means of perfecting their spiritual mission, assimilating in this way the Spiritist doctrine to the first step in their religious careers. This is how a new religious variant appeared in the United States in the 1960s, a mixture of Puerto Rican Spiritism and Cuban Santería, called Santerismo (Brandon 1993, 107–14). In this case, it is not merely a question of preserving African tradition—as in countries such as Cuba and Brazil—but rather a process of revitalizing African roots.

From the 1960s onward, African Americans set out to rediscover religions of African origin, leading to the adoption of Cuban Santería by black nationalists. Orisha-Voodoo was the fruit of this encounter, which al-

lowed African cultural roots to revive by purging African American religions of any Catholic influence. In 1970 the founder of this movement,
Walter "Serge" King—Oba Adefunmi I, king of the Yoruba of America—
founded a village of initiates near Beaufort, S.C., called the Oyotunji Village.[2] However, Orisha-Voodoo is just one aspect of the "back to the roots"
movement, which also gave rise to a large number of centers where the
study of the Yoruba language is combined with religious practices. As in
Brazil, this movement concentrates its efforts on revitalizing African roots
while getting rid of Christian influences, elaborating an African identity via
the learning of the Yoruba language—a "sacred" language and the symbolic
key to the world of African tradition.

With African American religions spreading outside *Latino* districts
(mostly Cuban and Puerto Rican) and the ever-increasing commitment of
African Americans, linguistic problems became inevitable. In Santería
houses of worship, religious instruction was usually given in Spanish and
lucumí (the name given to Yoruba slaves in Cuba). Several centers were
then created to offer language courses in the United States. Their main
goal was to purify ritual language of all that evoked the painful experience
of slavery and to reformulate religious concepts to reaffirm African heritage, erasing any reference to Catholic saints, holy water, and pilgrimages,
all signs of a colonized culture. We find there the same opposition between
the valorization of the Yoruba religious identity, chosen as the traditional
model, and the perpetuation of the religious traditions associated with the
diaspora.

However, the link between the different African American religions,
through the practitioners' circulation from one cult to another (from Umbanda to Omolocô and Candomblé in Brazil; from Spiritism to Santería and
Orisha-Voodoo in the United States), shows us how these cults are not
bounded realities but elements of a religious continuum. Each cult is connected to other practices, considered more or less traditional according to
the ritual actors' political agenda. Nevertheless, the idea that African American religions could be considered a continuum has not gained ground yet,
given the difficulty of considering "mixed cults" a valuable object of study.
In the case of Afro-Brazilian religions, Candomblé is still taken to represent
African purity compared with Umbanda, which is associated with ritual
change and syncretism. In Brazil as well as in international forums, the

celebration of Bahian Candomblé, identified with traditional houses of worship, continues to appear as a model of purity and African tradition. Today, Nagô is synonymous with African and remains the most commonly used term for all that concerns African roots in Afro-Brazilian identity. The locus of legitimation is a mythical Africa, a common cultural heritage which is shared by blacks and whites in Brazil. Paradoxically, being Nagô does not necessarily mean being black. As we have seen, the Afro-Brazilian religious identity crosses color lines: through initiation into Candomblé, whites can claim an African religious identity, as Roger Bastide did. Thus Candomblé, and Afro-Brazilian religions in general, see themselves as universal, in the sense that they are composed of a set of beliefs shared by blacks, whites, mestizos, and even Japanese descendants.[3]

Furthermore, by considering Afro-Brazilian religions a religious continuum, we are compelled to study carefully mixed religious practices, such as Omolocô and Umbandomblé, the mix of Umbanda and Candomblé so popular in the outskirts of large Brazilian cities. If we think of Afro-Brazilian religions as different elements of a system of transformation, the analysis of their different forms, including their mixed forms, becomes necessary. Ritual differences may, then, be analyzed as variations in the assembly of religious elements from distinct belief systems. In this way, instead of stressing a religious standardization legitimized by the work of anthropologists, it becomes possible to preserve the complexity of ritual practice, which is, as we have seen, constantly transformed and negotiated.

This reluctance to consider mixed cultural forms forces us to reflect upon the discipline of anthropology, which too often has accorded a normative central place to tradition. The complexity of the Afro-Brazilian religious field leads us to question a whole series of notions and practices which form the basis of this discipline. The analysis of the construction of African tradition in Brazil questions the ever-increasing temptation of a certain methodological idealism that prefers to gather the diverse explanations of informants into remarkably structured units, where everything finds its place, and any contradictions are brushed aside in order to give life to fascinating African metaphysics.

However, this task of smoothing out material that is too rough or not "noble" enough produces anthropological works that constitute "scientific" rereading of an African heritage, validating the Candomblé elites' claims of a purity that never really existed. In the typical example of Afro-Brazilian religions, we witness the epistemological tension between local sources of religious knowledge and anthropological works. The convergence of discourse of initiates and anthropologists is not always the proof of scientific accuracy. Initiates use anthropologists' categories just as anthropologists use initiates' religious categories. While religious elites gain legitimacy and authority because of their collaboration with anthropologists, anthropologists gain scientific authority when they produce remarkable analysis of traditional worlds, untouched by modernity.

In the world of Afro-Brazilian religions, legitimacy plays a key role. We have seen the constant play between the discourse of religious practitioners, the discourse of their initiators, and that of the spiritual beings who inhabit them, all claiming their links to an imagined and imaginary Africa. Even initiation does not really seem to be sufficient, since the initiatory religious origins and the underlying ritual procedure can always be contested. The Byzantine discussions in the houses of worship about orthopraxis—the "true" way to perform rituals—highlight the complexity of such a fragmented field, where the very idea of orthodoxy constitutes a paradox and even the word of the spirits and gods may be contested by accusations of simulation.

Legitimacy is also at the core of the relations between researchers and informants. Researchers are caught between two options: to keep secret by not translating or disclosing certain parts of their work that might not please their local public, or to take the risk of seeing their relationship with their informants irredeemably damaged. Initiates' ability to reclaim the anthropologist's work should not be underestimated. For my Brazilian informants, the simple fact that I took an interest in their religious group implied the traditionalism of the Efon nation, which had remained hidden until an anthropologist came to discover it. My protestations and efforts to explain that any tradition is constructed and constantly reinvented were useless; the fact that I took an interest in the Efon nation could only be proof of its traditionalism.

The Afro-Brazilian example is also a good illustration of the way in which anthropologists approach their field. In most cases, young researchers are introduced to the universe they wish to study by another anthropologist. With regard to Bahian Candomblé, it has become almost compulsory to work in the three terreiros considered as the keepers of African tradition. We have seen how they have attracted several generations of anthropologists, all connected in one way or another to these religious groups. There are even examples of anthropologists who have grown up in this universe, for their mothers were Candomblé daughters-of-saint—anthropologists, therefore, who know this religious world very well but are also an integral part of it. That an anthropologist may be perceived equally as a researcher and as a potential informant only renders the task more complex for those entering this universe for the first time, making thorough preparation essential for fieldwork on African American religions and initiatory religions in general. Pitfalls abound, linked not only to religious commitment but also to the relations one has with one's predecessors: by subscribing to one tradition of studies, anthropologists legitimize these traditions and perpetuate them. Analysis of the processes which lead to the construction of a model of African tradition thus becomes crucial for a real comprehension of the ever-changing reality of African American religions.

abian or *abiã*: A novice or candidate for initiation in Candomblé.

adjuntó: A second protector *orixá*.

adoxu: An initiate in Candomblé who has worn the *oxu*, the initiatory cone of herbs and other elements placed over the head during initiation.

aiyê: The material world of the living. From the Yoruba *aiyé*.

ajé: A witch. From the Yoruba *àjé*.

assentamento or *assentar o santo*: A ceremony to "seat" the *orixá*'s energy in an altar representing the initiate's head.

assento: The material representation of the sacred force of the divinity. It consists of clay, ceramic, or wooden containers holding a stone (*otan*), symbolizing the initiate's head, and various other ingredients.

awo: A secret or mystery. An *awo* is also a high priest, linked to the Ifá cult. See *fundamento*.

axé: The sacred force concentrated in objects and initiates. *Axé* is also a religious tradition transmitted via spiritual kin. From the Yoruba *àṣẹ* (order, command, authority).

axexê: A funerary ritual in Candomblé.

baba kekeré: See *pai pequeno*.

babalaô, babalawo: Priest of Ifá, diviner. From the Yoruba *babaláwo* (*baba ní awo*: father of the secret).

babalorixá: Nagô term for *pai-de-santo*. The female counterpart is *iyalorixá*. From the Yoruba *babalóòrìṣà* (*baba ní òrìṣà*: father of the *orixá*).

baculo: A Bantu ancestral spirit.

barracão: The main hall of a *terreiro*, where public ceremonies are held.

Bombonjira or *Bombagira*: One of the names of Exu in Bantu *terreiros*.

borí: A ceremony dedicated to the head, often a preliminary rite to initiation. From the Yoruba *bọ orí* (worship the head).

caboclo: Indigenous spirit, revered in Umbanda, as well as in Candomblé, and even in the most traditional *terreiros* of Bahia.

calunga: Cemetery (*calunga-grande* means ocean).

cambono: An assistant to the *pai pequeno* in Umbanda.

carrego: Burden or weight. The notion of *carrego* is linked to that of *despacho*. It is the negative charge resulting from *ebó* (magic work), which must be neutralized by being abandoned in a specific place (a crossroad, forest, riverbank, or beach). *Carrego* is also a ritual obligation inherited by a person who must care for the divinity of a deceased family member.

centro de mesa: A Kardecist center, also called *mesa branca* (white table).

charity: Work accomplished by the spirits in order to complete their evolution. They give consultations to human beings, helping them solve their problems.

crianças: Literally, children; childlike spirits in Umbanda.

curandeirismo: The illegal practice of medicine.

dagan: One of the oldest daughters-of-saint in the house, who has a ritual responsibility linked to the *padê*. Her assistant is called *sidagan* or *ossi dagan*, from the Yoruba *òsì* (left). See also *iyamorô*.

deká (to receive the): A ceremony accomplished seven years after initiation in Candomblé. The initiate then becomes an *ebomi* and can open his own *terreiro*.

demanda: A struggle between, or a magical attack on, members of an Umbanda center.

despacho: A ritual dedicated to Exu, performed before any religious ceremony. Sometimes called *padê*, it also designates the disposal of an offering or the negative charge resulting from magic work (see *carrego*).

dilogun: A divination method through which Exu speaks directly to a person via the way the cowries fall. Also called *jogo de búzios*, in Brazil it has replaced divination with *opelé*.

ebó: A sacrificial offering to an *orixá*, or a positive magic work. From the Yoruba *ẹbọ*.

ebomi: A *terreiro* elder, initiated for more than seven years. From the Yoruba *ègbọ́n mi* (elder sibling).

egun: A spirit of the dead. Contact with one may be dangerous for Candomblé initiates.

Egungun or *Egun* or *Baba Egum*: An ancestral spirit venerated on Itaparica Island, in Bahia. From the Yoruba *Egúngún*.

ekedi: A woman consecrated to a divinity who does not experience trances. She cares for initiates in trances and is present at all ritual ceremonies.

erê: A childlike manifestation of an orixá, with its own name and characteristics. It is a shallower trance, during which the initiate speaks and behaves like a child.

essas: The founding forefathers of the *terreiro* evoked in the *padê*.

Èṣù Ẹ̀lẹ́gbẹ́ra: Name given to Exu in Yorubaland. *Ẹ̀lẹ́gbẹ́ra* (or *ẹlẹgbá*) means "one who has strength or power" (*agbára*).

evolution: An organizing principle in Kardecism and Umbanda. A spirit is evolved when he is detached from the material world, through being indoctrinated and practicing charity.

exés: Parts of a sacrificed animal which are charged with divine power (*axé*). These parts (the head, feet, wings, tail, heart, lungs, esophagus, and testicles) are offered to the *orixá* and usually placed in front of his shrine.

Exu: In Candomblé, Exu is an orixá, through whose intercession communication takes place between the other gods and human beings. In Umbanda, exu is a disincarnated spirit.

Exu-Bara: A personal Exu, linked to an individual's destiny, who accompanies the initiate until his or her death.

Exu-egun: In Umbanda, a disincarnated spirit. The term is used by mediums from Umbanda who are initiated in Candomblé to differentiate the *Exu-egun* from the *Exu-orixá*.

Exu of the gateway: The guardian of the *terreiro*, who wards off negative influences.

Exu-orixá: A term used to differentiate the *orixá* from the other functions of Exu.

Exu-slave: An Exu servant of the *orixá*.

family-of-saint: Religious kinship within the cult group. Complex ritual genealogies link the initiate to different *terreiros* from the same *axé*.

feitura or *feitura de santo*: Initiation, ritual cermony to "make" (see) the orixá, "seating" his energy in the head of the new initiate.

fundamento: A founding principle or religious secret; everything containing *axé*.

fuxico-de-santo: The practice of gossip among initiates. This is a very important instrument of political control in the *terreiros*. Conflicts are expressed by incessant criticism of everything opposed to the dominant model of the tradition.

gameleira branca: A sacred tree (*Ficus doliaria Martius*), consecrated to the *orixá* Iroko.

geledé: A ritual mask representing female ancestral power.

guia: A spirit in Umbanda.

horse or *cavalo*: A medium embodying a spirit or divinity.

inkice: Bantu divinities, equivalent to Nagô orixás.

iyá kekeré: See *mãe pequena*.

iyalorixá: A high priestess and head of a Candomblé *terreiro*. See also *mãe-de-santo*. From the Yoruba *ìyálóòrìṣà* (*iyá ní òrìṣà*: mother of the *orixá*).

iyamí: A feminine ancestor who masters magic and often is associated with witches (*ajés*).

Iyamí Oxorongá: The principle of feminine power, head of the mythical mothers. She is evoked in the *padê* ceremony.

iyamorô: Ritual responsibility linked to the *padê*.

iyawó or *iaô*: An initiate in Candomblé of fewer than seven years, from the Yoruba *ìyàwó* (younger wife). Unlike the generic term "son-of-saint," *iyawó* indicates the hierarchical position of the new initiate, inferior to that of *ebomis*.

jogo de búzios: A divination practice in Candomblé. The priest interprets messages from the gods by tossing sixteen cowries. Also called *dilogun*.

Leba: The name given to a re-Africanized pombagira. Also called Exua or Lebara.

Legba: The Fon name given to Exu in Jeje *terreiros*.

line or *linha*: An Umbanda spirit division. Each line is ruled by an *orixá* or Catholic saint and is divided into phalanxes or legions, composed of disincarnated spirits.

mãe-de-santo: A high priestess in a *terreiro*; *mãe-de-santo* means mother-of-saint, where saint is the synonym of *orixá*, as a consequence of the Afro-Brazilian syncretism in Candomblé. See also *iyalorixá*.

mãe pequena: The direct assistant of a *pai-de-santo* or *mãe-de-santo*. She is also known as *iyá kekeré* (little mother, in Yoruba).

make: to give birth to a new initiate (*feitura de santo*) or to a new *orixá* in the initiate's body. Somebody is "made" when he has performed the initiation rites. Likewise, the initiator makes the novice's *orixá* or *santo*, "seating" his energy in the novice's head.

mesa branca: See *centro de mesa*.

Nagô: Name given in Brazil to Yoruba slaves. Also one of the Candomblé nations, including the subgroups of Ketu, Efon, and Ijexá, as well as the language employed in Candomblé rituals.

nation: Internal division of Candomblé. The concept of nation lost its original ethnic meaning and acquired a more political and theological meaning. The Candomblé nations are Ketu, Efon, Ijexá, Nagô-Vodun, Jeje, Angola, Congo, and Caboclo.

obrigação: Literally, obligation; a ritual ceremony to the *orixás* performed one, three, seven, fourteen, and twenty-one years after initiation to mark progress through Candomblé's initiatory grades.

odù: One of the divinatory configurations of the Ifá system, also known as the paths by which the *orixás* come, thus influencing their actions on men in a positive or negative way. *Odùs* are regarded as living, active entities, which must be fed and propitiated with sacrifices. It also refers to the notion of destiny.

ogan: A ritual position reserved for men who do not enter into trances but who serve as protectors of the cult, as well as drummers or sacrificers of animals.

ojé: A priest of the Egungun cult.

Oju Oba: Ritual title in Candomblé which means "the King's eyes" and is related to the Xangô cult.

opelé: A chain to which are attached eight palm-nut halves; the combinations of the halves refer to the *odùs* of the Ifá system.

oríkì: A series of laudatory epithets, praise names related to the *orixá*.

orixá: African gods venerated in Candomblé as mediators between Olorun (the supreme god) and mankind. Also called *santo*.

orun: The spiritual world. From the Yoruba *òrun*.

oyè : A ritual title in Candomblé.

padê: A propitiatory ritual for Exu, when ancestors can be invoked (*rodar a cuia*). From the Yoruba *pàdé* (meeting).

"pagan" Exu: An Exu in Umbanda who is not yet indoctrinated; an unevolved spirit.

pai-de-santo: A Candomblé priest and leader of a cult house. The religious terminology refers to a ritual kinship: the initiator is the father (*pai*) or mother (*mãe*) of sons and daughters-of-saint, initiates to the gods. See *babalorixá*.

pai pequeno: The *terreiro* head's direct assistant. Also known as *baba kekerê*.

Pombagira: A female Exu in Umbanda.

ponto cantado: A chanted invocation dedicated to the Umbanda spirits.

ponto riscado: A drawing made of cabalistic symbols that has the power to invoke the Umbanda spirits. The drawings are the spirits' signatures, as the specific combination of symbols (arrows, crosses, or circles) identifies the spirit invoked.

pretos-velhos: Spirits of an old African in Umbanda.

"qualities": Different manifestations of the same divinity. Each individual *orixá* is known by a specific name, corresponding to his "quality."

quartinha: A small clay amphora that is filled with water and placed near the *assentos*.

quiumba: An unevolved, obsessing spirit.

ronkó: The initiation room in a *terreiro*.

santo: *Orixá*. Both terms are synonymous as the consequence of the Afro-Brazilian syncretism that linked *orixás* to Catholic saints.

son-of-saint or daughter-of-saint: An initiate in Candomblé. The term refers to spiritual kinship.

terreiro: Both the house of worship and the community of initiates.

trocar as águas: Literally, to change the waters, meaning to change Candomblé nations. The initiate affiliates himself with another *terreiro*, passing under the mystical protection of another *pai* or *mãe-de-santo*.

Umbanda: A Brazilian religion, born from the combination of African rituals (especially of Bantu origin), indigenous cults, Catholicism, and the Spiritism of Allan Kardec.

vodun: A Fon divinity, venerated in Jeje Candomblé and Tambor da Mina.

xirê: Ritual invocations and dances for the *orixás* during public ceremonies.

NOTES

Introduction

All quotations from interviews in this book are from interviews that I conducted in Rio de Janeiro between December 1993 and March 1995.

1. The use of the term "Afro-Brazilian" presents some epistemological problems because we find, within the Afro-Brazilian religious field, religions such as Kardecism, which is not recognized as a cult of African origin but is closely linked to the other religions ("African" Umbanda, Omolocô, and Candomblé) claiming African heritage. We will see that mediums circulate from one modality to another, in a religious continuum that runs from the pole considered least African (Kardecism) to that considered the most African (Nagô Candomblé). Despite the problems that using this term can lead to, I have chosen to follow the accepted usage in literature about Candomblé and other cults known as Afro-Brazilian. We will return to this issue at the end of the introduction.

2. Candomblé is divided into "nations": Nagô, Ketu, Efon, Ijexá, Nagô-Vodun, Jeje, Angola, Congo, Caboclo. The concept of nation lost its original ethnic meaning and now has a more "political" and theological meaning. For an in-depth discussion of this concept, see Costa Lima 1976 and Parés 2006 (101–3).

3. A *pai-de-santo* is a Candomblé priest and leader of a cult house. The religious terminology refers to a ritual kinship: the initiator is the "father" (*pai*) or "mother" (*mãe*) of "sons" and "daughters-of-saint," initiates to the cult. See Costa Lima 1977.

4. The term "terreiro" defines both the cult house and the community of initiates.

5. The term "Nagô" is a contraction of the term used by the Fon of Dahomey (now Benin) to designate the Yoruba who live in their country. According to Cornevin (cited by Ceccaldi 1979, 178), this word derives from *inagonu*, a term used by the Dahomians to designate their Yoruba enemies. This was later transformed into *Anagonu*, then into *Anago*, which became Nagô in Brazil. Yoruba and Fon mythologies were always much syncretized. This mixture, found prior to slavery, is the basis of the *Jeje-Nagô* model, which for a long time was considered predominant in Bahian Candomblé. The word "Jeje" refers to the enslaved people from the Gbe-speaking area of Dahomey (Parés 2006, 47–52).

6. The term "Bantu" originates in linguistic studies—especially those of Guthrie and of Greenberg, who, following the model of Indo-European languages, classified African languages into several families, such as Sudanese and Bantu languages. The names of these two large linguistic groups also came to define the different African peoples who spoke these languages. Thus, in Brazil, the Nagô (Yoruba) and the Jeje (Fon) were classified with the Sudanese, and the Angola and Congo with the Bantu.

7. Angola Candomblé has been little analyzed. With the exception of Édison Carneiro's classic studies (1964, 1991), which confirm the mythical and ritual inferiority of the Bantu, at the time of my research there were only two anthropological works about Angola Candomblé: Gisèle Binon-Cossard (1970) and Ordep Trindade Serra (1978). While the first author abandoned anthropology to become a Candomblé mãe-de-santo, the second is now linked to Nagô Candomblé (see Serra 1995).

8. It should be emphasized that, although Binon-Cossard dedicated her doctoral thesis to a terreiro located in a suburb of Rio de Janeiro, her pai-de-santo, Joãozinho da Goméia, was from Bahia and well known in the world of Afro-Brazilian religions. Despite his "sins" of origin (Capone 1996), which brought his legitimacy into question, he is cited in various anthropological studies, such as Bastide 1971, Carneiro 1991, Landes 1967, and Ziegler 1975. The other study dedicated to Angola Candomblé (Serra 1978) is based on a terreiro in Salvador. Bahia has always been a powerful center for legitimation in Candomblé literature.

9. This geographic distribution among "pure" African religions and "degenerate" African cults never considered the presence, since the end of the nineteenth century, of a large contingent of Candomblé pais and mães-de-santo in Rio de Janeiro. For a detailed analysis of this question, see Moura 1983 and Capone 1996.

10. In 1944, Luis Viana Filho, speaking of the existence of several Bantu Candomblés founded before the studies of Nina Rodrigues, wrote that "it was remarkable that they had gone unnoticed by a scholar as intelligent as this illustrious master" (1988, 209).

11. Dantas (1988) analyzes the political role of the use of popular culture by the elites as a distinctive element of local and regional specificities, in response to the dislocation of the center of power from the Northeast to the Southeast in the 1930s.

12. A Brazilian religion, Umbanda revives a large part of the Macumba heritage, which is reinterpreted via the "whitening" of all the less "presentable" aspects of Afro-Brazilian religions, such as animal sacrifice or a long initiation period. Umbanda was born in the 1920s in Rio de Janeiro (Brown 1985), from which it spread to nearly all of Brazil. As with Macumba, Umbanda combines African

rituals (most of Bantu origin), Catholicism, indigenous cults, and the Spiritism of Allan Kardec.

13. We shall see that the existence of witchcraft accusations in terreiros, considered traditional, only confirms this hypothesis (see Landes 1994).

14. We shall return to this question in the part of the introduction on fieldwork.

15. The ogan is a ritual position reserved for men who do not enter into trances but who serve as protectors of the cult, as well as drummers or sacrificers of animals.

16. I use here the concept of religious field developed by Pierre Bourdieu (1971) to analyze the set of cult modalities that are part of a single religious universe considered to be Afro-Brazilian. This is built in relation to other religious universes, such as the Roman Catholic Church and the pentecostal churches, according to ties of inclusion or exclusion.

17. In an interview, Mãe Stella from Axé Opô Afonjá, the Nagô terreiro considered the most traditional, asserted: "In Candomblé the *ewọ* or *quizilas*, prohibitions, are not good things for us, either spiritually or materially. But if you do not respect the restrictions, your soul will not go to hell; if you do not comply with a particular *ewọ*, you are spiritually delayed, you cannot evolve" ("Mãe Stella" 1994, 46). Similarly, Olga de Alaketu, another renowned Nagô *mãe-de-santo*, explained the relationship between Catholic saints and *orixás* as "a transposition of spirits, in different times" (quoted in Costa Lima 1984). These notions of spiritual elevation and evolution stem from the Kardecist-Spiritist discourse, demonstrating its importance even in the most traditional terreiros.

18. "Umbandomblé" is another term of accusation, like Quimbanda. It indicates a Candomblé terreiro that is mixed—i.e., that has a strong Umbanda influence. The term is frequently used in Rio de Janeiro to contest the legitimacy of other terreiros.

19. The term "medium," used in Umbanda and Kardecism, emphasizes the specificity of the adept—his mediumship—rather than an ideal loyalty to the religious group expressed by the term *filho-de-santo*. This loyalty is constantly questioned by the circulation of mediums within the different nations of Candomblé.

20. The mãe-de-santo Olga de Alaketu, from one of the most traditional Nagô terreiros of Salvador, organized a festival every year for her caboclo Jundiara (Lopes dos Santos 1984). In 1983, one day after the decision to declare the Casa Branca terreiro a heritage site by the Historic Heritage Council, a photo of this traditional terreiro with a large picture of a caboclo was published in a Salvador newspaper. Despite his undeniable presence, the caboclo has been the object, like Exu, of a strategy of dissimulation in anthropological writings (see Teles dos Santos 1995)

21. The widespread practice among mediums of calling Umbanda exus by the name exus-eguns is not accepted by those who belong to the most "Africanized" pole of Candomblé. For them, the Eguns are ancestors—the Baba Eguns—venerated

on the island of Itaparica in Bahia. Nevertheless, I use this term, from mediums' discourse, to distinguish the exus of Umbanda from those of Candomblé: the Exu-egun from the Exu-orixá. In this book, I will use the term "eguns" (lowercased) to refer to the disincarnated spirits and the term "Eguns" (capitalized) to refer to the ancestors' spirits.

22. Accusations of witchcraft—as well as of simulation—are part of the internal logic of the Afro-Brazilian cults, having a central role in the reproduction of an ideal model of orthodoxy. The practice of gossip (*fuxico-de-santo*) also constitutes an instrument of political control very important in the terreiros. Conflicts are expressed by incessant criticism of everything opposed to the dominant model of the tradition. On this topic, see Paul Johnson 2002.

23. To respect this plurality of voices, I used a technique similar to that of Oscar Lewis (1961). When dealing with a "mystical triangle" in chapter 5, I opted for a cumulative and multiple vision of a single reality, creating a dialogue between different points of view: the husband, the wife, and her Pombagira, a constant character in the conjugal drama.

24. The history of the Efon nation in Brazil is presented in chapter 3.

25. Attitudes toward the object vary greatly according to the cult studied. While the majority of anthropologists who work on "traditional" religions, such as Candomblé, become involved with these cults, those who study Umbanda maintain a certain distance from their object. Peter Fry (1984) proposed the interesting hypothesis of an excessive cultural proximity to Umbanda that impedes the researchers' identification with it, while "African" Candomblé presents an exotic and fascinating image, with very important aesthetic dimensions that attract both mediums from Umbanda and researchers.

26. Initiation is the outcome of a long learning period, marked by various rituals corresponding to different levels of religious engagement. The divination session is followed by the preparation of the necklaces, the *borí* (a ceremony dedicated to the head, from *bo ori*, "to venerate the head"), and the *assentamento* (the seat of the divinities' energies in an individual altar representing the initiate's head), which eventually lead to the initiatory reclusion and the public ceremony announcing the new initiate's definitive entrance into the cult. These rituals may be accomplished over a long time, or concentrated in the three-week reclusion period.

27. *Axé* is the sacred force or religious power concentrated in objects and initiates. It also refers to the religious tradition transmitted via spiritual kin.

28. Nina Rodrigues and Arthur Ramos were chosen to be ogans in Gantois (Landes 1994, 72), Carneiro in Axé Opô Afonjá (ibid., 35), and Donald Pierson in the Ogunjá terreiro of the pai-de-santo Procópio. Pierre Verger was chosen to be an ogan in Axé Opô Afonjá, as were Vivaldo da Costa Lima and Marco Aurélio Luz. Júlio Braga received the ritual title of Onan Mogbá (head Xangô priest) in Axé

Opô Aganju of Balbino Daniel de Paula, a son-of-saint of Mãe Senhora from Axé Opô Afonjá (Braga 1988, 20). Serra embodies the best example of the "obligation" to affiliate with the cult group studied. After having been chosen as an ogan in the Angola Tanurijunçara terreiro of Mãe Bebê, where he conducted his early research (Serra 1978), he is now an ogan in the Ketu Casa Branca terreiro (Serra 1995).

29. The *ekedi* is a woman consecrated to a divinity, but who does not experience trances. She cares for the initiate in a trance and is present at all the ritual ceremonies.

30. *Babalorixá* is the Nagô term for pai-de-santo. His female counterpart is *iya-lorixá*, "mother of the orisha."

31. My ties to Candomblé were finally confirmed by initiatory rituals in 2002.

1. The Messenger of the Gods

1. I will use the Portuguese spelling of the Yoruba name Èṣù when referring to this divinity in Brazil.

2. Mac Ricketts defines the figure of the trickster as "the maker of the earth and/or . . . the one who changes the chaotic myth-world into the ordered creation of today; . . . he is also a prankster who is grossly erotic, insatiably hungry, inordinately vain, deceitful, and cunning toward friends as well as foes; a restless wanderer upon the face of the earth; and a blunderer who is often the victim of his own tricks and follies" (1965, 327).

3. Here I will consider the Èṣù Ẹlẹgbẹra of the Yoruba and the Legba of the Fon to be corresponding and equivalent mythical figures. Their place in the divination system justifies this choice, although the Fon Legba is considered to be a less negative divinity than Èṣù, "whose mood is perpetual evil" (Ellis 1894, 64–65; Thompson 1984, 20). This demonization of Èṣù, in opposition to the less frightening figure of Legba, is not confirmed by the work of Bernard Maupoil (1988), in which Legba is considered the incarnation of evil and misfortune. According to Joan Wescott (1962, 336), the difference between Legba and Èṣù resides in the intense sexual activity of Legba and in his transgression of sexual taboos. The cult of Èṣù probably spread from Nigeria to Dahomey, where this divinity took the name of Legba (Maupoil 1988; Verger 1995, 259).

4. E. Bolaji Idowu, however, sees in the figure of Èṣù "the inspector-general" of Olódùmarè (Ọlọrun), the supreme god of the Yoruba pantheon: "He is certainly not the Devil of our New Testament acquaintance, who is an out and out evil power in opposition to the plan of God's salvation of man. On the whole, it would be near the truth to parallel him with Satan in the Book of Job, where Satan is one of the ministers of God and has the office of trying men's sincerity and putting their religion to the proof" (1962, 80).

5. According to Melville Herskovits, *gbo* means "all categories of specific cures or supernatural aids, as well as their anti-social counterparts" (1938, 256).

6. Among the Yoruba, as in most of Africa, twins (*ibéjì*) are considered to be beings with great power and, for this reason, extremely dangerous. Their birth demands the realization of complex rituals that allow the socialization of the newly born. The firstborn is called Táíwò and the second Kéèhìndé (he who is before-behind).

7. Idowu (1962, 85) says that there are 200 different names for Èṣù, but among the Yoruba that number (and its double, 400) symbolizes multiplicity—that is, a large, undetermined quantity.

8. In Yoruba *erù* corresponds to the Brazilian *carrego* (burden, weight). In Candomblé the notion of carrego concerns not only religious ceremonies, because carrego is also the negative charge resulting from *ebó* (magic work), which should be neutralized by being abandoned in a specific place (crossroads, forest, riverbank, beach). Carrego is also a ritual obligation received as an inheritance by a person who must care for the divinity of a deceased family member.

9. Juana Elbein dos Santos provides a complete version of this myth in Yoruba, with its translation in Portuguese (1976, 139–61).

10. In the texts of the Apocalypse of Talmudic literature and the Kabbalah, we find belief in devils of both sexes. Like incubi and succubae, they have sexual relations with human beings, giving birth to a special category of devils who are part of human nature. This belief is the origin of demonology of the sixteenth and seventeenth centuries, and it finds its expression in the treatise called *Malleus Maleficarum*.

11. In Siegfried Nadel's study (1942, 194) about the Nupe kingdom in northern Nigeria, *bara* designates freed slaves, servants, messengers, or soldiers tied to their master's property. Nadel translates baraship as clientship. The king of the Nupe was called "Etsu" (ibid.). Until today, the possibility that Èṣù has a Nupe origin, like Yansan-Oya, has never been considered.

12. This discussion about the existence of a priesthood consecrated to Èṣù takes on significant importance in the discourse of Nagô Candomblé, which refuses initiation in the cult of Èṣù under the pretext that it does not conform to African tradition.

13. See Herskovits 1938, Herskovits and Herskovits 1958, Aguessy 1992, and Verger 1957.

14. All Candomblé initiates are known by the name of their god, as in Marcos de (of) Yansan or Alvinho de (of) Omolu. This and the following quotations without attributions come from interviews I conducted in Rio de Janeiro between December 1993 and March 1995.

15. An *opelé* is a divinatory chain to which are attached eight palm-nut halves; the combinations of the halves refer to the *odù* (divinatory configurations) of the Ifá

system. These odùs are considered Ifá's children; they can combine to give 256 different responses which the diviner must memorize. This form of divination still exists in Cuba, but was lost in Brazil. See chapter 8 on the reintroduction of this forgotten practice in Candomblé.

16. *Dilogun* is an abbreviation of the Yoruba *mérindínlógún* (sixteen).

17. The *assento* is the material representation of the sacred force of the divinity. It is made of clay, ceramic, or wooden containers holding a stone (*otan*), symbolizing the initiate's head, and various other ingredients.

18. "Qualities" are a divinity's different avatars, symbolizing his or her bonds with the other orixás. Each divinity has a different number of qualities.

19. *Dendê* comes from the Kimbundu *dendém* and refers to the oil extracted from the palm tree *Elaeis guineensis*.

20. The word "slave" is obviously an inheritance from colonial times: if Exu "works" for the orixá, he becomes his "slave." For a long time in Brazil, manual labor was only performed by slaves.

21. See Carneiro 1986, 68, and Lépine 1978, 259.

22. "Èṣù is an *orixá* or saint like the others, with his own brotherhood and adepts. In the Gantois temple or terreiro, the first day of the great festival is dedicated to Èṣù" (Nina Rodrigues 1900, 25).

23. In reality, Exu's replacement by Ogun shows the adaptation to Afro-Catholic syncretism: "because of the association the missionaries made between Exu and the devil, and in order to avoid complications for the terreiro, the blacks of the Ketu nation would say, here in Brazil, 'Exu has no son, for he does not have the right to manifest himself in anyone from the religion'" (Deoscóredes dos Santos 1988, 60). Here the author is referring to an adaptation strategy set up in the terreiro, which is today considered to represent the Nagô tradition, the Axé Opô Afonjá of Salvador. Likewise, Carneiro (1986) gives us a list of Exu's "qualities" known in the Casa Branca terreiro where he carried out his research. In the list are found, next to Yoruba-derived names such as Ekeçae (a corruption of Akessan) and Lona, the names Pavena, Maromba, Barabô, Tibiriri, Tiriri, Chefe Cunha, and Maioral, usually linked to the "less pure" cults of Bantu Candomblé and Macumba. This is important for the debate about the construction of an image of purity in the Nagô terreiros, of which the Casa Branca is the founder.

24. Seventeen years later Bastide (1975, 190) stated categorically that Exu was never incorporated in Candomblé, contrary to Macumba, where he provokes crises of possession and is considered a demonic entity.

25. He is, then, Maria de Xangô's "brother-of-saint." In Candomblé, the ritual kinship structures the religious group (see figure 3).

26. *Axé* indicates here a religious tradition linked to a house of worship considered the motherhouse. Religious energy—the other meaning of axé—is transmitted during the initiation rituals, when the novice's head is shaved with a razor.

27. Olga de Alaketu was the mãe-de-santo of the Ilê Mariolajé, better known by the name of Alaketu, one of the oldest and most respected Ketu temples of Salvador.

28. *Rodar a cuia* means "to turn the calabash." In fact, the cuia is a half-calabash, used as a ritual container in Candomblé.

29. *Acaçá* is a paste of a gelatinous constituency, made of white corn flour and water, and wrapped in banana leaves.

30. *Exés* are the parts of a sacrificed animal which are charged with divine power (axé). These parts are offered to the orixá and usually placed in front of his shrine. They are the head, feet, wings, tail, heart, lungs, esophagus, and testicles.

31. Juana Elbein dos Santos and her husband, Deoscóredes M. dos Santos, *asogbá* (a high dignitary in the cult of Obaluaiê) in the Axé Opô Afonjá, define the ritual as follows: "The Pàdé as it is practiced in the Ase Opo Afonja is a solemn and private ritual which can be attended only by persons who belong to the terreiro or by exceptional visitors. It is a ceremony fraught with danger, in view of the supernatural power of the entities that shall be invoked and of its purpose of propelling and maintaining harmonious relations with them and of propitiating or restoring, by means of suitable offerings, their favour and protection" (Santos and Santos 1971, 112).

32. The sacred trees of the iyamís-eleiye are *aridan*, *akoko*, and *apakoka* (Rego 1980).

33. Juana Elbein dos Santos (1976, 108–12) tells the same story but replaces the name of Odu with those of Iyamí and Odua. The changing of Odu into Odua was strongly criticized by Verger (1982b) because of the confusion with Oduduwa (or Odua), a male figure in the Yoruba pantheon. Odu is also linked to the cult of Ifá and must not be confused with *odù*, the divinatory configuration.

34. In Africa there are secret societies dedicated to the cult of the Eguns or Egunguns. In Brazil, this cult was perpetuated on the island of Itaparica, in Bahia. When invoked, the Eguns appear dressed in multicolored, embroidered robes which cover them completely. No one may touch them, for contact with them is considered fatal. Only men may become *ojés*, priests of this cult.

35. The connection between Iyamí Oxorongá and Exu is confirmed by an *itan* (story) from the body of knowledge of Ifá, linked to the Odù Osa Meji. He tells of how the vagina found its place in the human body thanks to the intervention of Exu and Iyamí Oxorongá, who placed it under Iyá Mapo's protection (Rego 1980).

36. According to the Drewals (1983, 3), the geledé festival began toward the end of the eighteenth century with the Yoruba from Ketu. It spread rapidly to other Yoruba groups and, following the slave trade of the nineteenth century, to Brazilian and Cuban groups of Yoruba influence.

37. In Sergipe, the opposition between a "pure" religion (Nagô) and a "degenerate" cult (Toré) does not follow the model of the Candomblé of Bahia. In fact the

Nagô of the Xangô of Sergipe shows a series of distinctive traits, which make it closer to the so-called degenerate cults in Salvador, while the Toré, a "mixed" cult at Serpige, shows traits which are considered "pure" in Salvador, such as the ritual shaving of heads (Dantas 1988).

38. The name given in the state of Maranhão, in the north of Brazil, to the religion of African origin considered traditional, just like the Candomblé of Bahia and the Xangô of Recife.

39. The line defended by this temple is very important, because it incarnates in São Luís—as well as the Casa Branca, the Gantois, and the Axé Opô Afonjá in Salvador—the religion's tradition and orthodoxy in the eyes of members of other terreiros.

40. The same relation between Exu-Legba and Averekete has been suggested by Nunes Pereira (1979, 79), Costa (1948, 79), and Bastide (1958, 178).

2. The Spirits of Darkness

1. The account of the revelation of Zélio de Moraes's mission, which led to the creation of a new religion, is considered by Diana Brown (1986) to be the founding myth of Umbanda.

2. According to Areia (1974), calundus are the spirits of ancestors in Angola. Generally they are warrior spirits and upholders of justice.

3. Laura de Mello e Souza (1986, 263–66) reveals the great importance of these calundus in colonial life, through the witchcraft trials led by the Inquisition in Brazil. She quotes the case of the slave Tomasia, who claimed to be possessed by fetishes called calundus, the souls of his deceased parents who spoke through his mouth. See also Harding 2000.

4. In Angola, Calunga-ngombe is also responsible for judgment after death, and the ensuing punishment or reward (Ribas 1958, 37). Calunga also means sea or ocean. We shall see how the figure of Calunga, representing death, has been preserved in Umbanda.

5. For an analysis of the categories of Umbanda spirits, see Montero 1985.

6. Absinthe was banned in France in 1915. It is still produced in Portugal, the country where the medium often worked, and from which he brought back this drink for his Exu. The connection between a drink belonging to a "cursed world" in France, where it was the favorite liquor of Charles Baudelaire, Arthur Rimbaud, and Paul Verlaine, and its insertion into the diabolical world of the exus does not seem to me to be mere coincidence. I see in it traces of a possible literary rewriting of religions of African origin.

7. According to Alva (n.d., 124), Maria Padilha was part of the "dynasty of the Cleopatras"; in another reincarnation, she was a Frenchwoman called Marie Padi (or Marie Padu or Marie Padille).

8. See Verger 1957, 119.

9. The spirits of exus or pombagiras may be invoked by chants (*pontos cantados*) or drawings (*pontos riscados*) which are their signatures (see figure 17).

10. The figure of Pombagira has seldom been analyzed, except by Márcia Contins (1983), Augras (1989), Meyer (1993), and Kelly Hayes (2004).

11. *Padilla* in Spanish has the same pronunciation as *padilha* in Portuguese.

12. We have seen how Iyamí is thought to control women through their menstrual periods.

3. The Religious Continuum

1. The circulation of spirits and men is not only characteristic of cities in the Southeast (the degenerated pole); it may also be seen in cities regarded as traditional. Unfortunately, researchers have always concentrated on "pure" terreiros and religious practices, leaving aside all that does not correspond to the orthodox model. My experience of four months (July to October 1991) at São Luís do Maranhão, a city considered to be one of the traditional centers of Afro-Brazilian religions, my time in Salvador (December 1983 to October 1984), and my more than ten years in Rio de Janeiro lead me to believe that the most common ritual is never that which the pure model refers to. While there is a strong interpenetration of different ritual practices, the study of mixed forms remains to be carried out.

2. Bastide (1978, 204) claims that the influence of Yoruba and Bantu nations in the city of Rio de Janeiro was strong until the first decade of the nineteenth century, "until urbanization of the Brazilian capital reached a peak." For Bastide, the similarity of Cariocas religious practices with Candomblé of Bahia was not the consequence of contact between the Northeast and Southeast, "yet these blacks were not in close contact with either Bahia or Recife. The similarity of their cults can therefore be explained only by their common ethnic origin" (Bastide 1978, 205). However, I have tried to show (Capone 1996) that contact has always existed, and that various representatives of traditional Candomblé of Bahia were also active in Candomblé in Rio de Janeiro at the beginning of the twentieth century.

3. The *mãe pequena* is the pai-de-santo or mãe-de-santo's direct assistant. She is also known as *iyá kekeré* ("little mother," in Yoruba).

4. Ziegler devoted a chapter of his *Les vivants et la mort* (1975) to funeral rites in João da Goméia's terreiro.

5. The history of the Efon nation was collected during my interview on April 6, 1994, with Maria de Xangô in the Pantanal terreiro in Rio de Janeiro.

6. Iroco (or Iroko), who lives in the tree *gameleira branca* (*Ficus doliaria Martius*),

and Oloque (or Oloroquê) are two gods considered to be brothers in the Efon nation. Both of them are associated with the god Xangô. Oloque is considered to be Xangô's forest brother, and his sacred necklaces are the same color as those used by initiates to Xangô: red and white. He is also called "the lion of the mountain." The close links between Iroko and Oloroke (or Oloke) are confirmed by Apter (1995, 389) who emphasizes the importance of these two orixás as dominant cults of different districts of the city of Ilemesho in the kingdom of Ishan, in Ekiti country (Nigeria). Verger (1957, 314) cites the name Oloroke among the twelve types of Xangô catalogued in Bahia.

7. In Candomblé it is forbidden to initiate a member of one's nuclear family, which is why Cristóvão's daughter was initiated by a mãe-de-santo from an allied terreiro. This ban is limited to sons, daughters or spouses and so a pai-de-santo may initiate his granddaughter without breaking the ritual rules.

8. Prandi (1990, 22) presents a slightly different genealogy for the Oloroquê's terreiro. This genealogy is not confirmed by the current mãe-de-santo of the house of Pantanal, or by Alvinho de Omolu.

9. "Changing the waters" (trocar as águas), where water represents the religious tradition or nation, is one of the most efficient ways of renegotiating ritual ties. By placing himself under the protection of another pai-de-santo, the initiate severs the ties of submission with his original terreiro. The purpose of this practice, which is extremely widespread in Afro-Brazilian religions, is often to legitimize one's religious origins, linking the initiate to a "purer" terreiro.

10. "Seating a divinity in someone's head" signifies initiating someone. The head is regarded as the place where the divinity connects with his son.

11. On this subject, see Prandi (1990).

12. The program's title refers to the Candomblé divination practice consisting of tossing cowries and interpretating the patterns in which they fall.

13. The principal function of federations of Afro-Brazilian religions is negotiation: with society to legitimize the cult, but also between the different practices within the cult. In reality, the federation has to guarantee that each terreiro can carry out "its own" Umbanda, by intervening as a mediator only in moments of crisis. The multiple variants which exist within any one cult make it impossible to carry out the project of normalization.

14. In 1950, there were 1,869 Spiritist religious associations registered in São Paulo, of which 1,023 were Umbandist, 485 Kardecist, and only 1 Candomblé. However, in 1970, there were 8,685 registered associations, of which 7,627 (87.8 percent) called themselves Umbandist, 202 Kardecist, and 856 Candomblé (Cancone and Negrão 1985, 48).

15. Here Bastide is referring to the Bahia pai-de-santo Joãozinho da Goméia, who moved to Rio de Janeiro in the early 1950s. Although without a pure pedigree, he

was nevertheless one of Brazil's most famous heads of terreiro. We find in these few lines by Bastide a concentration of the criticisms made by the partisans of "pure" religions: material advantage (financial success), the practice of black magic, contamination by Spiritism, and the lack of respect for "purely African norms."

16. On this subject, the words of Mãe Stella, iyalorixá of the Axé Opô Afonjá, regarded as the guardian of Bahia Candomblé traditions, are very significant: "Candomblé is not a black religion. It has black origins as it was brought by the Africans. The whites have joined it, adopted it, and asserted themselves in it . . . It is we, the poor people, mostly black, who run the terreiro, even though the white people who are integrated into Candomblé are sometimes more faithful and more responsible than most people of black descent" ("Mãe Stella" 1994, 44). See João Reis (1989) and Renato da Silveira (1988) about the presence of white people in Candomblé at the beginning of the nineteenth century.

17. Until the 1950s, Brazil, part of the Luso-Brazilian community, aligned its foreign policies with those of Portugal. The 1965 mission in West Africa led to a decisive change of direction. A publication by the Department of Culture and Information of the Brazilian Ministry of Foreign Affairs, dedicated to the first Festival of Black Arts at Dakar in 1966, clearly shows the effects of these new policies: "Upon the return from Africa of the successful Trade Mission in June 1965, the Government definitively decided that Brazilian vessels would call periodically at West African ports on the way to the Mediterranean, carrying Brazilian merchandise to Africa and picking up African products for shipment to Brazil in return" ("The African Contribution to Brazil" 1966, 106).

18. The importance of relations with representatives of African governments, and above all the central role played by the Nigerian ambassadors, is part of the process of re-Africanization which is the subject of my analysis in the third part of this book. The changes in Brazilian foreign policies led to a new cultural policy, with the creation of specific research centers and the diffusion of courses on Yoruba language and civilization in Salvador, São Paulo, and Rio de Janeiro.

19. Mãe Menininha was the great-granddaughter of Maria Julia da Conceição Nazaré, one of the founders of the Casa Branca, regarded as Salvador's oldest terreiro. She was born in 1894 and died August 8, 1986.

20. This difference in levels of mystical power is also established with regard to Kardecism, which is considered less powerful than Umbanda in the face of supernatural attack.

21. My interview with Palmira de Yansan, of the Ketu nation.

22. I have frequently engaged in long discussions about "things from Africa." Many interlocutors expressly asked me for references to books about religions in Africa. All information—from libraries, research centers, and universities—was

received with astonishing interest, blurring the limits between researcher and key informant.

23. My interview with Alvinho de Omolu, of the Efon nation.

24. My interview with Dina de Yansan, of the Ketu nation.

25. The *Mercadão* at Madureira, a district in the northern part of Rio de Janeiro, is a covered market spreading out over three floors. Everything necessary for Candomblé rituals can be found there—herbs and objects or animals for sacrifice. Unfortunately, there are no in-depth studies about the parallel economy connected with Afro-Brazilian religions.

26. My interview with Dina de Yansan, of the Ketu nation.

27. In Candomblé, the expression *feitura de santo* (making the saint) is used to describe initiation. During this period the initiator (the pai-de-santo) is supposed to give new life to the novice, who will be bound to his orixá forever. This personal orixá is thus "made" by an intermediary, the head of the terreiro, and the initiate's submission to him is therefore prescribed.

28. On this subject, see Maggie's (1977) analysis of a demanda in an Umbanda terreiro. The purpose of magical attacks is to redefine the hierarchical positions in the religious group. Maggie's analysis is one of the very rare studies dedicated to conflict in Afro-Brazilian religions.

4. Reorganizing Sacred Space

1. Here I refer to an egun (without a capital letter) as the spirit of a dead person who does not have the status of a collective ancestor, as opposed to the Egun in Itaparica. What makes things even more complex is that the same term also designates the bones used in various magical practices. This difficulty results from the loss, in Brazil, of the tones of the Yoruba language. In fact, in Yoruba, ancestors are called *egúngún* (or, in the contracted form, *eégún*), while the bones are called *egungun* or *eegun*.

2. In 1986, I attended a funerary ritual for an ojé. During the ritual, which lasted three nights, those present took great care to keep away from the Eguns who manifested themselves. The impromptu appearance of the deceased—a man covered with a white shroud—at the door of the house of worship provoked panic among the women there, and many of them went into a trance. Calm was restored by the rapid intervention of the ojés who chased away the spirit, thus reestablishing the necessary separation between the living and the dead.

3. In chapter 5 we shall see how this submission is always renegotiated, for most conflicts within the cult develop around exus and pombagiras. Obedience to the pai-de-santo and even submission to the master of the head (the individual orixá) are always called into question.

4. In the initiation process, it is said that the pai-de-santo "makes" the initiate, but

he also "makes" his orixá: he makes both of them be born and enables the divine nature (the initiate's liaison with the divinity who possesses him) to express. This orixá is deeply linked to the initiate's personality, becoming known as the Ogun of Maria or the Oxalá of José.

5. This tension is common to all terreiros, even the most traditional.

6. The razor (navalha) is used for the ritualistic shaving of hair, the incision in the initiate's head, and ritual scarifications—the symbol of initiation and belonging to the cult.

7. Orixás or spirits may be inherited by a family member. In the case of Maria de Xangô, she inherited her mother's caboclo.

8. It may be imagined that the reason this orixá's cult is so widespread in Brazil, as opposed to being very limited in Africa, is related to the erasing of the caboclo in orthodox discourse. According to Serra (1995, 23), Mãe Menininha do Gantois always used to tell him that "Oxossi is an Indian, my son." The closeness between Oxossi, patron orixá of the Ketu nation, and the caboclo enables a reinterpretation of the latter in the African universe.

9. In Candomblé, the role of the divinity's messenger may be played by the erê, the child's spirit which accompanies every orixá. But possession by the erê is not systematic, and his discourse, full of childish expressions, does not have the same strength as that of re-Africanized exus and pombagiras.

10. Interview with Sandra de Oxum, of the Efon nation.

11. In the following chapter, we shall see how in reality this conflict between spirit and orixá masks a conflict between initiate and initiator, where the same relationship of power upon which the Candomblé hierarchy is founded is called into question.

12. The coexistence of the two names is common to most initiates. Thus Miriam de Omolu, who embodies the Ciganinha da Estrada (Bohemian of the Road), introduces her by the African name of Akolojemin. Likewise, Baiana do Malandro, a daughter-of-saint of Alvinho de Omolu, showed me in her terreiro a couple of Exus, of which the male element, Jebará, was the African representation of the Umbandist Exu-Caveira (Exu-Skull), and the female element, Jebaraí, that of the Pombagira Maria Padilha.

13. Various informants have told me of the initiation, in the Angola nation, of Pombagira as being the medium's master of the head. Unfortunately, each time I tried to contact one of these initiates, the trail disappeared, and the meeting was impossible.

5. *Contesting Power*

1. One can change terreiro or nation by carrying out the ritual ceremonies (*obrigações*) bound to the initiation cycles—after one, three, seven, fourteen, and

twenty-one years—with another pai or mãe-de-santo. In this way, one goes under the protection of the latter, becoming his or her spiritual son.

2. This is a very common strategy. Six of the mediums I interviewed had resolved their conflicts with their initiators in this way (see figure 29).

3. This was the case with Cristóvão de Ogunjá, for example, who was obliged to accept caboclos after the healing brought about by these spirits.

4. Candomblé adepts establish a clear distinction between spiritual life and material life. The first is the exclusive domain of the orixás, while the second is a matter for exus and pombagiras. Problems encountered in daily life being linked to the material side of existence, their solutions will be sought in the intervention of exus (or other spirits such as caboclos or pretos-velhos).

5. Spiritism as used here is synonymous with Umbanda, for in Kardecist Spiritism one is not possessed by Exu or Pombagira. The term, like that of Macumba for Afro-Brazilian religions, can indicate anything to do with spirits.

6. Proof by fire is usually required when a doubt exists about the veracity of a possession. The proof consists of touching fire or swallowing something burning without getting burned.

7. Spirits are always regarded as subjects acting directly upon the lives of their horses. It is the spirit, therefore—not Rosinha—who earns this money because it is she who is holding the consultations.

8. The phalanx of the Pombagiras Meninas is made up of young girls aged between ten and twelve. These pombagiras seem to be linked to the group of exus-mirins—young exus acting like mischievous children.

9. When a medium has not developed his mediumship or has died, a member of his family may inherit his "saints" (orixás) and must then carry on his spiritual mission.

10. Márcia Contins (1983) analyzed a legal case where a woman possessed by Pombagira killed a man. In the various narratives related to this case, the opposition emerges between impotent and cowardly men, and powerful and courageous women. However, the power of these women, who are allied to spirits, is always a dangerous power, which can lead this opposition between men and women to extreme consequences. Within the symbolic framework defined by Pombagira, there is no place for strong men. It is always women who occupy the predominant position.

6. Exu and the Anthropologists

1. Since the end of the nineteenth century, almost all the studies on Bahian Candomblé have been dedicated to Nagô Candomblé, which is only one of the Afro-Brazilian cult modalities. Furthermore, all these studies were carried out in the three terreiros of the Ketu nation regarded as the most traditional: the Casa

Branca or Engenho Velho, the Gantois, and the Axé Opô Afonjá. The sole exception is Lépine's thesis (1978) on the classification system of psychological types in Ketu Candomblé of Bahia, developed in Olga de Alaketu's terreiro. After Carneiro's work (1937), Serra (1978) was the only person to take an interest in an Angola terreiro in Salvador. Recently studies have begun on other cult modalities, such as the Caboclo Candomblé (Teles dos Santos 1992).

2. Antônio Risério (1988, 161) talks of a "resocializing efficiency" in the Nagôs' religious practice, combined with a great ability to form political alliances, which enabled the Nagôs to assert themselves as the dominant model on the religious market. He quotes the work of George Rawick (1972) and Eugene Genovese (1976), who criticize the traditional view of blacks as total victims of slavery. The two authors defend the point of view according to which, even in the most totalitarian society, oppressed people always find room for maneuver in order to develop survival strategies, as much physical as cultural. Silveira (1988, 186) also sees in the predominance of Nagô Candomblé the sign of a political act of adaptation rather than of resistance. This ability to adapt and cover up the more disturbing elements of the religion (Exu's links with black magic) would not seem to be so different from the legitimation strategies put in place by Umbanda.

3. On rebellions in Bahia, see Verger 1987, 329–53, and Reis 1986, 1988, and 1992.

4. J. A. Gobineau's (1884) work on the inequality of the races, originally published in 1854, was much discussed in Brazil. Gobineau, who had lived there while acting as France's minister to the Brazilian court, prophesized the decline of civilization as a result of the mixing of races. Nonwhite races' inaptitude for civilization could not be corrected through education—only crossbreeding could raise the inferior races, but that had the drawback of lowering the superior races. For the debate on race and nation in Brazil, see also Thomas Skidmore 1989, Moritz Schwarcz 1993, and Capone 2000.

5. The relative inferiority of the people of Latin origin, such as the Portuguese, explained the inferiority of the Brazilian people: "The servility of the blacks, the idleness of the Indians and the authoritative and avaricious tendency of the Portuguese have produced a shapeless nation, lacking both creative and original qualities" (Romero 1888, quoted in Roberto Ventura 1991, 49).

6. The 1824 constitution stipulated that religious freedom in Brazil be limited to the Roman Catholic Church. Article 5 specified that all other religions were only to be tolerated as "domestic cults." When the republic was proclaimed in 1889, a new constitution was promulgated in 1891, granting full religious freedom: the state could no longer discriminate against its citizens on the ground of religious convictions. Roman Catholic faith was no longer the religion of the state, which therefore had to find other ways to distinguish between legitimate and illegiti-

mate religious cults. Sorcery and the illegal practice of medicine then became the pretext for the repression of Afro-Brazilian religions.

7. Nina Rodrigues created this term from Ellis's research, to designate the syncretism, prior to the slaves' arrival from Africa, between the religious beliefs of the Yorubas and the Fons (Jeje). The expression "Jeje-Nagô" became in Afro-Brazilian studies the synonym of traditional religion. In reality, no house of worship defined itself as Jeje-Nagô, and a nation of this name has never existed.

8. Maggie (1992) analyzed twenty-five criminal-court cases against those who practiced sorcery and "low spiritism" (Ramos 1951b, 221) between 1890 and 1945. She demonstrates the belief, shared by judges and the accused alike, in the reality of bewitchment and the possibility for human beings to embody a spirit with the aim of performing malevolent acts. As in the trials of the Inquisition, persecutors and persecuted shared the same worldview.

9. Dantas (1988) develops this idea, analyzing the election of Nagô purity, embodied by the traditional blacks of the Northeast, as a distinctive local and regional mark: the Northeast region became the seat of the updating of African heritage. Freyre's work has been criticized, owing to the regional nature of his data (from the Northeast and Pernambuco), by Ramos in 1934 (1951b) and Pierson in 1942. In reality, the generalization of the Northeast model was a response to the spread of the Paulist model, supported by the modernists.

10. For an in-depth analysis of this historical period, see Dantas 1988.

11. "Low spiritism" was prosecuted by the law, for it was synonymous with the exploitation of popular credulity. Defining Caboclo Candomblé as in the realm of low spiritism thus legitimized its repression.

12. In an interview given to *Diário de Pernambuco*, just before the Bahia congress was held, Freyre insinuated that the second congress lacked "scientific solidity" (Oliveira and Costa Lima 1987, 28). In fact, the issue at stake in the confrontation between Recife and Bahia was the hegemony of what was regarded as traditional, linked to the purity of African cultural heritage. Bahia, as Recife had been in Freyre's writings, became synonymous with a "good land" and the motherland of racial democracy, the theory at the origin of the national ideology extolled by the Estado Novo.

13. I shall return to this institution in chapter 7.

14. Pierson lived in Bahia from 1935 to 1937, studying interracial relations in Brazil —which, after the publication of Freyre's book (1946) in 1933, had become an example of racial democracy. Landes's (1967, 5) principal aim was also to study "how diverse races can coexist."

15. René Ribeiro (1982, 24) wrote that the Recife group, linked to Pernambucano, was strongly influenced by Herskovits and his assertion of the normality of trances, which until then had been considered the expression of psychopatho-

logical behavior. This was to change forever the manner in which possession cults were seen, removing them definitively from the medical influence which had characterized Afro-Brazilian studies.

16. It should be remembered that, at the time, the African people in Brazil were divided into two large families: the Sudanese, which included the Yorubas and the Fons, and the Bantus. On stereotypes associated with these two groups, see Capone 2000.

17. The question of the revalorization of the figure of Exu is present in all Carneiro's writings. He dedicated an article to Exu (1950), in which he reaffirmed the orixá's "un-evilness." In 1964, he established a difference between the Exu of Candomblé and that of the Macumbas of Rio and São Paulo, who had kept the phallic nature of his dances and was linked to the dead and to cemeteries (Carneiro 1964, 134).

18. It was not until the penal code of 1985 that explicit references to the practice of magic were removed from Brazilian law. However, the illegal exercise of medicine, charlatanism, and curandeirismo continue to be prosecuted as offences (Maggie 1992, 47–48).

19. In 1948 under Herskovits's direction, Eduardo Octavio da Costa, another researcher, also underlined the strategic erasing of all that could link houses of worship to sorcery in the ritual of the "orthodox" terreiros of São Luís do Maranhão, where, as we have seen in part 1, the cult of Exu is still denied today: "Members of the two 'orthodox' houses stated that in their opinion many people in São Luís held their ceremonies in ridicule; and stated that others had accused them of practicing black magic. Cult initiates know also that the Church has taken a stand against the dances of their groups. This feeling tends to make the members of the Dahomean and the Yoruba centers wary . . . In the Dahomean house, some ceremonies have been discontinued to avoid public criticism" (Costa 1948, 106–7).

20. Research was conducted in São Paulo by Florestan Fernandes and Roger Bastide (1955); in Rio de Janeiro by Luiz Aguiar da Costa Pinto (1953); in Recife by René Ribeiro (1956); and in Bahia by Thales de Azevedo (1953) and Charley Wagley, Marvin Harris, and Ben Zimmerman (Wagley 1952). This last study, led by researchers from Columbia University, showed the existence of an indicator of racial antagonism in the "good land" of Bahia.

21. An example of the use of these categories within the religious group is this quotation from Landes (1994, 182–83) about a power struggle between two priestesses from the Gantois, which gave rise to accusations of sorcery: "people later told me that Menininha's [the head of the Gantois] second in command, Dona Laura, did practice black magic, contrary though this was to the code of a priestess. But Dona Laura was said to make it her business to go contrary to the

wishes of Menininha, whom she regarded as a priestly rival, and she could not be halted; in fact, she was said to be popular and to have many clients."

22. In chapter 7, I shall analyze Verger's role in the foundation of Africanist studies in Bahia and in the re-Africanization process. For the moment, I shall only underline the importance of the publication of *Notes sur le culte des Orisa et Vodun* (1957), which incited Brazilian Africanists to develop studies comparing Brazil and West Africa.

23. Exu's identification with the revolutionary element of the religious universe still exists. Raul Lody (1982, 11 and 14) defines Exu as "the sign of resistance," "the most active liberator of the history and culture of the African in Brazil."

24. Carneiro (1986, 135) defined axé as "the magic foundation of the house of Candomblé, its reason for existing." According to Verger (1957, 29), the word "axé" (or *àṣẹ*) signifies "power, potential, sacred force linked to an *òrìṣà*." Yeda Pessoa de Castro (1971, 35) defines it as "force or power against malevolent influences," and also as "a house of worship's magic foundation." According to Ziegler (1975, 307), "axé" corresponds to "sacred objects endowed with a specific force." Bastide (1958, 59–60) refers to Maupoil's definition (1988/1938, 334) of axé, described as "the immaterial principle, the magic force" with which Legba (the Fon Exu) transports sacrifices to the divinities. This "magic force" is closely linked to the blood of sacrificed animals. In Afro-Brazilian literature, axé is generally identified with a spiritual force or energy. According to Abimbola (1976a, 187), Exu is endowed with àṣẹ, translated as "charm of command." In Yoruba, àṣẹ means "an order, a command" (Abraham 1958, 71). This term is also associated with the idea of authority, becoming an "instrument of command."

7. In Search of Lost Origins

1. We have seen how the use of magic was also present as a pattern of accusation in terreiros known as traditional, as in the example of the Gantois related by Landes (1994, 182). The opposition between religious practices and magic is made even more artificial by this observation from Landes: "I recalled too the newspapers in Rio de Janeiro, which several times a week carried stories about the bad magic practiced by Negro men there, fathers of the temples. The Bahia papers did not carry such reports, except rarely, concentrating instead on the religious performances of the mothers" (ibid., 183).

2. Landes's text (1994) also proves to be very interesting because of the differentiation it establishes between the quest for prestige in Nagô Candomblé and the quest for mere profit in Macumba and the "degraded" cults. The author, who carried out her research in Mãe Menininha's Gantois, writes that this traditional mãe-de-santo cared for the ill people who came to see her only "to the extent

that they could pay her" (ibid, 152). This behavior would have received divine approbation, for "all clients and novices had to pay in advance, by the god's mandate" (ibid.). This same greed made Menininha attack a Caboclo Candomblé mãe-de-santo, Sabina, accused of seeking her own personal gain (ibid., 158). However, this criticism reflects here more a pattern of accusation than a specific characteristic of less traditional cults. Despite this, Landes accepts the reality of this opposition, describing Sabina as a simulator, interested only in money, while she defends the Gantois "mothers" for their "good faith."

3. It must be pointed out that in spite of the sixteen years he spent in Brazil, Bastide had direct experience of Afro-Brazilian religions only during the brief trips he made in the Northeast, trips during which he worked mostly with local experts. In *Le candomblé de Bahia* (1958, 14), he himself admits that his enquiries were limited to nine months, of which no more than five were spent in Bahia, spread over seven years (from 1944 to 1951). His contract with the University of São Paulo obliged him to carry out his research only during the university vacations, "the result being that I could only really get to know Candomblé during the three months of the vacation. I could not attend the ceremonies that took place during term-time" (quoted in Cardoso 1994, 72). This extremely limited experience in the field was compensated for by intense collaboration with Verger, who held an official position in one of the traditional terreiros of Bahia (the Axé Opô Afonjá). In a March 1951 letter, Bastide announced to Verger his arrival in Bahia and his work schedule, asking Verger to make the preparations for the visit because Bastide had so little time (from July to August 1951). He then proposed to gather information about divining practices with a certain Vidal, probably a member of the same terreiro (Morin 1994).

4. Talking of Nagô Candomblé, he writes: "religion is not something that is dead, even if everywhere it is conservative; it evolves with the social context, with changes of place or dynasty, it gives itself new rituals in order to respond to the needs of the population, or the interests of the dominant families" (Bastide 1958, 232). On Bastide's theory of syncretism, see Capone 2007.

5. Verger (1987, 634) speaks of 2,630 Brazilian passports given to freed slaves before their departure from the port of Bahia, from 1820 to 1868. Jerry Turner (1975, 67 and 78) estimates that there were 1,056 passports issued between 1840 and 1880, and 3,000 former slaves who returned to Africa. Cunha (1985, 213) calculates 8,000 *libertos* who came from Bahia between 1820 and 1889, and gives 1909 as the probable date of the last departure from Bahia to Lagos. Many of these "Brazilians" came back to establish themselves in the city of Salvador, after short or long journeys to Africa. On travel between Brazil and Africa, see also Matory (2005).

6. I will keep the different spellings used by authors for the names of the founders of the first Bahian terreiros (for example, see the difference in spelling between

Costa Lima and Verger). However, I shall use standard Yoruba spelling for terms in that language.

7. Costa Lima (1977) contested the fact that the founders of the Casa Branca could originally be from Ketu, a Yoruba city which is now part of Benin. Iyá Nassô is in fact an oyè (an honorary title) exclusive to the court of Oyó and designating the woman responsible for the cult of Xangô, the patron divinity of the dynasty of the Aláàfin, the king of Oyó. Those who used the title would not, then, be originally from Ketu but from the city of Oyó. In the same way, the existence of the three founding mothers would seem doubtful, for in reality, Iyá Akalá is one of the honorary titles of Iyá Nassô. In fact, the *oríkì* of the founder of the Casa Branca was Iyá Nassô Oyó Akalá Magbô Olodumarê (ibid., 198). Àkàlà (or Àkàlàmàgbò)—which in Yoruba means a kind of bird, the ground hornbill (*atíálá*)—is linked to the cult of Iyamí Oxorongá (Abraham 1958). *Adetá* is an apparently masculine title, used, for example, by the *kakanfò* (chief of the army) of Jabata, in Nigeria (Samuel Johnson 1957, 75). Costa Lima stresses that the supposed Ketu origins of the first Candomblé terreiro arise from the "problematic of Yoruba nagô supremacy in the establishing of an ideal model of the Candomblé terreiros of Bahia" (Costa Lima 1977, 24). Verger's hypothesis, which asserts the superiority and the biggest religious structuring of Africans of Ketu origin, minimizes the contribution of the other Yoruba groups and thus legitimizes the Ketu nation, to which belonged the Axé Opô Afonjá, which is now synonymous with Nagô tradition. Today, talking of the "pure" Nagô cult is the same as talking of Ketu terreiros.

8. The Byzantine discussion about the degree of kinship, spiritual but also biological, between the founder Iyá Nassô and Obá Tossi is extremely important, as we shall see, for the legitimation of one of the most famous mães-de-santo of Bahia, Mãe Senhora (Maria Bibiana do Espírito Santo), who claimed that Obá Tossi was "her great-grandmother" (Costa Lima 1977, 46).

9. *Wassa*, which is a term that has not been found in any other text about the foundation of the Casa Branca, seems to refer to *waasi*, which means an Islamic sermon in Yoruba (an *aroowaasi* is a Muslim preacher). Islam's penetration into the kingdom of Oyó and a large part of Yorubaland during the nineteenth-century wars, is the reason for the presence of black *malês* (from the Yoruba *ìmàle*, meaning Muslim) in Bahia until the first half of the nineteenth century.

10. References to Martiniano do Bonfim may be found in the writings of many anthropologists and intellectuals connected with Candomblé, such Carneiro, Landes, Pierson, Aydano de Couto Ferraz, Ramos, and Jorge Amado.

11. Verger (1981) writes that, during his stay in Lagos, Martiniano worked as an apprentice joiner. Oliveira and Costa Lima (1987, 52) underline the commercial aspect of Martiniano's travels to Nigeria, where he bought coral and "fabric from the Coast" to then sell to Candomblé adepts. On the other hand, Bastide (1978,

165) justified his travels to Lagos by the desire "to learn the art of divination and later became the most prestigious babalaô in Bahia."

12. On Aninha's visits to Rio de Janeiro and the rivalry between the terreiro in Bahia and that of the same name in Rio, see Augras and Santos 1985 and Capone 1996.

13. It is not just a journey to Africa which is a source of prestige, it is a journey to a mythical land bound to African tradition, which can be Africa or the Bahia of the traditional terreiros, as René Ribeiro (1978, 106) underlines for the city of Recife: "A certain priestess, who was obliged to take refuge in Bahia because of police repression of Afro-Brazilian cults in 1937, drew enormous prestige from this enforced stay, and a great number of faithful followers came to the re-opening of her terreiro, even though her practices were far from orthodox, for her rivals from Recife accused her of practicing Amerindian and spirit syncretism."

14. In his 1982 book of photographs, Verger (1982a, 258) writes: "Ataoja, king of Oshogbo, whose dynasty is linked to the cult of Oshun, was delighted to know that there was a fervent cult to this divinity in Brazil, and sent Senhora, through me, copper bracelets and river pebbles from Oshun's shrine."

15. The Aláàfin Oyó is regarded as the descendant of Xangô, who, according to oral tradition, was the third king of this city and was transformed into an orixá. The cult of Xangô then, is the cult of the ancestor of the royal dynasty of Oyó. The close relationship between the Aláàfin (king of Oyó) and the Ìyá Nasó (priestess of Xangô) is emphasized by the obligation, on the king's death, to carry out a series of ritual executions including that of the Ìyá Nasó (Samuel Johnson 1957; Abraham 1958, 19).

16. Initially, Verger had no vocation for anthropological work, as he said himself: "I did this research for myself and my friends from Bahia. The idea of publishing the results for a wider public never occurred to me. It was Monod who persuaded me to write it up" (Verger 1982a, 257). Théodore Monod, who in the 1950s was the director of the Institut Français de l'Afrique Noire, invited Verger to publish a study on religious practices in Brazil and Africa, a study which appeared in 1957. Verger became part of the Centre National de la Recherche Scientifique in 1962 and was, from 1963 to 1966, a research associate of the Institute of African Studies at the University of Ibadan in Nigeria.

17. This is Verger's explanation of the Herskovits' disapproval of his work as a messenger: "Herskovits, the head of Northwestern University in Evanston, Illinois, did not like me. For him I was a terrible killjoy, because of him, Brazil and Africa were areas of predilection in which to exercise his observations on (let us use his terms) the phenomena of enculturation or acculturation of tribes in their original land and those transported elsewhere . . . and I committed the unpardonable sin of giving them each others' news!" (ibid.).

18. The oríkì of Obá Tossi was, according to Costa Lima (1977, 198), Axipa Borogum Congo Obatossi. "Congo" is transformed into "Gongôô."

19. Deoscóredes dos Santos (1988, 12) estimates 1935 as the date of the obás' establishment in the Axé Opô Afonjá. This is inconsistent, as we shall see, with the institution's transformations, which followed Martiniano's communication at the congress of 1937.

20. The Yoruba *móngbà*—or mangba, as Martiniano transcribes it—is transformed into obá (literally, king in Yoruba) in the Axé Opô Afonjá. Móngbà (the Yoruba pronunciation is close to the Portuguese transcription mangba) are Xangô priests in Nigeria. According to Verger (1981, 38), they are "responsible for the smooth running of the cult, and guardians of the axé," and do not enter into trances.

21. Martiniano's list in 1937 was different: Abiodun, Onikoyi, Aressa, Onanxokun, Obá Tela and Olugba, for those on the right; and Aré, Otun Onikoyi, Otun Onanxokun, Eko, Kaba Nfo and Ossi Onikoyi, for those on the left. The presence of two left-hand ministers with a name beginning with òtun (right) is puzzling from someone who, as Nina Rodrigues wrote (quoted by Verger 1957, 314), had translated Yoruba texts for Brazilian anthropologists for many years.

22. Abraham (1958, 63) notes that *ààrẹ*, used with *àgòrò*, is the "first title borne by a young chief of great promise, who, as the heir of a great war chief, has just succeeded to the leadership of a great house."

23. A secret society linked to the cult of the earth and to the administration of justice, the Ogboni was very important among the Egba. It was far more important in the New Oyó, after 1835, than in the old (Òyó-ilé), destroyed by war.

24. It would also seem that Martiniano was influenced by his Egba origins in his reconstruction of the Yoruba past. We have seen that the Ogboni were very important in the Egba kingdom, which liberated itself from the Oyó's control at the beginning of the nineteenth century. Many of the reactivated titles in Brazil are linked to the Ogboni in the town of Abeokuta, in Egba country. Johnson (1957, 78) explains the predominance of the Ogboni's cult among the Egba as follows: "amongst the Egbas and Ijebus, the Ogbonis are the chiefs executives, they have the power of life and death, and power to enact and to repeal laws: but in the Oyó provinces the Ogbonis have no such power; they are rather a consultative and advisory body, the King or Bale being supreme, and only matters involving bloodshed are handed over to the Ogbonis for judgment or for execution as the King sees fit."

25. The first to have emphasized the ogan's fundamental role in protecting the terreiros against the repression of Afro-Brazilian religions was Nina Rodrigues (1900), who pointed out the presence of a senator and a political leader among the terreiro's ogans. Silveira reveals the existence, in Catholic brotherhoods of Africans' descendants at the beginning of the nineteenth century, of a category of white protectors, "purely honorary members." He adds that "everything indicates that the title of protector, which already existed in Catholic brotherhoods,

was used again in the founding of the first national Candomblés" (Silveira 1988, 183). These white "allies" are part of a vast political project to make Nagô Candomblé "a new model, better structured and more firmly rooted in local society" (ibid., 186).

26. We have already seen how any ritual modification, even if it aims to purify tradition, is always a pretext to renegotiate power relationships within a religious group.

27. Costa Lima (1966, 25) points out that even the obás' confirmation ritual was modified to adapt it to the status of the new members, especially with regard to what touched mediumship, a faculty that the obá must not possess, at the risk of not being able to fulfill his functions. In Senhora's eyes, the risk did not exist, for "the new obás were chosen from the social classes which had little cultural engagement with the phenomena of religious possession." The fact that he himself was a member of the terreiro does not prevent Costa Lima from criticizing Senhora's criteria for choosing: "At the moment, the obás who have already been confirmed introduce their friends to the iyalorixá who may choose them to fill available places in the terreiro" (ibid.).

28. Among the obás of the Axé Opô Afonjá we find Jorge Amado (Otun Arolu), confirmed in 1959; Carybé (Otun Anaxokun), an Argentinean painter who had been living in Bahia since 1950, and who died there in 1997; and Vivaldo da Costa Lima (Ossi Odofin), an anthropologist at the Universidade Federal da Bahia (UFBa), confirmed in his post in 1977 by the current mãe-de-santo, Mãe Stella. The title of Ojú Obá, also linked to the cult of Xangô, was borne by Verger and by the anthropologist Marco Aurélio Luz, who was his replacement on the left.

29. The importance of this alliance between terreiros and anthropologists is very clear in Afro-Brazilian religious circles. During a meeting of Candomblé nations in 1981, a participant from an Angola terreiro appealed to anthropologists to carry out research on his nation's rituals, for "there are no books about Angola, and there are more Angola terreiros in Bahia than Ketu, Jeje or any other nation" (Santana 1984, 41). According to a member of Caboclo Candomblé, the anthropologists' omission was due to the "proximity" of Ketu Candomblés, which were located in the high part of the city of Salvador (Cidade Alta), and the "distance" of Caboclo Candomblés in the low part (Cidade Baixa), surrounded by "a lot of bush" and situated "far from the center" (Ferreira 1984, 59). A spatial metaphor thus symbolizes the invisibility of the "untraditional nations."

8. Which Africa?

1. On the COMTOC congresses, see Capone 2005, 279–97.

2. Castro (1981, 65) reveals an identical situation for Yoruba as it is spoken today in terreiros: "This supposed 'Nagô language' used in Candomblé is nothing

more than operational terminology, specific to ritual ceremonies . . . , which uses a lexical system composed of different African languages which were spoken in Brazil during [the period of] slavery."

3. Abimbola (1976b, 634–35) writes about the "contra-acculturative" experience to which Lashebikan was subjected. The first Yoruba professor in Bahia and a "well-known scholar of the Yoruba language," Lashebikan "was grossly ignorant of the ways of the orisa, since in Nigeria he regarded himself as a Christian. Therefore, when he first reached Brazil, he could not understand the people whom he had been sent to educate. But he soon adjusted himself and learnt more about the orisa as he himself taught the Yoruba language to his students who were mostly made up of babalorisa and iyalorisa."

4. During his four-week visit to Bahia in 1976, Wande Abimbola was accompanied by Olabiyi Babalola Yai and Pierre Verger, and attended the confirmation ceremony bestowing the title of *alapini* from the cult of the Eguns upon Deoscóredes dos Santos (Mestre Didi), whom he already knew well, as he had been the one "who arranged in 1968 the decoration of Didi as the Baale Sango of Bahia on the instructions of the Federal Government of Nigeria" (Abimbola 1976b, 620). With his friends, Abimbola visited the Axé Opô Aganjú terreiro of Balbino Daniel de Paula, "who has been greatly aided in his activities by Pierre Verger" (ibid., 622). This alliance between initiate and researcher seems to have been fruitful, for Abimbola writes that in the terreiro "the chanting and dancing in which we participated (Olabiyi Yai, Verger and myself) were rendered in clearer Yoruba than those which I had recorded elsewhere" (ibid.).

5. An awo is someone initiated into the cult of Ifá: "The Ifa diviners are most commonly called *babalawo* or "father has secrets" . . . or simply *awo*, secrets or mysteries" (Bascom 1969a, 81).

6. We have seen in chapter 3 that Tancredo da Silva Pinto was the promoter of "African" Umbanda. He was also the leader of the Omolocô cult, a mixture of Umbanda and rituals from Angola Candomblé.

7. Odùs are also known as the paths by which the orixás come, thus influencing their actions on men in a positive or negative way. Odùs are regarded as living, active entities, who must be fed and propitiated with sacrifices.

8. My interview with Fernandes Portugal.

9. In reality, a babalawo should not go into a trance, while Candomblé initiates (except if they are ogans or ekedis) are all possessed by their divinities. Although women's initiation into the secrets of Ifá is restricted, they as well as men are accepted in Torodê's course. In Cuba, where there are many babalawos, mediumship is not an indispensable condition for initiation in the orixá cult, and women can only receive the *kofá*, the first level of initiation to Ifá. About gender issues in Ifá worship, see Capone 2005, 236–46.

10. Luz was the national head of the Consultative Council of the INTECAB, whose

general coordinator at the time was Deoscóredes dos Santos. Juana Elbein dos Santos was the national head of the Science and Culture Commission and, at the same time, the general coordinator of SECNEB, created in Salvador in 1974. At the end of 1993, the address of the Editora Arembepe, which published *Siwaju*, the journal of the INTECAB, was the same as that of SECNEB's head office.

11. On Luz's passage from a "Brazilian" discourse—as opposed to the "cult of Africa" —to demands for African tradition in the terreiros which "revitalized the black civilizing process," see Sónia Giacomini (1988, 64).

12. This double structure clearly recalls the principle of compartmentalization in Bastide's work. It should be reiterated that Bastide shaped a whole generation of intellectuals in Brazil and was also Juana Elbein dos Santos's research director at the Sorbonne. The assertion of the hegemonic vocation of Nagô Candomblé is also based on the theory of the separation of the African world and the western world in the "pockets of resistance" of traditional Candomblé (Capone 2001).

13. Toward the end of his life, Bastide had significantly modified his position on the notion of cultural encystment. About the "society of the blacks," he wrote: "this society may only be understood by replacing it in the dialectic of the negro community versus the non-negro community; more precisely, we come to the conclusion that, in reality, an Afro-American culture does not exist, but rather a continual process of blacks' cultural adaptation to the vicissitudes of the social, economic and political life of the New World" (Bastide 1970b, 68).

14. The INTECAB is run by a national religious council made up of high-ranking priests from different Candomblé nations (Nagô, Jeje, Angola, etc.) as well as other Afro-Brazilian religions. It is divided into different executive commissions: science and culture, intercommunities, communications and public relations, secretarial and administration, and finance. There is also a consultative council, made up of representatives from the religious council and different commissions, whose national leader in 1992 was Marco Aurélio Luz. The quotations in this paragraph are from various INTECAB brochures.

15. The diverse religious federations never produced concrete results with regard to religious standardization. The INTECAB is trying to respond to the need for organization within the religious community.

16. "Indeed it is sometimes the case . . . that 'continuity' does not really exist, that it is but a simple ideology, either of the white class (aiming to better distinguish itself from colored people) or of the black class (attempting to better assert its originality), whereas what really exists, underneath, in the domain of facts, is on the contrary discontinuity—a pure and simple rupture with tradition . . . In any case, in every moment of rupture and everywhere discontinuity surfaces in the facts, a compensatory ideology emerges at the same time that valorizes rootedness in the past" (Bastide 1996a, 78).

17. "Ideologies aimed at demonstrating the continuity that links today's Afro-

American culture to the Afro-American culture of the past only highlight ruptures and discontinuities (Afro-American culture is a construction, not a 'sequence' or a 'continuity', and as such, it goes as far as betrayal, thereby accentuating all the more, for Africanists, the element of discontinuity which these ideologies reveal even as they aim to conceal it)" (Bastide 1996a, 85).

18. Pascal Boyer (1990, 95) claims that "whatever mystical knowledge is transmitted seems to focus on secrets either meaningless or empty . . . In some cases the communication of secrets can be delayed indefinitely. What they learn at each step is that the essential secrets, the ultimate explanations, will be given next time." The secret is thus a sort of empty cage. The loss of tradition, then, is not caused by the structure of secrecy, as Carvalho (1987) claims; it is the very void of the secret which is the basis of the tradition (the "black civilizing process"), for it feeds the circulation of the axé. There is no secret to reveal: the initiation process and hierarchical submission are the only ways to come into contact with the true black culture.

19. Several authors have drawn attention to the influence of anthropological literature on the re-Africanization of Afro-Brazilian religions (Ramos 1951b; René Ribeiro 1978; Leacock and Leacock 1972; Dantas 1988; and Vagner Gonçalves da Silva 1992, 1995). Bastide (1973, 168) wrote: "They read the books written about them and these books may have an influence on their beliefs and practices, mainly because they put the African data next to Brazilian data. Therefore, if they cannot go to Africa as they did in the past, today, pais-de-santo study Africa through books in order to reform their religion." This situation is even more evident today, because of the great number of pais and mães-de-santo in academic circles.

Conclusion

1. Practitioners of *Santería,* an Afro-Cuban religion that can be compared to Candomblé.

2. I have developed my analysis of this movement, as well as its ritual negotiation with Cuban Santería, in another work (Capone 2005). For more on Oyotunji, see Clarke 2004.

3. At the beginning of the 1980s, I met two mães-de-santo in Salvador, who were *nissei* (descendants of Japanese in Brazil) living in São Paulo, a city with a large number of descendants of Japanese immigrants. Despite their origins, they considered themselves members of an Afro-Brazilian community of believers, as their black initiator was one of the most famous pais-de-santo of the Jeje nation in Salvador.

BIBLIOGRAPHY

Abimbola, Wande. 1976a. *Ifá: An Exposition of Ifa Literary Corpus.* Ibadan, Nigeria: Oxford University Press.

———. 1976b. "Yoruba Religion in Brazil: Problems and Prospects." *Actes du XLIIe Congrès international des américanistes* 6: 619–39.

Abraham, Roy C. 1958. *Dictionary of Modern Yoruba.* London: University of London Press.

The African Contribution to Brazil. 1966. Rio de Janeiro: Departamento de Cultura e Informação do Ministério Brasileiro de Relações Exteriores para o Primeiro Festival de Artes Negras em Dakar.

Aguessy, Honorat. 1992. *Cultures Vodoun: manifestations, migrations, métamorphoses (Afrique, Caraïbes, Amériques).* Cotonou, Benin: Institut de Développement et d'Echanges Endogènes.

Alva, Antônio de. n.d. *Exu: génio do bem e do mal.* Rio de Janeiro: Espiritualista.

Andrade, Mário de. 1984. *Macunaíma.* Translated by Edward Arthur Goodland. New York: Random House. (Orig. pub. 1928.)

Andrade, Oswald de. 1972. *Manifesto da poesia Pau-Brasil.* 1924. In *Do Pau-Brasil à antropologia e às utopias, manifestos, teses de concursos e ensaios.* Rio de Janeiro: Civilização Brasileira.

Apter, Andrew H. 1995. "Notes on Orisha cults in the Ekiti Yoruba Highlands. A tribute to Pierre Verger." *Cahiers d'études africaines* 35, nos. 138–139: 369–401.

Areia, Manuel Laranjeira Rodrigues de. 1974. *L'Angola traditionnel: Une introduction aux problèmes magicoreligieux.* Coimbra, Portugal: Tipografia da Atlântida.

Aubrée, Marion, and François Laplantine. 1990. *La table, le livre et les esprits: magies et médiums,* Paris: Éditions J.-C. Lattès.

Augras, Monique. 1989. "De Yiá Mi a Pomba Gira: transformações e símbolos da libido." In *Meu sinal está no teu corpo,* edited by C. Moura, 14–33. São Paulo: EDICON/Editora Universidade de São Paulo.

Augras, Monique, and João Batista dos Santos. 1985. "Uma casa de Xangô no Rio de Janeiro." *Dédalo* 24: 43–62.

Azevedo, Thales de. 1953. *Les élites de couleur dans une ville brésilienne.* Paris: UNESCO.

Balandier, Georges. 1967. *Anthropologie politique*. Paris: Presses universitaires de France.

Barros, José Flávio. Pessoa de. 1993. *O segredo das folhas: sistemas de classificação de vegetais no candomblé jeje-nagô do Brasil*. Rio de Janeiro: Pallas/Universidade do Estado do Rio de Janeiro.

Bascom, William R. 1969a. *Ifa Divination: Communication between Gods and Men in West Africa*. Bloomington: Indiana University Press.

———. 1969b. *The Yoruba of Southwestern Nigeria*. New York: Holt, Rinehart and Winston.

———. 1980. *Sixteen Cowries: Yoruba Divination from Africa to the New World*. Bloomington: Indiana University Press.

Bastide, Roger. 1945. *Imagens do Nordeste místico em branco e negro*. Rio de Janeiro: O Cruzeiro.

———. 1952. "Le Batuque de Porto Alegre." Reprinted in Sol Tax, *Acculturation in the Americas. Proceedings and Selected Papers of the 29th International Congress of Americanists*, 195–206. Chicago: University of Chicago Press.

———. 1958. *Le candomblé de Bahia (rite nagô)*. Paris: Mouton.

———. 1969. "Le problème des mutations religieuses." *Cahiers internationaux de sociologie* 46: 5–16.

———. 1970a. *Le prochain et le lointain*. Paris: Éditions Cujas.

———. 1970b. "Mémoire collective et sociologie du bricolage." *L'Année sociologique*, 3rd ser., 21: 65–108.

———. 1970c. "Le rire et les courts-circuits de la pensée." In *Échanges et communications: Mélanges offerts à Claude Lévi-Strauss à l'occasion de son 60ème anniversaire*, edited by Jean Pouillon and Pierre Maranda, 953–63. Paris: Mouton.

———. 1971. *African Civilisations in the New World*. Translated by Peter Green. New York: Harper and Row. (Orig. pub. 1967.)

———. 1973. *Estudos afro-brasileiros*. São Paulo: Perspectiva.

———. 1974. *La femme de couleur en Amérique latine*. Paris: Éditions Anthropos.

———. 1975. *Le sacré sauvage et autres essais*. Paris: Payot.

———. 1978. *The African Religions of Brazil: Toward a Sociology of the Interpenetration of Civilizations*. Translated by Helen Sebba. Baltimore, Md.: John Hopkins University Press. (Orig. pub. 1960.)

———. 1996a. "Continuité et discontinuité des sociétés et des cultures afro-américaines." *Bastidiana* 13–14: 77–88.

———. 1996b. "État actuel des recherches afro-américaines en Amérique latine." *Bastidiana* 13–14: 11–28.

Binon-Cossard, Gisèle. 1970. "Contribution à l'étude des candomblés au Brésil: le candomblé Angola." Ph.D. diss., Paris I-Sorbonne.

Birman, Patrícia. 1980. "Feitiço, carrego e olho grande, os males do Brasil são: estudo de um centro umbandista numa favela do Rio de Janeiro." Master's thesis, Museu Nacional/UFRJ, Rio De Janeiro.

Bonfim, Martiniano Eliseu do. 1950. "Os ministros de Xangô." In *Antologia do Negro brasileiro. Trabalhos apresentados no II Congresso afro-brasileiro, Bahia, 1937,* edited by Édison Carneiro, 347-49. Rio de Janeiro: Civilização Brasileira.

Bouche, Pierre B. 1885. *Sept ans en Afrique occidentale: La côte des Esclaves et le Dahomey.* Paris: Plon, Nourrit.

Bourdieu, Pierre. 1971. "Genèse et structure du champ religieux." *Revue française de sociologie* 12, no. 3: 295–334.

———. 1977. *Outline of a Theory of Practice.* Translated by Richard Nice. Cambridge: Cambridge University Press. (Orig. pub. 1972.)

Boyer, Pascal. 1990. *Tradition as Truth and Communication: A Cognitive Description of Traditional Discourse.* Cambridge: Cambridge University Press.

Boyer-Araujo, Véronique. 1993. *Femmes et cultes de possession au Brésil: les compagnons invisibles.* Paris: L'Harmattan.

Braga, Júlio Santana. 1988. *O jogo dos búzios: um estudo da adivinhação no candomblé.* São Paulo: Brasiliense.

———. 1999. *Na gamela do feitiço: repressão e resistência nos candomblés da Bahia.* Salvador, Brazil: Editora UFBa.

Brandon, George. 1993. *Santería from Africa to the New World: The Dead Sell Memories.* Bloomington: Indiana University Press.

Brown, Diana. 1985. "Uma história da Umbanda no Rio." In *Umbanda e Política,* 9–42. Cadernos do ISER 18. Rio de Janeiro: ISER/Editora Marco Zero.

———. 1986. *Umbanda: Religion and Politics in Urban Brazil.* Ann Arbor, Mich.: UMI Research Press.

Brumana, Fernando G., and E. G. Martinez. 1991. *Marginália sagrada.* Campinas, Brazil: Unicamp.

Cacciatore, Olga Guidolle. 1977. *Dicionário de cultos afro-brasileiros.* Rio de Janeiro: Forense Universitária.

Camargo, C. P. Ferreira. 1961. *Kardecismo e umbanda: uma interpretação sociológica.* São Paulo: Livraria Pioneira.

Capone, Stefania. 1991. "A dança dos deuses: uma análise da dança de possessão no candomblé Angola Kassanje." Master's dissertation, PPGAS/Museu Nacional/UFRJ, Rio de Janeiro.

———. 1996. "Le pur et le dégénéré: le candomblé de Rio de Janeiro ou les oppositions révisitées." *Journal de la Société des américanistes* 82: 259–92.

———. 1999. *La quête de l'Afrique dans le candomblé. Pouvoir et tradition au Brésil,* Paris: Karthala.

———. 2000. "Entre Yoruba et Baiitou: l'influence des stéréotypes raciaux dans les études afro-américaines." *Cahiers d'études africaines* 157: 55–77.

———. 2001. "Regards croisés sur le bricolage et le syncrétisme. Le syncrétisme dans tous ses états." *Archives de sciences sociales des religions* 114: 42–50.

———. 2004. *A busca da África no candomblé. Poder e tradição no Brasil.* Rio de Janeiro: Contracapa/Pallas.

———. 2005. *Les Yoruba du Nouveau Monde: Religion, ethnicité et nationalisme noir aux États-Unis.* Paris: Karthala.

———. 2007. "Transatlantic Dialogue: Roger Bastide and the African American Religions." *Journal of Religion in Africa* 37: 1–35.

Cardoso, Irene. 1994. "Entretien avec R. Bastide." *Bastidiana* 7–8: 69–73.

Carneiro, Édison. 1937. *Os mitos africanos no Brasil.* São Paulo: Companhia Editora Nacional.

———. 1950. "Um orixá caluniado." In *Antologia do Negro Brasileiro*, edited by É. Carneiro, 344–49. Rio de Janeiro: Civilização Brasileira.

———. 1964. *Ladinos e crioulos: estudos sobre o Negro no Brasil.* Rio de Janeiro: Civilização Brasileira.

———. 1986. *Candomblés da Bahia.* Rio de Janeiro: Civilização Brasileira. (Orig. pub. 1948.)

———. 1991. *Religiões Negras/Negros Bantos.* Rio de Janeiro: Civilização Brasileira. (Orig. pub. 1936–37.)

Carvalho, José Jorge de. 1987. "A força da nostalgia: a concepção do tempo histórico dos cultos afro-brasileiros tradicionais." *Religião e Sociedade* 14, no. 2: 36–61.

———. 1990. "Xangô." In *Sinais dos tempos: diversidade religiosa no Brasil*, edited by L. Landim, 139–45. Rio de Janeiro: ISER.

———. 1993. "Antropologia: saber acadêmico e experiência iniciática." *Anuário Antropológico* 90: 91–107.

Cascudo, Luis da Câmara. 1972. *Dicionário do folclore brasileiro.* Rio de Janeiro: Edições de Ouro. (Orig. pub. 1954.)

Castro, Yeda Pessoa de. 1971. "Terminologia religiosa e falar cotidiano de um grupo-de-culto afro-brasileiro." Master's thesis, Universidade Federal da Bahia.

———. 1981. "Língua e nação de candomblé." *África* 4: 57–77.

Ceccaldi, Pierrette. 1979. *Essai de nomenclature des populations, langues et dialectes de la République populaire du Bénin.* Paris: CARDAN/CNRS.

Clarke, Kamari M. 2004. *Mapping Yorùbá Networks: Power and Agency in the Making of Transnational Communities.* Durham, N.C.: Duke University Press.

Clifford, James, and George E. Marcus, eds. 1986. *Writing Culture: The Poetics and Politics of Ethnography.* Berkeley: University of California Press.

Concone, M. H., and L. Negrão. 1985. "Umbanda: da representação à cooptação. O envolvimento partidário da umbanda paulista nas eleições de 1982." In *Umbanda e Política*, 43–79. Cadernos do ISER 18. Rio de Janeiro: ISER/Editora Marco Zero.

Contins, Márcia. 1983. "O caso da Pomba Gira: reflexões sobre crime, possessão e imagem feminina." Master's thesis, PPGAS/Museu Nacional/UFRJ, Rio de Janeiro.

Correa, Ana Maria. 1976. "Descrição de uma tipologia mítica: os orixás do candomblé'." Master's thesis, Pontifícia Universidade Católica do Rio de Janeiro.

Costa, Eduardo Octavio da. 1948. *The Negro in Northern Brazil: A Study in Acculturation.* New York: American Ethnological Society.

Costa Lima, Vivaldo da. 1966. "Os Obás de Xangô." *Áfro-Ásia* 2–3: 5–36.

———. 1976. "O conceito de 'nação' nos candomblés da Bahia." *Áfro-Ásia* 12: 65–90.

———. 1977. "A família-de-santo nos candomblés jeje-nagô da Bahia: um estudo de relações intra-grupais." Master's thesis, Universidade Federal da Bahia, Salvador.

———. 1984. "Nações-de-candomblé." In *Encontro de nações-de-candomblé*, edited by Vivaldo da Costa Lima, 11–26. Salvador, Brazil: Ianamá/UFBa/CEAO/CED.

Crowther, Samuel. 1852. *A Vocabulary of the Yoruba Language.* London: Seeleys.

Cunha, Manuela Carneiro da. 1985. *Negros estrangeiros: os escravos libertos e sua volta à África.* São Paulo: Brasiliense.

Cunha, Marianno Carneiro da. 1984. "A feitiçaria entre os Nagô-Yoruba." *Dédalo* 23: 1–16.

Dalmir, Francisco. 1992. "Ancestralidade e política da sedução: a pluralidade étnico-cultural brasileira." In *Democracia e diversidade humana: desafio contemporâneo*, edited by Juana Elbein dos Santos, 179–205. Salvador, Brazil: SECNEB.

Da Matta, Roberto. 1983. *Carnavals, bandits et héros: ambiguïtés de la société brésilienne.* Translated by Danielle Birck. Paris: Le Seuil. (Orig. pub. 1979.)

Dantas, Beatriz Góis. 1984. "De feiticeiros a comunistas: acusações sobre o candomblé." *Dédalo* 23: 97–116.

———. 1988. *Vovó nagô e papai branco: usos e abusos da África no Brasil.* Rio de Janeiro: Graal.

Dennett, Richard E. 1910. *Nigerian Studies, or the Religions and Political System of the Yoruba.* London: Macmillan.

Dopamu, Ade P. 1990. *Exu, o inimigo invisível do homem: um estudo comparativo entre Exu da religião tradicional iorubá (nagô) e o demônio das tradições cristã e muçulmana.* São Paulo: Oduduwa.

Drewal, Henry John, and Margaret Thompson Drewal. 1983. *Gelede: Art and Female Power among the Yoruba.* Bloomington: Indiana University Press.

Durkheim, Émile. 1912. *Les formes élémentaires de la vie religieuse.* Paris: Alcan.

Ellis, A. Burton. 1894. *The Yoruba-Speaking Peoples of the Slave Coast of West Africa: Their Religion, Manners, Laws, Language, etc.* London: Chapman and Hall.

Estudos afro-brasileiros: Trabalhos apresentados ao I Congresso afro-brasileiro, Recife, 1934. 1988. 2 vols. Recife, Brazil: Fundação Joaquim Nabuco/Editora Massangana.

Evans-Pritchard, Edward E. 1937. *Witchcraft, Oracles and Magic among the Azande*. Oxford: Clarendon Press of Oxford University Press.

———. 1962. "Religion and the Anthropologists: The Aquinas Lecture, 1959." In *Social Anthropology and Other Essays*, 155–71. New York: Free Press.

Favret-Saada, Jeanne. 1991. "Sorcellerie." In *Dictionnaire de l'ethnologie et de l'anthropologie*, edited by P. Bonte and M. Izard, 670–73. Paris: Presses universitaires de France.

Fernandes, Florestan, and Roger Bastide. 1955. *Relações raciais entre negros e brancos em São Paulo*. São Paulo: Anhambi.

Ferreira, Almiro Miguel. 1984. "Candomblé-de-caboclo." In *Encontro de nações-de-candomblé*, edited by Vivaldo da Costa Lima, 59–67. Salvador, Brazil: Ianamá/ UFBa/CEAO/CED.

Ferretti, Mundicarmo. 1993. *Desceu na guma: o caboclo do tambor da mina no processo de mudança de um terreiro de S. Luís (a Casa Fanti-Ashanti)*. São Luís, Brazil: SIOGE.

Ferretti, Sérgio F. 1986. *Querebentam de Zomadonu: etnografia da Casa das Minas*. São Luís, Brazil: Editora EDUFMA.

Fonseca, Eduardo, Jr. 1988. *Dicionário yoruba-português*. Rio de Janeiro: Civilização Brasileira. (Orig. pub. 1983.)

Fontanelle, Aluízio. 1952. *O espiritismo no conceito das religiões e a lei da umbanda*. Rio de Janeiro: Espiritualista.

———. n.d. *Exu*. Rio de Janeiro: Espiritualista.

Freyre, Gilberto. 1946. *The Masters and the Slaves (Casa-Grande & Senzala): A Study in the Development of Brazilian Civilization*. Translated by Samuel Putnam. New York: Knopf. (Orig. pub. 1933.)

———. 1967. "Manifesto regionalista." *Brasil Açucareiro* 70, no. 4: 20–23. (Orig. pub. 1926.)

———. 1988. "O que foi o 1° Congresso afro-brasileiro do Recife." In *Estudos afro-brasileiros. Trabalhos apresentados ao I Congresso afro-brasileiro no Recife. 1934.* 2 vols. Recife, Brazil: Fundação Joaquim Nabuco/Editora Massangana.

Frigerio, Alejandro. 1989. "With the Banner of Oxalá: Social Construction and Maintenance of Reality in Afro-Brazilian Religions in Argentina." Ph.D. diss., University of California, Los Angeles.

Fry, Peter. 1984. "Gallus africanus est, ou como Roger Bastide se tornou africano no Brasil." *Folhetim* (Folha de São Paulo), 15 July, 7–10.

Genovese, Eugene. 1976. *Roll, Jordan, Roll: The World the Slaves Made*. New York: Vintage.

Giacomini, Sónia Maria. 1988. "Uma dupla leitura: macumba, cultura negra e ideologia do recalque." *Comunicações do ISER* 28: 55–71.

Gobineau, J. A. de. 1884. *Essai sur l'inégalité des races humaines*. Paris: Firmin Didot. (Orig. pub. 1854.)

Gonçalves Fernandes, Anibal. 1937. *Xangôs do Nordeste*. Rio de Janeiro: Civilização Brasileira.

Goody, Jack. 1977. *The Domestication of the Savage Mind*. Cambridge: Cambridge University Press.

Halbwachs, Maurice. 1925. *Les cadres sociaux de la mémoire*. Paris: Félix Alcan.

Harding, Rachel. 2000. *A Refuge in Thunder: Candomblé and Alternative Spaces of Blackness*. Bloomington: Indiana University Press.

Hayes, Kelly Black. 2004. "Magic at the Margins: Macumba in Rio de Janeiro. An Ethnographic Analysis of a Religious Life." Ph.D. diss., University of Chicago.

Herskovits, Melville J. 1938. *Dahomey: An Ancient West African Kingdom*. New York: J. J. Augustin.

———. 1967. "Pesquisas etnológicas na Bahia." *Afro-Ásia* 4–5: 89–105. (Orig. pub. 1943).

Herskovits, Melville J., and Frances S. Herskovits. 1958. *Dahomean Narrative*. Evanston, Ill.: Northwestern University Press.

Hess, David J. 1992. "Umbanda and Quimbanda Magic in Brazil: Rethinking Aspects of Bastide's Work." *Archives de sciences sociales des religions* 79: 135–53.

Hobsbawm, Eric, and Terence Ranger. 1983. *The Invention of Tradition*. Cambridge: Cambridge University Press.

Hoch-Smith, Judith. 1978. "Radical Yoruba Female Sexuality: The Witch and the Prostitute." In *Women in Ritual and Symbolical Roles*, edited by Judith Hoch-Smith and A. Spring, 245–67. New York: Plenum.

Holmes, Douglas, and George E. Marcus. 2005. "Refunctioning Ethnography: The Challenge of an Anthropology of the Contemporary." In *The Sage Handbook of Qualitative Research*, edited by Norman Denzin and Yvonna Lincoln, 1099–113, Thousand Oaks: Sage.

Horton, Robin. 1990. "La tradition et la modernité revisitées." In *La pensée métisse: croyances africaines et rationalité occidentale en question*, translated by Yvonne Preiswerk and Jacques Vallet, 69–124. Paris: Presses universitaires de France/ IUED.

Hubert, Henri, and Marcel Mauss. 1902. "Esquisse d'une théorie générale de la magie." *L'Année sociologique* 7: 1–146.

Idowu, E. Bolaji. 1962. *Olódùmarè: God in Yoruba Belief*. London: Longmans.

Johnson, Paul C. 2002. *Secrets, Gossip, and Gods: the Transformation of Brazilian Candomblé*. Oxford: Oxford University Press.

Johnson, Samuel. 1957. *The History of the Yorubas*. London: Routledge. (Orig. pub. 1921.)

Kardec, Allan. 1875. *The Spirits' Book*. Translated by Anna Blackwell. London: Trübner. (Orig. pub. 1857.)

———. 1970. *The Book on Mediums*. Translated by Emma E. Wood. New York: S. Weiser. (Orig. pub. 1861.)

———. 2000. *The Gospel Explained by the Spiritist Doctrine.* Philadelphia, Pa.: Allan Kardec Educational Society. (Orig. pub. 1864.)

Kayodé, Benji Durojaiye, and Ornato J. da Silva. 1978. *A linguagem correta dos orisa.* Rio de Janeiro: Livraria São José Matriz.

Kiti, Gabriel. 1926. "Le fétichisme au Dahomey." *La reconnaissance africaine* 2, no. 25: 2–3.

Landes, Ruth. 1940a. "Fetish worship in Brazil." *Journal of American Folklore* 53: 261–70.

———. 1940b. "A Cult Matriarchate and Male Homosexuality." *Journal of Abnormal and Social Psychology* 35, no. 3: 386–97.

———. 1967. *A cidade das mulheres.* Translated by Maria Lúcia do Eirado Silva. Rio de Janeiro: Civilização Brasileira.

———. 1994. *The City of Women.* Albuquerque: University of New Mexico Press. (Orig. pub. 1947.)

Leacock, Seth, and Ruth Leacock. 1972. *Spirits of the Deep: A Study of an Afro-Brazilian Cult.* New York: American Museum of Natural History.

Le Hérissé, A. 1911. *L'ancien royaume du Dahomey: moeurs, religion, histoire.* Paris: Larose.

Lenclud, Gérard. 1987. "La tradition n'est plus ce qu'elle était . . . Sur les notions de tradition et de société traditionnelle en ethnologie." *Terrain* 9: 110–23.

Lépine, Claude. 1978. "Contribuição ao estudo do sistema de classificação dos tipos psicológicos no candomblé ketu de Salvador." Ph.D. diss., Universidade de São Paulo.

Letourneau, Charles. 1892. *L'évolution religieuse dans les diverses races humaines.* Paris: Vigot Frères.

Lewis, Oscar. 1961. *The Children of Sanchez: Autobiography of a Mexican Family.* New York: Random House.

Lody, Raul. 1979. *Santo também come: estudo sócio-cultural da alimentação ceremonial em terreiros afro-brasileiros.* Recife, Brazil: MEC/Instituto Joaquim Nabuco de Pesquisas Sociais.

———. 1982. *Sete temas da mítica afro-brasileira.* Rio de Janeiro: Altiva Gráfica e Editora.

Lopes dos Santos, M. C. 1984. *Caboclo: da África ou do Xingû.* Recife, Brazil: Fundação Joaquim Nabuco, Centro de Estudos folclóricos.

Luz, Marco Aurélio. 1983. *Cultura negra e ideologia do recalque.* Rio de Janeiro: Achiamé.

———. 1992. "Da porteira para dentro, da porteira para fora: a tradição africano-brasileira e a pluralidade nacional." In *Democracia e diversidade humana: desafio contemporâneo,* edited by Juana Elbein dos Santos, 57–73. Salvador, Brazil: SECNEB.

———. 1993. *Do tronco ao opa exin: memória e dinâmica da tradição africano-brasileira*. Salvador, Brazil: SECNEB.

Luz, Marco Aurélio, and Georges Lapassade. 1972. *O segredo da macumba*. Rio de Janeiro: Paz e Terra.

"Mãe Stella: sacerdotisa e guardiã do candomblé na Bahia." 1994. *Bahia, Análise & Dados* 3, no. 4: 42–46.

Maggie, Yvonne. 1977. *Guerra de Orixá: um estudo de ritual e conflito*. Rio de Janeiro: Zahar.

———. 1989. "Cultos afro-brasileiros: consenso e diversidade." In *Sinais dos tempos: igrejas e seitas no Brasil*, edited by Leilah Landim, 77–82. Rio de Janeiro: ISER.

———. 1992. *Medo do feitiço: relações entre magia e poder no Brasil*. Rio de Janeiro: Arquivo Nacional, Orgão do Ministério da Justiça.

Marcus, George E. 1997. "The Uses of Complicity in the Changing mise-en-scene of Anthropological Fieldwork." *Representations* 59: 85–108.

———. 2006. "Where Are All the Tales of Fieldwork Gone?" *Ethnos* 71, no. 1: 113–22.

Marques Pereira, Nuno. 1939. *Compêndio narrativo do Peregrino da América*. Rio de Janeiro: Academia Brasileira. (Orig. pub. in 1728.)

Matory, Lorand J. 2005. *Black Atlantic Religion: Tradition, Transnationalism, and Matriarchy in the Afro-Brazilian Candomblé*. Princeton, N.J.: Princeton University Press.

Maupoil, Bernard. 1988. *La géomancie à l'ancienne côte des Esclaves*. Paris: Institut d'Ethnologie. (Orig. pub. 1938.)

Mérimée, Prosper. 1994. *Carmen*. Paris: Librio. (Orig. pub. 1846.)

Métraux, Alfred, and Pierre Verger. 1994. *Le pied à l'étrier: correspondance 1946–1963*. Paris: J.-M. Place.

Meyer, Marlyse. 1993. *Maria Padilha e toda a sua quadrilha: de amante de um rei de Castela a Pomba-Gira de umbanda*. São Paulo: Livraria Duas Cidades.

Molina, N. A. n.d.a. *Pontos cantados e riscados de Exu e Pomba Gira*. Rio de Janeiro: Espiritualista.

———. n.d.b. *Saravá Maria Padilha*. Rio de Janeiro: Espiritualista.

———. n.d.c. *Saravá Pomba Gira*. Rio de Janeiro: Espiritualista.

Montero, Paula. 1985. *Da doença à desordem: a magia na umbanda*. Rio de Janeiro: Edições Graal.

Morin, Françoise. 1975. "Roger Bastide ou l'anthropologie des gouffres." *Archives de sciences sociales des religions* 40: 99–106.

———. 1994. "Les inédits et la correspondance de Roger Bastide." In *Roger Bastide ou le réjouissement de l'abîme*, edited by P. Laburthe-Tolra, 21–42. Paris: L'Harmattan.

Mott, Luiz. 1986. "Acotundá: raízes setecentistas do sincretismo religioso afro-brasileiro." *Revista do Museu Paulista*, n.s., 31: 124–47.

Motta, Roberto, ed. 1985. *Os Afro-Brasileiros. Anais do III Congresso afro-brasileiro, Recife, 1982*. Recife, Brazil: Fundação Joaquim Nabuco/Editora Massangana.

Moura, Roberto. 1983. *Tia Ciata e a Pequena África no Rio de Janeiro*. Rio de Janeiro: FUNARTE.

Nadel, Siegfried F. 1942. *A Black Byzantium: The Kingdom of Nupe in Nigeria*. Oxford: Oxford University Press.

Nina Rodrigues, Raymundo. 1900. *L'animisme fétichiste des nègres de Bahia*. Salvador, Brazil: Reis and Companhia.

———. 1938. *As raças humanas e a responsabilidade penal no Brasil*. São Paulo: Companhia Editora Nacional. (Orig. pub. 1894.)

———. 1988. *Os Africanos no Brasil*. São Paulo: Companhia Editora Nacional. (Orig. pub. 1932.)

Nogueira, Tateto Nelson Mateus. 1991–92. "Oferendes nos cultos." *Siwaju* 5–6: 8.

Nunes Pereira, Manoel. 1979. *A Casa das Minas: culto dos voduns jeje no Maranhão*. Petrópolis, Brazil: Vozes.

Oliveira, Waldir Freitas. 1976. "Desenvolvimento dos estudos africanistas no Brasil." *Cultura* 7, no. 23: 110–17.

Oliveira, Waldir Freitas, and Vivaldo da Costa Lima. 1987. *Cartas de Édison Carneiro a Arthur Ramos: de 4 de janeiro a 6 de dezembro de 1938*. São Paulo: Corrupio.

Ortiz, Renato. 1988. *A morte branca do feiticeiro negro: umbanda e sociedade brasileira*. São Paulo: Brasiliense.

Paine, Robert. 1967. "What Is Gossip about? An Alternative Hypothesis." *Man*, n.s., 2: 278–85.

Parés, Luis Nicolau. 2006. *A formação do candomblé: História e ritual da nação jeje na Bahia*. Campinas, Brazil: Editora da Unicamp.

Parrinder, E. Geoffrey. 1950. *La religion en Afrique occidentale*. Paris: Payot.

———. 1956. *The Story of Ketu. An Ancient Yoruba Kingdom*. Ibadan, Nigeria: Ibadan University Press.

Peel, J. D. Y. 2000. *Religious Encounters and the Making of the Yoruba*. Bloomington: Indiana University Press.

Pelton, Robert D. 1980. *The Trickster in West Africa: A Study of Mythic Irony and Sacred Delight*. Berkeley: University of California Press.

Pemberton, John. 1975. "Eshu-Elegba: The Yoruba trickster god." *African Arts* 9: 20–27, 66–70, 90–91.

Pierson, Donald. 1942. *Negroes in Brazil: A Study of Race Contact at Bahia*. Chicago: University of Chicago Press. (Published in 1945 as *Brancos e Pretos na Bahia*. São Paulo: Companhia Editora Nacional.)

Pinto, Luiz. Aguiar da Costa. 1953. *O Negro no Rio de Janeiro*. São Paulo: Companhia Editora Nacional.

Pouillon, Jean. 1974. *Fétiches sans fétichisme*. Paris: Maspero.

Prandi, Reginaldo. 1990. "Linhagem e legitimidade no candomblé paulista." *Revista brasileira de ciências sociais* 14: 18–31.

———. 1991. *Os candomblés de São Paulo*. São Paulo: HUCITEC/Editora Universidade de São Paulo.

Prandi, Reginaldo, and Vagner Gonçalves da Silva. 1989. "Axé São Paulo: notas preliminares de pesquisa sobre as origens e mudanças do candomblé na região metropolitana de São Paulo." In *Meu sinal está no teu corpo*, edited by C. Moura, 220–39. São Paulo: EDICON/Editora Universidade de São Paulo.

Querino, Manuel. 1988. *Costumes africanos no Brasil*. Recife, Brazil: Fundação Joaquim Nabuco/Editora Massangana. (Orig. pub. 1938.)

Ramos, Arthur. 1951a. *The Negro in Brazil*. Translated by Richard Pattee. Washington: Associated Publishers. (Orig. pub. 1934.)

———. 1951b. *O Negro brasileiro*. São Paulo: Companhia Editora Nacional. (Orig. pub. 1934.)

———. 1961. *Introdução à antropologia brasileira*. 3 vols. Rio de Janeiro: Casa do Estudante do Brasil. (Orig. pub. 1943.)

———. 1971. *O Negro na civilização brasileira*. Rio de Janeiro: Casa do Estudante do Brasil. (Orig. pub. 1939.)

———. 1979. *As culturas negras no Novo Mundo*. São Paulo: Companhia Editora Nacional. (Orig. pub. 1937.)

Rawick, George P. 1972. *From Sundown to Sunup: The Making of the Black Community*. Westport, Conn.: Greenwood.

Rego, Waldeloir. 1980. "Mitos e ritos africanos na Bahia." In *Iconografia dos deuses africanos no candomblé da Bahia*, edited by Carybé, 269–77. Salvador, Brazil: Fundação cultural do Estado da Bahia/Instituto nacional do livro/UFBA.

Reis, João José. 1986. *Rebelião escrava no Brasil: a história do levante dos malês (1835)*. São Paulo: Brasiliense.

———. 1988. "Um balanço dos estudos sobre as revoltas escravas da Bahia." In *Escravidão e invenção da liberdade*, edited by J. J. Reis, 133–40. São Paulo: Brasiliense.

———. 1989. "Nas malhas do poder escravista: a invasão do candomblé do Accú." In *Negociação e conflito: a resistência negra no Brasil escravista*, edited by J. J. Reis and E. Silva, 32–61. São Paulo: Companhia das Letras.

———. 1992. "Recôncavo rebelde: revoltas escravas nos engenhos baianos." *Áfro-Ásia* 15: 100–126.

Ribas, Oscar. 1958. *Ilundo*. Luanda, Angola: Museu de Angola.

Ribeiro, José. n.d. *Pomba Gira (Mirongueira)*. Rio de Janeiro: Espiritualista.

Ribeiro, René. 1956. *Religião e relações raciais*. Rio de Janeiro: MEC/Departamento de imprensa nacional.

———. 1957. "Religiões negras no Nordeste." Special issue. *Para todos, Quinzenário da cultura brasileira* 2, no. 31.

———. 1978. *Cultos afro-brasileiros do Recife: um estudo de ajustamento social*. Recife, Brazil: MEC/Instituto Joaquim Nabuco de pesquisas sociais. (Orig. pub. 1952.)

———. 1982. *Antropologia da religião e outros estudos*. Recife, Brazil: Fundação Joaquim Nabuco/Massangana.

Ricketts, Mac Linscott. 1965. "The North American Indian Trickster." *History of Religion* 5: 327–50.

Rio, João do. 1976. *As Religiões do Rio*. Rio de Janeiro: Nova Aguilar. (Orig. pub. 1904.)

Risério, Antônio. 1988. "Bahia com 'H': uma leitura da cultura baiana." In *Escravidão e invenção da liberdade*, edited by J. J. Reis, 143–65. São Paulo: Brasiliense.

Romero, Sílvio. 1888. *Estudos sobre a poesia popular do Brasil*. Rio de Janeiro: Tip. Laemmert

Salami, Sikiru. 1990. *A mitologia dos orixás africanos*. Vol. 1. São Paulo: Oduduwa.

Santana, Esmeraldo Emetério. 1984. "Nação-Angola." In *Encontro de nacões-de-candomblé*, edited by Vivaldo da Costa Lima, 35–47. Salvador, Brazil: Ianamá/UFBa/CEAO/CED.

Santos, Deoscóredes M. dos. 1988. *História de um terreiro nagô*. São Paulo: Max Limonad. (Orig. pub. 1962.)

———. 1990. "Vamos usar a joeira." *A Tarde* (Salvador, Brazil), July 7.

Santos, Juana Elbein dos. 1976. *Os Nagô e a morte*. Petrópolis, Brazil: Vozes.

———. 1977. "A percepção ideológica dos fenômenos religiosos: sistema nagô no Brasil, negritude versus sincretismo." *Revista de Cultura Vozes* 71, no. 7: 23–34.

———. 1982. "Pierre Verger e os resíduos coloniais: o 'outro' fragmentado." *Religião e Sociedade* 8: 11–14.

———. 1991–92. "A sedução dos novos africanos." *Siwaju* 5-6 (October): 2–3.

———. 2007. "A história do INTECAB." *Siwaju/SP. Boletim Informativo do Instituto Nacional da Tradição e Cultura Afro-Brasileira* 1: 3–4.

Santos, Juana Elbein dos, and Deoscóredes M. dos Santos. 1971. *Esu Bara Laroye*. Ibadan, Nigeria: University of Ibadan, Institute of African Studies.

———. 1993a. "La religion Nago génératrice et réserve de valeurs culturelles au Brésil." In *Les religions africaines comme source de valeurs de civilisation*, 157–73 (Actes de Colloques de Cotonou, 1970). Paris: Présence africaine.

———. 1993b. "A cultura nagô no Brasil: memória e continuidade." *Dossiê Brasil/Africa, Revista da Universidade de São Paulo* 18: 40–51.

Santos, M. R. Carvalho, and M. dos Santos Neto. 1989. *Boboromina: terreiros de São Luís, uma interpretação sócio-cultural*. São Luís, Brazil: SECMA/SIOGE.

Schwarcz, L. Moritz. 1993. *O espetáculo das raças: cientistas, instituições e questão racial no Brasil (1870–1930)*. São Paulo: Companhia das Letras.

Segato, Rita L. 1992. "Um paradoxo do relativismo: discurso racional da antropologia frente ao sagrado." *Religião e Sociedade* 16, nos. 1–2: 114–35.

Serra, Ordep Trindade. 1978. "Na trilha das crianças: os erês num terreiro angola." Master's thesis, Universidade Federal de Brasília.

———. 1995. *Aguas do Rei*. Petrópolis, Brazil: Vozes.

Silva, Ornato J. da. 1988. *Ervas: raízes africanas*. Rio de Janeiro: Rabaço.

Silva, Vagner Gonçalves da. 1992. *O candomblé na cidade: tradição e renovação*. Master's thesis, Universidade de São Paulo.

———. 1995. *Orixas da metropole*. Petrópolis, Brazil: Vozes.

Silveira, Renato da. 1988. "Pragmatismo e milagros da fé no Extremo Occidente." In *Escravidão e invenção da liberdade*, edited by J. J. Reis, 166–97. São Paulo: Brasiliense.

Sjørslev, Inger. 1989. "The Myth of Myths and the Nature of Ritual: Ideology and Practice in Afro-Brazilian Religion." *Folk* 31: 105–23.

Skidmore, Thomas E. 1989. *Preto no Branco: raça e nacionalidade no pensamento brasileiro*. Translated by Raul de Sá Barbosa. Rio de Janeiro: Paz e Terra. (Orig. pub. 1974.)

Smith, Robert S. 1988. *Kingdoms of the Yoruba*. London: James Currey. (Orig. pub. 1969.)

Sodré, Muniz. 1979. *Samba, o dono do corpo*. Rio de Janeiro: Codecri.

———. 1988. *A verdade seduzida: por um conceito de cultura no Brasil*. Rio de Janeiro: Francisco Alves.

Souza, Laura de Mello e. 1986. *O diabo e a terra de Santa Cruz*. São Paulo: Companhia das Letras.

Teles dos Santos, Jocélio. 1992. "O dono da terra: a presença do caboclo nos candomblés da Bahia." Master's thesis, Universidade de São Paulo.

———. 1995. *O dono da terra: O caboclo nos candomblés da Bahia*. Salvador, Brazil: Editora Sarah Letras.

Thompson, Robert Farris. 1984. *Flash of the Spirit: African and Afro-American Art and Philosophy*. New York: Vintage.

Trinidade, Liana M. S. 1985. *Exu: símbolo e função*. São Paulo: FFLCH/USP.

Turner, Jerry M. 1975. "Les Brésiliens: The Impact of Former Brazilian Slaves upon Dahomey." Ph.D. diss., Boston University.

Ventura, Roberto. 1991. *Estilo Tropical: história cultural e polêmicas literárias no Brasil (1870–1914)*. São Paulo: Companhia das Letras.

Verger, Pierre. 1953. "Le culte des voduns d'Abomey aurait-il été apporté à Saint Louis de Maranhon par la mère du roi Ghézo?" In *Les Afro-Américains*, 157–60. Dakar, Senegal: Institut Français de l'Afrique Noire.

———. 1957. *Notes sur le culte des Orisa et Vodun: à Bahia, la Baie de tous les saints, au Brésil et à l'ancienne côte des Esclaves en Afrique*. Mémoires de l'IFAN, no. 51. Dakar, Senegal: Institut Français de l'Afrique Noire.

———. 1965. "Grandeur et décadence du culte de Iyami Osoronga (ma mère la sorcière) chez les Yoruba." *Journal de la Société des américanistes* 35, no. 1: 141–243.

———. 1981. *Orixás*. Salvador, Brazil: Corrupio.

———. 1982a. *50 anos de fotografía*. Salvador, Brazil: Corrupio.

———. 1982b. "Etnografia religiosa iorubá e probidade científica." *Religião e Sociedade* 8: 3–10.

———. 1987. *Fluxo e refluxo do tráfico de escravos entre o Golfo do Benin e a Bahia de todos os Santos: dos séculos XVII a XIX*. Translated by Tasso Gadzanis. Salvador, Brazil: Corrupio. (Orig. pub. 1968.)

———. 1992. "O Deus supremo iorubá: uma revisão das fontes." *Áfro-Ásia* 15: 18–35. (Orig. pub. 1966.)

———. 1995. *Dieux d'Afrique*. Paris: Revue Noire. (Orig. pub. 1954.)

Viana Filho, Luis. 1988. *O Negro na Bahia: um ensaio clássico sobre a escravidão*. Rio de Janeiro: Nova Fronteira. (Orig. pub. 1946.)

Wagley, Charley, ed. 1952. *Race and Class in Rural Brazil*. Paris: UNESCO.

Werneck Sodré, Nelson. 1974. *Síntese da história da cultura brasileira*. Rio de Janeiro: Civilização Brasileira.

Wescott, Joan. 1962. "The sculpture and myths of Eshu-Elegba, the Yoruba trickster: Definition and interpretation in Yoruba iconography." *Africa* 32: 336–53.

Ziegler, Jean. 1975. *Les vivants et la mort*. Paris: Le Seuil.

Africanisms, search for, 13–14, 173
"Afro-Brazilian" as term, epistemological problems of, 31–32, 269 n. 1
Afro-Brazilian congress: of Bahia, 187,
188, 223–24, 226, 234; of Recife,
186, 188, 233–34
Afro-Brazilian religious field: constitution of, 7–9, 248, 255; hierarchiza-
tion in, 1, 6; power relationships in,
3, 16, 116–17, 229, 255, 292 n. 26;
religious continuum in, 8–9, 16, 76–
78, 95–96, 104–5, 257, 259–60, 269
n. 1
Alvinho de Omolu [Alvaro Pinto de
Almeida], 21, 53, 101–3, 106–7,
125–27, 129, 132, 138–39, 141,
151–52
Angola "nation": Exu in, 50–53; in Rio,
100
Aninha [Eugenia Ana dos Santos], 98–
99, 187, 213–15, 217, 223, 225–27,
290 n. 12
anthropological writings: influence of,
253, 295 n. 19; as source of legitimation, 24, 26, 222, 292 n. 29
arkhé, 14, 245–46, 251, 254
axé, 17, 25, 53, 129, 200–201, 230, 240,
245–46, 250–51, 253, 272 n. 27, 275
n. 26, 276 n. 30, 287 n. 24, 295 n. 18
Axé Opô Afonjá: religious engagement
of researchers in, 6–7, 107, 185, 187,
193, 198, 217, 253, 255, 272 n. 28,

276 n. 31, 283 n. 1, 288 n. 3; in Rio de
Janeiro, 99, 111, 146, 243, 290 n. 12;
in Salvador, 3–4, 59–60, 62, 98, 131,
199, 213, 215, 221, 223–27, 230–31,
247, 253, 255, 271 n. 17, 277 n. 39,
280 n. 16; 275 n. 23, 289 n. 7, 291
n. 19, 291 n. 20, 292 n. 28

Baba Eguns. *See* Eguns
babalaô. See *babalawo*
babalawo, 17, 43, 50, 98, 178, 180, 214,
218, 220, 222, 240–41, 243–44, 258,
289 n. 11, 293 n. 5, 293 n. 9
Bamboxé [Rodolfo Martins de
Andrade], 98, 213
Bantu: degeneration of, 2, 5, 7–8, 51,
184, 189, 205–7; origin of term, 270
n. 6
Bastide, Roger, 189, 192–96, 260; on
acculturation theory, 207–8; anthropological fieldwork of, 288 n. 3;
on Candomblé degradation in São
Paulo, 106, 207; on dialectic of continuity and discontinuity, 249, 294
n. 16, 294 n. 17; on Macumba as
degradation of African tradition,
193, 196, 198, 206–7; on opposition between "pure" religions and
"degenerate" cults, 5–6, 9, 107, 193–
95; on opposition between tradition
and modernity, 205–6; on principle
of compartmentalization, 208–9,

Bastide, Roger (*cont.*)
246, 294 n. 12; on "theory of the
mask," 246; Verger and, 189, 216–
17, 288 n. 3
Batuque, 3; Bará in, 62–63
Bombogira, 83, 85, 90, 132–33
Bonfim, Martiniano Eliseu do, 4, 99,
178, 187, 214–16, 222–25, 235, 289
n. 10, 289 n. 11, 291 n. 19, 291 n. 20,
291 n. 21, 291 n. 24
Brazilian policy, toward African
decolonized countries, 108–9, 196,
235, 280 n. 17, 280 n. 18
Brazilian returnees in Nigeria, 212–13,
288 n. 5

caboclo: in Candomblé, 12, 125–28,
130–32, 152, 250, 271 n. 20, 272 n. 7,
283 n. 3, 283 n. 4; strategy of dissimulation of, 131, 271 n. 20, 282
n. 8; in Umbanda, 12, 76–77, 96,
122, 158
Caboclo Candomblé, 6, 100, 184, 205,
211, 284 n. 1, 285 n. 11, 288 n. 2, 292
n. 29
Cabula, 71–72, 105
Calundu, 71–73, 277 n. 3
Calunga, 71–72, 82, 84, 277 n. 4
Candomblé: concentration of studies
on, 283 n. 1; conflicts in, 118–20,
281 n. 3, 282 n. 11; "nations" of, 269
n. 2; passage from Umbanda to, 11–
12, 15–16, 81, 105–7, 110, 113–16,
121, 124–27, 133, 136, 144–45, 153,
258; radio programs on, 100, 112–
13, 243; in Rio de Janeiro, 5, 11, 21–
22, 52, 96–103, 270 n. 9, 278 n. 2,
279 n. 15, 290 n. 12; ritual kinship in,
16, 269 n. 3, 275 n. 25, 289 n. 8; in
São Paulo, 11, 21, 101, 105–8, 129,
222, 237, 279 n. 14; as universal reli-

gion, 107–8, 260, 295 n. 3; whites in,
11, 107–8, 211, 260, 280 n. 16, 291
n. 25
Carneiro, Édison, 4, 184–90, 286 n. 17
Casa Branca terreiro, 3–4, 7, 62, 98,
178, 199, 213–14, 217, 222, 225, 271
n. 20, 273 n. 28, 275 n. 23, 277 n. 39,
280 n. 19, 289 n. 7, 289 n. 9; religious
engagement of researchers in, 6,
185, 189, 283 n. 1
CEAO (Centro de Estudos Afro-
Orientais), 196, 218–20, 235
change in religious affiliation, 282
n. 1; by "changing the waters,"
102, 240, 279 n. 9; by upward mobility within same family-of-saint,
147–48
collective memory: in Bastide's work,
13, 207, 210; in Halbwachs's work,
14, 210
COMTOC (International Congress of
Orisha Tradition and Culture), 233–
34, 247–48, 257–58, 292 n. 1
counterculture movement in Brazil,
109, 197–98
courses on Yoruba language and civilization, 18, 62, 113, 135, 212, 219,
233–42, 244, 252, 259, 280 n. 18, 293
n. 3
Cristóvão de Ogunjá [Cristóvão Lopes
dos Santos], 21–22, 53, 100–103,
126–30, 279 n. 7, 283 n. 3

Departments of Mental Hygiene, 183–
84, 186
divination: courses on *odús*, 134, 212,
233, 238–44; by *dilogun*, 43, 49, 275
n. 16; monopoly on, 145, 152; by
opelé, 43, 274 n. 15; system of, 112;
using cowries vs. possession by Exu
or Pombagira, 16–17

Efon "nation," 21–23, 53, 58, 125–26, 130, 151, 164, 261, 269 n. 2, 278 n. 5, 278 n. 6; Ekiti origins of, 22–23; history of, 100–103; in São Paulo, 106–8

Egungun. *See* Eguns

Eguns (deified ancestors), 81, 250, 271 n. 21, 281 n. 1; in Bahia, 121–22, 134–35, 276 n. 34, 281 n. 2; in *padê* ritual, 59; ritual relationship with iyamís, 61

eguns (disincarnated souls), 80–81, 122–23, 127, 281 n. 1; as spiritual polluting in Candomblé, 12, 121–22

Engenho Velho. *See* Casa Branca terreiro

Estado Novo, 104, 182, 285 n. 12

Exu: *assento* of, 44; Bara, 40–41, 45–47, 49, 53, 123, 133, 274 n. 11; in Batuque, 62–63; compadre, 16, 44, 144; dance of, 56–57; as disincarnated spirit in Umbanda, 12; divination, 43; egun, 81, 122–24, 133, 142, 152, 271 n. 21; female in Africa, 35, 40, 42, 86, 132–33, 140; female in Brazil, 16, 51, 78, 83, 86, 137, 140–41, 147, 186, 282 n. 12; of the gateway, 44; as pivot between religious systems, 10; possession of, 49–57, 81–82; as principle of revolution, 43; "qualities" of, 47–48; in Quimbanda, 78–79; *quiumbas*, 81, 123; ritual colors of, 54; sexuality, 16, 39–41, 74, 160, 163, 165, 167–70, 197, 273 n. 3; "slave," 12, 44–45, 47, 91, 123, 129, 132–33, 135, 142, 147, 152, 275 n. 20; sons' characteristics of, 149; as symbol of contradictions in modernity, 11; in Tambor da Mina, 64–67; Tranca-Rua, 80, 164, 169; as trickster, 11, 35–37, 66, 273 n. 2; as

unevolved spirits in Umbanda, 77–80; in Xangô, 63–64

Federations of Afro-Brazilian religions, 70, 104, 210, 250, 279 n. 13, 294 n. 15

feitura de santo. See initiation: in Candomblé

Freyre, Gilberto, 73, 120, 182, 186–87, 189, 216, 285 n. 9, 285 n. 12

fuxico-de-santo. See gossip

Gantois terreiro, 3, 51, 103, 199, 213, 222; religious engagement of researchers in, 4, 6–7, 178–80, 185, 216, 272 n. 28, 275 n. 22, 277 n. 39, 283 n. 1, 286 n. 21, 287 n. 1, 287 n. 2

gender issues, 84, 150: in Ifá initiation, 293 n. 9; balance of power within the couple, 154–55, 160–62, 168–70; woman's ambivalence, 16, 169

gossip: as catalyst of the social process, 215; as instrument of political control, 120, 216, 227, 272 n. 22; as resolution of conflicts, 118–19, 149, 151

healing, mystical, 127–28, 132, 150, 283 n. 3

Herskovits, Melville J., 41, 66, 111, 186, 285 n. 15; on acculturation of Africans' descendants in Brazil, 188–89, 290 n. 17; Verger and, 220, 290 n. 1

Ifá: in Brazil, 43, 239–44, 293 n. 9; divinatory system, 37, 39, 43, 60, 239–41, 274 n. 15, 293 n. 7; in Nigeria, 37–38, 61, 276 n. 33, 276 n. 35, 293 n. 5; role of Èṣù in, 37–38

initiation: in Candomblé, 12, 25–25, 28, 40, 45, 48–54, 63, 101, 109–11, 114, 118, 122–23, 125–27, 129–30, 134, 139, 141, 144–47, 151–52, 200, 206,

Ifá (*cont.*)
216, 218, 229–30, 237, 244, 249,
260–61, 272 n. 26, 274 n. 12, 281
n. 4, 281 n. 27, 282 n. 1, 282 n. 6, 282
n. 13, 295 n. 18; in Umbanda, 103,
106, 116, 270 n. 12
initiatory age, 116–18, 237
INTECAB (National Institute of Afro-
Brazilian Culture and Tradition),
233, 244, 248–49, 251, 254, 294
n. 10, 294 n. 14, 294 n. 15
International Congress of Orisha Tradition and Culture (COMTOC), 233–
34, 247–48, 257–58, 292 n. 1
Iyá Nassô, 213–14, 217–18, 289 n. 7,
289 n. 8, 290 n. 15
Iyamí Oxorongá, 60–62, 276 n. 33, 276
n. 35, 278 n. 12, 289 n. 7; Pombagira
and, 89–90, 140–42

Jeje: "nation" in Rio, 99–100; origin of
term, 269 n. 5
Jeje-Nagô model, 178–79, 188, 269 n. 5,
285 n. 7
Joãozinho da Goméia [João Alves
Torres Filho], 53, 100, 103, 107–8,
134, 240–41, 270 n. 8, 278 n. 4, 279
n. 15
jogo de búzios. See divination: by
dilogun
journey to Africa: of Candomblé initiates, 212–14, 216, 220–22; as means
of reinforcing cultural roots, 211–
12, 233; as source of prestige, 213,
216, 229, 290 n. 13

Kardec, Allan, 69–70, 270 n. 12
Kardecism, 8–9, 31, 69–71, 75–78, 80,
104–5, 125–26, 269 n. 1, 271 n. 17,
271 n. 19, 279 n. 14, 280 n. 20
Ketu: as birthplace of founders, 213–

14, 289 n. 7; history of, 221; as traditional "nation" of Candomblé, 54,
107, 194, 214, 218, 289 n. 7, 292 n. 29

Landes, Ruth, 185–86, 215, 285 n. 14,
287 n. 1, 287 n. 2
Legba: and Èṣù, 30, 35–42, 132, 273
n. 3, 287 n. 24; in *fa*, 37–38, 40; in
Tambor da Mina, 64–67, 277 n. 40
life stories, 19–20; of Edí de Omolu,
162–169; of Rosinha de Mulambo,
155–60; of Sandra de Oxum, 151–
53
"Little Africa" in Rio, 97–98

Macumba, 71–74, 78, 85, 95–96, 270
n. 12, 275 n. 24, 283 n. 5; as "degenerated" cult, 3, 5, 10, 108, 193–98,
206–7, 210, 257, 275 n. 23, 287 n. 2;
in Rio, 98–99, 183; as symbol of
rebellion, 197–98
Madureira market, 115, 281 n. 25
magical practices, in colonial Brazil,
73–74
Menininha do Gantois [Maria
Escolástica Nazaré], 109, 185, 240,
280 n. 19, 282 n. 8, 286 n. 21, 287
n. 2
military dictatorship, 105, 109, 112, 197
Moraes, Zélio de, 70, 104, 277 n. 1
mystical healing, 127–28, 132, 150, 283
n. 3

Nagô: origin of term, 269 n. 5; as predominant model of tradition, 1–2,
5–7, 53, 96, 107, 174, 188, 226, 260,
284 n. 2; *terreiros* as embodiment of
African tradition in Brazil, 3, 206–
10, 247–51, 289 n. 7
National Institute of Afro-Brazilian
Culture and Tradition (INTECAB),

233, 244, 248–49, 251, 254, 294
  n. 10, 294 n. 14, 294 n. 15
Nina Rodrigues, Raymundo, 3–4, 6–7,
  13, 49, 107, 176–80, 196, 272 n. 28,
  291 n. 25; on "black danger," 176,
  178, 284 n. 6; on criticism of Bantu
  supremacy, 3, 234, 270 n. 10; Martiniano E. do Bonfim and, 4, 178, 235;
  on valorization of Yoruba language,
  234–35, 291 n. 21

obás de Xangô, 187, 215, 223–24, 291
  n. 19, 291 n. 20, 291 n. 21, 292 n. 27,
  292 n. 28; as proof of traditionalism,
  225–26
Obá Tossi [Marcelina da Silva], 62,
  213–14, 218, 221, 226, 289 n. 8, 290
  n. 18
Olga de Alaketu [Olga Francisca Regis],
  221, 271 n. 17, 271 n. 20, 276 n. 27,
  283 n. 1
Oloque (Oloroquê), 21, 101, 278 n. 6
Omolocô, 31–32, 76–77, 105, 163,
  259–60, 269 n. 1, 293 n. 6
Oyó: Aláàfin of, 217, 224–25, 289 n. 7,
  290 n. 15; as birthplace of founders,
  289 n. 7; history and social organization of, 220–21, 224–25, 289 n. 9,
  291 n. 23, 291 n. 24

padê ritual, 57–59, 65, 200, 276 n. 31;
  ancestors in, 59, 98; in Efon "nation,"
  58; iyamís in, 59–60, 62, 140
Pantanal terreiro, 21, 53, 101–103, 126,
  129, 131, 278 n. 5, 279 n. 8
Pinto, Tancredo da S., 104–5, 239, 293
  n. 6
police repression, of Afro-Brazilian religions, 10, 104, 110, 178–79, 183,
  199, 205, 285 n. 6, 285 n. 11, 290
  n. 13, 291 n. 25

Pombagira: in *despacho*, 84–85; families of, 84; Menina, 162–69, 283
  n. 8; Maria Mulambo, 84–85, 135–
  36, 138–39, 146–47, 149–50, 155–
  60, 162; as negation of dominant
  female model in Brazilian society,
  170, 283 n. 10; as negative side of
  Exu, 83; Maria Padilha, 85–89, 133,
  135, 137, 139, 162, 277 n. 7, 282
  n. 12; sexuality and, 85–86, 89–90,
  160, 163, 165, 167–70; Tzigane
  (Cigana), 84, 89, 135, 151–52; as
  women's protector, 154–55, 168
principle of seniority, 117, 248
"pure" religions vs. "degenerate" cults,
  2–9, 15, 95–96, 105, 107, 111, 173–
  74, 184, 194–96, 207, 210, 270 n. 9,
  276 n. 37

Querino, Manuel, 25, 179
Quimbanda: as criticism of social
  structure, 77–79, 197–98; as
  pattern of accusation, 8–9, 78, 271
  n. 18

Ramos, Arthur, 6–7, 28, 72, 85, 96,
  107, 179–81, 183–84, 186, 188, 192,
  272 n. 28, 289 n. 10
re-Africanization: in Candomblé, 13,
  18, 31, 35, 113, 132–36, 139, 142,
  210–12, 231, 233, 237, 239–45, 250,
  252, 257, 280 n. 18, 287 n. 22, 295
  n. 19; *obás* of Xangô as first example
  of, 187, 222–25; rituals for Exu and
  Pombagira, 136–38, 147; in United
  States, 258–59
religious engagement of researchers, 6–
  7, 24–30, 229, 272 n. 25, 272 n. 26;
  in Axé Opô Afonjá, 6–7, 107, 185,
  187, 193, 198, 217, 253, 255, 272
  n. 28, 276 n. 31, 283 n. 1, 288 n. 3; in

religious engagement (*cont.*)
>   Casa Branca, 6, 185, 189, 283 n. 1;
>   in the Gantois, 4, 6–7, 178–80,
>   185, 216, 272 n. 28, 275 n. 22, 277
>   n. 39, 283 n. 1, 286 n. 21, 287 n. 1,
>   287 n. 2

religious hierarchy: in Candomblé, 25,
>   116–18, 210, 226; conflicts with,
>   143–48, 150–51, 153; criticism of,
>   16, 116; reversal of subordinate rela-
>   tionships in, 116, 150

religious market, 8, 10–13, 16, 111–12,
>   128, 238, 256, 284 n. 2

Ribeiro, René, 26, 183, 190–92, 285
>   n. 15, 286 n. 20, 290 n. 13

Santos, Deoscóredes dos, 7, 198, 217–
>   18, 220–21, 245–46, 276 n. 31, 291
>   n. 19, 293 n. 4, 293 n. 10

Santos, Juana E. dos, 7, 17, 52, 59, 62,
>   198–201, 218, 220, 230, 244–51,
>   253, 274 n. 9, 276 n. 31, 276 n. 33,
>   293 n. 10, 294 n. 12

SECNEB (Society of Studies of Black
>   Culture in Brazil), 247, 249, 294
>   n. 10

secret, and structure of secrecy, 210,
>   229, 242, 250–51, 295 n. 18

Senhora [Maria Bibiana do Espírito
>   Santo], 193, 213–15, 217–18, 220–
>   21, 226–28, 272 n. 28, 289 n. 8, 292
>   n. 27

slaves: abolition and, 7, 32, 70, 97, 174–
>   76, 194; rebellions of, 174, 176, 212,
>   284 n. 3

Society of Studies of Black Culture in
>   Brazil (SECNEB), 247, 249, 294 n. 10

Spiritism, 3, 69–70, 75–76, 111, 157,
>   163, 166, 169, 178, 258–59, 270
>   n. 12, 279 n. 15; influence of, 9, 72,
>   271 n. 17; low, 78, 85, 184, 285 n. 8,

285 n. 11; synonymous with
>   Umbanda, 106, 207–8, 283 n. 5

Stella de Oxossi [Stella de Azevedo
>   Santos], 221, 230–31, 247, 271 n. 17,
>   280 n. 16, 292 n. 28

symbolic and ritual spaces, 12, 128,
>   131–32, 134, 139, 145, 152, 162, 281
>   n. 2, 294 n. 12

Tambor da Mina, 3; Legba and Exu in,
>   64–67, 286 n. 19

tradition: loss of, 2, 107, 203–4, 206–7,
>   215, 229, 240, 245, 295 n. 18; making
>   of, 3, 203; political functions of, 14,
>   203–4, 227–28

Umbanda, 7–9, 11–13, 15–16, 70–71,
>   103–5, 257, 270 n. 12; "African," 31,
>   76–77, 79, 104–5, 163, 269 n. 1, 293
>   n. 6; legitimization of, 75; Kardecism
>   and, 75–76, 80; Macumba and, 74–
>   75; during military dictatorship, 105;
>   Quimbanda and, 8, 77–78; spirits
>   lines in, 76; spiritual evolution in, 76;
>   "white," 11, 31, 75–77, 79, 104

Umbandomblé, 9, 250, 260, 271 n. 18

UNESCO, 192–93

Union of Afro-Brazilian Cults, 187–88

Vargas, Getúlio, 104, 106, 182

Verger, Pierre, 41, 51, 65, 189, 193, 197,
>   200–201, 213–14, 227, 231, 272
>   n. 28, 276 n. 33, 287 n. 22, 287 n. 24,
>   288 n. 3, 290 n. 16, 292 n. 28, 293
>   n. 4; Herskovits and, 220, 290 n. 17;
>   initiation as *babalawo*, 218; mes-
>   senger of, 7, 216–21, 290 n. 17

Xangô: Exu in, 63, 183; in Recife, 3, 26,
>   71, 183, 187, 277 n. 38; in Sergipe,
>   64, 276 n. 37

Stefania Capone is a Research Professor of
Anthropology at the University of Paris and a senior
researcher at the French National Center for
Scientific Research (CNRS). She is currently working
at the Center for International Research in the
Humanities and Social Sciences at New York
University.

Library of Congress Cataloging-in-Publication Data
Capone, Stefania.
[Quête de l'Afrique dans le candomblé. English]
Searching for Africa in Brazil: power and tradition
in candomblé / Stefania Capone;
translated from the French by Lucy Lyall Grant.
p. cm.
Includes bibliographical references and index.
ISBN 978-0-8223-4625-8 (cloth : alk. paper)
ISBN 978-0-8223-4636-4 (pbk. : alk. paper)
1. Candomblé (Religion)
2. Cults—Brazil. 3. Gods, Afro-Brazilian.
4. Blacks—Brazil—Religion. I. Title.
BL2592.C35C3613 2010
299.6'7340981—dc22 2009047586